The Way to Win

THE WAY TO WIN

★ ★ ★ ★ ★

TAKING THE

WHITE HOUSE IN 2008

★ ★ ★ ★ ★

Mark Halperin

John F. Harris

RANDOM HOUSE · New York

Published in the United States by Random House,
an imprint of The Random House Publishing Group, a division of
Random House, Inc., New York.

RANDOM HOUSE and colophon are registered trademarks
of Random House, Inc.

ISBN 1-4000-6447-3

Printed in the United States of America on acid-free paper

www.atrandom.com

2 4 6 8 9 7 5 3 1

First Edition

Book design by Simon M. Sullivan

TO KAREN

with gratitude, respect, appreciation, friendship, optimism, and love.

MARK HALPERIN

TO LIZA, GRIFFIN, AND NICOLA

with love and awe.

JOHN HARRIS

CONTENTS

Section IX • Hillary Clinton, the Freak Show, and the Presidency

Section X • Conclusion

INTRODUCTION

★ ★ ★ ★ ★

THIS BOOK BEGINS IN THE RAIN—a cold, pelting, dismal rain that at times fell so hard it nearly obscured a remarkable moment in American politics. Up on the stage, huddled beneath umbrellas, were a father and son, the forty-first and the forty-third presidents of the United States. Joining them was the woman some believe is destined to become the forty-fourth president. All three of them—George H. W. Bush, George W. Bush, Hillary Rodham Clinton—had gathered in Little Rock, Arkansas, to pay tribute to the nation's forty-second president and dedicate the William J. Clinton Presidential Library and Museum. Rarely have the past, present, and potential future of American politics been on such vivid display. It was an arresting tableau, one that naturally evoked questions about the art of politics: what it takes to win the presidency, what it takes to survive in that office, and what has created a strange, generation-long cycle of Bushes and Clintons alternating as the preeminent figures in American life.

How has a supposedly egalitarian nation come to have its politics dominated by two competing dynasties? What have these families learned from observing and opposing each other? Why has American politics, during two decades of Bush-Clinton rule, turned so unruly, bitter, and destructive? As the country considers its next presidential choice, what lessons are there from the experience of these two clans?

This book is our effort to answer these questions.

Our conclusions all return to the same place. The long reigns of the Bushes and the Clintons are not a curiosity. They are more than a historical accident. These families have dominated American politics because, over years in the business, they have learned specific principles and practices. We call these the "Trade Secrets" of modern politics. The race for the presidency in 2008 will be framed by the examples of the past two people to hold the job. Cumulatively, their Trade Secrets are a formula: *The Way to Win.*

At the outset, we must clarify the intentions of this book. Bill Clinton won the presidency, and scuttled the efforts to blast him from it prematurely, in part because he is the most naturally gifted politician of his age. Some of his gifts flow from a combination of instinct and showmanship that will not be matched by anyone running for president in 2008, including his wife. But our focus is not on the unique aspects of Clinton's talent. It is on the prosaic ones. Clear lessons from his career are available to be borrowed by anyone from either party. The smart candidates already are doing exactly this.

We also must qualify our argument about George W. Bush. This book is not a history of his family or his political career. It is a book about political strategy. President Bush himself appears in these pages frequently, but the dominant character is his friend and longtime political adviser Karl C. Rove. This is not to suggest that Bush is a puppet, and Rove the brains behind the operation. Rove is an effective strategist because he has had exceptional rapport with an exceptionally capable politician who brought intuition, skills, and independent judgment to the task. But, in the Bush-Rove partnership, Rove's assignment was to master the theory and practicalities of *winning elections.* As with Clinton, our focus is not on the features of Rove's method that are sui generis, but on those that could be adapted by anyone serious about presidential politics.

Clinton and Rove understand how to win elections better than anyone of their generation. In making this comparison, it is not our intent to elevate Rove to the level of a principal. His power, while commanding, has been derivative. As with all campaign advisers and White House staff hands, he remains hired help. Nor is it our aim to reduce Clinton from president to campaign operative, nor to exaggerate his political talents. As detailed in these pages, his successes as a strategist were punctuated by extravagant failures. He won two elections in part because he had his own equivalents of Rove—people such as James Carville and Paul Begala in 1992, and Dick Morris in 1996. Still, when it comes to understanding presidential campaigns, Clinton and Rove are of equal stature. While they are famous for their political smarts, there is little understanding of what specifically makes them so smart—and makes them winners. Both gave interviews for this project.

There may be people who recoil at the suggestion that Clinton or Bush and Rove should be called winners. What is so impressive, Clinton critics might reasonably ask, about a Democratic president who never achieved a majority in either of his two presidential elections, and who helped steer his party to minority status in Congress? Does becoming the second president in U.S. history to be impeached represent the way to win?

Bush skeptics, meanwhile, might wonder why, if this book is about winning presidential elections, it does not celebrate Al Gore, who won more votes than Bush in 2000. Even Bush's unambiguous 2004 victory was achieved by coolly exploiting the advantages of being a wartime president. Now that same war threatens to sink his presidency. If Bush and Rove know the way to win, why can't they figure out how to do it in Iraq?

We answer by emphasizing again what this book is and what it is not. This is an effort to identify and explain the strategies and techniques of those who have won presidential elections and policy battles over the past generation, and identify their singular skills.

This is not a book about the justification for the war in Iraq, or the merits of tax cuts. It is not an attempt to relitigate the contested 2000 election. It is not an attempt to assess presidential records in a historical context.

Even in the context of contemporary politics, reputations are highly fluid. When we embarked on this project at the Little Rock library dedication in the wake of the 2004 election, many Republicans believed, and many Democrats feared, that the newly reelected president, through his political and policy victories, had shifted the balance of power in America in long-term ways—a realignment, in the parlance of political scientists. Demoralized Democrats, like the hapless pursuers of Butch Cassidy and the Sundance Kid, gazed at Bush and Rove and wondered, "Who are those guys?"

But by the fall of 2005, an assortment of political and policy debacles—the failure of Social Security reform, the bungled response to Hurricane Katrina, the grinding war in Iraq—had left Bush with some of the lowest job approval ratings of any modern president. In 2006, the war dragged on sullenly, congressional Republicans were mired in scandal, and the hope for the party was to avoid a rout in the midterm elections, never mind the dream of realignment. It seemed entirely possible that the twelve-year GOP reign on Capitol Hill would soon come crashing down, leaving Bush to limp through the balance of his second term. After nearly two years under the shadow of a criminal investigation in the Valerie Plame CIA leak case, Rove was cleared by special prosecutor Patrick Fitzgerald in June 2006. Still, Rove remained the chief political strategist for a crippled presidency—not exactly the mark of a genius.

Election success cannot be viewed as separate and distinct from governing failure. As adherents of the permanent campaign, in which politics and policy are always integrated, Clinton and Rove would agree.

But neither do the setbacks Clinton and Bush faced in their second terms negate their electoral achievements. Clinton in 1992 was the first Democrat to be elected president in twelve years, and in 1996 he was the first Democrat to win two consecutive elections since Franklin D. Roosevelt. Bush in 2000 defeated an incumbent party that was running amid peace and prosperity. In 2002, he defied historical trends by leading his party to big gains in the midterm elections. In 2004, despite deep public unease over the economy and the Iraq war, Bush beat a Democratic Party that had never been more energized or better organized. This record amply demonstrates that Clinton, Bush, and Rove know something about the way to win.

Conservatives who decried Clinton's alleged character defects as blatantly disqualifying still must wonder how he bested them so often. Liberals who regard Bush's political strategist as Satan scan the Democratic Party and ask plaintively, "Where is our Karl Rove?"

The Way to Win is meant partly for fun. We are not political strategists, and we do not presume to give advice to politicians. But as political reporters, we share the obsession with electoral strategy and maneuver, not to mention with the gaudy carnival of presidential elections.

But *The Way to Win* is meant mainly as serious argument. The United States is on the brink of what promises to be one of the most intensely fought and consequential presidential elections in its history. American politics has grown more heated, suspicious, and erratic. It is less apt to confront, illuminate, and resolve genuine issues. The Bushes and Clintons have governed in this deteriorating environment, and in certain ways they are responsible for the situation. People who think American politics is broken and needs fixing must reckon with the impact of these leaders and their political allies.

Divisive though they may be, both families have won political victories in this perilous new environment. Their Trade Secrets are not gimmicks or abstractions, but substantive ideas and tactics gleaned through tough experience. The candidate who masters their lessons will take the White House in 2008.

• • •

NOVEMBER 18, 2004, was very much Bill Clinton's day. His bid for historical immortality was ready to open its doors—a gargantuan glass and steel structure on the banks of the Arkansas River. How had the Bushes come to honor a Clinton on that slick stage in Little Rock? Twelve years earlier, Clinton's 1992 victory had sent George H. W. Bush into involuntary retirement. The elder Bush had spent the fall campaign alerting the country to Clinton's alleged misdeeds, and kept faith until nearly the end that voters ultimately would take heed of his warnings. A few days after the election, as they strolled through the Maryland woods at Camp David, Bush turned to Colin Powell, his top military adviser, and confessed, "I just never thought they'd elect him. Don't understand it."

Now, in the pouring rain, the first President Bush at last was ready with an explanation: "Of course, it always has to be said that Bill Clinton was one of the most gifted American political figures in modern times. Trust me, I learned this the hard way."

After years of enmity, the former presidents had in the preceding months developed a curious affection for each other, linked by the bond of shared experience in power.

Bush's son, when he took the podium, emphasized not Clinton's smooth Southern moves but his steely, unshakable strength. "The president is not the kind to give up a fight," his successor said. "His staffers were known to say, 'If Clinton were the *Titanic*, the iceberg would sink.' "

These were gracious nods to an old adversary, but the forty-first and forty-third presidents were indulging in a common tendency to view Bill Clinton's successes through the prism of his mystique, as though he had superhuman political powers and resolve. Again, it is our aim to dispense with the Clinton mystique and focus instead on the Clinton *method*—techniques devised through practice that includes errors and defeats as well as victories.

On this particular occasion it was easy for George W. Bush to be gracious. Just two weeks earlier, he had defied conventional wisdom in securing re-election, winning by a narrow percentage but with the largest number of votes for any presidential candidate in history. In so doing, he had thrilled his ardent supporters, surprised the national press corps, and confounded the thousands of Democrats sitting under umbrellas in Little Rock. The Democrats' candidate, John Kerry, had lost to a man most of them regarded as incompetent and immoral, defending a record they considered transparently appalling. The crowd was chastened by the defeat, but hardly more comprehending of why Bush had proved so formidable an opponent. Bill Clinton, however, professed an early insight into Bush's success. In his remarks at the library, he recalled a night in 1999 when he sat up late in front of the television and first saw Texas governor George W. Bush on the stump in Iowa: "I called a friend of mine and said, 'My God, that guy can beat us. He is a good politician.' " There is no higher praise that Bill Clinton knows how to offer.

Bush, Clinton, Bush, Clinton. The dynastic pattern of recent politics perhaps has grown too familiar for people to appreciate what a striking historical fact it represents. When the current President Bush completes his full second term, it will be the first time since James Madison and James Monroe almost two hundred years ago that back-to-back presidents both served all eight years of two elected terms. Put another way, two of the most divisive figures in this country's history will have commanded the White House for sixteen consecutive years. Hillary Clinton could extend this record, as someday could George W. Bush's younger brother Jeb, whose achievements as Florida's governor and own acute ambition make him a potent potential presidential contender.

These families are the era's preeminent politicians because they are preeminent political innovators. Much of what they know about politics they have learned from watching one another and reacting accordingly. They have self-consciously emulated the other side's accomplishments, and maneuvered to avoid their pitfalls.

The first President Bush certainly is part of this chain. But he is from a bygone era no longer relevant, or increasingly even recognizable, to our own. Even George W. Bush and Karl Rove, and perhaps George H. W. Bush himself, would agree that to the extent the elder Bush's career offers any lessons for candidates running in 2008, they are mostly in the negative: what not to do.

For her part, Hillary Clinton has had her eye trained on the current President Bush for six years. While she would run for president in 2008 trying to repudiate his policies, she and her team have studied Bush's success in several areas: maximizing the power of the executive branch; maintaining discipline in party ranks; and, especially, attempting to keep the national news media and Washington political Establishment at her heel rather than at her throat.

· · ·

WHILE THE BUSHES and Clintons have borrowed from each other, this filching is mainly in the realm of tactics. Their strategic assumptions about how to win and govern in divided America are quite different and over time have developed such distinct forms that there are now two leading brands in American presidential elections: Bush Politics and Clinton Politics. The two brands revolve around different answers to two questions. Why are the American people so choleric and divided? And what should a politician try to do about it?

Clinton Politics is the politics of the center. It holds that Americans for the most part, with the exception of irate groups at the edges, are less interested in ideology than in practical solutions to basic problems. People would prefer for politics to be polite, civil, and compromise-minded. And they would get their wish, Clinton maintained, were it not for the cynical maneuverings of interest groups and operatives who deliberately contrive to invent and exaggerate conflicts and make people frustrated and distrustful. The goal of Clinton Politics is not to clarify differences but to blur and ultimately bridge them. The great weapon of Clinton Politics is presidential approval ratings. Clinton's notion was that a president with a 50 percent approval rating or lower is living dangerously. A president with a 65 percent approval rating has enough clout that no adversary can lay a glove on him. But Clinton's critics—a group that very much includes Bush and Rove—suggest that this approach to politics produces "small-ball" policies that squander the true power of the office.

Bush Politics is the politics of the base. It holds that people are angry in the main because the issues and values dividing Americans are real and consequential. A successful leader will stand forthrightly on one side of a grand argument. Then he or she will win that argument by sharpening the differences and rallying his most intense supporters to his side. A president who wins by one vote—or even by five Supreme Court votes—has all the power he needs to make history. As president, Bush has not won every fight, and he has on occasion sought bipartisan legislative consensus, but his presidency primarily has used the energies and passions of conservatives to change the country, often well ahead of public opinion.

Karl Rove is the chief author and chief implementer of Bush Politics. At this moment, the legacy of Bush Politics is very much unsettled, as is Rove's reputation.

What is undeniable, despite recent setbacks, is that Bush and Rove together built a strategy that—from 1999 to 2004—produced a nearly unbroken string of political successes. Democrats and journalists trying to understand the future of politics ignore this accomplishment at their peril.

Fortuitously for Hillary Clinton, the closest Democratic approximation to

Karl Rove, as the individual with the finest strategic skills in her party, happens to be her top political adviser—and husband. Furthermore, Bill Clinton's own expertise has evolved, through eight harsh years in office and a half dozen more observing the Bush administration, making him significantly better prepared to participate in a winning presidential campaign than he was back in 1992. The next chapter in the Bush-Clinton rivalry is potentially in the offing.

Many Democrats are hungering for a presidential candidate who will rally a dispirited party and speak out on behalf of liberal values they feel were neglected even during Clinton's reign. In other words, they are looking for a Democrat who will run on Bush Politics. The most imposing figure on the Republican side, Senator John McCain, for years has presented himself as a unifying figure willing to defy his party's orthodoxy. He is a Republican who preaches something resembling Clinton Politics.

In practice, of course, every candidate will run on some composite of Bush Politics and Clinton Politics. There are moments when it makes sense to rally the base, and others when the imperative is to court unaligned voters in the center. The question is one of emphasis, and deciding which priority will be the dominant theme of campaign strategy.

Hillary Clinton especially must navigate this delicate balance. For the past twelve years, after the repudiation of her health care agenda and the Democratic disaster of 1994, she has been a disciplined devotee of Clinton Politics. As a senator from New York since 2001, she has avoided issue positions that could make her seem excessively liberal. She cultivates independent voters and strives to work, and be seen working, with Republicans. At the same time, Hillary Clinton by temperament is drawn to Bush Politics. Her instinct is to approach politics as combat. Far more than her husband, she is concerned about the need for Democrats to develop an infrastructure of aggressive advocacy organizations to match the ideological and communications infrastructure that has existed on the right. This reflects a worldview that, again far more than her husband's, is prone to drawing sharp lines between her side—selfless and enlightened—and the opposition—greedy and benighted. Oddly enough, it is conceivable that 2008 will see Hillary Clinton running for president on a strategy that owes practically as much to George W. Bush as to Bill Clinton.

This is, of course, if Hillary Clinton runs. We cannot divine her real intentions, and perhaps she does not yet know them herself. But if she chooses not to run it would be an abrupt break from the patterns of a lifetime, in which she rarely has failed to choose the most ambitious path. In tandem with her husband, she has spent three decades absorbed in the question of the way to win the White House and how to govern once inside. And in the past six years, she has become one of the most sure-footed actors in public life, no longer merely borrowing Trade Secrets but refining her own.

There is one essential continuity between Clinton Politics and Bush Politics. A cardinal Trade Secret of modern politics is: *Party nominations and the presidency itself usually are won by the candidate with the most impressive substantive claim on the job.* Presidential campaigns do not hinge solely on which hopeful seems more likable, or comes across better on television. We do not know who will win the presidency in 2008, but we feel sure it will be the candidate who has the smartest and most disciplined approach to three basic challenges: fashioning a political strategy that addresses the elemental changes in media and technology that have reshaped current politics; executing this strategy despite innumerable and unpredictable distractions; and combining personal ambition with credible and concrete ideas about how to change the country.

There are plenty of people—respected political scientists, winning political strategists, fellow journalists—who disagree with us on this point. Their view holds that campaigns do not matter all that much. By this light, the outcome of elections is preordained by larger factors, such as demographic trends or the performance of the economy, or by factors that have little to do with a candidate's public performance, such as fund-raising. Our view is emphatically the opposite. In a closely divided electorate, whoever wins either the Democratic or Republican presidential nomination has a clean shot at becoming the next president. It is folly to say, as many commentators do, that Hillary Clinton "could never win" because of her political past, or that the Republican nominee automatically will be "damaged goods," because of Bush's unpopularity in his second term.

The 2008 election, like most recent elections, will be a jump ball. Its outcome will hinge principally on which candidate capably implements the necessary practical Trade Secrets, most vividly understands what the electorate is seeking in a president—its ideological, emotional, and practical demands—and speaks to those demands in the most substantive ways.

• • •

NEEDLESS TO SAY, substance does not always play a starring role on the presidential campaign trail. Anyone who followed the past several presidential elections, in which the campaign narrative was dominated by personal attacks and controversies only tangentially connected to issues of governance, would be forgiven for wondering if serious ideas have any role at all. This book regularly invokes a phrase to describe the new arena in which presidential politics is waged: the Freak Show. The term comes from a late-night epiphany while channel surfing during the Clinton years. A cable news program featured a collection of reporters and commentators from the Left and Right shouting at one another about the Monica Lewinsky scandal. It was indeed a Freak Show, and one that seemed to embody the spirit of the age.

The Freak Show is about the fundamental changes in media and politics that have converged to tear down old restraints in campaigns and public debate. The power of the Freak Show has developed through a confluence of generational and technological forces, including the destabilization of political journalism practiced by the so-called Old Media, which includes the broadcast television networks, major newspapers, and national weekly newsmagazines. The relative decline of the Old Media has been caused partly by the rise of the New Media, which includes the Internet, talk radio, and cable television. These changes have contributed to polarization, the voguish word used to represent the divisions within the electorate. Polarization is not a new phenomenon in American history. The Freak Show is new. Its *incentives* for divisiveness are embedded deeply in political and media culture. These incentives—for publicity, for influence, for money, for votes—favor more extreme and uncompromising positions, provoking the ruthless tearing down of adversaries. Opponents are portrayed not simply as wrong but as morally flawed.

The supreme challenge for any presidential candidate is keeping control of his or her public image in the face of the Freak Show's destructive power. Successful candidates have a strategy for insulating themselves from the Freak Show (and, when possible, for exploiting it against their opponents). For both idealistic and realistic reasons, the best way to accomplish this is to have something important to say. The Freak Show is the enemy of ideas. But ideas are also the enemy of the Freak Show.

The first chapters of *The Way to Win* examine the history and modern workings of the Freak Show as the new backdrop of presidential campaigns. These include a sketch of one of the Freak Show's most influential and representative characters, Matt Drudge, and a case study of one of its most recent victims, John Kerry, a politician who exemplified the way to lose. From there we pivot to portraits of our two main characters. Bill Clinton's skills made him the dominant political figure of the 1990s. Karl Rove's talents helped make George W. Bush the dominant figure of the current decade. We close with some reflections on the woman who will, at least at the outset, dominate the 2008 campaign. All of these chapters are organized around Trade Secrets. Some Trade Secrets relate specifically to how candidates protect themselves and take advantage of the modern Freak Show environment. Others have less to do with the Freak Show than with the kind of methods smart strategists employ that lesser strategists do not. Several Trade Secrets reveal principles of victory that all the 2008 candidates, no matter their party or ideology, would be well advised to emulate. And a few Trade Secrets are not universally applicable, but require a choice between Clinton Politics and Bush Politics.

While politics has become defined by the Freak Show, its leaders are not representative of it. Karl Rove and George W. Bush are not freaks, nor are Bill and Hillary Clinton. They are serious people with the great talent required to reach the heights of their field. Nevertheless, each of them has had to reckon with and learn to manage the Freak Show, with its tendency to lunge toward personal attack. At times, all have benefited from the Freak Show, and its propensity to divide voters into camps united by resentment and outrage. These politicians are seeking to navigate a wild new age in our democracy, a challenge in which every American—including the next president of the United States—has a stake.

SECTION I

★ ★ ★ ★ ★

THE FREAK SHOW

★ ★ ★ ★ ★

THE WAY TO LOSE

★ ★ ★ ★ ★

THE COLLECTION OF WINNERS on that Little Rock stage was the most striking image from the Clinton Library opening. But also in attendance, sitting
in the crowd, was a pair of distinguished losers.

Al Gore and John Kerry had never been close, despite the many years they
served together in Washington. Now they shared a special bond. Both had
been beaten by a man they believed to be less articulate, less capable, less experienced, less virtuous, less worthy, and less intelligent than they. Both had
been preparing for the presidency since they were young men, spurred not
just by ambition, but by colleagues, friends, and mentors who for a generation had been anticipating their eventual candidacies. Gore and Kerry long
had stood out as quintessential strivers, even among fellow senators. Now
they looked up through the rain at a man whom almost no one had regarded
as presidential material until a couple of years before he got the job. Neither
Gore nor Kerry seemed to grasp the reasons for what both considered a cruel
hoax of history.

Gore had had four years to contemplate his loss, but for Kerry, the sting of
defeat was still fresh that morning. An instinctually competitive man, he had
served notice immediately after Election Day that he was eager to try again
for the presidency in 2008. To his face, Kerry got handshakes, praise for a
race well run, and condolences that the better man had not won. Behind his
back, in Little Rock hotel bars filled with visiting Democrats, the notion of
Kerry running again for president was greeted with derision and mockery,
even by people who two weeks earlier had been on his payroll.

If this were a book about all the reasons John Kerry lost the 2004 election,
it would be too heavy to hold. John Kerry was beaten by John Kerry, who

never overcame the limitations of his diffident personality. He was beaten by George W. Bush, who was by far the savvier politician. Deep thinkers might say Kerry was beaten by history, since Democrats for nearly forty years had been at a stark disadvantage when national security was the dominant issue in voters' minds. Here is another nominee for who beat John Forbes Kerry: Matthew Drudge.

If you are reading this book, you probably know who Matt Drudge is. It is a guarantee that most of the reporters, editors, producers, and talk show bookers who serve up the daily national buffet of news recently have checked out his eponymous website, and that www.drudgereport.com is bookmarked on their computers. That is one reason Drudge is the single most influential purveyor of information about American politics.

Drudge, with his droll Dickensian name, was not the only media or political agent whose actions led to John Kerry's defeat. But his role placed him at the center of the game—a New Media World Order in which Drudge was the most potent player in the process and a personification of the dynamics that did Kerry in. Drudge and his ilk made Kerry toxic—and unelectable.

Toxicity is the new defining trait of modern American politics. The toxins themselves are not new. Thomas Jefferson and Alexander Hamilton initially clashed like gentlemen (albeit venomously) over the limits of federal power and the future of the economy, but when news of Hamilton's saucy mistress Maria Reynolds surfaced, thanks to nonpartisan busybody James Callender, Jefferson was content to let the accusatory pamphlets fly.

Anger, prurience, invective, conspiracy theory—all are native flowers on the American landscape. What is new is the greenhouse in which these blossoms are cultivated and sold. This greenhouse was built on two beams. The first was the disintegration of editorial filters in the Old Media, which in an earlier age prevented the most salacious tales and bitter accusations (though certainly not all) from entering the public arena. The New Media—talk radio, cable television, Internet websites—for the most part never had these editorial filters. Many of its leading voices, Drudge among them, are openly contemptuous of the very idea. The Old Media, faced with filter-free competition, responded by loosening or discarding its own.

This in turn helped promote, and was promoted by, the second beam, the erosion of basic habits of decorum and self-restraint, in politics and media alike. In an earlier generation, these habits meant that people more often refrained from fully expressing how much they loathed one another. In the current generation, self-restraint is commonly regarded as a weakness and rarely

is rewarded economically or politically. The result is that the extreme and eccentric voices who always populated the margins of politics now reside, with
money and fame as the rewards, at the center. *Michael Moore, please say hello
to Ann Coulter.* The collapse of filters and the collapse of civility together
have changed the purpose of politics. The goal now is not simply to win, but
to persuade voters (and donors and viewers and readers) that an opponent
lacks the character and credibility even to deserve a place in the contest.
That is Freak Show politics.

Bill Clinton and George W. Bush were sitting on the stage in Little Rock
because they learned to navigate the Freak Show—and even to use it to their
advantage. Al Gore and John Kerry were sitting in the audience because they
did not. Were it not for the Freak Show, Kerry's title today likely would be
President of the United States. Instead Kerry's title is *Case Study.*

• • •

KERRY'S 2004 PRESIDENTIAL bid began in earnest, though unofficially, days
after the 2002 midterm congressional elections. These had been a disaster for
Democrats. Bush, invoking his party's credentials on national security, and
revving up a turnout machine run from the White House by Karl Rove, led
the Republicans to House and Senate gains. But the Massachusetts senator believed Bush might yet be vulnerable in his own reelection. What was
needed was a way to make plain to voters what seemed painfully obvious to
Kerry: Bush was an incompetent president. Kerry hired a campaign manager,
veteran Capitol Hill operative Jim Jordan, who set out with consultant Bob
Shrum and a wide circle of Kerry advisers to take inventory of the Democrat's
strengths and vulnerabilities. They might have been wise to start with his
hair.

By conventional measures, the thick mane atop Kerry's lean, craggy face
should have registered in the strengths column. His hair had grayed but not
receded by a single follicle over his six decades. Kerry was a bit vain about his
locks, and he gave them careful attention. As it happened, folks at the Republican National Committee had been paying attention, too. Sometime earlier, a tasty nugget of news raced around RNC headquarters. *Would you
believe that Kerry gets his hair cut at the Washington salon of Cristophe?* Yes, exactly, that Cristophe—the same guy who did Hillary Clinton's hair. Cristophe
was also the stylist who was trimming Bill Clinton that time in 1993 when
Air Force One sat on the tarmac in Los Angeles for two hours while the
whole world cooled its heels (never mind that reports about delayed air traffic turned out to be false).

No one at the RNC was surprised by the Cristophe news. Barbara Com-stock, the party's savvy research director, had been in television green rooms with Kerry and witnessed him fussing over himself before going on air, utterly oblivious to anyone or anything around him. Jim Dyke, the party's communi-cations director, sensed the Cristophe information would come in handy, and tucked it away for the right occasion.

On Sunday, December 2, Kerry publicly announced his candidacy to Tim Russert on NBC's *Meet the Press*. Ordinarily, this was the kind of news that would echo positively through the media for the rest of the week. With a well-timed placement, however, Dyke and his colleague Tim Griffin made sure that something else was waiting for Kerry, first thing Monday morning.

"**Exclusive**" promised the *Drudge Report*. "Cash and Coif!" read his headline, using the alliteration Drudge favors. "Democrat all-star John Kerry of Massachusetts is positioning himself as a populist politician while he takes the first step for a White House run. . . . But the self-described 'Man of the People' pays $150 to get his hair styled and shampooed—the cost of feed-ing a family of three for two weeks!"

Like many *Drudge Report* exclusives, this one implied rigorous reporting, including direct quotations from well-positioned sources to whom the author supposedly talked on a not-for-attribution basis. In this case, it was a "stylist source," who allegedly told him: "When it comes to his hair, Mr. Kerry is very, very particular. The coloring and the highlighting, the layering. But the re-sults are fabulous." Drudge also claimed he had spoken to a "green room in-sider" at Fox News's Washington bureau: "It's always a fight to get mirror time. He obsessively primps and poses before he goes on the air." Drudge items often quote from his roster of breathless White House insiders, top media "suits," or highly placed campaign aides, all furtively but authorita-tively telling Matt Drudge the way it is. Does Drudge really get on the phone and converse with such people? Some in the Old Media speculate that he takes his tips from a single source by phone or e-mail, then creates hyperven-tilated quotes based on (entirely plausible) speculation about what someone somewhere probably is saying. The assumption that Drudge is casually em-broidering his stories—what would be career-ending fraud for an Old Media journalist or author—has not caused reporters to remove Drudge from their daily reading. *Whatever. It's just Drudge. And maybe he's got something there.* As Jim Dyke knew, any superiority reporters and editors feel toward Drudge does not inhibit them from pouncing on his best items.

Within hours, the Cristophe story was everywhere. Rush Limbaugh chortled over it for an hour on his radio show. Later in the day, conservative commentator Pat Buchanan gave the website credit ("We learn from Drudge this morning . . .") on his MSNBC cable show. Kerry's team knew they had a genuine problem on their hands when they saw the next day's newspapers filled with accounts of "Senator Kerry's Bad Hair Day," as one newspaper put it. A Kerry spokeswoman noted indignantly that Drudge had erred: The senator did not pay $150 for his haircut, only $75—Cristophe charges less for men. This gave Drudge a new hook. Why, he crowed, was the would-be president patronizing an establishment that practices sexism? Inevitably, the whole fuss caught the attention of Jay Leno. By the end of the week he was joking on *The Tonight Show* that the "winds were so strong yesterday" in Massachusetts that "John Kerry's hair actually moved." Acknowledging that the line was a little lame, Leno explained, "You see, he's running for president—I wanted to get the first joke in."

Leno's tone suggested the ruckus over Kerry's hair was all in good fun. And a sensible person might have paused to wonder how a candidate's hair possibly could have any impact on a presidential race in an era of war, terrorism, and looming global calamity. But the Cristophe story was a serious portent of a much larger problem for Kerry, with which he would live almost daily for the next two years.

• • •

PRESIDENTIAL CAMPAIGNS ARE about storytelling. A winning presidential campaign presents the candidate's life story to voters. A losing campaign allows someone else to frame that story. In 1992, Bill Clinton's race vividly exemplified the phenomenon of competing narratives. There was plenty in Clinton's life to support his self-description as "The Man from Hope": an exceptional young fellow who grew up with few advantages but through brains and cheerful hard work had made a difference for his struggling Southern state. There was also plenty in that life to justify his opponents' description of "Slick Willie": a double-talking, temporizing, womanizing opportunist, whose private life and public record raised troubling questions about how he might behave in the White House.

In the end, more voters believed Clinton's version of his story. Kerry's personal life was not nearly as complicated as Clinton's, but his political challenge was bigger. Clinton had a detailed agenda, which he cared about and helped create. This is not true of all presidential candidates. Even rarer, Clinton had been the dominant voice in crafting that agenda. The most underappreciated assets in presidential politics are a coherent rationale and the ability to defend that rationale, not just with words but with convictions that flow from life experience. Clinton had these in abundance, as did George W. Bush. Kerry understood the issues, but had not harnessed them to a greater vision. He had not compiled an impressive record of legislative achievements in the Senate. Nor had he been an influential or consistent voice in the conversation over the direction of the Democratic Party, a debate that overlapped precisely with his Senate career. In the public mind, he stood for no particular ideas beyond a mild and conventional brand of liberalism. His advisers believed that Kerry's primary claim on the presidency was his personal biography. In this, they were indulging an obsessive desire of the political world, and reporters most of all, for a familiar plot line, in which a heroic life climaxes in a rendezvous with history at the White House. In the past generation, Bob Dole, Jack Kemp, John McCain, Bill Bradley, and John Glenn all have been lead characters in such dramas. None (so far) has ever gone to the White House except as a visitor.

A candidate who runs *principally* on his or her biography is acutely vulnerable to the accusation that this biography is embellished. Such a candidate, in other words, is a fat target for the Freak Show. One signature of Freak Show politics is a fixation on personality and alleged hypocrisy. Another is the ease with which shrewd political operatives can manipulate the Freak Show's attention to hijack the public image of an opponent.

Kerry and his political team knew exactly the story they would impart to voters. To paraphrase Henry Kissinger's famous line, the story had the added advantage of being largely true. It began with a bright, earnest young man whose interest in politics was sparked in the early 1960s by John F. Kennedy, and whose idealism led him to don a Navy uniform and fight heroically in Vietnam. Coming home, and recognizing that the war had become a terrible national tragedy, he stood on principle to oppose that war, and in so doing revealed his patriotism as valiantly as when he was fighting. Devotion to public service carried him to the United States Senate. The 2004 presidential campaign would bring this forty-five-year journey full circle, as the legacy of one JFK in the White House would be honored by a new JFK in the White House—a nearly mystical convergence of history. It was a powerful enough narrative to help make Kerry the Democrats' consensus front-runner for the presidential nomination from late 2002 through the spring of 2003.

But there was another way to tell the story. It was of a man who had been nakedly ambitious since his youth and had been willing to trim his sails to suit the moment ever since. The decision to go to Vietnam had been an obvious stepping-stone to politics. His tales of combat valor had been deliberately inflated, perhaps even manufactured. Sensing an opportunity to preen for the cameras in the antiwar moment, Kerry made a big show of discarding his war medals, but secretly hung on to a prized few. He affected a Kennedyesque accent and went before a Senate committee and prattled on fallaciously about alleged war crimes by his fellow servicemen. Elected to the Senate, Kerry found a natural home for himself as a vain and, thanks to two advantageous marriages, wealthy politician, with his finger in the wind and his hair under a blow-dryer.

Would the real John Kerry please stand up? Of course, *both* versions of his life had truth to them. Whenever Kerry's self-image tried to stand up, it was knocked over by a Freak Show interpretation. Every positive element of Kerry's existence was neutralized or turned into a weakness. Every vulnerability was maximized. By the end, this proud man was lying on the bloodied ice like a freshly clubbed harp seal.

One reason political operatives such as Jim Dyke value Freak Show politics is that it is never entirely clear who is swinging the club. From the average voter's vantage point, the Cristophe item just seemed to materialize. But the purpose and timing of Freak Show attacks are almost never coincidental, and they always landed at inopportune moments for Kerry.

• • •

A MONTH AFTER the Cristophe exposure, Kerry took his first trip as a candidate to Iowa. The Republican National Committee researchers again had done their jobs well. They had found a *Boston Globe* story from 1996 in which Kerry said: "I hate going to places like . . . Dubuque to raise large sums of money. But I have to. I hate it. I detest it." Kerry no doubt did not even remember saying such a thing, or the context in which he said it, but others made it their business to unearth these kinds of statements. Drudge was again the beneficiary of the RNC research. He reported this "breaking news" during an appearance on the Fox News show *Hannity & Colmes*. The date was January 16, 2003. By design, this was only two days before Kerry was scheduled to make an appearance in Dubuque. Hannity closed his interview by telling Drudge: "It's great for the country that you are out there. And keep giving the elites a tough time." On the *Drudge Report,* the dispatch quoted an outraged "Dubuque resident Marsha Vittal" who demanded to know where Kerry gets off by claiming he "wants to be my president, but he detests, detests coming to where I've chosen to live my life to ask for my support."

Curiously, the *Dubuque Telegraph Herald* could not find anyone named

Marsha Vittal listed in local phone books, Internet directories, or county voting records. By this point, though, it did not matter whether she existed or not. The *Drudge* item was dominating advance coverage of Kerry's visit in both the Iowa and the national media. Kerry and his aides were left to brainstorm over how to put the best face on their circumstances. As he stood up before Dubuque Democrats, Kerry said, "I'm thrilled to be here, contrary to all . . ." The next phrase was drowned out as the crowd erupted in laughter.

• • •

THE *DRUDGE REPORT* may be the leading platform for Freak Show politics, but it is not the only one. Under the right circumstances, even the *New York Times* can play a role. In April 2003, a *Times* story by chief political writer Adam Nagourney and White House reporter Dick Stevenson quoted an unnamed Bush adviser commenting on Kerry's appearance. "He looks French," the adviser cracked. Whether a planned insult or a spur-of-the-moment inspiration, it was one of the most ingenious remarks of the entire campaign. It brilliantly combined two Freak Show themes that were central to the Bush case against Kerry. One was that he was an exotic, even feminine, character. The other was that he was a virtual quisling, since the French were the most vocal foreign opponents of Bush's war in Iraq. Nagourney and Stevenson played the dig deep in their story, but it hardly went unnoticed. Teresa Heinz Kerry, the candidate's wife, perhaps did not help her husband's cause the next day when she responded with a shot of her own at White House advisers: "They probably do not even speak French." The *Times* story showed that one of the Trade Secrets of politics is truer than ever in the new environment: *Little things can become big things.*

The "looks French" line was picked up on Rush Limbaugh's show. Ann Coulter devoted a column to it. House Republican leader Tom DeLay delighted audiences with his new opening line: "Good afternoon. Or, as John Kerry might say, 'Bonjour!'"

As 2003 stretched on, Kerry faded as a laugh line. But only because his presidential ambitions were similarly fading, under the weight of his own lassitude and disorganization, and in the face of the fleeting rise of Howard Dean. Jim Jordan was sent packing by Kerry; some other staff, startled by the candidate's lack of loyalty and the discord he tolerated on his own team, chose to leave with Jordan. Yet one of Kerry's virtues as a politician had always been an ability to rise to the occasion. In January of 2004, he roared past erstwhile front-runner Dean and a field of others to win the Iowa caucuses, and then the New Hampshire primary. For a flickering moment, people seemed to be viewing Kerry in a new, more favorable light.

The golden light quickly turned harsh again. In mid-January, there had been passing references in the *Chicago Tribune,* the *Boston Herald,* and elsewhere to speculation that Kerry was freshening his look through injections of Botox. But this speculation did not ignite until it was highlighted on the *Drudge Report* on January 28: "New and Improved Kerry Takes New Hampshire." There were before-and-after photographs with analysis of the respective furrows. Kerry and his spokeswoman, Stephanie Cutter, both denied that he had received Botox injections. Former *Washington Post* editor Ben Bradlee once described a certain type of especially delicious story: "Too good to check!" Kerry's alleged Botox treatments fell in this category. Whether true or not, it fit so neatly into the existing image of Kerry as a popinjay that the story scurried through the news.

CNBC, MSNBC, the *Washington Post,* the *Washington Times,* the *Philadelphia Inquirer*—all of them, and lots of others, did Botox stories. Dean, then fighting vainly for a comeback, made a public gibe. The former Vermont governor, who had hardly concealed his dislike for Kerry, laughed aloud in conversations with reporters about the Botox rumor. *You know it's true,* he roared, throwing his head back in mirth. By March, even Vice President Dick Cheney was joining in the fun. At the Gridiron Dinner, an annual gathering of the Washington Establishment, he joked that the administration had dispatched weapons inspectors to "search for the bio-warfare agents we believe are hidden in Senator Kerry's forehead."

Another Drudge-driven story was not such a laughing matter. On February 12, the *Drudge Report* posted a "World Exclusive" stating various news outlets were investigating suspicions that Kerry had had an affair with a young woman, and that she had "fled the country, reportedly at the prodding of Kerry." Drudge wrote, accurately, that rival candidate Wes Clark had earlier told reporters, in an off-the-record session, that he believed Kerry's campaign would "implode over an intern issue." (Trade Secret for candidates: *Make sure journalists you are speaking with have the same understanding of "off the record" as you do.*)

In an earlier era—after Gary Hart but before Monica Lewinsky—rumors about a Kerry affair would have prompted editors and producers to hold lengthy, brooding meetings about what to do with the information. These discussions would drag on inconclusively for weeks or months. Reporters would be dispatched to investigate discreetly, and perhaps confront the campaign with the suspicions, but perhaps no story would run, even if the rumor proved true. This essentially took place in 1996 at the *Washington Post,* where editors debated how to handle the account of Bob Dole's affair in the 1960s, before finally tucking it in a story buried inside the paper.

Kerry's rumored dalliance, as with all such stories in the Internet Age, unfolded in real time. It soon was known to every American with a modem and a discernible interest in politics. On cue, Limbaugh devoted the first hour of his show to the story. Kerry, meanwhile, kept a previous appointment on the Don Imus radio program and, when pressed, said only, "There is nothing more to report." Later in the day he was more emphatic: "It's untrue, period." The denial was widely reported, earning a few lines from ABC's Peter Jennings on that evening's *World News Tonight.* From Africa, the woman in question, journalist Alexandra Polier, also issued a denial. Polier later traced the story to its apparent source: a former high school acquaintance who was aware that Kerry and Polier had once shared dinner after meeting at the annual World Economic Forum in Davos, Switzerland, and had wrongly assumed a romance. Polier theorized that the gossiping friend told her boss, who happened to be Republican lobbyist Bill Jarrell. He allegedly gabbed to others, and a rumor was born.

After the denials, the affair story quickly faded, if only because there was no oxygen, in the form of new details, to feed it. The news organizations Drudge claimed were working on the story never published a word about the alleged facts of the accusation, only about Kerry's denials. But at least some damage had been done to Kerry's image, set off by whoever gave the initial tip to Drudge.

By March, with the nomination in hand but many scars to show for it, Kerry felt he had earned a vacation. The candidate and his wife decamped for a skiing holiday in Idaho. Drudge was still hovering: "Spring Break: Kerry Retreats to His Sun Valley Mansion for 5-Day Luxury Unwind." As Republicans delighted in emphasizing, the Kerrys between them owned five properties. Drudge highlighted the fruits of some excellent Republican research on Kerry's Idaho home, including reference to the size, value, and taxes on the "compound," and the detail that the "mansion's 'Great Room' is a 500 year old barn" imported from England and reconstructed on site. Several newspapers began reporting on the other lavish Kerry-Heinz homes as well.

If retreating to Sun Valley was a dubious choice, it was aggravated in the coming days. The athletic candidate was snowboarding when he collided with a Secret Service agent detailed to him and took a spill on the snow. A reporter and cameraman were there for the encounter. "I don't fall down," Kerry snapped defensively, when the reporter asked him what happened, and he called the agent a "son of a bitch."

Kerry had been in the Senate for twenty years and in public life for more than thirty, but he appeared not to appreciate the reality of a presidential candidate's life. While the *New York Times* put the snowboarding morsel far down in its story about how the weary candidate needed a rest, Drudge trumpeted it on his site, and added, based on his own quasi-reporting, that Kerry and the agent had clashed before. The *Boston Globe* picked up the baton and noted, "Republican operatives even circulated to reporters and party members news of Kerry's jab at his Secret Service escort," and quoted one GOP strategist as pronouncing the incident "perfect material showing that Kerry will say anything, and can't control what he says." Republican officeholders fanned the flames. Weeks later, Republican congressman Jack Kingston of Georgia went to the House floor to give a speech about Kerry's five residences, listing the locations and prices of them all. "I will ask you, Mr. Speaker, how many guys do you know over 60 years old who know how to snowboard?" Kingston said. "I guess he bought five ski resorts to learn how. He wanted to flaunt it a little bit. But, to me, if you have a guy that age and he knows how to snowboard, he has not only too much money, but he has too much time on his hands as well."

As Kingston's remarks demonstrated, there were so many cartoon image themes available in the Republican toy chest that sometimes it was difficult for Kerry's opposition to choose which characteristic to mock. In the GOP conception, Kerry alternatively wore sandals (hippie), French loafers (*mon dieu!*), or flip-flops (enough said). And a negative Kerry theme, once floated, never really evaporated.

Eleven months after the *New York Times* got the Gallic ball rolling, a new round of the Jacques-ification of Kerry started up. In a March 15, 2004, story with a Paris dateline, the conservative-leaning *New York Sun* wrote that "the French are going wild for John Kerry." The line Drudge picked up was from the director of the French Center on the United States, Guillaume Parmentier, who described Kerry as having "a certain elegance." A few days later, an Associated Press story quoted Kerry's French cousin, Brice Lalonde, the mayor of St.-Briac-sur-Mer, the town where Kerry spent his boyhood summers, saying helpful things such as "John Kerry is incredibly American. He has absolutely nothing French about him."

Right around the same time, Kerry played into his opponents' hands by boasting of support he claimed to have from unnamed foreign leaders with whom he had met in New York (presumably some French among them). The Republican Party produced a video entitled *John Kerry: International Man of Mystery*. It was put on the Internet with the goal of earning free television news coverage, which it did, with its irresistible homage to the popular *Austin Powers* movies. By now, some Americans may have been convinced, Monsieur Lalonde's assessment notwithstanding, that there actually *did* seem something French about John Kerry.

Republicans also were quick to take advantage of Kerry's more blatant errors, most significantly when he declared at a West Virginia town meeting that he "was for" funding of the Iraq war "before he was against it," and when he decided to go windsurfing within camera view while vacationing on Nantucket, the graceful Massachusetts island where he and his wife owned a sumptuous multimillion-dollar oceanfront cottage. These two episodes, one about a serious matter and the other trivial, were cited by Bush aides as turning points in the election.

Kerry's opponents also leapt on his embrace of some Hollywood liberals who performed distinctly blue sets at a Radio City Music Hall fund-raiser he attended. President Bush and his campaign made Kerry pay over and over again for praising coarse-tongued entertainers as the "heart and soul of America" (a phrase highlighted on *Drudge* before it hit the newspapers and network TV). The line encroached on coverage of the selection of John Edwards as his running mate, which had occurred three days before.

The big controversies coupled with the petty images (John Kerry ordering a Philly cheesesteak with—take a deep breath—*Swiss* cheese; Teresa Heinz's barking at a conservative reporter to "shove it" on the eve of the Democratic convention; Kerry mispronouncing the name of the Green Bay Packers' fabled Lambeau Field) added up.

The stories about Kerry's vacation habits, his houses, his ties to Europe, his complexion, his hair, and all the rest had been deliberately promoted in order to exploit what Republicans long recognized as the candidate's greatest vulnerability: that he lived a life beyond the experience or even imagination of most of the people he hoped to lead.

• • •

THE PIÈCE DE résistance of the Freak Show in the 2004 campaign was taking Kerry's greatest asset, his military record in Vietnam, and transforming it into a liability.

In the winter of 2004, this thirty-five-year-old period in Kerry's life was resurrected, as Dean faded and Kerry improved his campaign trail performance. The final lift came when former Navy colleagues—the "Band of Brothers," as they became known—showed up in Iowa to vouch for the candidate. A flailing campaign was revived. The political logic seemed unassailable to Democratic voters in Iowa and New Hampshire: There is no way a candidate with Purple Hearts on his chest and shrapnel in his leg can be portrayed as weak. The old Republican strategy of painting Democrats as unreliable on national security could not possibly work against this Democrat. Within days of the New Hampshire triumph, however, there were signs that such a strategy might indeed be effective.

Once more, the *Drudge Report* served as a leading indicator of the potential potency of an anti-Kerry scheme. On February 11, Drudge's opposition-research friendships were again in evidence. Someone alerted him to a 1970 *Harvard Crimson* article, which he rendered into the headline "Radical Kerry Revealed. Old Harvard Interview Unearthed." The story was interesting and relevant, too, as a historical document illuminating the thinking of the candidate as a young man. "I'm an internationalist," Kerry said then. "I'd like to see our troops dispersed through the world only at the directive of the United Nations." He also said he wanted to "almost eliminate CIA activity." A few days later in the *New York Times,* Newt Gingrich announced that Republicans were not going to allow Kerry to go through the campaign portraying himself as a war hero. The reality, Gingrich said, was that he was a "Jane Fonda anti-war liberal."

In April, several Republican members of Congress marched to the House floor to deliver speeches about Kerry. The occasion was the thirty-third anniversary of his 1971 antiwar testimony to a Senate committee, when Kerry had alleged, among other things, that war crimes by U.S. servicemen were commonplace in the Vietnam theater. The congressmen, themselves Vietnam veterans, assailed Kerry for the "slander." One of them, Sam Johnson of Texas, showily entered Kerry's 1971 testimony into that day's Congressional Record.

In any era, the complexities and puzzles about Kerry's life in Vietnam and his subsequent return as a prominent antiwar leader would have been a subject of widespread attention in the Old Media. It was only in the context of the Freak Show, however, that this convoluted tale was forged into a powerful weapon by Kerry's opponents.

As the story of Kerry's Vietnam-era history played out, the Bush campaign and the White House made it a point to avoid addressing the allegations directly. The strategy was clear: Rhetorically honor Kerry's war service, selectively question his protest activity, repeatedly savage his "votes and quotes" on national security over the years, and make sure the Old and New Media received the results of their top-notch opposition research in a well-timed manner.

Most of this was on display during two critical days in late April—Sunday the 25th and Monday the 26th. First, Bush's close confidante Karen Hughes appeared on CNN and was asked by Wolf Blitzer if too much was being made of Kerry's past. Hughes said she wanted to divide her answer into two parts, the first of which was a splendid critique (and denunciation) of the Freak Show's basic dynamics as she experienced them in Bush's 2000 campaign:

> [D]uring our own campaign, there was all kinds of gossip and innuendoes and rumors, and many of them were reported, and they were put on the Internet, and then the mainstream media thinks they have to pick them up. And I think that's very troubling to people. It's almost as if . . . a candidate has to disprove a negative, rather than someone has to come forward and make a charge against the candidate. And I worry that does prevent good people from entering the democratic process.

Hughes then went on to say that she was "very troubled" by Kerry's charges of atrocities committed by Americans, although she acknowledged that Kerry had retreated somewhat from his statements of the 1970s.

She also said that she was "very troubled by the fact that he participated in the ceremony where veterans threw their medals away, and he only pretended to throw his. Now, I can understand if out of conscience you take a principled stand and you would decide that you . . . were so opposed to this that you would actually throw your medals. But to pretend to do so, I think that's very revealing."

It was one of the first (and last) times that a Bush campaign adviser directly raised questions about Kerry's Vietnam-era conduct. Kerry spokesman Phil Singer told CNN that Hughes's remarks "confirmed her membership in the right-wing smear machine . . . with her misleading attacks."

Whatever impact Hughes's words by themselves would have had was overtaken a few hours later when Matt Drudge posted the following dispatch:

XXXXX DRUDGE REPORT XXXXX SUN APRIL 25, 2004 16:52:38 ET XXXXX

1971 VIDEO: KERRY ADMITS THROWING OWN MEDALS; CON-TRADICTS CURRENT CLAIMS

In an interview published Friday in the LOS ANGELES TIMES, Dem presidential hopeful John Kerry claimed he "never ever implied" that he threw his own medals during a Hill protest in 1971 to appear as an antiwar hero.

But a new shock video shows John Kerry—in his own voice—saying he did!

ABC's GOOD MORNING AMERICA is set to rock the political world Monday morning with an airing of Kerry's specific 1971 boast, sources tell the DRUDGE REPORT.

The video was made by a local news station in 1971.

It directly contradicts Kerry's own website headline: "RIGHTWING FIC-TION: John Kerry threw away his medals during a Vietnam war protest."

Kerry's campaign refused comment Sunday afternoon, citing a policy not to respond to the DRUDGE REPORT.

Developing . . .

How did Drudge know what would be on *Good Morning America* the following morning? And how was it that the *New York Times,* also that Monday, would have a story based on the same 1971 video? (CNN's Candy Crowley, a believer in the divine, reported that the *New York Times* and ABC "found" the tape. But the *Washington Post* stated that "copies of the tape were provided to [the] two news organizations by the Republican National Committee, according to several media staff members familiar with the situation.")

In the fourth paragraph of its Monday story, the *Times* antiseptically noted that it "obtained a videotape of the interview late last week." The only indication of where the tape might have come from was in the comment "Republicans, nervous about questions regarding President Bush's Air National Guard service, have raised the issue to revive accusations by some veterans that the discarding of medals dishonored those who served and died in the war. At the same time, the Republicans have said that Mr. Kerry's explanation of what happened at the ceremony is an example of his proclivity to fall on both sides of every issue."

As for the *Good Morning America* airing of the tape, the stakes were raised by Hughes's remarks and the anticipation fostered among the Chattering Class by Drudge's hype. The stakes were raised even higher when Kerry agreed to appear live to proffer a response. The interview with ABC News's Charles Gibson was contentious, and after the segment ended, a heated Kerry, still wearing his microphone, bellowed, "God, they're doing the work of the Republican National Committee."

Kerry's aides posited that there was a coordinated effort by Hughes and the RNC, whose communications director, Jim Dyke, told the *Washington Post,* "It is interesting that John Kerry, confronted with his own words, blamed the RNC. Where the tape came from, the place to start would be the National Archives."

There are several Trade Secrets of the Freak Show represented by this episode. First, getting Drudge to build suspense for an exclusive is very helpful. Second, if you have a vintage video of the opposing candidate saying something controversial, exercise the patience to hold it until the candidate's contemporary words contradict the video. Third, if your opposition research not only forces your opponent to lose control of his public image but also makes him lose his temper on network television, give yourself bonus points.

For days, talk radio, cable TV, and the blogs were consumed with the tape, Kerry's emotional response, and the question of his veracity. Politics has always been an unpredictable business—more so, without question, in the Age of the Freak Show. And yet this strategy worked as if plotted play by play on a locker room chalkboard. By taking advantage of the new media environment, Kerry's foes painted him as an angry, unpatriotic liar. And the effective efforts to damage Kerry using his Vietnam-era past barely had begun.

• • •

IN 2004, THE Swift Boat Veterans for Truth started out on the margins of the presidential race. In an era of Old Media domination, they might have stayed there. When the group's founders held a news conference at the National Press Club in Washington on May 4, there was nothing in the next day's *Washington Post,* and the episode got scant attention elsewhere. A conservative website, FreeRepublic.com, however, covered the news conference and listed the fax numbers of Establishment news organizations, urging readers to send missives demanding to know why they were "blacking out" the event. A day later, the *Post* and *New York Times* carried short stories inside the paper. The *Post* report included the Kerry campaign's response that the Swift Boat

Veterans was a "politically motivated organization with close ties to the Bush administration."

The Swift Boat Veterans for Truth was organized by Vietnam veterans who profoundly resented Kerry's role in the antiwar movement. Some of the men personally had served with Kerry in Vietnam. The group was funded and promoted by prominent Republicans, several of whom had ties to both President Bush and Karl Rove, though no evidence of a coordinated effort ever emerged.

As it happened, the Swift Boat Veterans for Truth need not have worried about the amount of coverage they would receive, in either the New Media or the Old. And the spasm of publicity would come at the worst possible time for Kerry. On July 28, one day before Kerry formally accepted the Democratic nomination at the party's national convention in Boston, Drudge touted the imminent release of *Unfit for Command: Swift Boat Veterans Speak Out Against John Kerry.* On the morning of Drudge's report, the book was ranked at #1,318 on Amazon.com. The next day it had jumped to #2, and within a couple of days it hit #1. The book, published by the conservative Regnery Publishing, alleged that key elements of Kerry's account of his Vietnam service were false. Most dramatically, it claimed that Kerry's Bronze Star for heroic service, earned on March 13, 1969, was based on fraud. The group also questioned other aspects of Kerry's versions of his tour of duty and his involvement with the antiwar movement.

Beyond the book, the Swift Boaters started with relatively modest purchases of television advertising time. But their sophisticated political advisers knew that cable TV, talk radio, and, eventually, the Old Media would pick up on the ads themselves as controversial content, and give them the equivalent of millions of dollars in free coverage. This, of course, promoted their message and drove up awareness of their cause, traffic to their website, and donations to their coffers. In the end, the group was able to purchase additional millions' worth of television ads. Democratic polling showed widespread awareness of the group's message, even in places where the advertisements never aired. The group's work also lit up the blogosphere and talk radio for weeks, giving the Old Media another hook in covering the coverage of the story.

The Swift Boaters pointed out authentic flaws and contradictions in some of Kerry's assertions about his war service and protest activity. But their most sensational claims were either unsupported by evidence or contradicted by independent journalistic inquiries. This nevertheless did nothing to diminish the group's significance in the 2004 campaign: It inflicted crippling damage on Kerry. Many of his strategists in retrospect regard the Swift Boat Veterans as the single biggest reason he is not president today.

Initially, coverage was limited, and what did appear was sympathetic to Kerry. A *Washington Post* story from August 6 led with John McCain, a prominent Republican but a longtime Kerry friend, defending his fellow senator. The *Post* cited McCain's interview with the Associated Press in which he attacked the group's campaign as "dishonest and dishonorable."

Yet within a couple of weeks the Swift Boat Veterans charges were dominating the front pages, and reporting teams were assigned to ascertain the truth of the group's charges.

One reason the controversy moved from the margins to front-and-center was that Bush's reelection team—which had been watching the story with delight—helped push it there. While there is no evidence that the Bush campaign orchestrated the group's allegations, surrogates gave the charges respectable validation. The party's 1996 nominee, war veteran Bob Dole, appeared on CNN on August 22 and declared that the Vietnam criticism was fair game. If nothing else, Dole said, it exposed Kerry as a hypocrite: "I mean, one day he's saying that we were shooting civilians, cutting off their ears, cutting off their heads, throwing away his medals or his ribbons. The next day he's standing there, 'I want to be president because I'm a Vietnam veteran.'" As for the merits of the accusations, Dole suggested that the Swift Boat Veterans could not all be "Republican liars—there's got to be some truth to the charges." What about Kerry's war wounds? "I respect his record. But three Purple Hearts, and [he] never bled, that I know of. I mean, they're all superficial wounds. Three Purple Hearts and you're out [of the combat zone]." A week later, the president's own father weighed in similarly on CNN. From what he could tell, the forty-first president said, the claims of the Swift Boat Veterans were "rather compelling."

The Swift Boat Veterans' offensive presented Kerry with a classic political dilemma. If he responded, it might only elevate the prominence of the allegations. The alternative was to let damaging charges go unrebutted. It was not an easy question at the time but, in retrospect, there plainly was a right and a wrong answer. Kerry chose the wrong one. He and his team allowed themselves to imagine that, because the Swift Boat Veterans at first were not getting wide coverage in the Old Media, they could not be gaining much traction with the public.

Like many Democrats, Kerry and his team believed that presidential campaigns are fundamentally about which candidate has the best thirty-two-point policy plan and who snags the most endorsements from top-tier newspapers. The reality is that campaigns are also character tests. And, unlike gossip about a possible affair, the Swift Boat controversy went to the heart of Kerry's leadership character. As August dragged on, a debate grew in Kerry's campaign about whether to get off the sidelines and defend aggressively against the Swift Boat Veterans. The debate was resolved with a bold decision: *Let's wait for polling to settle the matter.* By the time the numbers came back, it confirmed for Democrats what Republicans already knew. The Swift Boat blitz was raising serious doubts among some swing voters about Kerry's veracity and values. Kerry's team finally responded, with a demand that Bush apologize for the Swift Boat attacks. That wan parry, which Bush swatted away, was so late and so lame that it hardly projected an image of strength, or solved the problem.

• • •

THE ENTIRE EPISODE, like Kerry's earlier encounters with the Freak Show, revealed the combination of indignation (*How dare they attack me!*) and insecurity (*This is a crisis—let's take a poll!*) that was at the heart of Kerry's campaign. In his defense, it must be said that this combination is characteristic of many Democrats. So, too, was the reaction of his party: pervasive grumbling to Old Media reporters about its candidate's incompetence in standing up to New Media abuse.

Kerry was hardly blameless. Most of the attacks against him were predictable, however unfair. Indeed, they were predicted. The failure of Kerry and his team to anticipate and prepare for such assaults was a lapse that fully justified the grousing of Democrats in Little Rock about their defeated nominee.

Bush certainly had his own Freak Show moments. The September 2004 controversy over whether he had evaded his commitments to the Texas Air National Guard was an example. That story, however, promoted by the Old Media warhorse CBS News, promptly was demolished by New Media critics. And though Bush survived it, the episode illustrated that he, too, had a life of competing narratives. According to some, he was a man born to privilege but with a common touch, whose life had been infused with new purpose once he embraced religious faith. This faith was the core of a presidency that had led the nation through the worst attacks on native soil in American history and was keeping the country safe in a dangerous new era.

There was another narrative, too. Bush was a daddy's boy and a lifelong mediocrity who was comically unprepared for the presidency and was elevated to the office by a Republican-weighted Supreme Court. With hawkish surrogates making the decisions, Bush had blundered into a disastrous war and had led the nation to the brink of catastrophe. As in 2000, the country in 2004 divided almost perfectly down the middle over which version of George W. Bush they found more plausible.

But new negative information coming to voters about Bush during the 2004 campaign was less likely to hurt him than negative data about the challenger. As Kerry's pollster Mark Mellman explained, "When an incumbent faces a challenger there is a fundamental asymmetry in information. Voters knew very little about John Kerry so each new fact, each new impression constituted a very large proportion of their total storehouse of knowledge about Kerry. That [made] attitudes toward him quite malleable. By contrast each new fact about or impression of George Bush constituted an infinitesimally small percentage of their knowledge about the President, making attitudes toward him harder to shape."

Sometimes in focus groups during the campaign, Mellman remembers, voters would have no idea Kerry had fought in Vietnam, but they would bring up Botox treatments and Kerry's "rich" wife.

Mellman's polling data demonstrated the impact the Swift Boat Veterans had on his candidate's public image. Just after the Democratic convention, voters who thought Kerry would keep America strong militarily outnumbered by 19 percentage points voters who said he would not. After Labor Day the margin was 3 percentage points. Over the same time period, Kerry saw comparable declines on "strong leader" (from 18 to 1) and "trust John Kerry to be commander in chief" (16 down to 3).

Because of the Swift Boat attacks, Kerry had to shy away from discussing Vietnam, which the campaign had planned to use as its entrée into presenting Kerry as a regular guy (through his crewmate relationships), illustrating his mettle, displaying his ideas for national security, and positioning him as a wartime president. Within Kerry's campaign, there was a roiling debate about when and how to take the issue on, but there was always more talk than action.

The Bush campaign and the Republican Party simply were better organized than the Democrats. Their research files on Kerry (and on Howard Dean, Dick Gephardt, and John Edwards) were significantly more thorough than the Democrats' files on Bush—and on themselves. Republicans had thick and frequently updated research books, clip files, video archives, and real-time tracking of new data, as well as a full appreciation of the value of such tools. With the speed of a cable modem and the ease of finger painting, Bush's supporters regularly circulated to New Media allies tidbits about Kerry's actions and statements. Kerry, meanwhile, often seemed uncertain about the facts of his own life. And his staff was unwilling and unable to get its reticent and private candidate to cough up enough details to mount a serviceable defense. Some of the anti-Kerry stories were patently false, some were patently true, some hovered in between. But over time, the accumulation of negative imagery was left largely unchallenged. And the merits of Kerry as a man, as a senator, and as a possible president were lost in the shuffle.

It should be noted that just because Republicans used the Freak Show's vast powers of simplification and amplification to disseminate these attacks does not mean they did not reveal some information to voters about what kind of president John Kerry might be. But the Freak Show is decidedly indifferent to the truth of such charges and elevates the personal and the negative over an impartial appraisal of an allegation's relevance in determining a person's qualifications for the office.

The bottom line was that the Bush campaign and its allies did a better job than the Kerry campaign and its allies in using the Freak Show—its magnification of the personal and negative—to define the opposing candidate. But the story as told in this chapter is a *tactical* one. What is more important for the next presidential election is the strategic reality that the Freak Show does not affect both parties equally.

The dynamic in 2008 will be the same as it was in 2004. There are structural issues in politics and media that now favor Republicans over Democrats. Freak Show politics will represent only a moderate threat to Republicans and give them a major advantage as they try to define the opposition on unfavorable terms. On the other side, Freak Show politics offers virtually no advantages for Democrats, but will again present a huge threat to any politician hoping to keep control of the narrative of his—or her—life story.

The Profile Primary

★ ★ ★ ★ ★

ONE OF THE EARLY THRESHOLDS any presidential candidate must cross is the Profile Primary. This is the point in a campaign at which a politician is being taken seriously enough by the news media that he or she will be the subject of lengthy biographical features in outlets such as the *New York Times,* the *New Yorker,* and the *Washington Post.* These stories will not be read by many voters. But they will be read (and filed for future reference) by the so-called Gang of 500.

The Gang of 500 is the group of columnists, consultants, reporters, and staff hands who know one another and lunch together and serve as a sort of Federal Reserve Bank of conventional wisdom. While the Gang of 500 is not as important as it used to be, it still has plenty of power—enough to punish a politician who tries to flout its residual authority. That is why a candidate's participation in the Profile Primary, in the form of long and self-revelatory interviews, is compulsory. Gang members believe it is crucial, before real votes get cast, that someone—specifically, *500 someones*—probe deeply and pass judgment on a candidate's intellectual timbre, applicable ambitions, philosophical journey, and telling life choices.

The Profile Primary holds both peril and opportunity. It is a chance to explain the embarrassments and family secrets that shadow every human life and place them in the context of a trajectory of achievement and personal growth. Perhaps the candidate dropped out of college for a semester in the early 1970s after an unfortunate projectile vomiting incident. (*"I woke up and got my act together. And those six months in the stockroom of that shoe store taught me more about hard work and marginal tax rates than I could have learned on any campus."*) Perhaps at age fourteen the candidate discovered his father was a cross-dresser. (*"No one needs to tell me about the importance of South Carolina's textile industry."*)

There is one question that invariably comes up as part of the Profile Primary that is so predictable its existence cannot even qualify as a Trade Secret: "What books have you been reading lately?" As it happens, most political reporters are more likely to collect books (from the book parties of colleagues or freebies from publishers) or even to write their own than they are to read them. Nevertheless, they believe it is important that the politicians themselves read books, and be duly inspired. Unless a candidate intends to run an avowedly anti-intellectual campaign, he or she must order the staff to prepare a plausible answer to the *what-books-lately* question. In 2000, for instance, the book of the year was a biography of diplomat Dean Acheson, which Texas governor George W. Bush said he was reading. Bush confirmed that, yes, the book was having a profound influence on him.

In the history of presidential politics, no candidate has ever been more skilled at winning the what-books-lately competition than Bill Clinton. At one point during the 1992 campaign, his press secretary Dee Dee Myers noted that her boss recently had reread the *Meditations of Marcus Aurelius,* and was at that moment also plowing through a historical biography and a Tom Clancy thriller.

As a service to those thinking of running for president in 2008, here are other questions that are sure to come up in the Profile Primary:

- *How did you meet your spouse?*

- *What is your favorite food, drink, movie, and Dwarf (of the Seven)?*

- *How often do you attend your chosen house of worship?*

- *What is your favorite vacation destination?*

- *Have you ever had illegal drugs, therapy, or a dustup with the law?*

- *Would you please say a few words in Spanish?*

The low point of John Kerry's campaign may have occurred when he first entered into the Profile Primary. It was the late spring of

2002, months before any voter would go to the polls with the option of choosing Kerry. But a novelist might argue that the Massachusetts senator that day ended his chances of being elected.

The setting was Kerry's Georgetown home—or, more precisely, the home he shared with his wife, Teresa Heinz ("Heinz" being the last name she was using at that point, acquired, along with the house itself, through her marriage to the late Republican senator from Pennsylvania, John Heinz, a handsome, wealthy, and popular figure, who died tragically in a 1991 plane crash). The Gang of 500 had sent as its representative Mark Leibovich (then of the *Washington Post,* and currently of the *New York Times*), a tart and keen-eyed writer who performed many of the 2004 presidential campaign cycle's Profile Primary duties.

Leibovich's story ran over four thousand words and was filled with favorable biographical details about both Kerry and his wife, none of which was retained for even two seconds by the Gang of 500. What the Gang remembered—all the way through Election Day 2004— were the less favorable moments, starting with the piece's opening scene, an edgy marital spat conducted in Leibovich's presence. (Trade Secret: *Don't fight with your spouse in front of the help, the Secret Service, or profile writers.*)

From the very first line ("Teresa Heinz is getting up a full head of rage while her husband, Sen. John Kerry, fidgets") to the fact that she referred to John Heinz as "my husband" and "the love of my life," and that she still wore "the blue sapphire engagement ring that Heinz gave her," the story was an unmitigated disaster for the couple and the campaign, creating instant and intense buzz among the Gang of 500.

As it got to the time when voters actually were about to vote, the image of the couple that Leibovich had imprinted into 499 other brains endured. *New York* magazine cited the "damaging" profile and said it "portrayed her as an outspoken, needy diva and her husband as a stoic wimp." In January of 2004, *Newsweek* said "reporters on the campaign trail" were "still talking about *The Washington Post* profile of the Kerrys . . . in which she challenged her husband in front of a reporter and talked freely of 'the love of her life'—her late husband."

Thus, for candidates in 2008: Just as your four-year status in high school was set in stone the first week of freshman year, so will your image be established with those first brushes of a profiler's pen.

The rules:

- Affix your happy face (and make sure your spouse dons a corresponding unwavering smile).

- Remember who liked you in grade school (and whom you beat up during recess).

- Visit a supermarket in an average-sized Midwestern city. Check the prices of a gallon of milk, a package of diapers, a box of cereal, and a six-pack of beer. Memorize them.

- Prepare a clever, equivocal answer about whichever movie, reality show, celebrity, or trivial media hullabaloo is stirring controversy at any given time.

- If you say something weird, rest assured: The tape recorder will record it, the transcriber will transcribe it, and the reporter will plop it right into the story, in quotes.

- If, during the interview, you consume more than three cups of coffee, more than two Diet Cokes, more than one candy bar, or a single sloppy sandwich, it *will* make it into the piece.

- Pick a Dwarf (recommended: Happy, Bashful, or Doc).

FREAK SHOW POLITICS

★ ★ ★ ★ ★

THE FORCES THAT CAUSED John Kerry to lose control of his public image in 2004 flowed from incentives that now influence the daily routines of people in the media and in politics, and dominate the interaction between the two professional cultures. These incentives for fame, money, power, are a basic feature of presidential campaigns. It was no surprise that the turbulence they caused, while buffeting both sides, hurt Kerry and helped George W. Bush. Republicans understood the new environment of presidential politics more keenly than did Democrats, and were far better positioned to benefit from it.

The term *Freak Show* might suggest images of exotic figures scheming at the fringes of presidential campaigns, but the reality is that the engines of the Freak Show operate at the center of national politics, not just at the margins. While the Freak Show's most flamboyant characters, such as Michael Moore, the director of the anti-Bush film *Fahrenheit 9/11*, or Jerome R. Corsi, co-author of the anti-Kerry book *Unfit for Command,* may have a dubious aroma, they have merged into a new mainstream. They regularly interact with the political strategists who run campaigns and the principal players of Old Media news organizations who, despite the competition that has encroached on their franchise in recent years, continue to direct political coverage. It is the cross-pollination between these two groups, the fringe and the Establishment, that produces the politics of personal attack and division that are Freak Show specialties.

The Freak Show was a decisive factor in George W. Bush's 2004 win. Bush was running for reelection at a time when polls showed many voters were not satisfied with the general direction of the country and his job approval ratings were below the levels at which a president is considered safe to retain the office. Bush's strategists knew their candidate would be in danger if the election was viewed primarily as a referendum on the previous four years. The race had to be seen as a *choice* between Bush and Kerry. The principal goals of the Bush campaign, therefore, were to persuade undecided voters that Kerry was an unacceptable alternative and to energize core supporters who were devoted to the president and disliked the senator. The Bush team pursued those targets by harnessing the poisonous strength of the new political-media environment.

This strategy almost certainly would not have worked in a past era when the major newspapers and television networks of the Old Media controlled the climate. But in the modern era, the power of the Old Media has weakened, challenged by the ideologically driven news organizations, websites, and pundit-provocateurs that make up the New Media. The simultaneous stumble of the Old Media and the rise of the New have had a disproportionate impact on the two warring sides in American politics. While there are plenty of conservatives who have been singed (or even burned at the stake) by the Freak Show, on the whole these changes have been beneficial for conservatives and bad for liberals, since the New Media overwhelmingly favors conservatives. There is no liberal equivalent of the Fox News Channel, or Rush Limbaugh, or the *Drudge Report,* all of which have significant audiences and a demonstrated ability to promote controversies and story lines that affect the Old Media. The Left, enraged by Bush's presidency and humiliated by the Right's successes in message control, lately has moved to promote its own New Media agents, especially bloggers. In the same manner as their conservative counterparts, these liberal voices seethe with contempt for what they regard as the hypocrisy and incompetence of the Old Media. The Left likewise has embraced its own brand of Freak Show politics, with a similar emphasis on accusation and ideological fervor. There is no reason to expect, however, that by 2008 the Left will have altered the fundamental balance of the right-leaning Freak Show.

The New Media's bias toward Republicans is unfair. But the New Media's growth was fueled by a widespread perception on the right that the Old Media's favoritism toward Democrats, while less overt, was itself unfair. Conservative complaints often were overheated, but they were not all fanciful. An Old Media tilt to the left existed for decades before the Freak Show, and still exists, albeit with diminished potency. The Right took its grievances and embraced a brand of New Media journalism that was less responsible and more blatant in its personal and ideological prejudices. Alarmed by this challenge to its primacy, the Old Media too often responded not with a recommitment to high standards, but by allowing the New Media to commandeer the Old Media agenda. This downward cycle has defined coverage of recent presidential campaigns, and it will be even more pervasive in the next one. The Old system had a referee, even if a flawed one. The New system has no referee.

A primary characteristic of Freak Show politics is the deterioration of Old Media filters. In the past, the Old Media tended to sift and suppress the angriest and most sensational elements of politics, using its editorial sensibility to shape voters' judgments. Technology and competition have weakened that power and shaken the self-confidence of many Old Media decision-makers regarding their own continued relevance and survival. The result is a willingness to let New Media interests infect editorial judgment.

This leads to the second, and most defining, aspect of the Freak Show: the rise of incentives for extreme behavior. In every arena of politics and media, there are rewards to be had—publicity, ego gratification, power, and financial gain—for going on the attack, for indulging the personal and the prurient, for eschewing the temperate middle.

In the Age of the Freak Show, centrist values—rhetorical restraint, ideological moderation, compromise with opponents—are increasingly impoverished. Extremist values—rhetorical invective, ideological purity, partisan loyalty—are richly rewarded.

These incentives exist in the media. They exist in the Congress. They exist among activists and interest groups. And, increasingly, they exist within the foundations of presidential campaigns. As a result, the competing sides of the electorate view each other with contempt, even hatred. To be sure, it is rational to seek power, fame, and wealth. But the cumulative effect of these incentives and the actions they inspire is a political system constantly staggering toward the irrational.

Intense and often violent disagreements over ideology, influence, and basic human rights have marked every generation in American history. The Freak Show, though, is a contemporary phenomenon. Its incentives breed division even when the underlying issues are of minimal relevance. It obscures legitimate debates behind clouds of accusation and spite. Moreover, the rewards encourage the players to keep the Freak Show stoked for electoral and financial gain, with 24/7 cable television, the Internet, direct mail fundraising, and publicity-hungry candidates enmeshed in a glutted, endless loop. This is an environment so quantitatively different from anything in America's past that it is qualitatively different, too. And the way to win in 2008 involves understanding these incentives and finding a strategy to transcend and exploit them.

The Freak Show's roots can be traced to a president who knew all about John Kerry. He would not have been surprised to learn that Kerry ran for president, but would have been deeply impressed by how Kerry was defeated.

• • •

"WELL, HE IS sort of a phony, isn't he?" Richard Nixon growled to his loyal aide Charles Colson, as they contemplated a twenty-seven-year-old John Kerry, who that week was making his national debut by testifying to the Senate Foreign Relations Committee in opposition to the Vietnam War. Nixon saw the patrician bearing and handsome features, and heard the Kennedyesque accent, and concluded that Kerry was a potentially dangerous man.

"He was in Vietnam a total of four months," Colson scoffed to Nixon. "He's politically ambitious and just looking for an issue." While other protesters spent the night camped on the National Mall, Kerry, in keeping with Nixon's image of him, stayed at the home of a Georgetown socialite.

At the time of this Oval Office conversation, in April 1971, Nixon had been in the White House for just over two years, and he had been at war— on the home front as much as in Vietnam—for all of them. By most measures the most powerful man on the planet, he nevertheless felt persecuted by the East Coast Establishment, which loomed over American life and included the liberal intelligentsia at the universities and in think tanks; the representatives of the big newspapers and network newscasts; and those wealthy Georgetown socialites who looked down sneeringly at a Republican president.

The battle ended when Nixon was routed from power, his criminality exposed, his legacy ruined. But the initial clash was sparked by his conviction that, as a Republican and a conservative (by the standards of his time), he was governing in a media and political atmosphere that was intrinsically hostile to him. He also had a vision of what he could do about it.

Years later, in a reflective mood, Nixon wrote in his memoirs: "I felt that the Silent Majority of Americans, with its roots mainly in the Midwest, the West, and the South, had simply never been encouraged to give the Eastern liberal elite a run for its money for control of the nation's key institutions."

In a less reflective mood, while still in power, he said to Colson: "One day we'll get them—we'll get them on the ground where we want them. And we'll stick our heels in, step on them hard and twist, right, Chuck?"

Nixon's great hope was for a brand of politics conservatives could use to manipulate the divisions and resentments of the electorate to their advantage, liberating themselves from having to worry about what either partisan critics or the news media said about them. In his own time, Nixon's faith was misplaced. But his vision has since come to life for his political legatees.

Richard Nixon is the godfather of the Freak Show and the philosophical inspiration for conservative efforts to defy the liberal Establishment. It is perhaps his only legacy to modern conservatism. Ken Mehlman, a protégé of Karl Rove who ran George W. Bush's 2004 reelection campaign and later became chairman of the Republican National Committee, explained: "Nixon understood before other people . . . that the elites and the media no longer reflected the values of the American people. . . . We became a populist party under President Nixon because of that, because of the resentment [toward] those elites."

• • •

ONE OF THE most important statements in Nixon's challenge to the Establishment came in a speech assigned to Vice President Spiro T. Agnew, and designed to confront network television news. Nixon himself studied the draft, leafing through the pages with an expressionless gaze, before finally looking up in delight. "This really flicks the scab off, doesn't it," the president said to the speechwriter, a clever young polemicist named Patrick Buchanan, as they huddled together in the Oval Office.

On November 13, 1969, Agnew flew to Des Moines, Iowa, to level the administration's attack. The specific complaint was the networks' habit of following major presidential addresses with "instant analysis" provided by correspondents and commentators. As the White House saw it, these analyses revealed arrogance and liberal bias, since the commentary inevitably dripped with contempt for Nixon and his policies.

But Agnew was not really making a narrow criticism of "instant analysis." By unmistakable implication he was questioning the values and legitimacy of the Establishment media generally—not only the three networks but also the elite newspapers and national newsweeklies that collectively set the agenda for how a president was covered.

Agnew was a previously obscure Maryland governor who as vice president became famous for his diatribes against liberals and his addiction to alliteration ("nattering nabobs of negativism," "pusillanimous pussyfooters"). With a taunting tone that suggested how much he was enjoying the task, the vice president delivered words that long had been commonplace in living rooms and taverns in conservative precincts across Middle America. What was remarkable was that now such sentiments were invested for the first time with the authority of an administration in power.

Network news, Agnew said, was run by "a small group of men, numbering perhaps no more than a dozen anchormen, commentators, and executive producers," who reserved the right to determine what their audience of tens of millions would learn about the "great issues in our nation." The vice president noted that "to a man these commentators and producers live and work in the geographical and intellectual confines of Washington, D.C., or New York City." And what about these places? "Both communities bask in their own provincialism, their own parochialism. We can deduce that these men read the same newspapers. They draw their political and social views from the same sources. Worse, they talk constantly to one another, thereby providing artificial reinforcement to their shared viewpoints."

Agnew's assault carried a loud echo. Thrown on the defensive, the networks felt obliged to cover the speech live. It made the front pages of both the *Washington Post* and the *New York Times*. Agnew's and Nixon's targets responded with indignation. Frank Stanton, the president of CBS, called Agnew's speech an "unprecedented attempt to intimidate a news medium," comments that were echoed by executives at the other networks. Senator Edward M. Kennedy said Agnew had delivered "an attack designed to pit American against American." He had that part right. A few weeks earlier, Agnew had given another speech declaring the administration's intentions: "It is time for the preponderant majority, the responsible citizens of this country, to assert their rights. If, in challenging, we polarize the American people, I say it is time for a *positive polarization*."

* * *

NIXON'S WAR AGAINST the Establishment was bold, but it was also foolish. For one thing, he had no effective means to win it. Unlike now, there was not a conservative anti-Establishment with an infrastructure of media organizations, advocacy groups, and think tanks to aid him in battle. For another, both Nixon and Agnew were so flagrant in their criminal behavior that they were acutely vulnerable to the Establishment's counterattack. Indeed, Nixon's resignation over the Watergate scandal represented the historic high point of Establishment news media power. But this should not obscure the historical relevance of the Nixon-Agnew indictment.

Today, one strains to recall that not that long ago there really was a "small group of men"—and at that time they were all men—who served as gate-keepers for what the public learned about national politics. It included the anchors and top producers of the evening newscasts; the editors of the *New York Times, Washington Post,* the wire services, and perhaps a handful of other papers read closely by elite opinion-makers; and the editors of the weekly newsmagazines. Of course, these people did not assemble in regular meetings to reach shared judgments about the news. By virtue of their cultural and ideological perspectives, they inexorably arrived at the same place.

Some of the most serious journalists of the period acknowledged the obvious: Nixon's complaint was partly justified. One day during those years, *Washington Post* reporter Richard Harwood returned to the newsroom from an antiwar protest on the Washington Mall and confronted his editor, Ben Bradlee: "Jesus Christ, how am I supposed to write this story? The first god-dam person I ran into in the demonstration was my wife. And the second person was yours."

Like Harwood forty years ago, a journalist today is more likely to run into his spouse, or his boss's spouse, at a rally on the Mall for a liberal cause than for a conservative one. During Bill Clinton's first presidential campaign, a major profile of him in *U.S. News & World Report* magazine carried three by-lines. Two of the writers later took jobs in Clinton's White House, while the third ended up marrying one of Clinton's top political consultants. This type of cultural affinity is not by itself evidence of bias. But it is one reason many Republicans are suspicious of the Old Media.

• • •

THE SEEMINGLY ANCIENT history of the Nixon era is relevant to the 2008 presidential campaign. To understand the Freak Show, one must understand its birth and the disparate lessons that different groups took from the triumph of the Old Media during Watergate, when corruption was exposed by persistent truth seekers.

For Democrats, the legacy of Watergate was that the good guys won. Nixon's surrender was a mutual victory for clean politicians and a valiant press, epitomized first by the brave reporting of the *Washington Post* and later by other Establishment platforms such as CBS News and *Time* magazine. Democrats could gloat, *Republicans are press-bashers, because they have something to hide. We are the virtuous ones, so journalists are our friends. By day, we can be professionally supportive. By night, we can trade off-the-record gossip and enjoy fancy dinners at the expense of the publishers.*

Today, things have changed. Democrats feel a sharp sense of betrayal toward the Old Media, which they believe has let them down. *First the press equated Clinton's oral exploits with Nixon's subversion of the Constitution. Then they went limp against George W. Bush, who if anything is more dangerous than Nixon. Those press guys make me so angry! Still, it would be nice if we could be friends again.*

For many Republicans, the lesson of Watergate was that the system was tilted against their kind, that reporters voted Democratic, but that it was necessary to make the best of a skewed situation. *Reporters are not so bad if you keep them well fed and in the loop.* Ronald Reagan was far more conservative than Richard Nixon, and had his share of disdain for the ingrained liberalism of the Eastern Establishment and its news media allies. But he never considered conducting systematic Nixon-style combat against the press or other Establishment power centers. Neither did Gerald Ford or the first President Bush. And if any of those three Republican presidents had been inclined to challenge the Establishment, they would have found insufficient allies in their effort. Congress was still controlled by the Democrats. Liberal elites in the media, the lobbying world, the federal bureaucracy, academia, the labor movement, think tanks, and the publishing business reinforced a common worldview. Ford, Reagan, and Bush 41 were friends and drinking partners with powerful Democratic lawmakers such as Democratic Speaker of the House Tip O'Neill. This was not simply a matter of temperament (or nontemperance). Washington's culture was predicated on a functioning center in which politicians felt it was in their interest to be on amicable terms with the opposition, even if that meant accepting an unfair status quo.

For another breed of Republican, the lesson of Watergate was quite different. The heirs of Nixon's true bequest to the modern conservative movement allowed that Nixon might have been a flawed messenger, but the message itself was valid: The established order, in particular what they viewed as the liberal orientation of the news media, had to be toppled.

These acolytes took small but steady steps. It was during the Nixon years that the watchdog group Accuracy in Media (AIM) was founded by an irascible yet indefatigable conservative named Reed Irvine. For decades, the group has churned out an unbroken skein of examples meant to show how the Old Media leans to the left and a log of the revolving door between journalism and Democratic politics. AIM exists to this day, though it is no longer the lonely voice in the wilderness it was in the 1970s and 1980s. Now, the essence of Irvine's media critique, once regarded as eccentric and extremist, is echoed daily by Rush Limbaugh and legions of other commentators on cable television, talk radio, and websites, and sometimes directly from the Bush White House briefing room podium.

Another outgrowth of the Nixon years was the Heritage Foundation, a think tank founded in 1973 in the belief that the Right needed to aggressively cultivate and promote policy ideas in order to counteract the influence of supposedly nonpartisan but pervasively liberal places like the Brookings Institution. There was a common theme to these efforts by the Right. *The liberal Establishment will never give us a fair break, and complaining will do no good. We should not stop fighting, but start fighting smarter—by creating our own voices and institutions.*

• • •

FOR A FULL generation after Nixon's fall, the old order prevailed. Only with the arrival of a young new president in 1993 did it collapse. Bill Clinton took power just as several distinct trends that had been building for years converged, creating a chaotic new order in the relationship between the media and the political Establishment.

The first of these trends was in nearly every respect a positive development. The Cold War was over, a cause for relief and optimism. The gravity of the contest, with the prospect of nuclear annihilation in constant orbit, had imposed a certain restraint on U.S. domestic politics. It is hard to imagine Bill Clinton, a boyish and informal man with few national security credentials, being elected in 1992 if the Cold War had not ended. But it is also hard to imagine a newly elected president being subjected to such systematic disrespect by the opposition in a Cold War context. Republican congressman Dick Armey stood on the House floor during Clinton's first term and told Democrats, "Your president is just not that important to us." Republicans, who a few years earlier had deplored any efforts to weaken the prerogatives or mystique of the Oval Office, now cheered as independent counsel Kenneth Starr and other prosecutors publicly disrobed the president. Describing such treatment, Clinton himself later reflected: "I think the end of the Cold War had something to do with it. Some irresponsible people thought they could afford to play fast and loose because they believed there were no serious consequences in politics. They seemed to believe it was okay to tear down the presidency in the service of ideological, professional or financial goals." Clinton, of course, further opened the door to attacks through his personal conduct.

The second historical trend was the ascent of members of the 1960s generation—Bill and Hillary Clinton's generation, as well as Newt Gingrich's and Rush Limbaugh's—into positions of prominence in public life. As numerous demographers and cultural historians have noted, the baby boomers came of age with a different set of political values, and a starkly different style of argument, than their elders in the 1950s "Silent Generation" or the World War II–era "GI Generation." Those senior groups placed a higher premium on societal consensus as a paramount value in national life. When they did disagree, it tended to be over economic issues, like the power of labor unions. The 1960s generation, raised amid relative affluence, was more prone to clash over cultural issues, like the rights of women and minorities. Opponents can split the difference over an economic issue, such as the proper level for the minimum wage, while cultural politics encourages fiery language and fervent conflict. Its practitioners presented their arguments not as a contest between wise policies versus unwise, but as a mortal struggle of good people versus bad. Gingrich draped his own agenda in almost messianic terms, claiming that he was a "transformational figure" whose aim was to "renew American civilization." Few leading Democrats spoke in quite such exaggerated language, but the instinct for grandiose and unabashedly moralizing rhetoric was by no means confined to conservatives. Hillary Clinton in the first year of her husband's presidency gave a searching speech about the spiritual poverty of modern life and called for a new "politics of meaning." Al Gore, as environmental evangelist, advocated eliminating the internal combustion engine by 2016 and said that halting global warming should be "the central organizing principle for civilization."

The third trend was the advent of a political culture of attack and revenge, characterized by the rise of independent counsels; congressional investigations into Iran-contra, Whitewater, and other executive scandals; confirmation fights over presidential nominees of both parties; and the "sack the quarterback" approach, described by Claremont McKenna College professor John J. Pitney as a tactic in which both parties attempt to score political bonus points by taking out the other side's congressional leaders through ethics investigations or at the ballot box (as in the cases of Gingrich and South Dakota Democratic Senate leader Tom Daschle). Well-funded interest groups on both sides became increasingly oriented toward this type of combat.

The fourth trend related to the technology of media. Nixon could only fume impotently against the power of mass media. His successors increasingly were able to abandon mass media in favor of niche media that spoke directly to the grievances of their followers. Conservative talk radio flourished with Clinton's arrival, as Limbaugh and scores of accordant commentators made their careers by attacking the new president. Cable television soon followed with its own conservative voices, and conservative websites arrived shortly after that. At every turn over the past two decades, said Bush adviser Ken Mehlman, "the de-massification of the media has benefited conservatives."

These four historical trends were engines of the phenomenon called polarization. Unlike Spiro Agnew, who celebrated "positive polarization," virtually no one in either major party publicly says that polarization is a good thing.

There have been many periods in American history that have produced polarized politics, complete with riots, lynchings, and bloodshed. On May 19, 1856, Senator Charles Sumner of Massachusetts launched into a two-day speech on the Senate floor denouncing the efforts of slavery advocates to bring Kansas into the Union as a slave state. The pro-slavery agitators, he said, "were picked from the drunken spew and vomit of an uneasy civilization." In response, a South Carolina congressman named Preston Brooks approached Sumner at his desk on the Senate floor and flayed his skull thirty times with a gold-headed cane. Sumner lay in a pool of blood, and suffered maladies the rest of his life. Across the Southern states, people cheered Brooks's gesture as noble. As an example of polarization, that is hard to top. What Vice President Dick Cheney did on the Senate floor 147 years later in 2003—suggesting that Vermont senator Patrick Leahy perform an anatomically impossible sexual act on himself—seems downright civil by comparison.

In Sumner's time, however, there were not the lavish rewards for everyday extremism and conflict that now define Washington politics.

Most members of Congress come from districts whose lines are drawn overwhelmingly to favor one party; therefore, they have no reason to court independents or opposition party voters with centrist language and positions. To the contrary, moderate stances or statements might invite a primary challenge from a more ideological candidate. Alienating the party leadership could result in a loss of committee assignments or assistance with election fund-raising. The number of party-line votes, which mirror hardened partisan sentiments in the electorate, has increased dramatically in the past decade.

Hand in hand with this development, the institutional elements of the conservative movement grew substantially larger than they were forty years ago. At the same time, liberal group power (such as that of labor unions) shrank. The Clinton White House spent little effort trying to build up the Democratic Party, its allied interest groups, or the corresponding think tanks to make them modern and efficient. In clashes of substance and style, from the 1990s into the new century, the Left was several steps behind.

With a Democrat in the White House in the 1990s, conservatives looked beyond the old methods to dispatch and receive their information and analysis. The alternative voices that conservatives embraced do not serve as a corrective to bias and a spur to more fair-minded coverage. To the contrary, these voices make little pretense of neutrality, nor do their listeners, viewers, and readers expect it. As Limbaugh has proclaimed, "I don't need equal time, I am equal time!" The Right years ago gave up on the notion of journalism or commentary that is detached from the struggle for power. Every news story and every opinion is regarded as either weapon or shield in the daily ideological brawl. And every purveyor of information is either a member of the home team or of the enemy. This radical view of the role of information and the absence of agreed-upon facts to frame debate is another essential aspect of the Freak Show.

In an ideal world, the values of accuracy, fairness, and relevance espoused by the Old Media would be a countervailing force against the Freak Show values of malice and agitation. At some news organizations, the reality approximates this ideal. In general, however, the Old Media finds itself on the brink of the 2008 campaign in an enfeebled position.

Most of the main organs of the Old Media that existed in Nixon's time are still around. Every operation, from the network news to the wire services to television stations, even back then had down-market elements and the need to balance commercial success with public interest journalism. Every one has its own history of decline since the 1990s.

This across-the-board deterioration was impelled by more pressure to control costs; less public appetite for the existing products; weakened market share because of amplified competition; fewer experienced reporters; more profit-driven corporate ownership; fewer family-run, civic-minded prominent media properties; dwindling audiences, with younger people less inclined than their parents to consume news; shrinking concern about politics and government because of the end of the Cold War; and a public perception of journalists as members of a spoiled, sensationalistic special interest focused more on embarrassing people in public life than protecting the public good.

Hampered and distracted by all of these problems and facing an identity crisis, every Old Media news organization in the country acted more or less the same way, either contributing or acquiescing to the Freak Show. Serious news outfits still covered issues, filed Freedom of Information Act requests, and spent the resources required to hold powerful interests accountable, especially government officials and presidential candidates. But those efforts were no match for the volume and pervasiveness of the Freak Show. The roles of providing objective facts, of adjudicating disputes, of helping citizens understand complicated policy debates—all of that gave way with greater frequency to a different type of journalism.

The Old Media landscape now is cluttered with trivial stories with a prurient angle (the misfortunes of young women such as Chandra Levy and Natalee Holloway); dubious stories manipulated by overzealous sources (questionable leaks about the integrity of nuclear scientist Wen Ho Lee) and personality-driven stories that favor process over policy substance (read almost any newspaper story in the heat of a presidential campaign).

In terms of both standards and business models, news organizations changed in fits and starts—or off-the-cliff plummets—throughout the 1990s. The *New York Times* started a gossip column (mercifully killed in the spring of 2006). The network news divisions became addicted to the O. J. Simpson trials, and in some cases bestowed White House beats on correspondents whose primary national journalism experience was earned in Judge Ito's courtroom. Foreign bureaus were closed. The "flagship" evening newscasts that once defined the networks were superseded in budget and significance by prime-time television newsmagazine shows and the weekday morning programs, featuring lighter fare. Newspapers experienced declines in both revenue and circulation, and increasingly saw their once hugely profitable print editions lose advertising and readers to the Internet.

At the same time, the New Media was burgeoning. Tabloid programming like *A Current Affair* and *Inside Edition*, cable news, and the increasingly influential talk radio offered serious competition, and the Internet exploded. The political discussion progressively was shaped by the Freak Show sensibility that defined these outlets. All this has led the Old Media to be increasingly attracted to the Freak Show's emphasis on conflict, personality, and scandal over substance, and to find it increasingly difficult to just say no to the salacious stories that dominate the New Media on radio, local and cable TV, e-mail, and the Web.

If you have that trendy twenty-first-century job of activist/paid speaker/ blogger/TV commentator, your capacity to get attention and work is based almost exclusively on how shrill and negative you can be. The Old Media increasingly borrows content and talking heads from the New Media specifically for shock value. So Rush Limbaugh gets a seat on NBC News's fabled *Meet the Press* (with Tim Russert introducing "the world according to Rush Limbaugh"). Or the *New York Times* invests divine meaning in Matt Drudge's treatment of a flashy story (the *Times*'s short-lived coverage of rumors about John Kerry's alleged extramarital affair was light on the facts and heavy on the Drudge references). Or *Good Morning America* covers the day's political developments by inviting Ann Coulter to pull up a chair. Spend a few thousand dollars to make an inflammatory television ad, or an "Internet video" that you post on a website, and you can be fairly sure that pliable Old and New Media conveyor belts will reward you with ample—and free—additional distribution to their wider audiences. That in turn will give you more publicity, which will allow you to raise more money, which will increase your influence.

Politicians also are drawn to the new venues in which the extreme is rewarded. Most members of Congress, for example, almost never turn down appearances on TV, seldom asking with whom they will debate, because they can reach potential supporters and donors in one short visual blast. The need for twenty-four-hour content, fast and snappy, has served to obscure the distinction between advocates and journalists. Partisans often are booked as guests on TV, but appear on platforms that might seem to the ordinary viewer to be journalistic.

For some, the enticement of the camera is so great that they permanently leave politics for punditry, further blurring the lines for viewers and voters. In fact, right-leaning New Media programs, aware that a number of Old Media figures once worked as partisan Democrats, feel morally justified in giving prominent roles to Republicans as talk show hosts or contributors.

In this new environment, the Old Media has lost much of its power—and too much of its moral authority—to referee disagreements or provide universally reliable facts. Meanwhile, the financial success and growing market share of New Media organizations serve as another temptation for old-timers to get out of the impartial refereeing game and into the Freak Show. There is decreasing commercial reward in producing the kind of tough and fair-minded journalism that requires serious resources.

Happily, there are news organizations that have resisted this trend. They include ABC News, the Associated Press, the *New York Times,* the *Wall Street Journal,* and the *Washington Post.* Unhappily, these organizations lack the relative authority they had in an earlier age to raise the overall tone of

presidential coverage. That means the full roster of defects in modern journalism will be on excruciating display in the 2008 presidential race. These
include the shredding of Old Media standards by New Media competition,
short attention spans, and general lack of seriousness. In the campaign context, journalists spend way too much time on polls, too little on policy and its
consequences. Of course, it takes no particular nerve to denounce these
maladies. Within the business, doing so is nearly obligatory. But what about
the most notorious journalistic sin of all?

Discussions about ideological bias in the news media are a drag. From a
journalist's perspective, few conversations are more awkward or tedious. One
strain of argument holds that most journalists are liberal, so they skew presentation of the news in the direction of their own views. The critics cite
surveys of newsrooms (some of dubious methodology) showing that most reporters are more liberal than the general public on such questions as abortion
rights, gay rights, gun control, and the proper role of government in helping
the poor. This certainly rings true to us, never mind the surveys. A contrary
argument posits that the more significant bias in the news media is conservative, because most news organizations are owned by big corporations concerned above all with protecting their economic interests. This notion seems
weak—the problem with too many corporate owners is indifference to the
news product, not a determination to instill it with their own ideological preferences. Finally, the Bush years have seen a surge in the double-backflip-
with-a-half-gainer take on the media bias argument. This version contends
that, while most journalists are liberal, the media has become so spooked
after years of complaints about liberal bias that reporters and editors lean the
other way, thus ensuring that news about politics carries a conservative bias.
This is possible, but the view corresponds with little or nothing in our own
experience.

These arguments get made exhaustively and exhaustingly—never reaching resolution and almost always illuminating more about the bias of the
debaters than the journalism they critique. Yet it would be a mistake to
dismiss the entire bias debate.

First, there is no way to understand modern presidential campaigns
without recognizing that nearly all Republican strategists begin with the assumption that the Old Media's ideological prism works against their party.
Additionally, although Democrats and most reporters are reluctant to admit
it, those Republicans are sometimes right.

It is true that the cry of "liberal bias" often is made frivolously, by people whose real objection is being the subject of unflattering but accurate journalism. It is true also that the accusation sometimes gets made cynically, by operatives who know that attacking the news media is an effective way of riling up the base. To the extent that there is an ideological slant to the Old Media, it is attenuated by professional habits and customs that do not exist in the portion of the New Media that celebrates a flagrant and unapologetic brand of conservative bias. Additionally, members of the Old Media do not self-consciously operate as partisans rooting for one side, as is common in the New Media. In June 2006, Fox News's Sean Hannity, for example, said of Hillary Clinton's presidential prospects, "She will not win. That more than anything is my solemn vow." No Old Media commentator would comfortably make such a partisan statement.

• • •

BUT DISCLAIMERS DO not erase the fact that there often is a tilt to media assumptions—most important, about which side gets the benefit of the doubt and which side gets roasted. And the tilt is most likely to evidence itself in campaign coverage. Often the best examples are stories that do *not* become big controversies. The news media's cultural, ideological, and personal sympathies can be revealed by the dog that doesn't bark. To illustrate the point, let's take a brief excursion into an alternate universe.

Imagine for a moment that five of the richest conservatives in America—one of them a billionaire—had decided in 2003 to give tens of millions of dollars to fund two new legally independent organizations that would work in all the battleground states and pay for media advertising aimed at defeating the Democratic presidential nominee.

Over the course of 2004, imagine that these five self-avowed conservatives gave over $70 million to the two groups for the express purpose of defeating John Kerry. Say these groups were headed by George W. Bush's former campaign manager; a senior member of the Republican National Committee; the top political operative of the Christian Coalition; and the head of the National Rifle Association. Other board members would be representatives of the Chamber of Commerce, the National Federation of Independent Business, and National Right to Life. These strategists met regularly and secretly, sometimes in the homes of their very wealthy benefactors, to plot and plan. At one point, a widely distributed e-mail invitation to one such meeting would describe it as a "hate Kerry" session.

Also, assume that one of the groups' lawyers was also the lawyer for the RNC. Picture that the groups' five hired-gun pollsters, with close ties to many senior Republican officeholders, conducted polling and focus groups to shape their anti-Kerry themes, testing various attack messages around the country. Suppose the groups' chief ad-maker created the ads for the previous two Republican presidential nominees and also had close ties throughout the Republican Party. Imagine that the groups' vicious TV ads attacking Kerry's record were more negative than most of those aired by the Bush campaign itself. Also assume that the groups distributed negative information about Kerry directly to voters, often using paid staffers bused in from out of state. Say, too, that there was a controversy involving convicted felons employed to do door-to-door canvassing.

Imagine this scenario. Then ask yourself how much coverage such an enterprise would have received from the broadcast networks, the major newspapers, and the newsweeklies. How much scrutiny would have been given to the donors' records, right-wing positions, and sources of income? How much would the press have examined the ties among all the parties involved and demanded to know what improper contacts there were between the Bush campaign, the RNC, and this shadowy newly formed cartel?

Everything described above actually did happen—only with the ideology reversed. The benefactors were all liberal tycoons, a significantly less sinister variety as perceived by Old Media organizations. Their largesse financed the groups America Coming Together and the Media Fund. There were plenty of stories about this venture, and how it might work to Kerry's advantage. But few of these stories conveyed a prosecutorial tone; to the contrary, almost all were infused with appreciation for the ingenuity of the endeavor and a certain anticipation that it would succeed. The people involved with ACT and the Media Fund—labor organizer Steve Rosenthal, Clinton White House veteran Harold Ickes, veteran Capitol Hill operative Jim Jordan, as well as representatives from EMILY's List, the Sierra Club, and other liberal groups—were not thought of as menacing types, but were familiar faces to the Washington press corps. Indeed, to some reporters, they were longtime sources or personal acquaintances. If a comparable right-wing effort had been launched, the press coverage would have been suspicious, antagonistic, and uncompromising.

The non-uproar over ACT was not the only revealing example of media assumptions influencing the campaign narrative of 2004. There were plenty of stories that year about the melding of religion and politics. Bush's ability to inspire devout Christian supporters was an important phenomenon that appropriately generated vast coverage. There were controversies about Republicans using church rosters to contact parishioners and nudge them to the polls. But how many stories do you recall comparing which party's nominees were campaigning most overtly from the pulpit?

If there had been many such stories, and there were not, they would have noted that Bush often cited the influence of religion on his personal life and public responsibilities, but his campaign trail ended outside church doors. John Kerry and John Edwards, by contrast, routinely went into houses of worship and served notice that righteous voters would be for the Democrats. Kerry often used religious metaphors and passages from the Bible to strike at President Bush. Kerry and Edwards both made numerous campaign stops at churches with mostly black congregations in an effort to encourage church-goers to be poll-goers, and Democratic ones at that. At a stop at the Allen Temple AME Church near Cincinnati, Ohio, John Edwards took the pulpit and warned the congregation that only a Democratic White House would in-crease funding for public schools, safeguard Social Security, and appoint affirmative action–friendly Supreme Court justices. When introducing Ed-wards to his flock, Pastor Donald H. Jordan Sr. dismissed concerns about the appropriateness of church involvement in politics: "I'm not worried about the [nonprofits] law. I'm asking you to support him."

If you ask Republican operatives what would have happened if Bush or Cheney had campaigned visibly in churches, they will answer without a mo-ment's hesitation that the Old Media news coverage would have been in-tense and disapproving. And if you ask them why Kerry's efforts were deemed unremarkable, they will tell you that on subjects like this one, the news media's cultural and political assumptions tilt toward Democrats.

We both work for news organizations where the effort to identify such as-sumptions and push back against them is admirably common. In the Old Media more broadly, the shrinkage and fragmenting of audiences is one fac-tor that has caused more searching discussions about the possibility of bias, both explicit and subconscious. Perhaps it should not have taken thirty-five or forty years of complaints, and the rise of New Media competition, for such introspection to begin. Among liberals, these internal debates are regarded as evidence that conservatives have succeeded in "working the refs," resulting in timid coverage. But this Old Media rumination is a positive development. Bias is the enemy of tough-minded journalism. The only way news organiza-tions can preserve the credibility to enforce accountability on politicians is to have reporters and editors who are divorced from cultural, partisan, or ideo-logical sympathies.

When the New Media sprang up to correct the imbalance caused by liberal bias, albeit while warping journalistic ethics, liberals were caught off-guard. They at first were oblivious to the New Media's rise, then indignant about the way it was changing a comfortable status quo. Only in the past few years have they begun to feel similarly victimized as the Old Media no longer provided its cozy cocoon. Now the Left is making belated efforts to create and exploit its own favored New Media platforms and interest groups, and claim a bigger slice of the Freak Show pie. Toward the end of the Clinton presidency, the Left began to develop a list of criticisms against the Old Media, a list that swelled rapidly in the Bush years. The Old Media's failure to more effectively challenge Bush's rationale for and conduct of the Iraq war has drawn special censure. According to the Left, so-called mainstream journalism has become beholden to Republican sources who starve reporters for information and ensure docility in exchange for scraps. The Left believes that the press has become captive to artificial notions of evenhandedness in which false statements from President Bush and true ones by Democratic critics are given equal footing, even when the facts are not ambiguous.

Disgusted by what they regard as the fecklessness of the Old Media, the Left does exactly what the Right does: it relies on its own agents, who will cheer for its side and heckle the opposition. Al Franken has found great success with his string of best-sellers and his radio show, and an audience that embraces both his irritable humor and his snappish commentary. Yet there remains an elemental imbalance. The favorite voices on the left are less likely to succumb to reflexive partisanship. Jon Stewart, for instance, is willing to condemn Democrats for incompetence or hypocrisy, yet it is relatively rare for Rush Limbaugh or conservative bloggers to criticize Republicans.

Despite attempts by the left-wing proponents to erect a New Media stronghold, they will still fall short in the 2008 presidential race, for a number of reasons. The Right's critique of the Old Media has coherence and a solid foundation. The Left's critique, on the other hand, has an internal contradiction. It celebrates the decline of Old Media power (*Thank goodness the bloggers are here to speak the truth*), but simultaneously rages at Old Media's impotence (*Why can't they stand up to the Bush-Cheney lies?*).

In addition, the Right's echo chamber has demonstrated repeatedly, as during the Kerry campaign, an ability to create controversies that resonate in the Old Media. The New Media Left is not big or powerful enough to match this feat.

Over his first four years in office, George W. Bush was the beneficiary of these changes. Without the burdens of Nixon's neurotic compulsions and acute anger, Bush organized the 2002 midterm elections, his 2004 reelection campaign, and some of his broader strategy as president to escape the power of the Old Media and reap the electoral advantages of a polarized electorate much as Nixon once proposed.

The Right's New Media infrastructure, unlike the Left's, is large enough that conservative partisans can receive all their news from it—effectively delegitimizing and marginalizing any Old Media story line to which they object. Old Media journalists can challenge Republican politicians, but these politicians can choose to ignore them, confident that their supporters will pay no heed to the criticism, and that they have effective venues to make their case. And there has been no more effective venue for promoting the Freak Show agenda in presidential politics than a particular website run out of a Miami apartment.

Watergate and the Freak Show

★ ★ ★ ★ ★

WOULD RICHARD NIXON have survived Watergate had he governed in the Age of the Freak Show?

What if Nixon had had at his disposal all the modern platforms and polarizing techniques that have shielded Republican politicians from the criticism of the Old Media and the attacks of the Democrats, and allowed conservatives to communicate and rally around the cause?

Suppose that, as in the 1970s, the Democrats controlled both chambers of Congress, but the media and political arenas otherwise were exactly as they are today.

Nixon would have had a multitude of ways to push back against accusers and sustain his political viability. On the political front, with party discipline high, congressional Republicans would accede to White House pressure to hold their ranks and preserve GOP control of the presidency. The goals would be to stop impeachment and removal, and to delegitimize any independent investigation.

To reassure allies, it would be important to boost Nixon's poll numbers, inhibit and confuse congressional and prosecutorial inquiries, and sully the president's critics. A host of livid surrogates would hit the airwaves armed with talking points composed by chief of staff H. R. Haldeman himself.

Keeping the base intact would be the first order of business. To help the cause, televangelist Pat Robertson would explain on *The 700 Club* that the efforts to get Nixon were really "a campaign to take the country away from Christians." Dr. James Dobson's radio commentary would assert that Nixon's enemies were trying to weaken him in order to impose school busing on communities all across the country.

The next task would be to discombobulate the opposition and

have its leaders worry more about their own future than Nixon's. An article in the *Weekly Standard* would examine Senator Sam Ervin's past statements about race and question his moral fitness to sit in judgment of the twice-elected president. Republican National Committee researchers would persuade Fox News Channel correspondents and anchors to do stories on why the country was not getting to hear the secret White House tapes of Presidents Kennedy and Johnson ("Why don't you support the release of the LBJ tapes, Senator Talmadge?" Sean Hannity would demand of one Democratic guest, lured on as chum. "Is it because they include coarse talk about crooked Texas schemes?").

Woodward and Bernstein would hardly be immune. A flashing red light on the *Drudge Report* would herald "Combined Book-Movie Deal in Works . . . Developing Hot." Drudge's "publishing sources" would divulge that the two "WaPo sleuths" were spotted with "super-lawyer Robert Barnett and celeb-editor Alice Mayhew" lunching at the Hay-Adams hotel for a "behind-the-scenes tell-all of their efforts to bring down the president—all just weeks before his 1972 re-election!!!" "I think this tells you all you need to know about the real motivations of the president's enemies," White House press secretary Ron Nessen would sneer at his daily press briefing the following day.

Nor would WoodStein have the only book deal. Regnery Publishing would be even quicker out of the gates with *Cox-Suckers: Why the Liberal Media Loves the Special Prosecutor and Loathes America,* by Ann Coulter.

Quite likely the White House would still lose a few skirmishes along the way. But even disgraced Nixon subordinates would not abandon the playing field. Tired of trailing Fox News in the nightly ratings battle, MSNBC would pay vast sums to launch an evening show with the former vice president himself. "Tune in tonight for *Nixon-Agnewistes,* as Spiro and the Nattering Nabobs debate whether President Nixon should burn the tapes." CNN, meanwhile, would have high hopes for its new show, *Hit Job with Gordon Liddy.* ("Put your hand in the flame! Tonight after *Larry King Live.*")

Nixon could count on a few friends up and down the media food chain. The *National Enquirer* would speculate about Elliot Richardson's drinking habits, while FreeRepublic.com would pick apart the ties between Peter Rodino and other New Jersey citizens who happened to be Italian-American.

Editorials and op-ed pieces written by distinguished national security experts and retired military officials conveniently would appear in the *Wall Street Journal,* the *New York Times,* and numerous big-city and regional papers stating that only a strong Nixon could continue to consolidate the gains made in Vietnam and win the war for the nation and the planet.

A new 527 group, Trustworthy Americans for Pride (TAP), funded by wealthy California conservatives, would begin an Internet campaign to encourage supporters to call and e-mail congressional Democrats from Red States, especially Southerners such as North Carolina's Ervin, urging them to support the president and stop the investigation. The group would produce an ad to be run on Washington cable TV (but guaranteed to get hours of free media coverage), which would blare: "Ted Kennedy wants to tell America what is right and what is wrong. And he wants to be our president. Is the judgment Ted Kennedy showed at Chappaquiddick the kind of judgment we need now?" Accompanying the voice-over would be slow-motion images of a plunging vehicle superimposed over a jowly, bulging Senator Kennedy, brow furrowed, fist aloft, and mouth ajar. On the radio, Rush Limbaugh and Laura Ingraham would seize upon the text of the ad as talking points, supplemented by curiously similar research provided by the RNC. Republicans on Capitol Hill would use floor statements and press conferences to make identical arguments.

Polling would show Americans divided straight down the middle on the question of whether Nixon was right to fire longtime Kennedy retainer Archibald Cox as special prosecutor. Instead of announcing the move furtively on a Saturday night, the president would give an exclusive weekday interview to the *Washington Times.* A *Wall Street Journal* editorial the next day would ask, "Who is Leon Jaworski?" and note disapprovingly that the supposedly independent-minded new prosecutor actually was once the attorney for none other than Lyndon Johnson.

How would the plot have ended in this alternate history? It is likely Nixon's behavior and the crimes of his political operation were so egregious that no amount of maneuvering could have saved them.

It seems possible, however, that Republican Arizona senator Barry Goldwater would not have visited the Oval Office with a delegation of fellow Republicans to tell Nixon it was time to go. Perhaps Goldwater instead would have announced on the Senate floor that he was so weary of Washington's vicious partisanship he was resigning his office to take over the chairmanship of a new right-wing group dedicated to stopping this insane drive by liberals for impeachment of the reelected commander in chief.

The name of Goldwater's new group? MoveOn.org.

HOW MATT DRUDGE RULES OUR WORLD

★ ★ ★ ★ ★

SOMETIMES THE QUESTION arrives with squeals of gossipy delight. Other times it is accompanied by groans of resentment and fear. *Have you seen Drudge?*

In an instant these four words spread through newsrooms and campaign headquarters.

The case study of John Kerry was about *hijacking*—the way political adversaries can exploit the media to take over a candidate's public image. The chapter that followed was about *incentives*—the ways that campaign and media cultures are influenced by Freak Show values that reward attacks and personality-based politics. These twin phenomena merge in the single person of Matt Drudge. No one has facilitated more political hijackings than he has. No one has a better grasp of the economic, ideological, and psychological incentives that power the Freak Show. Few journalists would count Drudge as a colleague. But in the past decade, he has contributed to the change in how American politics has been covered, and his impact will be a major factor in the 2008 presidential race. The root of his power lies in that four-word phrase. This chapter is about what happens after people ask, *Have you seen Drudge?*

Every day, many people indeed see *Drudge*. According to Nielsen Net Ratings, he receives between 180 and 200 million page views a month, along with around three million unique visitors. Some scrutinize his page religiously, others glance at it occasionally. Many use his site as their home page.

Such readers count on him to be a clearinghouse for the latest bizarre, or inflammatory, or salacious stories moving in the world of news or popular culture, and especially in politics. Among those who regularly click on the page is Karl Rove. Vice President Cheney does not commonly surf the Internet, but his wife, Lynne Cheney, frequently checks the *Drudge Report*. When some intriguing item appears, she or one of their two daughters is likely to tell him about it. Television news producers read *Drudge*. So do newspaper editors. So do publishing executives, Hollywood hotshots, and public relations agents. Members of the Gang of 500—which according to the *New Yorker* includes "the campaign consultants, strategists, pollsters, pundits, and journalists who make up the modern-day political establishment"—all read the *Drudge Report*. Gang members have the site bookmarked.

Drudge may be omnipresent, but his power is oddly obscure. It often goes unacknowledged even by his most influential readers. Many members of the press regard the *Drudge Report* as nothing serious—a good source of gossip and a mildly guilty pleasure, the professional equivalent of a cigarette break or an afternoon trip to Starbucks. Yet Drudge's decisions (or carefree hunches) affect whether millions of people will know of one story or another.

Drudge's chief influence derives from the links he chooses to highlight on his site, although his own exclusives (however inaccurate they may be at times) certainly stir up conversation. If a political item is prominently displayed on the *Drudge Report,* it is guaranteed that the topic will be talked about by people who matter in modern campaigns. It will color the perceptions of journalists, and campaign strategists and even candidates. It will prompt questions at news conferences and White House briefings. All of this trickles down to the voters, many of whom habitually read the *Drudge Report* themselves. If the greatest challenge of any person seeking the presidency is keeping control of his or her public image, and the great obstacle to this control is the Freak Show, then Matt Drudge is the gatekeeper. In this sense, he is the Walter Cronkite of his era.

This is not to say that Drudge has anything like Cronkite's audience. Drudge, to put it mildly, will never be known as "the most trusted man in America." But over the past two presidential elections, no single organization or individual has exercised as much influence in shaping what Americans learn about their presidential candidates. In the fragmented, remote-control, click-on-this, did-you-hear? politico-media world in which we live, revered Uncle Walter has been replaced by odd Nephew Matt.

A few points must be clarified. Describing Drudge's power is not the equivalent of celebrating it. What's more, when we speak of Drudge, we are not referring to him as a symbol for the New Media generally. We do not invoke him as a universal metaphor for the way politics is now defined by sensation and scandal. We are talking about Drudge *specifically*—a clever and erratic man who made his fortune working from his computer in apartments in Los Angeles and Miami, a self-described "loner" and former slacker whose keen grasp of politics, pop culture, and media, and of how to exploit the vulnerabilities of all three, mark him as one of the biggest success stories of his generation.

Drudge's power derives only in part from the colossal number of people who visit his site. Even the most devoted of his fans, hunched over basement computers or killing time at company expense, are sensible enough not to put full faith in his punchy communiqués. Drudge himself estimates that only 80 percent of the original material he posts is fully accurate, and he is being generous to himself. His power comes from his ability to shape the perception of other news media—Old and New alike.

With the exception of the Associated Press, there is no outlet other than the *Drudge Report* whose dispatches instantly can command the attention and energies of the most established newspapers and television newscasts. The AP, of course, is a sober, decades-old news enterprise that employs thousands of reporters and editors. Drudge is more or less what he was when he started: one oddball collecting provocative tips and posting weird, catchy news links from his personal computer.

One place in Washington where no one doubts Drudge's clout is at 310 First Street SE, the headquarters of the Republican National Committee. Peddling items to the *Drudge Report,* according to several current and former RNC staff members, is an essential part of the party's communications strategy.

Drudge, in fact, is important enough that senior operatives devote time and expense to ensure that their avenue to his website remains open. In early 2005, when RNC research director Tim Griffin left his job, he traveled to Florida with his replacement, Matt Rhodes, for a meeting with Drudge that marked an official baton passing. Griffin flew in from Arkansas, Rhodes from Washington, and Jim Dyke, the former Republican National Committee communications director, from Charlestown, South Carolina.

They dined at the Forge, one of Miami Beach's top steakhouses, described by one travel website as a "rococo Miami institution [that] celebrates the joys of living (and dining) large." Drudge was a longtime fan of the place. Griffin had known Matt Drudge for years and considered him one of the most valuable "journalists" of his acquaintance. Drudge might have been a shadowy, distant presence for many of his readers and even for most of his tipsters, but not for Griffin, who had dealt with him face-to-face before. Both Griffin's predecessor Barbara Comstock and Griffin himself believed that the RNC research department should not be staffed by a bunch of kids who just put newspaper clips together, but should employ sophisticated operatives with significant professional relationships in the real world and an understanding of how the press operated. The RNC thought there was no more significant relationship to have than the one with Drudge.

The point of the meeting was for Rhodes, who did not really know Drudge, to establish a personal tie with him, just the way an operative would court key Old Media journalists. It was a night of fun, a two-hour social dinner with little or no formal business discussed. Over steaks, seafood, salad, and wine, the four men reminisced about the 2004 campaign, talked about Miami culture, and chatted about life in general. When the shrimp arrived at the table, they were so gigantic that the men posed for photographs with the crustaceans.

This pleasant Florida tableau vividly captured how an ostensibly anti-Establishment figure like Drudge, a man disparaged in polite journalistic and political circles, was in fact central to how principal Establishment operatives such as Dyke, Griffin, and Rhodes do their jobs and communicate in the modern media marketplace. In the Freak Show, old lines between reputable and disreputable are obsolete.

The Miami courtship has paid off, by all evidence. Throughout 2005 and 2006, a steady flow of negative items about people such as Democratic National Committee chairman Howard Dean and Democratic Senate leader Harry Reid of Nevada have been highlighted on the *Drudge Report*. Many of the postings were direct products of RNC opposition research. Others, while originating from different sources, were brought to Drudge's attention by RNC staff members.

Ken Mehlman, the RNC chairman, said he values his party's pipeline to the *Drudge Report* and the website's ability to drive the editorial decisions of more conventional news organizations. "He puts something up and they have to cover it."

There are three Trade Secrets suggested here. From a campaign's perspective, there is a basic rule of twenty-first-century political communication: *The conflicts between the Old Media and the New Media are less important than the linkages.*

Some may find it comforting to imagine that the New Media is reckless and will run with anything, while the Old Media is respectable and restrained. The New Media, however, does its part to directly influence the Old Media.

Although he leans right, Drudge is not averse to linking to negative items about George W. Bush and other Republicans. A few savvy Democrats have established their own pipeline to Drudge to place research on his site. But they are exceptions. Drudge's greatest impact occurs with his more frequent and more biting attacks on the politicians of the Left. When it comes to Drudge, the table is not level, which leads to two more Trade Secrets:

• *A Republican politician will thrive in the 2008 presidential campaign by understanding the singular power of Drudge, and crafting a strategy to take advantage of this power.*

• *No Democratic politician will survive in the 2008 presidential campaign without understanding the singular power of Drudge, and crafting a strategy to defend against this power.*

Drudge also posts items about shark attacks, celebrity feuds, six-headed snakes, and gruesome small-town crimes that are interesting but generally don't create buzz in newsrooms the way his political items do. Here is what happens when people start asking, *Have you seen Drudge?*

His scoop will be electronically copied off the Web, pasted into an e-mail, and sent to news organizations' full internal distribution lists. Television producers and even anchors will call political journalists and ask, *Do you know anything about this?* Editors will wander across the newsroom to reporters and ask, perhaps sheepishly, *What do you think we should do?*

The overwhelming first impulse of Old Media agents is to respond defensively, *Why should we take our cues from Drudge?* The overwhelming second impulse, however, is to say, *Maybe we ought to make a few calls.* Such conversations occur simultaneously all over Washington and New York whenever Drudge posts a provocative item, especially if it is accompanied by his trademark red siren graphic, and most of all when it asserts that one news organization or another is hot on the trail of the story.

A dramatic Drudge posting sets off a competitive pulse because all journalists who see it know that they are not alone. So many media elites check the *Drudge Report* consistently that a reporter is aware his bosses, his competitors, his sources, his friends on Wall Street, lobbyists, White House officials, congressional aides, cousins, and everyone who is anyone have seen it, too.

So those "few calls" get made. Within minutes, press secretaries and political operatives will feel their cell phones vibrating. The calls will almost never be answered right away, because these people are all on the phone with their superiors asking, *How the hell should we deal with this?* Voice mail messages try to convey the right tone of nonchalance (*You know I don't actually take Drudge seriously*) and urgency (*I really, really need to hear back from you*).

The messages are not returned. New messages are left, no pretense of nonchalance this time. *Where are you? We've got to decide soon what we are doing with this. Call me right away.*

More often than not, at Establishment institutions, the result of these conversations and phone calls and voice mails is nothing. Or a trifling item might appear in a gossip column. Perhaps something like this: "Trouble in paradise? Political circles are buzzing about Internet reports that John Kerry and wife Teresa Heinz Kerry are squabbling . . ."

But even if national Old Media outlets do nothing, the *Drudge Report's* imprint will echo far and wide. Drudge's choices inform the rip-and-read planning at local TV and radio news stations for all of their newscasts throughout the day. The ladies of *The View*, with their millions of daily viewers, rely on Drudge's picks for their political story topics, though they almost never acknowledge his role. And should Old Media outlets ignore Drudge, his fellow travelers in the rightward organs of the New Media invariably do not. Drudge's standards for sourcing and checking are dangerously low, but the standards of the talk radio show hosts and bloggers who parrot his message are lower still, because they have no idea how credible the original source of his information is, and do not care.

Most of all, Drudge molds the mind-set throughout the national and local media—Old as well as New. Once a Drudge entry has burned some narrative thread or character trait into the brains of his readers, it can have a lingering effect on coverage. That item Drudge first reported in the summer of 2004 about the bickering Democratic presidential candidate and his spouse was not widely reported at the time, but it was widely *remembered* by every journalist on the Kerry press plane and their editors back home. In this case, many reporters believed that there was probably something to it. Not long after the election, *Newsweek* made clear that it thought there definitely was something to it. The story of an irritable row between the Heinz-Kerrys was the most talked-about plum in its special election issue.

• • •

DRUDGE HAS BUILT up such a loyal following that he no longer needs to obsessively update the site. Sometimes, he appears to take weekends off, or sleep in. But he understands his audience well enough to know how often he has to freshen up the content to maintain his page hits. (Additionally, he is aware that the site's unusual practice of automatically self-refreshing the page every few minutes allows him to record more hits and increase his Internet status.) Drudge also knows his economics. He did not get into the Internet gossip business to get rich, but that has been the result. His site produces considerable income with virtually no expenses. He remains, relatively speaking, a one-man operation.

The site draws plenty of advertising, including from large corporations and leading conservative politicians and causes, alongside more typical Internet patrons such as online mortgage brokerages and obscure universities. Drudge has hosted a Fox News cable television program and published a book, and has had a weekly nationally syndicated radio show since 1999. The *Miami Herald* quoted him in 2003 as saying he earned about $1.2 million a year, from the site and his radio program. Whatever the current figure, it is enough to afford frequent trips to Europe and a really nice car. But he reportedly has turned down many offers for partnership, marketing, and other deals that would have made him richer still. Drudge appears more inspired by noneconomic incentives.

The growing synergy between Old and New has been the most significant trend in the decade since Matt Drudge burst onto the public stage and computer screen. At the beginning, the commentary about his emergence put the emphasis on his anti-Establishment mission and values, and the Establishment's dismissiveness of him. This emphasis was always a bit misleading. From the start, much of the *Drudge Report* was devoted to electronic links to material published in the Old Media. Even his original reporting frequently consisted then, as now, of leaks about projects on which Old Media news outlets were working, or disputes and embarrassments within those organizations. Sometimes, journalists have found themselves wondering: *Does Drudge know something about our workplace that we don't?*

What has changed in recent years is the Old Media's move away from its posture of proud disdain for Drudge. While some in the Old Media now decry Drudge's influence, in the months following his role in the revelation of the Monica Lewinsky affair, his authority was feted, with major print profiles and network television appearances that increased his fame and validated his semi-legitimacy. Just over a year after NBC News invited Drudge to appear on *Meet the Press* on January 25, 1998, the show's moderator, Tim Russert, told the *Washington Post* that several items Drudge posted about Russert's news judgments and rumored ambitions for the New York governorship were false. "All three stories—they are just plain dead wrong," Russert was quoted as saying. "And he never called me about them, never." Today, the Old Media's attitude is one of public acquiescence, and, behind the scenes and away from polite company, an acceptance of the way the Drudge game is played.

When publishers have a new book to promote, the *Drudge Report* often is the first stop in a publicity campaign. In 2005, a series of obviously orchestrated leaks touted months in advance the coming release of Edward Klein's anti–Hillary Clinton book, *The Truth About Hillary*. Drudge's initial report claimed, " 'The revelations in it should sink her [presidential] candidacy,' a source close to Klein warns the DRUDGE REPORT." The book, from Penguin's Sentinel imprint, featured almost no new material about the Clintons except for a handful of lurid but weakly supported allegations. The book was uniformly lambasted by critics from all ends of the ideological spectrum. Even so, the drumbeat of Drudge-driven publicity, complemented by a few avowedly conservative websites, helped push Klein briefly onto the bestseller lists.

Others have learned the value of a Drudge publicity campaign as well. Publicists for glossy wide-circulation monthly magazines and television networks regularly plan early sanctioned "leaks" to him as part of their promotion of major stories. The situation at the *New York Times* may be most indicative of Drudge's current status. On several occasions in the 1990s and 2000s, *Times* editors and reporters were enraged by Drudge's ability to learn about stories in the process of being readied for publication. His sources apparently were comprised of the paper's own sources, newsroom personnel, and story budgets, the outlined summaries sent to subscribers to the paper's syndication service. In September 2000, after the *Drudge Report* disclosed details of an upcoming piece about Hillary Clinton's campaign contributors enjoying overnight visits to the White House, Drudge crowed raucously to the *New York Observer*: "This is just the first flare that I'm shooting up. It's going to be a long, long protracted battle with the *Times* and what they do internally. I have only just begun. I have access to all their internals. . . . Budgets, communications, what reporters are working on." This preening struck even Drudge as absurd. "'Access to all their internals'—what an arrogant statement. Hee, hee, hee."

Responsible *Times*men were not amused. "I understand and appreciate that there's an extraordinary interest in what *The New York Times* is doing, thinking and working on, and I appreciate that we operate in an extremely competitive environment," said veteran reporter John M. Broder. "That said, The Drudge Report is so flawed, so fantasy-ridden and, at times, [so] destructive to our efforts at fairness that it's disturbing. It's infuriating at times, not to mention annoying in the extreme."

In recent years, however, some *Times* executives have risen above their annoyance to recognize the marketing power Drudge possesses. Major *Times* stories are now flagged on *Drudge* in advance of their posting on the paper's website. These promos do not look or feel like the work of enterprising Drudge reporting or disgruntled *Times* employees leaking material without authorization. *Times* executives have stopped complaining publicly.

Meanwhile, although there is no system for authorized leaks to the *Drudge Report* at the *Washington Post,* editors at the website and main newspaper are delighted when Drudge does link to stories at washingtonpost.com. Invariably, traffic to the site soars. And there is evident frustration when the *Drudge Report* does not acknowledge significant *Washington Post* pieces. Speaking of the *Washington Post,* one of its reporters had direct experience with Drudge's astonishing power—both intoxicating and dangerous for those who come into contact with it. We will call this reporter "John Harris."

In 2005, like Ed Klein, Harris was promoting a book on the Clintons. Harris's volume, a history of the Clinton presidency, was by a wide margin less racy, if also less marketable, than Klein's. On the other hand, Harris knew particular sections had the potential to draw publicity-driving buzz in the news media. He wanted that publicity.

Two weeks before the official publication, he gave a series of talking points, along with an advance copy of the book itself, to a producer for a morning news program. The producer thanked him and wished him good luck, but told him that the book was not really up their alley. Later, the day before the book's publication, a friend with Harris's permission gave a set of the talking points to Drudge. A total of perhaps twenty minutes elapsed between his e-mail to the friend, the friend's e-mail to Drudge, and Drudge regurgitating the material into a banner headline and a dispatch in his own distinctive style. "Summer starts with a bang!" Drudge's "exclusive" read.

"Swearing, Screaming, Steaming—White House as Hot House." Within five minutes of that posting, another producer from the same morning show called: Was Harris free to come on the next morning? As it happened, he was committed elsewhere. But Drudge was no small part of the book's jump from 9,527 to 9 the next day on Amazon.com's sales ranking.

• • •

MATT DRUDGE IS salacious, reckless, superficial, and unfair—an eccentric man perfectly in tune with the eccentricity that now pervades politics and journalism. "I go where the stink is," he was fond of saying when he first shot to fame during Bill Clinton's presidency. Skeptics would add that where he has gone the stink has followed.

But Drudge is more than the impresario of the Freak Show. He is also a visionary, and deserves full credit for his perceptions. He arrived on the scene at the moment the Old Media was enjoying increasingly robust mass audiences. Well before it became obvious to everyone, Drudge understood the frailty that lay just beneath the Old Media's ostensible power.

Drudge exploits the universal human hunger for private gossip about public people. He knows the appeal of gazing unfiltered behind the scenes of movie studios, newsrooms, and political campaigns, as well as the thrill of being the secret source of such information. Drudge's insight was that this combination of institutional vulnerabilities and human appetites presented an enormous opportunity. Perhaps this does not seem like such an ingenious insight now, with a thousand websites offering daily photographic updates of Angelina Jolie or transcribed text messages from Bono. A decade ago, one strains to recall, e-mail and the Internet were still exotic technologies. Drudge was the first to recognize that someone sitting in his underwear at his living room computer could take control of the national news agenda. Across the spectrum of American life, this is a phase of history when the institution has yielded position to the entrepreneur. Matt Drudge counts as one of the most important entrepreneurs of his era.

• • •

DRUDGE DID NOT set out to be an entrepreneur. His attraction to the business of news and celebrity was more visceral, but for a while this interest was harnessed to no clear life purpose.

He was raised in Takoma Park, Maryland, the most liberal suburb of Washington, D.C. By his own recollection, he was a weak student and a social misfit in high school. Like many misfits, however, he seemed to grow up with an acute awareness of status as it matters to a young person—the rigid divide between cool and uncool. And, like many ultimately successful people who start out on the losing side of this divide, he brooded on and nurtured his resentments until they flourished. When his 1984 graduating class prepared a mock last will and testament, Drudge's entry was puckering: "I leave a penny for each day I've been here and cried here. A penny rich in worthless memories. For worthless memories is what I have endured."

More than a decade later, after Drudge hit it big, and had the Establishment news media roiling over the implications of his skewed brand of online journalism, he was invited to discuss the topic in Washington at the National Press Club. He gave a speech at once coldly penetrating about the vulnerabilities of the modern news business and mawkishly self-revealing about his own ambitions and neuroses. As an "aimless teen," he recalled, he used to walk the streets of Washington and gaze at doors he believed were closed to him. Those doors were not to Congress or the White House, but to the capital's dominant news organizations.

Journalism might fancy itself an egalitarian craft, but Drudge imagined its main institutions to be elitist redoubts. So he would "walk by ABC News over on DeSales, daydream; stare up at the *Washington Post* newsroom over on 15th Street, look up longingly, knowing I'd never get in," he recalled. "Didn't go to the right schools, never enjoyed any school, as a matter of fact, didn't come from a well-known family."

With these sullen words, Drudge revealed a powerful psychic connection with one of the lodestars of modern conservatism: resentment against the power and cultural values of so-called mainstream media. At the press club, Drudge even sounded a bit like Richard Nixon—another kid who grew up uncool and whose sense of outsiderness fueled a powerful drive to infiltrate and triumph over worlds that seemed closed to him.

Drudge drifted into his twenties with no higher education and no life plan. With his interest in media and celebrity, he migrated to Hollywood, taking an apartment in a seedy section of town. One of his jobs was as a runner on the game show *The Price Is Right*. Eventually he landed as manager of the gift shop at CBS Studios. In such a setting he could at least feign intimacy with an industry that fascinated him, as he traded gossip with other people trying to eke out a living in the ambient light of Hollywood. Back in Washington, his parents were understandably worried about their intelligent but directionless son. During one visit, Bob Drudge, a social worker, presented his son with a computer, hoping it would stir something more constructive.

In 1995, the notion of an online community, where individuals could traffic in news, rumor, commentary, and self-revelation, was novel. Hooking his new toy up to a phone line, Drudge became one of the very first Information Age explorers. He soon quit his CBS job and began spending the bulk of most days in his apartment, bent over the keyboard. This could not have been exactly what Bob Drudge had in mind. (Drudge Père would become something of an Internet pioneer himself, creating refdesk.com, a website that touts itself thusly: "On the Internet since 1995, refdesk indexes and reviews quality, credible, and timely reference resources that are free and family-friendly.")

When Matt Drudge was in his late twenties, computer modem at the ready, his life at last seemed infused with purpose. In short order, a new publication was born. In those days, the *Drudge Report* was sent to subscribers via e-mail for a $10 annual fee. In the exterior of his life, Drudge remained a peculiar and pasty-faced young man, exuding the unmistakable air of a washout. But on the computer, he was an instant success, a broker of fact and gossip in a rapidly growing online community of surfers who thrived on such insider information. Within a year or so of launching, he had a few thousand subscribers.

He delivered to them a rapid succession of mid-1990s news breaks. He posted that the actor Jerry Seinfeld was demanding a million dollars per episode in contract negotiations for his television sitcom. He alerted readers that anchor Connie Chung was about to be fired by CBS, apparently before Chung herself heard the news. Every Saturday, he was the first to report the box office take for newly released movies from the night before.

In contrast to the taut, exclamation-spiked style that would later become his signature, in those early days Drudge laced his reports with meandering personal commentary. "Nothing is sacred," he wrote. "I was having my usual Sunday morning breakfast of blueberry pancakes at the Source restaurant on Sunset when my beeper went off. I think Rod McKuen was singing MacArthur Park on the restaurant's sound system at the time . . ." Even then, updates on the legal and personal travails of the first family were part of his stock-in-trade. "Is the WALL STREET JOURNAL about to land a clop in the chops to Hillary Rodham Clinton?" he teased. Some reports turned out to be wishful thinking, such as one 1995 dispatch in which he speculated on the "imminent indictment" of the first lady.

If Drudge's dispatches were not always accurate, they were very often at least in the neighborhood of the truth. His "Exclusives!" could be faulty in detail but right in signaling that something was afoot. Even this loose standard raised a vexing question: *Where was he getting this stuff?* Drudge's work reflected a basic insight. For all their exterior power, the institutions and people who fascinated him and provided his copy had two abiding weaknesses. First, people at the top of these businesses cared desperately about what was written about them. Once people learned that Drudge's small audience included relatively large numbers of people who counted as cultural and journalistic tastemakers, Drudge had all the leverage he needed. The second great weakness is that people are malicious. They want to destroy someone's reputation, settle a score against a grumpy boss, or just stir some chaos for sheer enjoyment.

Drudge claimed he even had some gold-plated sources, such as studio chiefs. But much of what he did was report on reporters. Cannily, he tried to find out early what traditional news organizations were about to report—or were debating *whether* to report.

He elevated his newsroom snooping to a matter of high principle. He was knocking down editorial filters, which in his mind were instruments of elitism and even oppression. If journalists knew tantalizing things about celebrities and public officials—even if the items were not yet fully checked out—who were they to keep that information to themselves?

Thanks to his delving inside news organizations, he said, "We get to see the kinds of cuts that are made for all kinds of reasons; endless layers of editors with endless agendas changing bits and pieces, so by the time the newspaper hits your welcome mat, it has no meaning."

What the prissy inhabitants of the Old Media regarded as anarchy looked to Drudge like freedom: "Now, with a modem, anyone can follow the world and report on the world—no middle man, no Big Brother."

It would be these kinds of revelations—scooping reporters on their own scoops—that would first rocket Drudge to fame during the Clinton presidency. The impresario of the Freak Show had found the ideal content-provider.

★ ★ ★ ★ ★

BILL CLINTON'S TRADE SECRETS (AND AL GORE'S)

★ ★ ★ ★ ★

INTRODUCTION

★ ★ ★ ★ ★

THE THESIS OF THIS BOOK is that political success can be demystified—reduced to tangible rules that can be labeled and replicated. Is it possible to bottle Bill Clinton's approach to politics? Would such a potion even be safe for any conventional politician to drink? The question is complicated by evidence that often it was not safe for Clinton himself to imbibe. Across two presidential elections and a succession of political crises, the forty-second president showed that he knows the way to win. Together he and Hillary Clinton have created one of the most powerful brand names in the history of American politics. But nearly as often Clinton demonstrated the way to lose. He lost control of his public image and his governing agenda shortly after coming to the White House in 1993. His party lost power in the Congress and in a majority of statehouses during his tenure. He failed to reach 50 percent of the popular vote in both presidential elections. This section of the book aims to explain the Clinton record—wins and losses—by ignoring the Clinton mythology and his unique performance level, and concentrating on the Trade Secrets derived from concrete principles of political strategy.

The section has five chapters. The first examines the Trade Secrets that emerged from Clinton's 1992 presidential campaign. His victory that year is shrouded in the melodrama of *The War Room,* the documentary created from the behind-the-scenes access that Clinton's top campaign aides lavished on the filmmakers. The staff's tactical mastery depicted in the film is without question part of that election's story. But their well-chronicled campaign moves overshadowed less obvious strategic decisions—most of them made by the candidate himself rather than by his camera-happy advisers. Many of the lessons of 1992 remain deeply relevant to the people who will seek the presidency in 2008.

Of course, the triumphs of 1992 were followed by a series of setbacks once Clinton arrived in Washington. He proved that one can be the best politician of a generation and still make terrible choices. Thus, a second chapter will explore Clinton's reverse Trade Secrets—similarly still useful to the people who will run in 2008 and especially to whoever wins. The chapter that follows will document Clinton's remarkable rehabilitation from the sure loser of 1995 to the man who coasted to reelection in 1996. Then comes a chapter on the role of Matt Drudge in the events leading to Clinton's impeachment. Finally, this section closes with a cautionary tale about what happened to the first Democrat not named "Clinton" to try to get elected president in the Freak Show era.

1992

★ ★ ★ ★ ★

IN 1987, BILL CLINTON WAS THINKING seriously about running for the Democratic nomination for president the following year. As he saw the situation, he was a smart guy with a good head for politics. Then forty-one, he had been imagining himself in the White House since he was a boy. He had served as governor of Arkansas for most of the previous decade. He had no doubt he was as qualified as those other fellows whose names were being tossed about. *Why not do it?*

It was a question posed in a mood of extreme self-delusion. Fortunately for Clinton, he had someone at hand who could open his eyes.

His tutor was his longtime aide Betsey Wright. As the writer David Maraniss later reconstructed the scene, Wright faced the governor a few days before he planned to announce his decision in July 1987. Old friends were flying in from around the country to be present for what they had been told would be the launch of a presidential campaign. This was only two months after Democratic Colorado senator Gary Hart's candidacy had collapsed following the disclosure of an allegedly randy weekend with Donna Rice. But Clinton seemed to believe that Hart's experience was practically irrelevant to his own circumstances. After all, Hart had flaunted his behavior, even inviting the press to "put a tail on me." Clinton acknowledged to friends that his personal life was hardly free of blemishes, but he believed that he had been more circumspect than Hart, and therefore was less vulnerable to scandal. That was when Wright sat the would-be candidate down and confronted him with a list of names of the women with whom, if Little Rock gossip were to be believed, the governor had had affairs. "Now," she demanded, "I want you to tell me the truth about every one." They went over the list twice, Wright later recounted, the second time to discuss whether any of the women might spill their stories to reporters. After a couple more days of equivocation, Clinton made his public announcement, saying that he required "family time" and that the personal side of his life needed "renewal." He therefore would not be a candidate for president in 1988. He told supporters to wait for another day, "because it's coming."

When that day came four years later, a conventional analysis suggested that Clinton remained delusional about his chances. Most Democrats of presidential caliber had concluded in 1991 that incumbent president George Bush was too formidable in the wake of the U.S. victory in the Persian Gulf War to be beaten in his reelection bid. And, as Gennifer Flowers would soon demonstrate, Clinton still had abundant vulnerabilities on the personal front. But Clinton had keener insight into the politics of 1992 than other Democrats. He accurately perceived that a struggling economy and a widespread sense of national drift had left Bush far weaker than his high personal approval ratings indicated. In such an environment, Clinton believed that his own message would resonate. Importantly, it was a message that took into account the frailties of his own party just as much as the shortcomings of Bush and the Republicans. Clinton knew that, after the real and presumed failures of 1960s-era liberalism, a Democrat needed to offer voters ample reassurance that he represented a break from the old party tradition to be electable. After studying the problem for years in Arkansas—*how can a progressive politician win support among instinctively conservative voters?*—Clinton had good reason for confidence that his record as governor (stressing education and economic development) and his rhetoric (a message of "opportunity for all, responsibility from all, and community of all") would make him a credible national candidate. So in October of 1991, Bill Clinton got into the race. That same year, such far better known names as Dick Gephardt, Mario Cuomo, and Al Gore stayed out.

Clinton's decisions in 1987 and 1991 point to one of the most important Trade Secrets for presidential candidates: *Pick your moment.*

In earlier generations, candidates could run for president with a what-the-heck outlook. That's because serious politicians could be fairly certain that they would get more than one opportunity. The 1968 nominees, Democrat Hubert Humphrey and Republican Richard Nixon, both had made attempts in 1960 (in Humphrey's case as a main competitor to JFK and in Nixon's case as the nominee). Ronald Reagan ran for president twice before becoming his party's nominee in 1980. In that period, it was reasonable to figure, *why not run?* In the Freak Show era, that question has a definite answer. The incentives for the destruction of reputations mean that unless a candidate wins on the initial try, that first time out is likely to be the last. John McCain may attempt to disprove this point in 2008. John Kerry and John Edwards may as well, and perhaps even Al Gore. All four men would carry baggage from their previous bids. Gore and Kerry would enter the race with less credibility as prospective winners than when they ran in 2000 or 2004, regardless of any accomplishments in the interim. The second chance is almost never as promising as the first, which is why smart politicians choose their moment with care.

It is especially worth noting that Clinton did not obsess unduly about the practicalities of a campaign. One such practicality—*Will I be able to raise enough money to fund a serious campaign?*—was and is essential. But other commonplace anxieties—*What is my name ID in New Hampshire? What other candidates will enter the race? Can I sign up top consultants?*—were for Clinton second-tier concerns. Almost everyone who was privy to Clinton's decision to seek the presidency recalls him focusing on substantive and personal questions: *Is the country ready to hear the message on which I would run? Am I ready for the exposure and pressure that will follow me if I make the race?*

Clinton had the self-confidence in 1987 to believe that he could wait for a better moment. And he had the self-confidence in 1991 to believe that that moment had arrived.

• • •

IF POLITICAL REPORTERS in 1992 were polled on the question "Do you hate Fleetwood Mac?" the results would find 100 percent responding "Yes!" (with a margin of error of zero percent).

Perhaps not every song by the 1970s pop supergroup was reviled. But one song in particular certainly was. It actually was not so bad the first few times, hearing that familiar chorus fifteen years after it topped the charts. It was tolerable even the first few dozen times. But after the first few hundred times, it inspired a primitive loathing—the peppy rhythms, the cloying message, the ceaseless repetition. The deplorable song is "Don't Stop (Thinking About Tomorrow)." (Almost no one besides print reporters is aware that the precise name of the song places the last three words inside parentheses.) At virtually every Clinton campaign rally in 1992, the song blared from loudspeakers. The crowd rocked and swayed. The candidate was revved. Reporters might have hated the song, but they could not deny that it was a powerful anthem for a presidential campaign.

It therefore is painful to admit that it is also a Clinton Trade Secret: *Don't stop thinking about tomorrow.* (In our version, we have excised those maddening parentheses.)

There would appear to be a perilously thin line, in this case, between a Trade Secret and a cliché. All politicians profess to believe that "this election is about the future." Nearly all claim that they are running because they want to implement their "positive vision." But not many presidential hopefuls actually manage to liberate themselves from the gravitational pull of the past or to resist the temptation to let negativity dominate their message.

This is partly because politics is organized around grievance. The groups and activists who care most about politics, and those who dominate nominating contests, usually are drawn to participate because they have a complaint. They might be against abortion, or unequal wages, or pollution, or excessive regulation. They are pressed into battle for these causes, soon acquire battle scars, and years later are eager to sustain still more scars on behalf of the cause. But they remain resolutely focused on familiar old fights.

What such people want to know from a presidential candidate is where he or she stands on the past battles that still resonate for them: Were you for or against the confirmation of Clarence Thomas? How vigorously did you support or oppose Reagan's tax cuts, Bill Clinton's impeachment, and the Iraq war? These people have not stopped thinking about yesterday, and they insist that candidates do not either.

The other great force for negativity is the news business. Presidential campaigns in the early stages crave publicity. Reporters are willing to furnish it. To get coverage, candidates often must accept media premises about what matters most: controversies over staff (*Sir, do you plan to change consultants after your performance in the Florida straw poll?*); controversies over obscure corners of the past that supposedly illuminate character (*When you say you experimented "a few times," does that include all four years, or just sophomore year?*); and controversies between candidates (*On* Hardball *this afternoon your opponent called you a hypocrite for telling Iowans you support ethanol when you voted against research funding in committee in 1995. Would you please comment?*).

Throughout 1992, no matter how dire his political situation—and it was extremely dire on several occasions—Bill Clinton almost always conveyed optimism about the future and his ideas. (Significantly, George W. Bush shares this ability.) The temptation is to suppose that this was simply a function of a sunny personality. The truth is that Clinton, like most politicians, often could slip into self-absorption and anger toward the hypocrisy of his opponents, the small-mindedness of the press, the unfairness of it all. One day in 1992, after months of negative news coverage about his draft record, his relationship with Gennifer Flowers, and other flaps, he erupted to his staff: "I don't think you can minimize how horrible I feel, having worked all my life to stand for things, having busted my butt for seven months, and the American people don't know crap about it." This was a familiar side of the candidate to the people who saw him in private, but not to those who saw him in public. Clinton *seemed* optimistic and cheerful because of a trait rarely attributed to him: self-discipline.

This was never more vividly on display than during the 1992 New Hampshire primary. A letter Clinton had written in 1969 surfaced publicly, indicating that he had not been forthright about how he had avoided military service during Vietnam. Clinton's poll numbers started sinking precipitously. The campaign seemed doomed. It was then that Clinton demonstrated how even the most frightening ghosts of the past can be chased away with a relentless focus on the future. The people of New Hampshire, he said, in what soon became one of his most famous lines, "desperately want this election to be about their tomorrows, their future, their problems, not about my yesterdays."

That line might have been corny. But it accurately conveyed the spirit and strategy of Clinton's campaign, as he scrabbled back to a second-place finish in New Hampshire—good enough to keep going. He was still going, with the same script, eight months later. In the first debate of the general election, incumbent George H. W. Bush tried to force his rival to admit to showing a lapse in judgment and character by protesting against the Vietnam War while in England in the late 1960s. The charge never stuck—because Clinton would not let it. "Invest in American jobs, American education, control health care costs, bring this country together again," he responded. "I want the future of this country to be as bright and brilliant as its past, and it can be if we have the courage to change."

People who think this kind of unyielding focus is simple must ask themselves: Why is it so rare? Even casual observers of politics can close their eyes and imagine Clinton or George W. Bush speaking with manifest, abundant optimism about the future and putting forth plans to make it better. As an exercise, try to conjure John Kerry doing that, or, say, Bob Dole.

• • •

WHEN IT COMES time for the 2008 election, the privileged (albeit imaginary) Gang of 500 will have a special way of selecting the president. Members of this group (congresspeople, journalists, lawyers, lobbyists, political operatives, entertainment moguls, administration officials) can be found at the Palm and Lauriol Plaza restaurants in Washington, D.C., the Ivy on Robertson Boulevard in Los Angeles, and the Regency Hotel in New York City (for breakfast only). None of these places is celebrated primarily for its good food. All of them, however, were years ago granted long-term Gang of 500 service contracts, ensuring a revenue stream for decades to come.

Some readers may consider the Gang of 500 to be no more than a metaphor for a certain class of people who live on both coasts and by virtue of their interests and relationships exercise special influence in presidential politics. But, make no mistake, its impact is real.

In its own way, the Gang actually votes—as often as needed. It votes countless times every day on what is going on in Washington. It votes through a consensus reached via informal discussions, e-mail messages, luncheon tête-à-têtes, dropped hints, cocktail party gossip, pithy quotes, prominently placed op-eds, and cable TV chatter. These ballots can measure the current value of a rising or falling presidential candidacy. But what the Gang specializes in, above all else, are votes declaring a presidential candidate who has lost control of his public image to be a dead man running—whose time before withdrawing from the race can be measured in hours or days, rather than weeks. Or so the Gang decrees.

In the 1992 presidential cycle, the Gang of 500 went through more than a half-dozen roll calls on Bill Clinton alone. In October 1991, he was elected to serve as Mario Cuomo's vice president. When Cuomo decided not to run in late 1991, the Gang, with some misgivings, nominated Clinton to be the Democratic standard-bearer.

But the Gang's concerns soon proved justified. In February, amid the draft letter uproar and "bimbo eruptions," the Gang stripped Clinton of the nomination and his career was declared at an end. The Gang subsequently rethought the decision, and again bestowed the nomination on Clinton following personal appeals on his behalf from several longtime Gang members. But this decision was made in tandem with a special Gang of 500 emergency Security Council resolution declaring the 1992 Democratic nomination Not Worth Having, and with a demand for an old-fashioned "open convention" resolved by a brokered backroom deal. At the time, Clinton was running in third place in public polling, behind incumbent Bush and independent Ross Perot. Only after Perot backed out, and Clinton tapped Al Gore (who was back then a Gang of 500 favorite son) did the Gang finally endorse Clinton, clinching his success with voters that fall.

Clinton had a complicated relationship with the Gang of 500, but then *every* presidential candidate has a complicated relationship with the Gang of 500. It almost always begins as a courtship, since all candidates want the bounty—credibility, money, buzz—that the Gang has the power to bestow, and since the Gang loves to fall in love. The courtship can become shaky, as the new sweethearts begin to take one another for granted, and betrayal is a constant lurking threat. But the result is inevitable. In a Freak Show environment, no politician wins a major party nomination without confronting a moment when the Gang turns—when the consensus among political elites is that he is a goner.

George W. Bush confronted such a moment right after he lost the New Hampshire primary in 2000. So did John F. Kerry in the months just before New Hampshire in 2004. (Mickey Kaus wrote in *Slate*: "Democratic Senator John Kerry, once proclaimed the frontrunner in the press, faces not just defeat but utter humiliation in the New Hampshire primary. . . . Shouldn't he save his pride . . . by withdrawing from the race before this harsh popular verdict is rendered?")

Less sturdy candidates (Bob Kerrey in 1992, Bill Bradley in 2000, Elizabeth Dole in 2000) tend to accept the Gang of 500's judgments. With everyone (who's anyone) pronouncing their campaign over, they are no longer able to raise money, stay on message, or describe a realistic path to victory. So they quit.

The strongest candidates do what Clinton did: refuse to accept the death sentence. Even a less-talented politician, like John Kerry, can through force of will reject the Gang of 500's reality (*Give him the hook!*) and replace it with his own (*I'm not leaving this race except in a casket!*). That determination allowed Kerry to withstand a near-ruinous 2003 and win his party's nomination in 2004.

When Clinton's staff, during the toughest days before the New Hampshire primary, delicately suggested to the candidate that it might be time to think about withdrawing, Clinton responded: "If the voters want to withdraw me they will withdraw me on Election Day."

Clinton became president because he understood this Trade Secret: *When the Gang of 500 votes you out of the race, demand a recount.*

• • •

HERE IS A sad truth about presidential politics: Many of the people who seek the highest office in the land are not especially knowledgeable about national matters. They are drawn to politics because it is a great arena for competitive personalities. They find campaign strategy and tactical maneuvers fascinating. They think that most elections are determined by which candidates raise more money or are more attractive on television. This is not to say they have no genuine passion for improving the country. But they think about politics in very much the same way as the journalists who cover politics do. (That is not meant as a compliment.)

Perhaps the most important of Bill Clinton's Trade Secrets is the most prosaic. It is also the most attainable for any bright person: *Know your stuff.* That means having a campaign staff that has developed plausible policy prescriptions for the most serious questions of the day. It means taking the time to read and understand these plans in more than superficial detail. It means being able to answer questions about any major issue without pausing to take a breath, and without finishing each response with a look of mingled relief and self-satisfaction that a bullet has been dodged.

Many people who run for president do not meet this standard. Bill Clinton always cleared the bar, and cleared it by a wide margin. He has many exceptional assets as a politician—charm, intuition, stamina—but none of these would have counted for much if he did not have this thoroughly conventional talent. Once again, it is important to separate the mythology of Clinton from the reality. The myth holds that Clinton knew his stuff because he was an inexhaustible "policy wonk." It is certainly the case that Clinton had a lot of curiosity and experience with many domestic issues, particularly ones he had grappled with as Arkansas's governor. But there were a number of subjects that were important in 1992, such as macroeconomic policy, and almost all national security questions, on which he was not previously well versed. He passed the credibility threshold on these subjects simply by working hard to master them, through reading, tutorials, meetings, staff consultation, and deep thought.

Foreign policy, in particular, could have been a fatal weakness. But Clinton was never discomfited in the 1992 campaign by a question on foreign policy, and on some issues, such as what to do about China and the ethnic cleansing crisis in Bosnia, he even scored points on the incumbent. (This despite George H. W. Bush's classic taunt to Clinton and Gore that "my dog Millie knows more about foreign affairs than these two bozos.") Clinton's emphasis on issues was shared and amplified by his staff, including young aides such as Bruce Reed and Gene Sperling.

The policy book they wrote for Clinton, *Putting People First,* helped frame the argument for the general election, and even made it to the *New York Times* best-seller list. To this day, it is the only such book whose title is well known (unless you are the type who recalls Dick Gephardt's *An Even Better Place,* Wes Clark's *Winning Modern Wars,* Howard Dean's *Winning Back America,* John Kerry's *A Call to Service,* or, on the Republican side of the bookshelf, Lamar Alexander's *We Know What to Do: A Political Maverick Talks with America,* or Bob Dole's *Trusting the People: The Dole-Kemp Plan to Free the Economy and Create a Better America*).

One can readily anticipate the protests to this Trade Secret. If knowing your stuff is important, how do we explain Jimmy Carter, who knew a lot, losing to Ronald Reagan, who knew a lot less? More recently, how do we explain Al Gore, who possibly knew even more than Clinton, losing to George W. Bush? Part of the answer is that on the subjects most central to those campaigns, both Reagan and Bush knew more than they commonly were given credit for. More important, Carter and Gore had liabilities that outweighed their formidable knowledge. To the skeptics, we can merely state the obvious: Having a candidate who knows his (or her) stuff can't hurt. And there are many ways in which not knowing definitely *can* hurt.

There is no way to disguise the problem for long when a candidate is winging it. When the journalists on a campaign plane talk and joke among themselves about how the candidate knows less about policy than they do, the candidate is deeply vulnerable. Advisers hold their breath and cross their fingers whenever the boss is asked an unexpected question. The staff's lack of confidence will be palpable, and will infect the general mood of the campaign. The moment will come—and reporters eagerly will seize on it—when it becomes obvious in a public setting how shallow the candidate's knowledge is. A certain very nice, very intelligent, very well-spoken politician, with a great head of hair and a smooth Southern accent, often was compared to Bill Clinton when he first ran for president in the 2000 race. The biggest difference between Clinton and John Edwards is that Clinton seemed enthusiastic to master his facts (which can take days for a big speech or interview) and Edwards seemed tempted merely to know enough to get by (which takes a few hours). In discussions with journalists, Edwards on occasion showed a lack of familiarity on details of homeland security and poverty, areas in which he professed expertise.

Although current and former governors are thought to be the strongest presidential candidates, they face a special challenge to be prepared when they consider a bid for the Oval Office. New York's George Pataki, in many ways a highly intelligent and sure-footed politician, left an indelible impression in February of 1998, when, at a lunch with a roomful of Washington journalists, he displayed a wide-ranging ignorance of federal issues. Things got so bad that the event's host, Godfrey Sperling of the *Christian Science Monitor* (and the influential Sperling Breakfast), asked, "If you decide to run for President, aren't you going to have to spend a little time catching up on some of the national issues?" "Oh, I think I can probably fake it," Pataki joked in reply. Few found this witty.

Truly knowing your stuff allows a candidate to avoid awkward mistakes, but that is not the most important advantage. When Clinton was preparing for a debate or a major news conference, his staff did not have to waste time testing him on substantive answers. The preparation instead was devoted to figuring out how best to present the correct response. "What if we said it like this," Clinton might propose, searching for the right words to explain a controversial policy in soft reassuring tones, and he would practice over and over until he liked the sound of it. That is a luxury not enjoyed by most campaigns, who know that they are always one wrong answer away from disaster. (*Sir, Freedonia was the country in the Marx Brothers movie* Duck Soup. *Our position is that we support NATO membership for* Latvia.)

At this stage, there is only one possible 2008 candidate who can remotely approximate the mastery of issues that Bill Clinton brought to the 1992 campaign. Not coincidentally, her name is "Clinton," and she arguably knows more about substantive policy than any of her potential rivals—unless Gore chooses to run. Other sitting Democratic senators, John Kerry for instance, know plenty, but they are not in Senator Clinton's league. On the Republican side, one of the many reasons John McCain appears to be such a strong candidate is his evident policy depth, but he, too, has wide gaps in his expertise (which he smoothly deflects with glibness). For all the other candidates, here is some advice that they probably will ignore: Hit the books and study hard while there is still time.

• • •

IN THE FALL of 1991, Bill Clinton's presidential bid seemed like an implausible venture. By the fall of 1992 it seemed like an inevitable one. In retrospect, it is hard to re-create the madcap, flirting-with-disaster ethos that pervaded his campaign from beginning to end. It is a mistake to suppose that

Clinton's victory was entirely the result of rational forces. Politics is often a game of odd bounces and close calls that are outside a candidate's control.

But his win was *mostly* the result of rational forces. Clinton quite methodically did the things that good candidates do, and did them better than the candidates he defeated. He worked hard, showed self-confidence, and developed an intelligent basis for his campaign. These Trade Secrets, to be sure, may sound a little like Boy Scout mottoes for presidential candidates. But good intentions and good deeds can pay off—sometimes. Other times, good intentions are not enough, as Clinton would learn once he arrived in the White House.

Changing the Conventional Wisdom
About Bill and Hillary Clinton

★ ★ ★ ★ ★

BY THE SPRING OF 1992, Bill Clinton had locked up the Democratic nomination. But the consensus within the news media and his own party was that Clinton's chances of winning the White House were approximately zero. Clinton was in third place in the polls, behind the incumbent and a cocksure billionaire running as an independent. In Tennessee, Democratic senator Al Gore was said to be contemplating running for vice president—on Ross Perot's ticket. Clinton and his controversial wife, Hillary Clinton, were regarded as morally flawed. They had lost control of their images to a greater degree than (tank-riding, Vulcan-souled) Michael Dukakis had four years earlier, or than (French-speaking, windsurfing) John Kerry would in 2004. But Clinton had some things those candidates did not. One of them was an inherent quality that cannot be learned—an extraordinary talent for resilience in the face of setback. But another was a campaign team that understood an essential Trade Secret: *In the modern media environment, it is possible to reclaim an image that has been hijacked.*

What it requires is taking advantage of big events.

The upcoming big event Clinton's team was focused on that spring was July's Democratic Party national convention, scheduled for New York City's Madison Square Garden. The candidate himself was in a kind of psychic retreat, frequently bitter and depressed about what had happened to him and his wife. But among his more focused advisers, a steady stream of memos went back and forth, trying to identify the essential nub of the Clintons' problem and what could be salvaged and amended through the convention. Working with the campaign's traditional political advisers were the Clintons' old friends, the Hollywood producing team Harry Thomason and Linda Bloodworth-Thomason.

On April 13, Harry Thomason sent a memo to Clinton's chief pollster, Stan Greenberg, entitled "SUGGESTIONS FOR ATTACKING THE 'CHARACTER' ISSUE." Thomason thought the situation was so dire that there should be a separate advertising group, called the "Rehabilitation Team," in charge of making "ads that would have nothing to do with politics" but whose "sole objective would be to ease any doubts the public" had about Bill Clinton.

Around the same time, Bloodworth-Thomason sent a memo to the members of the "Clinton Election Project" with the evocative subject line "WHERE THERE'S BILL, THERE'S A WAY." She told her colleagues that "there is never going to be one speech, one comment, or one bullet that will put the character issue to rest," but she said they had to find "a discernable new beginning." Issues events, she argued, would make up 85 percent of the battle, but 15 percent involved personality and character. Clinton had the issues part aced, but work was needed on that 15 percent.

Moving to her favored ALL CAPS style, she boomed: "BILL AND HILLARY HAVE BEEN RADICALLY MISREPRESENTED TO THE AMERICAN PEOPLE IN AN EXTREMELY PERSONAL WAY AND NO BRILLIANT ENUMERATION OF THE ISSUES IS GOING TO ECLIPSE THAT."

Calming down a bit, at least in font, she added: "I believe they now need to go on a series of 'dates' with the American people. We have to let the public know them as we know them and allow them to fall in love."

She recommended "a number of informal popular culture forums," including Oprah, *The Tonight Show,* Rush Limbaugh [cough *mistake!* cough], and Bill Moyers. She suggested Clinton talk about his childhood, defiance of special interests, race, and the down-on-their-luck Americans he had met along the campaign trail.

On April 27, Greenberg and strategists James Carville and Frank Greer sent a memo to Clinton warning that "the 'character question' poses a critical threshold, blocking whatever message we choose to communicate—reducing messages to mere manipulation. . . .

"Bill and Hillary need to talk much more of their own family, including Chelsea, and their affection for each other," they wrote. "We need to make much more of Chelsea faxing her homework to Bill or something that Hillary does with Chelsea."

In a May 12 memo from Greenberg and his colleague Celinda Lake that focused on the Clintons' image problems, the two wrote, "What voters find slick in Bill Clinton, they find ruthless in Hillary." Voters "perceive her to be a rich woman with a nanny, if they know about Chelsea at all. . . . [V]oters believe that both Bill and Hillary Clinton were born with silver spoons in their mouths."

In conclusion, they argued, ". . . [V]oters need to hear more about the personal side of the Clinton's [*sic*] marriage; they need to understand that their relationship is more than a political partnership. Most importantly, they need to meet a much less political Bill and Hillary Clinton in this age of anti-political fervor. Voters want both the President and the First Lady to show commitment to policy, passion, advocacy, and to be outsiders. They need to learn of a couple—one who grew up poor and one who grew up as part of the middle class . . . and who share a strong family life and a great love of their daughter."

With little progress having been made, Greenberg argued in a July 1 memo that the convention was vitally important as "the only stage left in this election where we are alone—able to present Bill Clinton on his own terms. . . . [W]e must show that Bill Clinton is a man with good values who believes in something."

It seems like a foregone conclusion now. It seemed like a miracle at the time. But the 1992 convention did indeed show Clinton as that man. On Thirty-fourth Street and Seventh Avenue, less than a mile from Broadway's famous theaters, Clinton took back his public image with a really big show. As Margaret Carlson wrote in *Time* magazine, "Bill Clinton came into Madison Square Garden with a second chance to explain who he is and what he cares about. He did it by grabbing control of the convention in a way only Republicans have known how to do until now: with an unapologetic appeal to sentiment and a relentless approach to organizing." Slick Willie became the Man from Hope.

Audiences at home and in the arena were treated to the Thomasons' elaborate Hollywood video biography. Clinton began the narration: "I was born in a little town called Hope, Arkansas, three months after my father died," and closed with: "All I am or ever will be came from there. . . . I still believe in a place called Hope." The magical black-and-white 1963 footage of a teenaged Bill shaking hands with his idol John Kennedy in the Rose Garden was artfully included.

Voters insufficiently aware of the more appealing aspects of Clinton's family life were exposed to a radiantly gawky Chelsea, visual proof that Bill and Hillary were the proud parents of a real-life tween-aged girl, via calculated references to her in the Thomason video and in the acceptance speech. Clinton burbled, "[The] future entered my life the night our daughter Chelsea was born. . . . As I stood in the delivery room, I was overcome with the thought that God had given me a blessing my own father never knew: the chance to hold my child in my arms," and Chelsea herself endearingly recalled in the film, "When I was little when I would squeeze his nose, he would talk in a really weird voice."

A contentedly second-banana Al Gore, fully back in the Democratic fold, sold one-liners ("I've been dreaming of this moment since I was a kid growing up in Tennessee: That one day, I'd have the chance to come here to Madison Square Garden and be the warm-up act for Elvis"); the word "change" was tossed about every sixth sentence, and held aloft like a banner; and the final night ended with a giddily embarrassing yet undeniably jubilant group boogie to "Don't Stop (Thinking About Tomorrow)."

The show over, the bonded boomers boarded buses for their tour across America, equal parts Ricardos and Mertzes and Flintstones and Rubbles (and, at least, subliminally, a little Bob and Carol and Ted and Alice).

Never again would Clinton be in anything but first place in the race for the presidency.

WEAK AND WRONG

$\star\ \star\ \star\ \star\ \star$

By the first week of June 1993, less than five months after Bill Clinton's inauguration, *Time* magazine took stock of his debut. It presented an endless procession of bungled appointments, legislative setbacks, and public embarrassments, and awarded him one of the most devastating covers it had ever published about a politician. A tiny picture of Clinton was accompanied by a huge headline: "The Incredible Shrinking President."

By Election Day 1994, the man who was supposedly the smartest politician of his generation was thoroughly demolished, his party routed in what was an unmistakable midterm referendum on his presidency. With Newt Gingrich ascendant, Clinton soon was on national television invoking the Founders in an appeal for his own significance. "The Constitution gives me relevance," Clinton was forced to argue in an April 1995 prime-time press conference. "The president is relevant here." Reelection in 1996 seemed a dim prospect. What went wrong?

It was a long list. Some of the choices Clinton made in 1993 and 1994 were errors of policy and governance. Some of his travails were related to problems that other candidates are not likely to share. (Such as an idiosyncratic Arkansas personal history that included a former business partner with manic-depressive disorder and state troopers with ripe stories and loose lips.) Finally, some of the bad things that happened to Clinton were unique to the circumstances of the time—a moment when the Cold War's conclusion put momentous national security issues temporarily in the background, and Democrats were spent and complacent after a decades-long majority reign in Congress. Yet the principles of political strategy that shaped Bill Clinton's experience during this two-year period nevertheless apply broadly to the fortunes of the 2008 contenders.

These lessons—*the way to lose*—are the focus of this chapter. If failure is a better teacher than success, this passage in Clinton's career may be the most relevant of all to the 2008 candidates. The setbacks Hillary Clinton saw her husband (and herself) suffer more than a dozen years ago certainly remain tattooed on her psyche. Her closest advisers note that such defeats influence virtually every decision she makes about how to manage her public persona. They will guide her rivals, too, if they are wise.

Bill Clinton believes he was mugged during his first years in the White House. The analogy is apt. In real crimes, of course, it is not acceptable to blame the victim. In political journalism, it is part of the job. On the streets, the best way to avoid an ambush is to project confidence and power. It is no different in politics. In 1993 and 1994, Clinton was wandering around some of the roughest neighborhoods in Washington like a tourist with an expensive watch and a visible billfold, moving slowly, looking lost.

• • •

IT IS, OF course, important to project confidence and power to the opposition. But successful politicians know that it is just as important to communicate strength to influential people in their own party. Sometimes the most dangerous people are friends.

Just twelve days after winning the 1992 election, Clinton invited some new pals over to dinner. The guests at the Governor's Mansion in Little Rock were the Democratic leaders of Congress: House Speaker Tom Foley, House Majority Leader Dick Gephardt, and Senate Majority Leader George Mitchell. They were an imposing bunch, all older than Clinton, and with deep Washington experience of the sort Clinton lacked. But Clinton's guests assured him that they were eager to help however they could. After being locked out of the White House for twelve years, Democrats would soon run Washington. This was cause for celebration. Beef tenderloin was on the menu. The conversation stretched on for three hours. Participants later said that Hillary Clinton spoke nearly as much as her husband, and on some subjects was better informed.

But sometime between cocktails and dessert, Clinton began to give away to his fellow Democrats the power that he had just won from voters. His visitors were only too happy to lighten his load.

The congressional leaders made it plain that they were not enthusiastic about certain aspects of the president-elect's agenda. They did not like his proposal for a presidential line item veto to trim wasteful projects in spending bills. They hoped he was not too serious about his pledge to promote campaign finance reform. And if Clinton wanted to cut the White House staff by 25 percent that was fine by them, but he should mind his own business when it came to his notion that lawmakers should do the same with their staffs.

Clinton listened intently, and reassured the Democrats that none of these issues was a priority for him. Indeed, as a substantive matter, none represented a huge concession. But the evening was a disaster for Clinton even so. Once the details were publicized, Clinton had served notice to Democrats and the world that his presidency would be a shared project—everyone would have a say.

"He wants to help, he wants to participate," Mitchell said afterward. "He wants to know what senators to meet with, when to meet them, where to meet them, how he could be most helpful." Mitchell's comment suggested that he, like a proud but anxious mentor, had agreed that Clinton could be his apprentice.

Clinton's articulated analysis was not all that different. "We've got a big job to do, and we've got to do it together," Clinton told reporters of the relationship he wanted to have with congressional leaders. He heralded a "new ethic of shared responsibility."

Wrong. The modern presidency does not allow for shared responsibility, or shared power. The Constitution may say something about coequal branches of government, but the political and psychological realities of the office are different. Clinton either was going to assert power, or have power asserted upon him.

In time, he would come to understand a Trade Secret that applies to presidents and presidential candidates alike: *Never allow yourself to be bullied by your own party's legislative leaders and interest groups.*

This is among the most difficult principles to follow. Presidents and candidates urgently need to win support from powerful people in their own party. If these people are going to give their backing they will want things in return. Perhaps they require a pledge that the politician will never promote a merit pay plan for public school teachers. Or they might need a promise of a prime-time speaking slot at the party convention. Their interests could be rather more pedestrian, such as a demand that someone's cousin be given the contract to print the campaign's bumper stickers and yard signs in Michigan.

Most politicians are like Clinton: They find it more agreeable to say yes than no. What's more, no politician ever succeeded by saying no gratuitously. The key for anyone competing at the presidential level is to say yes or no the right way. That is, by never surrendering the position of dominance.

Voters do not want to think of a president as just another pol in a mass of pols. That is one reason that governors in recent history have had a vast advantage over senators—who almost by definition are perceived as one person among a hundred equals—in winning the presidency. That does not mean that Hillary Clinton and John McCain are not credible presidential material. But they are exceptions because both have established national reputations and personae that put them on a distinctly higher plane than their colleagues.

The challenge for all presidential candidates is to put themselves on that plane. They must through words and comportment project one message: *I expect to be the most important person in national life for the next eight years.* Those with whom the candidate has contact should be made to feel the same way and to gauge their self-interest accordingly. *Now, do you really want to talk to me about the yard sign contract?*

Once an aura of dominance is surrendered, it is hard to retrieve. A few weeks after the Little Rock session, Clinton was again harassed by his own side as he struggled to live up to his promise to appoint a cabinet that "looks like America," with racial and gender diversity. Under the normal course of things, liberal interest groups might be expected to want to stay on the good side of a president-elect. But having signaled that he responded to pressure, Clinton was subjected to even more of it. Rather than praising the number of women and minorities he was appointing—more than any predecessor—his so-called followers complained that he was not naming as many as they had hoped. One day he snapped testily at a news conference about the "bean counters" in his own party who were criticizing him, and accused them of playing "quota games and math games." But then he sent emissaries to meet with those same groups and assure them that he was trying to accommodate their wishes as best he could.

Many of the most significant mistakes of Clinton's first two years were variations on this theme—allowing the interests of allies to interfere with his own self-interest. Clinton should never have allowed himself to be maneuvered into making the question of permitting gays to serve openly in the military his first big public policy fight, but his fear of a liberal backlash forced his hand. If Clinton had been as savvy in 1993 as he was in 1992, he would have pursued a popularity-building policy like welfare reform before tackling a popularity-draining measure like health care reform. His solicitousness of congressional leaders—as well as his wife—caused him to take leave of his political instincts. The result was the most politically damaging public policy initiative of his presidency.

Specific circumstances call for specific strategies for how candidates and presidents choose to align themselves with their own party. Clinton, after his early stumbles, concluded that it sometimes made sense to put distance between himself and congressional Democrats. George W. Bush, at a different time and for different reasons, more frequently ran in tandem with congressional Republicans, but Bush always rode in the lead car. In fact, Bush might have taken this Trade Secret to an imperious and self-defeating extreme. But whether the strategy calls for hugging one's party or stiff-arming it, the principle is the same: *Never forget who is boss, and never let others forget either.*

• • •

CLINTON DID NOT establish that he was boss even with people who literally worked for him.

One characteristic of virtually every political or policy decision Clinton made in those early years in the White House was that his own team of advisers was divided into obvious factions. Moreover, these factions were publicly identifiable. Budget Director Leon Panetta thought Clinton needed to propose a plan heavy on deficit reduction. Political advisers such as Paul Begala felt the emphasis on deficits was all wrong. Moderates, including Treasury Secretary Lloyd Bentsen, wanted Clinton to push for passage of a free trade agreement with Mexico. Liberal staffers worried this would cause a backlash with pro-labor Democrats in Congress. Any reader could pick up the paper and learn who was on which side, and realize that Clinton's own mind was unsettled on basic questions of what he stood for and where he wanted to lead.

Nowhere was Clinton's penchant for allowing his internal deliberations to go on public display more damaging than in foreign policy—the very place it is most critical for a president to project confidence and consistency. Clinton's policies on Bosnia and Haiti in 1993 both veered from one halfway initiative to another. Voters who in 1992 had swallowed doubts about his lack of foreign policy experience now coughed them back up.

Whatever intellectual or psychic benefits Clinton gained from his management style, they were not worth it. Encouraging new ideas and robust debate is fine. But just as a president or presidential nominees must project confidence and power outward, they must project it inward to their own team as well. The failure to do so invariably has damaging consequences—first in private, and inevitably in public.

The factions that Clinton tolerated and even fostered by projecting uncertainty and weakness to his own team are the norm, not the exception, in presidential campaigns. In 1996, Republican Bob Dole, a man who had been in public life for thirty years, long enough to decide what he believed, watched as his own advisers conducted a semipublic debate about whether and how much to cut taxes, a debacle diligently recorded by the media. In 2000, the battle among Al Gore's campaign team about whether Gore should embrace Clinton or disown him was plainly visible. So, too, was the row about whether he should run as a roaring populist, fighting for the "people not the powerful," or as a more restrained consensus-minded "New Democrat." Anyone who cared could know from news accounts which advisers were on which side. And the debate itself revealed that, however the matter was finally resolved, the decision was merely tactical rather than a reflection of the candidate's core values.

Additionally, there were public schisms on John Kerry's campaign team about how vigorously to respond to the Swift Boat Veterans, and how the candidate should answer the question of whether he would still have supported going to war in Iraq if he knew in 2002 what he knew in 2004.

In general, Bush has avoided these semipublic internal debates. In the main, people do not know on what issues Karl Rove disagrees with Josh Bolten. The one major exception—division within the administration prior to the invasion of Iraq—only underscores how important the principle is. Secretary of State Colin Powell's misgivings about the war were widely known. There are few things more damaging to any campaign for public support than a widespread knowledge that some of a president's or candidate's closest advisers do not agree with his position.

In a media-saturated age, the imperative of projecting power to your own team has become vastly more important, in at least two ways. The first is that, because everything in politics, from the rotation of the news cycles to the dissemination of information to the cementing of a character trait, happens much more quickly, there is far less time to react. Given the speed with which a politician can lose control of his public image or governing agenda, there is no time for the paralysis that comes when advisers do not understand or share the values and strategic vision of the politician for whom they work.

Just as important is a phenomenon that did not exist before mass media.

Back then, advisers might complain among themselves about presidential indecision or the maddening way some leaders, such as Franklin D. Roosevelt, played different advisers off one another, but the public was none the wiser. These days, the pervasiveness of news media means that a politician's decision-making process, as much as the decisions themselves, is on public display. If there is internal chaos within a campaign or a White House, that means there is also external chaos—not exactly an attractive image of leadership.

The most damaging consequence of warring advisers is that it encourages people to demonstrate their loyalty in disloyal ways. This is the main reason the Clinton White House was vexed by leaks. The people in one Clinton camp always believed that they represented the best side of Clinton and it was their job to protect him from his unfortunate susceptibility to bad advice from another camp. An atmosphere of chronic tension is a gift for reporters, who learn to extract information about internal debates by manipulating the resentments and insecurities of each faction. Hillary Clinton attributed the leaks to her husband's young advisers being undisciplined and more concerned with tending to their own reputations than protecting his. In our experience, the leakers usually believed that they were advancing the president's interests, certain they knew best what those interests were.

An effective campaign or White House operation simply cannot tolerate destructive intramural contests over basic principles. A successful enterprise must be filled with people who have clarity about the goals and values of the politician they serve. Decisions about both policies and the political strategy necessary to promote them must be made quickly and without undue drama. It was a Trade Secret Bill Clinton learned slowly: *If you let your advisers battle over your soul, you will lose the battle.*

• • •

THE MOST IMPORTANT constituency to which a president must project an image of conviction and strength is not his enemies, nor his allies, nor his staff. What nearly sank Bill Clinton's presidency in his first term was failing to project an image of leadership to the public at large. Voters are not always watching a president *closely,* but they are keeping one eye on Washington, forming conclusions about personality, values, and job performance from a vast number of random episodes. Quite often, these judgment moments are not the ones for which presidential staffers have planned.

Instead they are ones such as what happened to Clinton on April 19, 1994, when he famously answered a question about whether he wore boxers or briefs in an appearance on MTV. Commentators everywhere discussed how he had answered the question and wondered: *What was Clinton thinking?*

In fact, he was due a measure of empathy. While he was a candidate, Clinton for the most part had been rewarded by styling himself as a new, hipper, and more accessible breed of politician. He wore sunglasses and played the saxophone on *The Arsenio Hall Show.* He conspicuously dined at fast food restaurants. He felt comfortable enthusiastically belting out Elvis Presley's "Don't Be Cruel" when prompted by Charlie Rose. It was incidents like these that were one reason Clinton always scored so well on the classic polling question of whether a politician "understands the problems of people like you." Clinton understood, the theory went, because he really was like the Middle Americans with whom he was trying to connect—a friendly, garrulous, informal fellow.

It was only once Clinton arrived in office that he and his advisers realized, after many stumbles, that people do not actually want a president who is that much like them. Even an egalitarian culture prefers to assign a special status to a president. And from this a Trade Secret flows: *Do not ever squander the dignity of the presidency.*

To be sure, all politicians want and need promotion. As Clinton showed in 1992, there is a payoff for a candidate who can creatively use publicity to communicate an appealing image. What's more, in the Freak Show environment there are more opportunities than ever for politicians to reap the exposure they crave. The problem is, many of these opportunities involve behavior—embarrassing self-revelations, unbecoming personal attacks, immersion in a vulgar celebrity culture—that is incompatible with the expectations people have for a president. If a candidate engages in acts unbecoming the office being sought, it can have a palpable impact on voters' perception of that person's fitness for the job.

In Clinton's case, maintaining the dignity of the office was more difficult because it ran counter to his basic nature. He was authentically a familiar, accessible man. Self-restraint did not come naturally to his ebullient, in-the-moment personality.

So when Hollywood stars Sharon Stone and Richard Gere invited Clinton to party in a hotel suite during an international summit in Canada, he went.

When reporters asked Clinton questions as he finished up his morning jogs, wearing short-shorts and dripping in sweat, he slowed to a walk and answered as the cameras rolled.

When on one of those jogs an attractive blond stranger cried out, "I wanna jog with you," Clinton waved her over and they chatted and huffed for the remainder of Clinton's route.

His close-to-the-surface emotions were forever erupting in ways that diminished his own professional stature. In the middle of an interview, he hissed that he had "not gotten one damn bit of credit from the knee-jerk liberal press, and I am sick and tired of it, and you can put that in the damn article."

In a variety of deliberate and unconscious ways, he neither invited distance from the public nor received it. Some of his advisers realized the effect this was having. "You know, he eats too much, he loves sports too much, he talks too much," said James Carville, his friend and 1992 political consultant. "He is not remote in the way that other presidents have been, so you are more free to love him or hate him the way you would anyone."

• • •

CLINTON DISCOVERED THAT perceptions of weakness are like gangrene. Once one portion of a politician's public image becomes infected, the entire body soon can be in mortal danger.

The simple analysis of what happened to Clinton upon taking office is that he abandoned the agenda that had proven so appealing on the 1992 campaign trail and foolishly advocated unpopular policies, like gays in the military or a supposedly "large and bureaucratic" health care program.

The problem, though, was more complicated. In 1992, just as in 1993, Clinton was walking around with separate bundles of popular and unpopular positions. This is true of all politicians competing at the presidential level. The necessity of winning support from the diverse and powerful interests that hold sway in both parties—to say nothing of staying true to one's own principles—guarantees that there will be things a politician supports or opposes that he or she would just as soon not talk about with the general public. George W. Bush, for instance, won election in 2000 and 2004 with positions on school vouchers and a constitutional amendment banning most abortions. Strong majorities of the public disagreed with him about these issues. But they were not decisive in shaping his public image.

An effective politician follows this Trade Secret: *Ensure that you are defined principally by your popular positions, and that the political damage from unpopular ones is effectively contained.* This may seem obvious, but most politicians fail to do so and suffer the damage. Clinton in 1993 did some very popular things. He enacted the Family and Medical Leave Act, which mandated time off for workers with new babies or serious family illnesses, and advanced an effort to help local governments hire 100,000 police officers. Even his health care plan included popular provisions. But Clinton never managed to be defined principally by these actions.

Clinton's lack of discipline in protecting his image as a personality (movie star pals, short-shorts, and tantrums) vastly amplified the problems caused by his lack of discipline in maintaining perceptions of his governing agenda. As a result, when people discussed Clinton, they usually were talking about things the news media or his political opponents thought were important, and only rarely about the things he thought were important. Clinton witnessed a stark illustration of the phenomenon in his first year in office. During a town hall meeting, an impassioned man confronted him about why he was devoting so much time to the issue of gays in the military. Coincidentally, Clinton's staff had just conducted a study of Clinton's work schedule. Since becoming president, Clinton assured him, he had held only two extended meetings on the matter.

The man stared at Clinton and said he did not believe him. He had simply heard too much about the issue to find it plausible that this was not an important priority of the new president's. Clinton listened in dismay. It was a bracing lesson in how powerfully news media coverage shaped public perceptions of his presidency.

· · ·

NEARLY A DECADE later, Clinton gave a speech that reflected the lessons he learned during his painful first years in office, shortly after his party had been clobbered by George W. Bush's Republicans in the 2002 midterm elections. His address at New York University stands to this day as one of the most explicitly political talks he has given since leaving the White House. The context was the way in which the Republican Party had made historic gains in the House and Senate by casting Democrats as national security wimps, but Clinton's words applied equally well to his own failure to project power at the start of his presidency.

Clinton never used the word "Bush" in his remarks, but it was clear what he had in mind when he unfurled this signature Trade Secret: "When people are insecure, they'd rather have somebody who's strong and wrong than somebody who's weak and right."

That line is the ultimate analysis of Freak Show politics, and it explains what had gone wrong for Clinton after he took office. He was seen as neither *strong* nor *right*—the worst of all worlds. He surrendered to Congress, to the interest groups, and to the press. He let his staff run wild and his public image be seen as undignified and soft. And he allowed his enemies to define him through his unpopular stands on gays in the military, bureaucratic health care plans, and tax increases. *Weak and wrong.*

After George W. Bush's first two years in office, Clinton marveled at NYU, a president seen by large numbers of Americans and by the Gang of 500 as strong could get away with a lot, including supporting some policy positions that were "wrong" in the eyes of a majority of voters. After his own first two years in office, Clinton knew he needed a change. He had to go from *weak and wrong* to *strong and right* if he was to save his presidency and get re-elected.

Making that change, it would turn out, required a terrible national tragedy at Oklahoma City, the return of a brilliant but eccentric longtime adviser, and a midcourse correction that replaced old bad habits with a set of new good ones.

Bubba Does Imus (and Vice Versa)

★ ★ ★ ★ ★

EMBLEMATIC OF BILL CLINTON's deals with the New Media devil was his relationship with radio personality Don Imus, the longtime host of an edgy, irreverent nationally syndicated morning program. For years, politicians and journalists of all types not only consented to appear on *Imus in the Morning*, but positively begged to be included. The media marriage, and subsequent divorce, of Clinton and Imus was especially charged. Clinton reached his hand inside the lion's cage, stroked the beast's fur, fed it some raw treats, and ultimately suffered a nasty bite.

The Clinton-Imus bond was forged in April during the 1992 campaign, when Clinton's past was making his present miserable. Months of shocking allegations and embarrassing revelations had left him limping on the eve of the critical New York Democratic primary. Throughout his campaign, Clinton had turned to New Media venues to reach a diverse audience and offer up a different image, but there was something about his daring appearance on *Imus* that caught Oxford-by-way-of-Arkansas lightning in a bottle.

At 7:20 A.M. on April 2, Clinton, sitting on his hotel suite's sofa wearing a tatty workout T-shirt, shorts, and a baseball cap, phoned Imus on the air. ABC News's Ted Koppel and a *Nightline* camera were on hand with the candidate to record it all. Imus had been mocking Clinton for weeks, referring to him as "Bubba," ridiculing his wife, and questioning his morality, yet the governor had agreed to an interview. Amused by the fuss over this potentially significant dialogue, Imus had laughed to the press the previous day: "All the media types believe I have all this influence. And then they turn that perception into a reality by covering what it is I do, and then people watching this stuff on TV or in the papers buy into it." Imus nevertheless gave some thought to the interview beforehand, informing his listeners that he planned to address Clinton directly as Bubba and grill him about his playing golf at an all-white country club.

With such a handy heads-up, Clinton was armed with the perfect riposte for both his host and the audience. After exchanging polite good mornings, Imus asked, "How are you," to which Clinton replied, "Well, I'm all right. I'm disappointed you didn't call me Bubba," adding the golden line, "It's an honorable term where I come from. It's just Southern for *mensch*." The two joshed obliquely about Clinton's various alleged character problems, dropping references to womanizing, marijuana, and the saxophone ("The great thing about playing the saxophone," Clinton explained, "is that you don't have to inhale"). They also chuckled over Clinton's interminable 1988 convention speech, mocked scrappy Democratic candidate Jerry Brown, and discussed Phil Donahue, on whose talk show the previous day Clinton had spent an hour dodging questions about adultery.

Imus, always appreciative of a relaxed sense of humor and a willingness to parry insults, adopted a tone of admiration. By 7:29 A.M., the interview was over and Imus wished Clinton well: "Governor, good luck. Hang in there, huh?" As Imus later admitted, "If he hadn't been funny, we would have blown him up." But Clinton's affability had been disarming and Imus's previously disdainful attitude now was dispelled. He ceased flogging the "Slick Willie" jokes and threw his support to Clinton. An untold number of listeners followed suit, or at least opened their minds to a more nuanced representation of the candidate.

The New York tabloids, always so tough on the Southerner, lapped up the "mensch" remark and splashed Clinton's minor triumph all over their pages. Hard-nosed columnists such as Jimmy Breslin of *Newsday* and Pete Hamill of the *Daily News* extended grudging respect, while the conservative *New York Post* offered an actual endorsement.

It became a classic case of "If you can make it there, you can make it anywhere." Clinton made it in New York and regained his momentum in the process. He took on one of his most scathing detractors, a man with a huge audience of savvy fans, a man who had labeled him "Butter Butt" and pegged Hillary Clinton as "psychotically ambitious," and turned him into an ally. Clinton won the New

York primary to boot. It seemed to be the perfect symbiotic match between a pop presidential candidate and a pop culture venue.

Clinton appeared on *Imus* a few more times before winning the presidency in November. Despite his newfound august position as leader of the free world, he continued to phone in, albeit rarely, as a guest on the show.

Imus ceased functioning as a Clinton cheerleader once the administration was up and running, however. He jammed his show with jokes about White House scandals, foolish missteps, colorful episodes, and an irresistibly garish first family circle (Imus even included Chelsea Clinton as a target). "Bubba" became a "lying weasel" whose girth was a constant opportunity for ridicule, while Hillary Clinton was serenaded by an Imus minion with a lewd ditty titled "That's Why the First Lady Is a Tramp."

One might imagine that in the face of such extreme hostility and disrespect a United States president would cut all ties with an insolent shock jock, particularly when Imus encouraged frequent caller and Clinton challenger Bob Dole during the 1996 campaign. But the bond remained, somehow, wispily suspended in the fabric of history, with a more-famous-than-ever Imus pleased with the evidence of his own influence, and Clinton and his staff tacitly aware of their debt.

The ties were broken—pulverized, actually—on March 21, 1996, when Imus was invited to be the featured entertainer at the Radio and TV Correspondents Association dinner, one of the annual gatherings of media luminaries and political players at which presidential attendance is all but mandatory. Imus had barely begun his routine when words such as "indicted," "subpoena," "Go, baby," "AstroTurf in the pickup" and "pot-smoking weasel" came spilling out of his mouth. The president and first lady, seated on the dais, were forced to maintain their composure in front of three thousand spectators and the television cameras. (Imus also slammed a number of prominent "TV scum.") In the wake of the humiliating event, the Clintons were presented with a letter of apology from the correspondents association, and White House press secretary Mike McCurry prevailed upon C-SPAN to desist from rebroadcasting the speech as scheduled. Imus, meanwhile, was unrepentant. "Let's not all pretend we don't know what the deal was," he said. "They knew what they were getting when they asked me."

STRONG AND RIGHT

★ ★ ★ ★ ★

BILL CLINTON, says a political adviser who worked with him for years, is an "optimistic, brilliant, principled, sincere, good-willed, empathetic, intellectual, learned and caring" leader, whose eight years heading the nation comprise "one of the most successful presidencies of our time." His wife, this adviser believes, is entitled to much of the credit. Hillary Rodham Clinton is a "sound, practical thinker." What's more, she is "usually a very, very warm person. She is loving and caring, quite the opposite of her strident public image."

This glowing impression, it must be noted, is hardly universal. One adviser who worked just as closely with the Clintons in Arkansas and the White House concluded at the end of a stormy relationship with the couple that Bill Clinton "has the nervous system of a shark, dividing everyone he meets into two categories—edible and inedible—depending on whether the person meets one of his needs or not." Hillary Clinton is even worse. She is "bitter and sarcastic, a partisan who is always looking for—and finding—enemies, plots, and conspiracies." The closest historical analogy, this aide suggested, was Richard Nixon. Just like Nixon, "Hillary hides a personality driven by paranoia, fear, and hatred for enemies, and a willingness to get even and do what it takes to prevail, behind a facade of sincerity and good nature."

It would be interesting to stage a debate between these two longtime aides with such different perspectives. But that would be impossible. They are the same person. His name is Dick Morris.

You may have seen Morris on television, where he regularly can be heard lambasting the Clintons as a commentator for Fox News. Or perhaps you have read his books. There have been seven of them in recent years, all trading to various degrees on his twenty-year collaboration with the Clintons.

The quotes above—both the positive and the negative—are from those books, though he has furnished very few favorable characterizations in recent years. The anti-Clinton industry is large and thriving, but only one of its leaders can claim to actually know the Clintons well.

With the exception of Hillary Clinton, there is no person more intimately familiar with the evolution of Bill Clinton's Trade Secrets and the career they made possible than Dick Morris. The consultant began working with him in 1977, when Clinton was Arkansas attorney general and worked out of a tacky office with metal chairs, false-walnut paneling, and a poster of Dolly Parton in a bikini pinned up on the bathroom door. Morris was by Clinton's side for nearly his entire Arkansas career, even as the consultant's business gradually shifted until all his clients except Clinton were Republicans.

Morris was absent from Clinton's life during the 1992 campaign and the first two years of his presidency during a down period of their up-and-down relationship. In late 1994, when Morris returned, Bill Clinton was a beaten man. The president was so demoralized he was taking meetings at Camp David with personal empowerment gurus such as Tony Robbins, the author of *Awaken the Giant Within,* who has helped train people to walk across hot coals as an exercise in purportedly turning fear into power. Robbins had been invited by Hillary Clinton. Notably, the first lady also was the sponsor of Morris's return to the Clinton fold. Distraught after the 1994 election, which some saw as a verdict on her conduct and character nearly as much as on her husband's, Hillary Clinton, Morris claims, confided: "I don't know which direction is up or down. Everything I thought was right was wrong."

No one in Washington would have disputed those two points. Newt Gingrich and his band of Republican revolutionaries had exploited the Clintons' mistakes to win the midterms and install themselves in power. The president's reelection prospects looked dim. Little more than a year later, however, the situation was reversed. Gingrich was in retreat and Bill Clinton's second term seemed assured. He had transformed his position from *weak and wrong* to *strong and right.* In the process, Dick Morris became the most influential political strategist in the history of the modern presidency. He would not hold that distinction for long, of course. Under George W. Bush, Karl Rove wielded even more influence, and for a far longer period of time.

Morris does not deserve singular credit for Bill Clinton's remarkable comeback. Yet his insights allowed Clinton to save himself in 1995 and 1996, and handily beat longtime Republican senator Bob Dole of Kansas in the presidential election. Morris helped Clinton overcome some of the flaws in his leadership style and take maximum advantage of his formidable gifts. Together their performance was a tour de force of electoral strategy.

· · ·

MORRIS'S FIRST ORDER of business in 1995 was to stop Clinton from projecting timidity and indecision. Clinton's early presidential advisers believed that his limited experience and lack of self-confidence in foreign policy was a weakness. Their response was to circumscribe Clinton's profile on foreign policy issues as much as possible. Morris advised him not to run from weakness but to confront it and then reverse it. "Use foreign situations to demonstrate your strength and toughness to the American people," he wrote in his first White House memo to Clinton. "Show by your actions in foreign situations, where you have control unfettered by Congress, that you are in charge and the boss."

The same memo did not mince words about Clinton's penchant for public vacillation: "Don't add to the damaging perception that you have flip-flopped on issues. It is never worth the price. If we've said something before, we're bound by it. We won't change it. The American people aren't against you because of your positions nearly so much as because of their perception of weakness and indecision. Don't ever, ever, change your mind."

Occasionally Morris's advice sounded perilously close to New Age mysticism, even as its essential diagnosis was dead-on. An October 1995 memo elaborated on how Clinton ought to study and project "images of Father." Until now, Morris noted, Clinton too often presented himself as a peer. Voters did not want that.

"Country craves fathers—Cosby, Lion King," Morris wrote in his trademark staccato style, adding that "women crave men who act responsibly—Romance novel themes are now of women done wrong and rescued by Mr. Right." In outline form, Morris explained how Clinton could be Mr. Right:

Fathering style in speeches and Q & A

1. Don't explain yourself overly—fathers don't.

2. don't complain (about lack of credit for accomplishments, for example).

3. No contemporary images like Blues Brothers.

4. Correct style: Memphis speech [in which Clinton had movingly sermonized on race relations].

5. don't have peer group conversations with audience—speak to them.

6. don't be self-depricating [*sic*]

7. don't ask questions—give answers.

8. don't be around unkempt kids, they need to show respect.

9. maintain sense of distance not eye to eye.

10. lectern should be small enough to tower over it.

Morris's hectoring memos, his swaggering self-assurance, and his aggressive television advertising strategy all played a vital role in Clinton's comeback. They restored the president's self-confidence, and imbued him with the sense that he could control his own fate and that there was a logical path to victory.

Morris illuminated a Trade Secret that has as much to do with psychology as politics: *There is no problem that cannot be solved with the consistent application of the right strategy.*

• • •

MORRIS BELIEVED THAT the most useful instrument for solving any political problem was a poll.

From 1995 onward, there was no pressing policy question that was not subjected to intensive surveying by pollster Mark Penn, who was brought into Clinton's fold by Morris and who stayed after Morris's departure. Penn today remains among Hillary Clinton's most valued advisers. Bill Clinton had an intellectual fascination with and even emotional attachment to public opinion data. Morris's numbers, recalled Clinton aide Harold Ickes, had a "supernatural hold" on the president.

But Clinton did not always do what polls said was the most popular move. To believe that, as many of his critics do, is a misreading of Clinton, who had strong convictions on many subjects and frequently acted on them even when it was politically risky. It is also a misunderstanding of effective political strategy. A president or presidential candidate who slavishly follows polls does himself no favors, since such an approach projects weakness. Clinton's overall approval ratings as president went *up* in 1995, after he sent U.S. troops on a peacekeeping mission in Bosnia, even though polls cautioned that the public disapproved of the action itself.

With Morris's help, Clinton was making full use of another Trade Secret: *Do not use polls to tell you* what *to do. Use polls to tell you* how *to do what you* want *to do.*

Clinton looked at polls to isolate points of strength and weakness in his public positions. Then he would use arguments—with language that it-self had been tested by polls—designed to maximize the strong aspects and minimize the vulnerable ones. That sounds simple. But it requires uncom-mon discipline to craft a message, adhere to it in the face of public pressure from allies and adversaries alike, and have faith that the message will work if you stick with it diligently.

In early 1995, for instance, most Democrats were eager for Clinton to de-nounce a Republican version of welfare reform that they regarded as too punitive to the poor. Clinton agreed that it was a bad plan. But he insisted on framing the rationale differently than his party proposed. His polling estab-lished that the only argument that resonated with the public was that the bill did not have tough enough work requirements for welfare recipients. "Do not fight," Morris urged in his weekly memo, over such provisions as the GOP's plan to cut off legal immigrants, or restrict aid to unwed mothers under age eighteen. "Work quietly with [the] Senate to eliminate as many of the above as you wish but make public issue only over work requirements being ade-quate."

Along the same lines, Republicans called for a moratorium on new regulations—an appealing position in the abstract. Polls helped Clinton move the debate from the theoretical to the specific—and on to more favor-able terrain for him. When it came to airline safety and protecting against *E. coli* bacteria in the food supply, both subjects that had recently been in the news, the data demonstrated the public was all in favor of the heavy hand of government. So Clinton stressed those features.

On affirmative action, polling indicated that at first blush Republicans had by far the better position with their fierce opposition to racial prefer-ences designed to offset past discrimination. The issue had Clinton and his advisers panicked for a time in 1995. But polling also showed that there were ways to neutralize the power of the issue with specific narrow reforms. "Mend it, don't end it," became Clinton's catchphrase, and what had been ex-pected to be an explosive issue played no significant role in the 1996 election.

In employing this kind of fancy footwork, Clinton was doing exactly the opposite of what he had done in 1993 and 1994, when his self-interest as president was subordinated to the collective interests of his party. Morris, with his love for metaphor and high-concept phrases, came up with a complex word for a fairly simple concept: *triangulation*. As Morris defined it for Clinton one evening, "to triangulate" meant to "create a third position, not just in between the old positions of the new parties but above them as well. Identify a new course that accommodates the needs the Republicans address but does it in a way that is uniquely yours."

Not surprisingly, Democrats in Congress did not appreciate the strategy. But Clinton's moves increased his public approval ratings, muting his party's criticism.

• • •

THE MOST CRITICAL factor in Clinton's political recovery in 1995 was an accident of circumstance, not a triumph of political strategy. The ghastly attack by domestic terrorists against the Alfred P. Murrah Federal Building in Oklahoma City on April 19 put the focus on Clinton in a way that it had not been in the months after the Republicans roared into power. Clinton's steady and empathetic performance during the tragedy increased confidence in his leadership in a manner that somewhat anticipated the boost in George W. Bush's support following the September 11, 2001, catastrophe.

Crass as it seems, capitalizing on these moments involves a heavy element of political calculation—much of it, ironically, about how to avoid seeming political. White House aides reacted indignantly that spring when reporters asked about the political implications of the bombing. Years later, Morris released copies of his Oklahoma City memos that made plain he had been busy doing just that type of strategizing. "A. Temporary gain: boost in ratings," Morris wrote in one memo. "B. More permanent gain: Improvements in character/personality attributes—remedies weakness, incompetence, ineffectiveness found in recent poll. C. Permanent possible gain: sets up Extremist Issue vs. Republicans."

• • •

NOTABLY, MANY OF the issues on which Clinton effectively employed polls were not about popular positions but about managing unpopular ones.

Morris himself observed: "In a room, [Clinton] will instinctively, as if by a canine sense of smell, find anyone who shows reserve toward him, and he will work full-time on winning his approval and, if possible, affection. . . . America is the ultimate room for Clinton. For him, a poll helps him sense who doesn't like him and why they don't."

This quote acknowledged one of Clinton's most distinctive, but least appreciated, Trade Secrets: *Run toward your weakness*.

The natural human instinct—and the conventional political one—is to avoid talking to people who dislike you, and avoid talking about subjects on which your positions are unpopular. Clinton always was willing to engage with people with whom he disagreed. This may have been a function of his temperament. But it is also an element of his political strategy that could be emulated by anyone. It is something of a mystery why the two Democratic nominees who succeeded Clinton did not try this disarming tactic.

In an interview, Clinton cited two examples of how he confronted conflict. The first was the issue of firearms. The National Rifle Association had used Clinton's enactment of gun control provisions to mobilize hunters in rural areas against Democrats. Among the targets was New Hampshire, an important state in Clinton's 1996 Electoral College strategy. On a trip to the Granite State during the middle of deer hunting season, Clinton was determined to talk about guns.

"And our guys in Washington thought I was crazier than the March hare, you know," he said. "I said, 'I'll go up there and I want to meet with the deer hunters, bring the deer hunters in.' And they looked at me like I was nuts and I said, 'You don't understand, we've got to carry New Hampshire and they can beat us up there.' And they said, 'Well, you don't want to talk about this.' I said, 'Oh, yes I do.' "

Clinton believed it was imperative to draw attention to his vulnerability if he hoped to address it. "I know here in New Hampshire, where like my native state of Arkansas there are a lot of people who love to hunt, when we passed the ban on assault weapons, when we passed the Brady Bill, there were hunters who were frightened into opposing our policies, who were told that their guns were going to be taken away," Clinton said at a stop in rural Keene, New Hampshire. "Well, we just had a great duck season in Arkansas and a great deer season in New Hampshire, and not a single hunter lost their guns. They were not told the truth. But I'll tell you who did lose their guns: over 40,000 criminals could not buy guns because of the Brady Bill. We are not going to repeal it."

Clinton ordered his Education Department to produce a pamphlet for distribution to public schools emphasizing that they had far more latitude than commonly believed to allow religious expression in schools. Students were free to pray privately or share religious views in homework assignments; extracurricular religious groups were permitted to use school facilities.

Many commentators rolled their eyes at what seemed like craven pandering. If so, it was pandering that worked. In 1996, in part by running straight into weaknesses on issues like guns and prayer, Clinton won New Hampshire, as well as Arkansas, Tennessee, and West Virginia, states that Democratic presidential candidates have not carried since.

The key, Clinton said, is to speak to people who disagree with you—even if you have no reasonable chance of winning a majority of them. Clinton cited polling that indicated he lost white, married evangelical voters to Dole by a margin of nearly 2–1. But Gore lost this same group to Bush by closer to 3–1, as did Kerry, Clinton claimed. "You know, if you want to run this country, particularly if you are a Democrat and you're going to push for change," Clinton said, "you have to be able to talk to everybody. . . . We give other people permission to define us if we don't even enter the conversation."

• • •

PRAYER AND GUNS were values issues on which Clinton skillfully played defense. Yet the 1996 campaign was the last time a Democrat used values issues to go on *offense*.

Morris believed, and Clinton readily agreed, that modern presidential elections hinge on values voters. This is a hard concept for many Democrats to embrace. For decades, the party was organized principally around economic interests, such as protecting labor unions and consumers against exploitation by business. The cultural issues on which the party was identified—for example ending discrimination and legalizing abortion—put the emphasis on rights. A majority of voters generally agreed with the party on these issues, but at a time when most people were uneasy about the direction of the culture, they were more receptive to a message that accentuated *responsibilities* over rights. Republicans had done better reacting to this change in public mood.

In 1996, Clinton turned the tables with this Trade Secret: *Advertise your values with policy proposals, especially ones that the opposition cannot support.*

This is done by touting symbolically resonant, specific policies. Rhetorical pronouncements alone are not good for much. This was especially true for Clinton, whose reputation had been hurt by his personal controversies. But he won the values debate by using polling to shape the right battles.

To voters upset about sex and crime on television, Clinton promoted the V-chip, allowing parents to block objectionable material. This seemed sensible enough, and Mark Penn's polls showed that independent voters especially liked the idea. The bonus political appeal was that many Republican politicians opposed the V-chip because their allies in the broadcast industry did not like it.

Clinton similarly led a public crusade for new regulations to curb youth smoking. The GOP's ties to the tobacco industry put Bob Dole and others on the opposing side, and even many Democrats were nervous about the political impact in conservative border states like Kentucky. Polls showed that even in those places Clinton's proposal was popular (and Clinton carried Kentucky over Dole on Election Day).

On it went. Expanding the Family and Medical Leave Act to require employers to give time off for children's doctor appointments and teacher conferences was wildly popular. Republicans' ties to business made them wary of endorsing the plan. Polls registered high support for proposals to track "deadbeat dads" across state lines and garnish wages. Republicans feared this could be an unnecessary burden on states. Clinton urged states to end "social promotion" by making students pass tests before advancing to the next grade. Conservatives recoiled at an idea that, to them, smelled too much like federal intrusion in education.

There is no reason Clinton's approach cannot work for any candidate. George W. Bush, for instance, knew that his proposals to reduce lawsuits were popular with the public, and were as much a values issue as an economic one. He also was aware that Democrats' ties to trial lawyers made it impossible for them to get on board. Bush's support for the government-funded delivery of social services by faith-based groups was viewed favorably, but it offended the sensibilities of many of the civil libertarian and secular voters typically allied with Democrats.

Skeptical 2008 presidential candidates should note that Clinton achieved his 1996 victory on values at a time when Dole was running against the president's character, and polls suggested that many voters agreed with Dole's condemnation, during a time of intense media attention to Whitewater and other controversies.

A political cartoon in 1996 depicted a woman with hair in curlers and rolling pin in hand talking to a pollster at her doorstep. "I'm for the scumbag," she said.

• • •

BY THE END of 1996, Clinton had bested Gingrich and trounced Dole. Republicans claimed that Clinton and his allies had distorted Republican ideas and used negative campaigning to make the opposition an unacceptable alternative to voters. "There is no grotesquerie, no distortion, no dishonesty too great for them to come after us," Gingrich once complained.

This is all plausible, except for one problem. It is virtually impossible to back up with anything Clinton actually said about his opponents.

Which leads to the final Trade Secret from Clinton's reelection triumph, even more relevant today because of the Freak Show's ever-rising incentives: *Be ruthless without being personal.*

It is easy to find quotes of Gingrich saying nasty things about Clinton and the Democrats ("the enemy of normal Americans"). It even is easy to find Democrats saying nasty personal things about Clinton. ("I think most of us learned some time ago, if you don't like the president's position, you simply need to wait a few weeks," Congressman David Obey bitingly complained.)

People who make such comments always will be rewarded with attention. "The number one fact about the news media is that they love fights," Gingrich once accurately observed. His own political action committee at one point produced a strategy memo advising Republicans on terms to use to describe the opposition in advertising and speeches, including "pathetic," "sick," "traitor," and "corrupt."

Earlier in his career, Dick Morris also had been a devotee of these kinds of attacks, and they had worked effectively. Over time, however, he concluded that negative politics had lost its efficacy. "For negatives to work, they usually have to rely on a simplistic, knee-jerk reaction from voters that can be brought to a fever pitch in thirty seconds," he explained. "But voters' greater subtlety in understanding both the variables of personality and the intricacies of issues make negatives a harder sell than before."

The Clinton style of negative campaigning almost never involved a personal attack on the character of an adversary directly from the candidate. (George W. Bush has used the same Trade Secret throughout his political career.) To the contrary, Clinton generally made a show of trying to understand and objectively explain where the other side was coming from—though not exactly framing its position in the most favorable terms. "These people are honest and genuine in their beliefs," he said in one speech, as he offered his view of why Republicans favored Uzis and AK-47 assault weapons.

Clinton in 1995 and 1996 successfully cast his opponents as the enemies of Medicare, education, and the environment. His team exploited the Republican nominee's verbal stumbles to label him as someone who believed that milk is as addictive as cigarettes, and even succeeded in branding him "DoleGingrich." He made his rival unacceptable in the public mind, and topped it off by having the audacity to be *polite.* "I want to begin by saying again how much I respect Senator Dole and his record of public service," Clinton said at the first presidential debate.

Dole was driven to distraction. "Where's the outrage?" he brayed on the campaign trail. "I can't believe any thinking American except the real partisans want four more years of this." But they did.

. . .

CLINTON MADE IT to the end of the 1996 campaign, but Morris did not. "White House Call Girl Scandal," read the *Star* tabloid. "Bill's Bad Boy," read the *New York Post,* in its report on the *Star* story. The news of Morris's indiscreet relationship with a prositute broke late in the evening on August 28. The next morning, Morris resigned from the campaign, on the day Clinton accepted his party's nomination for a second term.

Clinton and Morris stayed in regular contact for more than a year. The president even reached out to him for informal consultations when the Monica Lewinsky controversy erupted in January 1998. But that month, when Morris offered lurid speculation about the state of the Clinton marriage during a radio interview, he was banished for good from the Clinton fold.

No other person has as varied a perspective on contemporary politics. Morris has been a master of the Freak Show, helping Clinton rise above its attacks. He has been a victim of the Freak Show, with his own excursion into tabloid scandal. He is now an enthusiastic participant in the Freak Show, profiting from the personal attacks he aims at the Clintons. He has been supported by Rupert Murdoch, whose News Corp. empire is the most potent corporate promoter of the conservative Freak Show: In addition to his role on Fox News, Morris also writes an acidic, and occasionally brilliant, column for the *New York Post.*

For all the ill will that exists between them, Morris will be monitoring Hillary Clinton's possible 2008 presidential campaign as one of its original authors. The strategic assumptions behind her politics—on the primacy of values, the need to transcend partisanship, and the effectiveness of issue polling—all have their origins in his season of influence in 1995 and 1996. And no one should be surprised if sometime in 2008 or before, should Hillary Clinton hit a rough patch politically, her husband decides to place a surreptitious call to someone who has helped them out of jams in the past . . . *Say, Dick, you probably saw in the papers. Hillary is in a world of hurt. What do you think we should do?*

CLINTON VERSUS DRUDGE

★ ★ ★ ★ ★

ON THE EVE OF HIS REELECTION in November 1996, as his long battle for a second term ended in a blur of round-the-clock campaigning, Clinton made his final appearance at midnight in an arena in Sioux Falls, South Dakota. He told the crowd he was savoring "the last rally of the last campaign I will ever run."

For a moment, it did indeed seem that Clinton's presidency, and his life, had entered a new, rosy phase. The Republicans still held power in Congress, but they were now in political and ideological retreat. Washington arguments were waged on the president's terms. Kenneth Starr, the prosecutor appointed to investigate the Clintons' Arkansas business dealings, still was doggedly at work, but all signs indicated that he would be unable to pin criminal wrongdoing on the first family. Meanwhile, Clinton had a full second term in front of him, and it was not unreasonable to suppose, as many commentators did, that the president finally had transcended the familiar cycles of victory, misjudgment, and rehabilitation that until then had governed his life and politics. His battles over, who knew what great things might be possible in the coming four years?

Of course, Clinton's battles—and his campaigns—were hardly at an end. Only this time around his political acumen would be directed not at winning elections but at preventing enemies from ejecting him from office. One of the most important weapons in the war against Clinton was that odd young man with a computer who boasted that he could follow his nose to the good stories.

It turned out Matt Drudge's sense of smell was superb. Clinton conducted his personal life so recklessly within the White House that perhaps it was just a matter of time before some thread got pulled. But Drudge's role in the unraveling of Clinton's personal and political life in 1997 and 1998 was central—so much so that it is hard to imagine the strange drama unfolding without him as a player.

Monica, Linda, Lucianne, lawyer William Ginsburg, the secret tapes, the wagging finger, the blue dress, the grand jury testimony, the impeachment vote, the acquittal—they are all distant and even hallucinatory memories now. In these graver times, the temptation is to dismiss the episode as gaudy burlesque, the kind of thing that could have happened only during the holiday from history America experienced after the Cold War and before 9/11. But the significance of Clinton's encounter with the world of Matt Drudge should not be discounted. The standards and methods of the news media were forever altered. A sitting president was nearly evicted from office, and only a politician of Clinton's gifts could have survived. The scandal transformed politics in ways that will still be echoing in 2008.

• • •

BILL CLINTON IN the summer of 1997 had never heard of the *Drudge Report*. But as political hipsters, his young staffers delighted in being wise to the still obscure site and recommended it to their friends. Most Democrats at the time regarded the *Drudge Report* as gossipy and cool. They did not appreciate how closely its creator was aligned with the conservative forces arrayed against Clinton. This would soon become evident. And the opening shot was about not Monica Lewinsky but a woman named Kathleen Willey.

On the Fourth of July the *Drudge Report's* biggest scoop to date came when it detailed internal deliberations at *Newsweek* magazine, where reporter Michael Isikoff was pursuing a tale about Willey, once a Clinton White House aide. An ambivalent source, Willey had told Isikoff off the record that in 1993 the president had made a sexual advance on her in his private study off the Oval Office. Isikoff—a man his former colleague Bob Woodward extolled as a "junkyard dog" of a reporter—scrambled to find corroborating sources. And his *Newsweek* editors brooded over what information would be both sufficiently reliable and relevant to merit publication in the country's second-largest newsweekly, where it would undoubtedly cause a national sensation.

Thanks to Drudge, the sensation preceded *Newsweek's* eventual publication by a month. His website revealed that Isikoff was "hot on the trail" of an unnamed woman claiming harassment by Clinton. Neither Isikoff nor his editors then had any idea how Drudge could know such a thing. But

Newsweek was receiving an early lesson in how the New Media was changing the rules for the Old Media. The Clinton White House was learning the
same lesson.

Among the first people in Clinton's circle to hear of the breaking news was
White House deputy counsel Cheryl Mills. Few people in the administration
harbored such bilious feelings about the Old Media's political coverage as
she. A dazzlingly intelligent, aggressive young lawyer, Mills had seethed as
she watched reporters pursue a series of what she regarded as ever more trivial and sometimes downright fictitious scandals about the Clintons. Even so,
Mills was an avid consumer of political gossip and pop culture news. When
she noticed Drudge's item about a story in the works by *Newsweek,* she asked
Lanny Davis, a White House spokesman, to call Isikoff and find out what
was going on.

"What's this all about?" Davis demanded of the reporter.

Maintaining his poise and his discretion, Isikoff scoffed, "Come on,
Lanny, you're asking me about something in an Internet gossip report?"

The very same Independence Day when Drudge posted his report, Clinton greeted Monica Lewinsky in the Oval Office. Their sexual affair was now
over, but the president was desperately trying to keep the former intern in his
orbit so that she would not share details of their relationship. Clinton soon
would find out that it was a little late for that. Ten days later, after a European
trip, Clinton again met Lewinsky in the Oval Office. She gave halting answers to a series of questions that signaled to Clinton that there was a circle
of people who knew about his private life. In ways that were not yet fully
clear to him, there was somehow a web of connections among Lewinsky, Willey, Isikoff, and Lewinsky's friend and eventual betrayer Linda Tripp. Clinton
mentioned to Lewinsky that the Willey allegations were showing up on some
website called "The Sludge Report."

Throughout that month, Isikoff kept digging—and so did Drudge. On
July 29, Drudge posted his signature siren and trumpeted news of his
"WORLD EXCLUSIVE." He was the first to mention Kathleen Willey by
name, and he claimed—with enough corroborating detail to back it up—to
know all about the details of the presidential "sex pass" Willey had described
to Isikoff.

At *Newsweek,* and other news organizations, the anguished deliberations
that ordinarily would precede a decision about whether to publicize such a
salacious allegation were over. News of Willey's accusation drew widespread
coverage in the days that followed, combined with word that she had re-

ceived a subpoena to testify in a sexual harassment suit that was then pend-
ing against Clinton on behalf of a former Arkansas state employee named
Paula Corbin Jones.

Drudge delighted in the distress he had caused Isikoff by forcing
Newsweek's hand. "I outed the story," he chortled to the *Washington Post.* "I
was totally driving him crazy. There was nothing he could do."

When Isikoff was quoted by a reporter criticizing Drudge as "totally reckless," the *Drudge Report* gave it a blaring headline, with a link to the article.
Isikoff sent his tormentor an e-mail calling him "insane." There was a kind
of madcap quality to his site, Drudge admitted. One moment he was posting items on a penis-shrinking scare in Senegal or the location of Barbra
Streisand's wedding, and the next he was breaking news about the president
of the United States.

"It's a freak show," he explained, "but then we're in freaky times, on the
edge of insanity."

To any reporter who listened, he boasted of his computer records showing
that thousands of hits received by the *Drudge Report* came from White
House computers.

Trade Secret from the story so far: *Old Media restraint will not save you
from an embarrassing story, which can show up on the Internet at any time.*

• • •

WITHIN DAYS OF his Kathleen Willey triumph, Drudge broke another exclu-
sive that drew notice at the White House. "CHARGE: NEW WHITE
HOUSE RECRUIT SIDNEY BLUMENTHAL HAS SPOUSAL ABUSE
PAST."

Drudge claimed that sources told him Blumenthal, the journalist and
longtime Clinton supporter, had a violent past as a wife-abuser. Supposedly,
there were court records to document the allegations. Drudge's story was
posted the evening before Blumenthal was to begin his first day of work at
the White House as a communications aide, a job for which he temporarily
had left his journalism career.

The accusation was plainly false. By the next day, Blumenthal was threatening suit, and his lawyer had faxed Drudge a letter demanding a retraction.
Drudge complied, though in decidedly smaller type than his original charge:
"I am issuing a retraction of my information regarding Sidney Blumenthal
that appeared in the *Drudge Report* on August 11, 1997."

Drudge's response to the resulting furor was wan: "I apologize if any harm has been done," he said. "The story was issued in good faith. It was based on two sources who clearly were operating from a political motivation. . . . Someone was trying to get me to go after [the story] and I probably fell for it a little too hard. This is a case of using me to broadcast dirty laundry. I think I've been had."

Unappeased, Blumenthal filed suit anyway, against Drudge and against America Online, the Internet provider that had signed a special promotional agreement to carry the *Drudge Report* to its customers.

Trade Secret: *Beware the Internet's low bar for scandalous news. Anyone on your staff who makes a mistake (and even some who do not) can become embroiled in controversies for which you will have to answer.*

• • •

BOTH DRUDGE'S SUCCESS on the Kathleen Willey story and his rare renunciation of the bogus Blumenthal story illustrated how modern technology was dethroning editors and their historic role in American journalism.

One could lament this change, as all manner of chin-pulling commentators of the journalistic old guard did that summer of 1997. Or one could revel in it as a historic shift that was dragging democracy into a wondrous new age, which is how Drudge himself saw it. "I have no editor, I can say whatever I want," he noted contentedly. He saw this not as a perversion of traditional standards but a restoration of ancestral ideals: "You don't get a license to report in America," he said. "We have a great tradition of freedom of the press in this country . . . time was only newsrooms had access to the full pictures of the day's events, but now any citizen does."

In his crowing, Drudge put the emphasis on technology, as did many likeminded analysts. Yet the significance of Drudge was not the medium he used—the novelty and the notability of hyper-transmitted insta-scoop would wear off in due course—but the way he altered the psychology of news. The essential relationship between how people distilled and reacted to the information they learned had changed.

In the old regime of news organizations, a mistake of the sort Drudge had made about Blumenthal would have dealt a grievous blow to an institution's credibility. But Drudge was not interested in defending his reliability or precision, and the public did not respond to Drudge's Blumenthal error with a backlash. To the contrary, the episode supplied him with a bonanza of publicity. His personal celebrity and the audience for his website grew exponentially almost overnight.

Sure, some of what he published might be unverified bull, the public seemed to conclude, *but let's see it anyway.* By the end of 1997, his audience was larger than ever. Of Sidney Blumenthal, Drudge later chortled, "He made me."

Trade Secret: *When Drudge comes after you with a false report, take no solace from the fact that it is inaccurate. Being wrong does not matter to Drudge or his readers.*

. . .

MORE THAN BLUMENTHAL, needless to say, it was Bill Clinton who made Matt Drudge.

What the Kennedy assassination of 1963 was for television news, the writer Michael Kinsley observed, the opening weeks of 1998 were for the Internet: "Its coming of age as a media force. Or some might say media farce."

The pattern of the previous summer was repeated almost exactly, this time with far larger stakes. Once again, Isikoff was hot on a lead about a sexual scandal involving Clinton. And again there were intense internal debates within *Newsweek* about whether the story was solid enough to report, an argument preempted by Drudge. He broke his exposé about *Newsweek* sitting on the story of a still unnamed intern on a Saturday night. Earlier that day, Clinton had given his deposition in the Paula Jones sexual harassment case. Under oath, he repeatedly denied having a sexual relationship with Monica Lewinsky. But the questions were so insistent and so detailed—referring to gifts that Clinton had given Lewinsky—that it was evident the Jones lawyers were on to something. Clinton returned to the Oval Office in a panicked mood, even before the inevitable *Drudge Report* item. Scattered events in diverse legal and personal arenas were starting to merge. Clinton's vulnerability was the common theme.

Drudge's sketchy scoop arrived in time for the Sunday talk shows. Conservative commentator William Kristol brought up the gestating *Newsweek* investigation, and the likelihood that there was something to it, on the round-table discussion of ABC News's *This Week* program. Fellow panelist George Stephanopoulos tried to interject: "And, Bill, where did it come from? The *Drudge Report.* You know, we've all seen how discredited . . ."

"No, no, no," Kristol replied. "They had screaming arguments in *Newsweek* magazine yesterday. They finally didn't go with the story. It's going to be a question of whether the media is now going to report what are pretty well-validated charges of presidential behavior in the White House."

A week later, it was apparent that Kristol had been right. The panel on *This Week* speculated openly about a possible Clinton impeachment. The scandal had exploded into the Old Media a few days after Drudge's initial posting, when the *Washington Post* and ABC News followed up with their own reporting that identified Lewinsky by name. They also shared the startling news that Clinton's extramarital relationship—and his alleged efforts to suppress testimony and his apparent willingness to lie about it—now were under investigation by Kenneth Starr, who had pivoted from business affairs to sexual affairs. Conservative commentator George Will opined to laughter on the *This Week* telecast that Clinton's presidency in January 1998 "is as dead—deader really—than Woodrow Wilson's was after he had a stroke."

Trade Secret: *People in the Old Media with millions of readers or listeners closely monitor the Internet, and they are prone to be influenced by, or cite, Freak Show postings that would otherwise be seen only by a limited audience.*

· · ·

SHORTLY AFTER THE story broke, one of the mysteries about the *Drudge Report* was solved: Where was he getting this stuff? It turned out he was receiving his exclusives thanks to his membership in a loose but well-informed network of fellow conservatives whose lines reached into every aspect of this growing story—from Linda Tripp, to Paula Jones's attorneys, to Ken Starr's stable of prosecutors.

Drudge's main source was a conservative literary agent and public relations provocateur in New York named Lucianne Goldberg—the same woman who earlier had brokered an introduction between Isikoff and Linda Tripp. Drudge's social circle included the conservative writers and television pundits Laura Ingraham and Ann Coulter, and the author David Brock, who was then beginning his initial steps on an ideological journey from right to left. These writers had knowledge of—indeed, had played a part in facilitating— one of the most arresting facts to emerge in the case. There had been close cooperation between Paula Jones's legal team and Starr's prosecutors in their respective cases against Clinton; this collaboration had begun in the days before the president gave his deposition in the Jones case. In essence, Starr and the Jones attorneys jointly had set a trap for Clinton in that deposition, a trap Clinton walked into when he gave his false testimony about Lewinsky.

It was this alliance that First Lady Hillary Rodham Clinton was referring to when, soon after the scandal erupted, she went on the *Today* show to denounce the allegations as the product of a "vast, right-wing conspiracy." Those words sounded more paranoid when wrested from context than they did in the full interview. In any event, the first lady obviously was wrong about the Lewinsky claims—they were true enough—but she was right about the secret coordination among Clinton's enemies. She knew all about it from an unusual source. David Brock had struck up a surprising, covert friendship with Sidney Blumenthal. Brock gave Blumenthal regular reports about Drudge's activities, and passed on what he knew about the behind-the-scenes maneuvering of the Jones and Starr teams. Blumenthal in turn expeditiously communicated this information to Hillary Clinton.

Previously, the ideological tilt of Drudge had not been apparent. But his role in the Lewinsky drama made starkly clear that his conservative affiliations were central to the work of the *Drudge Report*. Drudge did not pretend to be a deep philosophical thinker or zealot. He was happy to report sensational news whatever its political implications. But he recognized that a big reason for the *Drudge Report's* rocketing influence was its use as an ideological weapon of the Right.

• • •

CLINTON SURVIVED THE Lewinsky scandal at the cost of a year of his presidency, and by some measures much more than that. As the uproar receded, there was a widespread expectation that Matt Drudge's moment on the public stage was over. The Fox News Channel had set him up with his own talk show in 1998, but then canceled it a year later. Traffic on the *Drudge Report* reportedly was trailing off. *New York Times* columnist Frank Rich in 1999 devoted a column to Drudge's "brief reign as the national press mascot." Rich argued that Drudge was consumed by the same voracious forces that he once represented: the explosion of new sources for news and commentary, the public's vagrant attention span, the relentless search for the latest cutting edge.

Rich and others who reasonably expected Drudge to fade into irrelevance watched as he grew more influential than ever. In the next six years, dozens of references to Matt Drudge would appear under Rich's own byline. The young man with the porkpie hat who leapt to the national stage at age thirty was still there as he approached his forties.

This is a curiosity. There is nothing that Matt Drudge did that could not be done—indeed is done on a daily basis—by multitudes of other people. There is no longer a technological freshness in running a website or hosting a bunch of links. The thrill is gone, but Drudge's influence remains pervasive, thanks to one of the most basic Trade Secrets of modern politics: *The Internet did not make editors obsolete, it just disempowered one set in favor of another.*

For all of Drudge's exclamations about how the Internet had made editors outmoded, we do not by any means live in an age without editorial filters. Who but the most committed consumers would want to spend their days sorting through the endless flow of news, gossip, and arguments circulating in the modern media bloodstream? But now the *old* filters of Establishment news values have been jostled aside by the *new* filters of Freak Show values.

Drudge became the most important filter because he got there first, and never let go. Clinton survived impeachment to serve out his term. The first presidential election of the post-Clinton era was coming up, and Drudge and his New Media colleagues would have to prove their power again. They recognized that success meant treating the next potential Democratic president the same way they had treated the one who made Matt Drudge rich and famous.

How to Run for President
and Let the Freak Show Destroy You

★ ★ ★ ★ ★

- Have little or no sense of how others perceive you.

- Be arrogant without being truly confident.

- Display a sense of entitlement tinged with bitterness and belligerence.

- Be foggy about your past controversial statements and actions.

- Be prone to dissemble about those statements and actions, and attempt to conceal the truth even from your staff by indignantly refusing to divulge facts.

- Fail to formulate an explanation for changes or discrepancies in your public policy positions.

- Treat your campaign advisers badly, thereby encouraging them to reward disrespect with disloyalty (through leaks, hostility, laxity, and shoddy work).

- Surround yourself with advisers who coddle you and reinforce your worst instincts.

- Allow your spouse and/or children to spook, intimidate, and meddle with the campaign staff.

- Refuse to make any decisions about how to respond to attacks on your character or on shifting events until you have seen polling data.

- Refuse to respond to character attacks you personally deem unworthy, inaccurate, or unfair.

- When you do respond to character attacks, do it in a manner that exhibits the very personality traits that were the basis of the original attack.

- Care more about the whims of the *New York Times* editorial board than about the views of middle-class families in the suburbs of Ohio.

- Treat the presidential debates as an opportunity to prove how clever you are, as if you are competing in an Ivy League forensic society event, and ignore the fact that you are addressing viewers who watch debates with the same degree of gravity and scrutiny with which they watch *America's Next Top Model*.

- Bask in the presumption that the "smarter" candidate will win.

- Speak and act as if you work in Washington, D.C., and as if everyone else works there, too, or at least would like to.

- Ignore the fact that the media is an active player (not a referee) in the contest and neglect to use its obsession with process stories to your advantage.

- Be convinced that the truth about your shining superiority ultimately will come through to the voters, that the Freak Show is just a sideshow and not the main event, and that you are owed a happy ending.

HOW THE FREAK SHOW KILLED AL GORE

★ ★ ★ ★ ★

AL GORE INHERITED EIGHT YEARS of peace and prosperity from Bill Clinton. Many Democrats believed that would be enough to keep the White House in party hands. Along with that record of policy successes, Clinton also bequeathed to Gore other less desirable legacies, including a still expanding Freak Show, which favored the political Right and which had grown accustomed to chewing Gore up and spitting him out.

Part of Gore's problem in 2000 was the paradox of the vice presidency. For all the humiliations of the job, ambitious people accept the second slot on the ticket not just for the varied honors but because they know the actuarial and political odds. Due to assassination, illness, and scandal, there is no more promising path to the presidency than being vice president. At the same time, it is historically rare to be *elected* to the presidency directly from the vice presidency. Over more than two centuries, only four people have managed the feat (John Adams in 1796, Thomas Jefferson in 1800, Martin Van Buren in 1836, and George H. W. Bush in 1988). Much more common has been the miniaturizing effect of the office. As the historian Arthur Schlesinger Jr. has noted, the job took outsized, hyperkinetic politicians like Lyndon B. Johnson, Hubert H. Humphrey, and Nelson Rockefeller and turned them into diminished and even pathetic figures as vice presidents. Gore's burden was heavier. He was the first sitting vice president to run in the modern Freak Show media environment. The Freak Show swoops upon any public figure who projects weakness or leaves himself open to easy caricature. Vice presidents, who owe their power wholly to another politician, are vulnerable to caricature almost by definition. The Freak Show's bullying tendencies against vice presidents presumably will not figure in 2008, since Dick Cheney has suggested he does not intend to seek the presidency.

But Gore, just like John Kerry, is a compelling case study in the way to lose. The two men lost control of their public images and therefore lost elections in markedly similar manners. In Gore's case, the tragedy seemed especially acute. He had, over twenty years, compiled a record of exceptionally serious study and advocacy on issues such as technology and global warming. But on the 2000 campaign trail, he was reduced to a clownish figure. Throughout the Clinton administration, Gore had worked determinedly to avoid two common humiliations of the vice presidency. Unlike some predecessors, he had not been turned into an official errand boy, flying off to attend the funerals of obscure foreign leaders. And he had the support of his boss; unlike Richard Nixon in 1960 or George H. W. Bush in 1988, Gore did not have to contend with a president who seemed a tad ambivalent about whether he wanted his vice president to succeed him. To the contrary, Bill Clinton would tell anyone who would listen that Gore was the most substantive, most influential person ever to hold the vice presidency. By 2000, however, the only thing Gore wanted from Clinton was for him to slap on a muzzle and stay off the stage. The Freak Show exerted intense destructive pressure on Gore. It seized his substantial strengths as a man and politician and shriveled them. It took a long roster of somewhat petty frailties and made them defining.

Although Gore won the national popular vote and likely had a majority of the votes of the people who went to the polls on Election Day in Florida, he failed in two ways. First, he did not sufficiently exploit Bush's slim record and the positive elements of the Clinton legacy. Second, he did not take office. Responsibility (or blame) for that can go to the bungling voters of Florida and some poorly designed ballots, the manufacturers of balky voting equipment, the impetuosity of television news organizations in calling the race prematurely on election night, the acumen of Bush's recount team, and/or the United States Supreme Court. But the fact is, Al Gore did not become the forty-third president of the United States, after being outdueled by George W. Bush.

The next section of this book will examine in detail how Bush, Karl Rove, and their political operation won national elections in 2000, 2002, and 2004. All of their Trade Secrets were exhibited in that first race against Gore, in which they demonstrated superiority in the strategy, tactics, and mechanics of presidential politics.

But their biggest advantage came from the way they utilized the Freak Show. Bush and Rove pried Gore's public image away from him with the same efficacy with which they captured John Kerry's four years later. The narrative of this chapter illustrates one of the major Trade Secrets of this book: *The presidential candidate who better keeps control of his public image wins the election.*

• • •

AL GORE'S TENNESSEE featured rough campaign combat, with a rising Republican Party, powerful pro–gun rights and anti-abortion contingencies, and a deep-seated distrust of the well-bred, such as a Harvard fancy pants who grew up living in posh Washington hotels (as Gore did).

But Gore had spent his whole life aware of the Freak Show seeds, and should have been prepared when they sprouted, blossomed, and mushroomed. He had seen his father, Al Gore Sr., lose control of his own public image—and his Senate seat—during the Vietnam War. The younger Gore's senior thesis in college was entitled "The Impact of Television on the Presidency, 1947–1969." He had been a journalist, a member of Congress, and a presidential candidate once before, in 1988.

Gore understood that becoming a winning presidential candidate was about storytelling. He knew he had lived a complicated life, marked by occasions when principle gave way to expediency and by the kind of embarrassing moments that most people struggle to avoid. But Gore and his strategists also knew that the key was to edit his life story, so that its best parts were displayed in the most favorable light, eclipsing the bad parts, and repeated over and over again.

In addition, Gore and his advisers recognized that *beating* a presidential candidate was also about storytelling. The race would come down to finding the weak points in the opponent's personality and character, and looking for every possible narrative, large and even small—the small ones often worked better—that reinforced those vulnerabilities.

Al Gore had a positive tale to tell in 2000, just as John Kerry did in 2004. He was a son of the South, a devoted husband and father, a religious man, and a public servant who had been the first to see and promote important issues relating to the environment and technology. He was a rudder of an administration that had made strong strides on the economy and the deficit, and whose policies were acclaimed by most Americans. A lifetime of preparation had come together for what seemed an almost predestined next step, the presidency.

Gore advisers knew there was also a negative story waiting to be told. Voters had an ill-defined sense of who Gore was and what he stood for. He had never really explained his positions on some issues, such as his shift from being morally and politically opposed to abortion to supporting it as a legal right. Personally, he was a brooding, insecure man renowned for his public stiffness. Many of his former aides could not stand him. Through faulty judgment and bad advice, he had become the poster child of the Clinton-Gore fund-raising scandals during the reelection cash harvest. He had a penchant for tailoring his rhetoric to the occasion and for exaggerating his achievements.

George W. Bush likewise had a story to tell in the 2000 campaign—and a story to suppress. He was an upbeat, practical, successful governor, who came from privileged circumstances but had experienced the kind of setbacks to which all people can relate. An irresolute youth and early adulthood, colored by excessive drinking, had taken an inspiring turn as Bush matured, found God, and gave his life new purpose. Or perhaps this was not the real Bush. Others assessed his history and saw a man who had never done much more than skip lightly through life, was seemingly not so bright, and was ridiculously unprepared for the presidency.

Many of Gore's advisers were so confident they could tag Bush with this negative image that they paid insufficient attention to making sure Gore's positive side got through to the voters. Bush faltered at times, and Gore succeeded on occasion. But those were the exceptions. By Election Day, Bush ended up with more cumulative news cycles in his favor than did Gore.

The vice president's reputation for not telling the whole truth, particularly about his record, contributed mightily to his losing control of his public image. The campaigns of both his opponents—former New Jersey senator Bill Bradley (the sole Democrat to attempt a nomination challenge) and George W. Bush—made Gore's propensity to shade the facts the centerpieces of their efforts to undermine him.

When the attacks came, almost always generated by opposition research pumped into the New and Old Media and kept alive by conservative Freak Show elements, Gore regularly compounded the violation of one Trade Secret (*Do not exaggerate or bend your own record*) with the violation of two additional ones (*Make sure your staff has all the facts and gets them out to the public,* and *Do not let attacks mess with your head*).

Gore's repeated breaches of all three rules were detrimental to his pursuit of the White House. What is perhaps most amazing is that, beyond Gore's own extensive personal experience with these issues, he had been warned repeatedly by his presidential campaign staff that the Old Media had seized upon the concept of Gore-as-exaggerator. And these warnings started not in the 2000 campaign, but in Gore's first White House run back in 1988.

Two old memos from that race surfaced just as the Bradley campaign was trying to reinforce Gore's image as a serial pretender. Written five months apart by two of his press advisers, they make it clear that his staff felt Gore's campaign was threatened by a growing perception in the media that he had trouble with the truth.

The first one, sent in September 1987 from campaign press aide Mike Kopp to Gore, bore the subject line "Attacks on your credibility," and it started this way:

> We've been hearing an increasing number of remarks from members of the press corps (national, and regional) about your tendency to go out on a limb with remarks about your campaign. . . .
> In the past few reporters cared if you stretched the truth to make a point or as an applause line. . . . Because of your steady climb in the polls . . . we are becoming increasingly scrutinized.

Kopp told his boss that the *Washington Post*'s Maralee Schwartz was saying Gore had "a growing reputation as a politician who 'stretches the truth to suit a political moment.'" Kopp listed a series of Gore claims that were still reverberating in the press, including one about how much campaigning he had done in the South and another about how many women worked on his campaign.

Gore apparently did not fully honor the caution, because on February 15, 1988, his communications director, Arlie Schardt, felt compelled to send "AL" a similar memo, the first line of which was "This is very important."

Schardt alerted Gore that Knight Ridder reporter Nolan Walters "wants to discredit your resume, primarily as it concerns your claims to be or have been (1) a farmer and (2) homebuilder."

Preparing Gore for a scheduled interview with Walters, Schardt warned his candidate, "[D]o not overstate your degree of involvement" in those fields. Schardt concluded: "[Y]our main pitfall is exaggeration. Be careful not to overstate your accomplishments. . . ."

• • •

GORE'S FAILURE TO win his party's nomination in 1988 was not attributable to his failure to curb his exaggerations, but it clearly worried his advisers. Just short of a decade later, a new crop of aides to then Vice President Gore had similar concerns about his image, but they now were broader. In the interim, Gore had seen his reputation rise (when he was added with dramatic and triumphal flourish to Bill Clinton's ticket and was hailed as handsome, vital, smart, experienced, and loaded with gravitas) and then fall somewhat during Clinton's first term (when he was caricatured as wooden and phlegmatic).

On top of the image problems that came with his job and his public stiffness, Gore added an additional piece of trouble in 1996 even before he was securely reelected as vice president. For the next four years, Gore would be punished for his role in the manic push for campaign donations to ensure the Clinton-Gore ticket's reelection. There was his April 1996 visit to a California Buddhist temple for an event that turned out to be a fund-raiser; his numerous telephone calls, some made from his government office, his pressure on potential donors for money (a *Washington Post* story dubbed him the "solicitor-in-chief"); his participation in coffee meetings at the White House with major contributors, some of whom were also rewarded with stays in the Lincoln Bedroom; and his famous March 3, 1997, press conference in which he defended his actions by repeatedly invoking the phrase "no controlling legal authority" to suggest that nothing he had done had technically broken the law. All of these actions were shrouded in confusion about the specifics of Gore's behavior and whether they were criminal or simply politically suspect.

Gore's advisers believed he did not have a moment to waste in planning for his own presidential campaign. So in the spring of 1997, just three months after he was sworn in for a second term, they wrote a lengthy memo to Gore and his wife, Tipper. Their recommendations covered every aspect of presidential election planning, from fund-raising, to scheduling, to staffing, to organizing, to policy.

But throughout the April 18 document, his advisers turned repeatedly to the imperative that Gore recapture control of his public image. Victory was impossible unless Gore was able to recast how the Gang of 500 and the voters viewed him.

One challenge was to get Gore more closely associated with the popular and important matters on which he worked. "The first message priority," aides Ron Klain and Karen Skelton wrote, "is to enhance your identity on the issues where you have an extensive history and a program and agenda.

National polling shows that most Americans . . . are wholly unaware of your work on your core issues of the environment, technology, ReGO [government reform], urban policy, and foreign policy. . . . We need to work harder than ever to bolster your identification with these issues . . . in a way to enhance your public image and profile.

They called for an effort "to build better relations with the press, by having small dinners, lunches, and one-on-ones designed at relationship building."

And they proposed a series of steps to "Continue Improvements on Likeability":

The public does not actually need to like its Presidents (the public does not really "like" Clinton), but you are different. From national polls that say you are "stiff" or "boring," to elite critiques of your performance as an obstacle to your electability, to the anecdotal stories we all here [sic]—everyone involved with you knows that we have to address this problem.

The good news is that we know that your private personality can only benefit you if it were transmitted to the masses. It is important that you continue to develop your public image as a guy that people "like," "relate to," and believe "understands their problems." One life-long Democrat and grade school teacher in Northern California put it this way: "Clinton is a person you want to go up and hug. Gore is a person you'll give a curtsy to." While Presidents deserve the more respectful curtsy than the informal hug, it is very important that you find ways to "connect" with voters by becoming more "warm and approachable."

Klain and Skelton proposed a series of steps to achieve this goal, including: "Highlight your sense of humor"; "Use more personal anecdotes to explain policies"; "Expose you in more informal settings: with Mrs. Gore, as a father, and without a suit (not at the same time)"; and "Booking network prime time appearances on a comedy show."

Gore's team was particularly concerned about the fund-raising scandal's potential to damage his image. After the vice president was interviewed by FBI agents in November 1997, his staff prepared for an announcement from the Justice Department regarding possible prosecutions or a widening of the inquiry. They put together a seventeen-page memo entitled "Communications & Political Plan," which addressed the implications should there be a full-blown investigation into the matter.

But in the event of the expected total or partial exoneration, they listed the following objectives:

- "Portray Decisions as Vindication and Closure"

- "Seek to Put Controversy 'Behind Us' "

- "Show VP Momentum, 'Doing his Job' "

- "Regain *Some* of Lost Strength in Polls"

They also included several "Cautions," such as "Do Not Set Expectations for 'Instant Recovery' too High" and "GOP Likely to Mount New Attack."

Those warnings turned out to be prescient. Although in early December Attorney General Janet Reno declined to name an independent counsel to look into Gore's fund-raising, the whole mess continued to dog him. The vice president was interviewed several more times by the FBI and his enemies ceaselessly flogged the topic. The phrase "no controlling legal authority" attached itself to Gore's persona like a "Kick Me" sign stuck to his back.

Despite the fund-raising controversy and other image problems, Gore was able to win the Democratic Party's presidential nomination. His only rival, Bill Bradley, initially brandished a sparkling public image as an Old Media favorite with formidable fund-raising capacity, and for a time appeared to be a viable alternative. Additionally, Bradley, a former basketball superstar and senator from New Jersey, had been dealing with the national media since he was a teenager, and was in most ways a very smart man. Yet he, too, suffered his fair share of genuine liabilities and Freak Show embarrassments. When the pressure hit, igniting controversies over his personal medical history, his congressional voting record on agriculture, and his health care plan, Bradley indignantly refused to defend himself. Gore enthusiastically ripped him apart just before the Iowa caucuses and the New Hampshire primary, thus proving more adept at dismantling Bradley's public image than at defending his own. Gore effectively sewed up the party's nomination shortly after trouncing Bradley in the first two nominating contests.

· · ·

IF THE ONLY Freak Show uproar hounding Gore during his face-offs with Bradley and George W. Bush had related to his 1996 fund-raising, perhaps the 1997 strategy put together by his consultants would have allowed him to reclaim his image. But Bush's advisers took advantage of old Gore controversies and a steady stream of new careless remarks to keep him off balance for most of the campaign.

There were dozens of furors, large and small, that bedeviled Gore. None of them involved illegality. Many of them were genuinely unfair to Gore. But all of them were skillfully used by the Bush campaign and its allies to frame Gore as the Republicans wanted him to be seen: an out-of-touch, privileged, peculiar, phony exaggerator. Among the story lines that entertained the popular consciousness and coursed throughout the Freak Show until Election Day (and up to the present time):

- Gore's alleged claim that he and Tipper Gore were the models for the main characters in the novel *Love Story*.

- Gore's alleged claim that he "found" the toxic waste danger at New York's Love Canal.

- Gore's campaign reportedly having four billion gallons of water costing $7 million released to facilitate a boating photo opportunity.

- Gore's assertion that "I took the initiative in creating the Internet."

- Gore's joking claim that when he was a child, his mother had sung him a labor union tune as a lullaby; the song was not written until he was in his twenties.

- Gore's flawed claim about the cost of his mother-in-law's prescription drug coverage.

(There are plenty more, but you get the point.)

The Freak Show, with substantial aid from the Bush campaign and the Republican National Committee, twisted Gore's original words and meaning in many of these cases, and made sure that every development was quickly and thoroughly disseminated. That nearly every one of these controversies was overplayed or mischaracterized by the Old and New Media might be unfair, but that does not alter the fact that Gore violated numerous Trade Secrets by neglecting to confront the stories.

One of Gore's communications directors, Mark Fabiani, acknowledged after the election that the campaign had failed to take the steps necessary to protect and rehabilitate Gore's public image: "The challenge of a campaign is to give people something to think about instead of the pre-existing story line. If you let people's pre-existing notions prevail, you deserve what you get."

No one who kept a close eye on the media coverage of the 2000 campaign would deny that the press corps assigned to Gore was more aggressive and more hostile toward the candidate than those assigned to Bush, a vivid reminder that liberal bias is hardly the only factor influencing Old Media coverage, and often not the most important. This discrepancy made Old Media reporters much more likely to buy into political party press releases, late-night comic jokes, and the general story line that mirrored the Bush campaign's crafted version of Gore.

A number of members of the Gang of 500 are convinced that the main reason George W. Bush won the White House and Al Gore lost was that Gore's regular press pack included the trio of Katharine "Kit" Seelye (of the *New York Times*), Ceci Connolly (of the *Washington Post*), and Sandra Sobieraj (of the Associated Press).

Those three journalists were known collectively in some corners of the press bus as the "Spice Girls." But by Gore's staff, the trio was called a word that, as Barbara Bush might say, rhymes with "witches." Journalism publications and blogs galore have appraised the fairness of their coverage.

Those three influential reporters—and the influential news organizations for which they worked—certainly played their part in churning out negative copy about Gore, but they were more representative of Gore's problem than they were the cause. At some point along the way, those reporters contributed to the vice president of the United States losing control of his public image. Seelye, Connolly, and Sobieraj most assuredly never resolved to confer with the Gore campaign to help the candidate recover his image. But a more adept campaign (and candidate) would have worked to defuse the danger early on.

And it was not just those three tone-setters who latched on to a negative image of Gore. Nearly every major newspaper and television network in the country did stories at some point during the campaign raising the question of whether the vice president was a big liar or merely a small one. As *Rolling Stone* pointed out long after the election, "Journalists just refused to drop unflattering Gore stories, no matter what the facts revealed."

The coverage of the presidential debates were particularly influenced by these themes, with minor Gore misstatements about the overcrowded conditions in a Sarasota, Florida, school and his travels with James Lee Witt of the Federal Emergency Management Agency turned into high crimes of character.

And the image problems did not stop with "liar." Most colorfully, Gore was branded as "out of touch" and "elitist" when Tracy Mayberry, a tenant on his Tennessee farm property, got into a dispute with him over the run-down conditions of the rented home she shared with her children and disabled husband. After threats of an eviction, Gore tried to set things right, but the Freak Show and the Old Media loved the story. (Trade Secret: *Avoid the label "slumlord" as best you can during a presidential campaign.*)

And the fund-raising controversy from four years earlier never stopped. In April of 2000, Gore, by then the Democratic Party's presumptive nominee, once again was hauled before Justice Department lawyers and FBI agents to answer four hours of questions about his fund-raising from the previous campaign, including the infamous Buddhist temple event. Bush allies in Congress, knowing an image-warping set of facts when they saw one, continued to demand throughout the 2000 general election that Reno appoint an outside investigator to examine Gore's role. The video of Gore at the temple with robe-clad monks played in what appeared to be a continuous loop on cable and broadcast television.

Gore made mistakes, and had some bad luck (including that infamous Florida butterfly ballot), but the biggest Trade Secret that explained what happened to him applied to Bill Clinton before and John Kerry afterward: *Not every election is a fair fight.* The media, the New leading the Old, helped Bush tell his good story about himself, and helped Republicans tell a bad story about Gore. And, once again, the pervasive influence of Matt Drudge was a big factor.

All the damaging stories about and embarrassing images of Gore were first highlighted on the *Drudge Report,* or received aggressive promotion there—from the flap over the creation of the Internet, to the searing image of Gore appearing at the Buddhist temple, to the sad plight of the Mayberrys. There was one particular damaging story line that Drudge hammered. With Clinton's days in the White House winding down, and the prospect of a Gore presidency, there was nothing more intoxicating to Drudge and his readers than the tensions between the impeached president and his flummoxed subordinate.

• • •

IN THE EYES of Washington's elite reporters and political operatives, Al Gore's biggest public image problems all derived from Bill Clinton. Gore had defended Clinton on the day of his impeachment, then condemned his conduct when he entered the presidential race. He continued to evince a confusing and confused ambivalence in public about the Lewinsky matter and the Starr investigation. He had trouble getting his share of the credit for what the Clinton-Gore administration had accomplished. He had to worry about the side-by-side comparisons between him and the greatest politician of his generation. And he tied himself in knots figuring out what role Clinton should play in his drive to inherit the White House.

The Bush campaign watched with pleasure as Gore struggled with the question of how to handle Clinton—the man and the issue. Both campaigns had reams of polling data showing that many voters in swing states were turned off by Clinton personally, but the Bush campaign nonetheless was surprised that Gore did not more openly embrace the administration's record and use Clinton regularly on the hustings. In Austin, they amused themselves observing Gore's typically inartful performances, as he got enmeshed in the negatives of Clinton (Lewinsky, impeachment, fund-raising scandals), without enjoying the benefits (years of prosperity and relative peace, strong job approval ratings).

In addition, Clinton occasionally would do something that threatened to overshadow Gore, and discombobulate his vice president. Clinton's dramatically staged long walk to the podium at the Democratic National Committee convention in Los Angeles was the perfect manifestation of his unwillingness to relinquish the spotlight to his would-be successor. And the press coverage of that walk reinforced Gore's instinct that it was in his interest for Clinton to be neither seen nor heard. Gore took steps to rein in his boss, and Clinton's campaign schedule was curtailed.

Most of Gore's advisers believed the research was conclusive that Clinton would alienate the swing voters they needed at the end of the campaign in states such as Tennessee, Ohio, and Missouri. Clinton's advisers argued that those voters were lost to Gore no matter what, and that the president should be deployed to energize Democratic voters.

The tie was broken by Gore himself, who had become completely psyched out by the Clinton Factor and insisted the president mostly be kept off the trail.

The Bush campaign was perfectly aware of these tensions and happy to make mischief. With speculation at a fever pitch that Gore would change his mind, and the Republican team convinced it was in their interest for Clinton to remain out of the picture, Bush executed a masterstroke on the campaign trail. Speaking to several hundred voters at a town meeting at a school in Arlington Heights, Illinois, he was asked a question that alluded to Clinton's Lewinsky affair.

"I'm not running against President Clinton," Bush replied. "This is the first chapter of the 21st century. I don't think there's a lot of politics to be gained by talking about him. As a matter of fact, I think most Americans would rather move on, and that's what I'm going to do."

Then Bush added the clever bazooka shot: "If he decides he can't help himself, and gets out there and starts campaigning against me, the Shadow returns."

The Shadow indeed. Who knew what motives lurked in the heart of the Texas governor that day? Not us. But Bush continued to taunt Clinton into (and out of) the race later that evening on ABC News's *Nightline,* saying Clinton's presence would "remind people that my opponent was not standing on his own, that there must be something amiss, if after having stiff-armed a president so to speak, all of a sudden they urge him to come back in the waning days of the campaign."

Most reporters and citizens who heard Bush's Shadow line probably thought it was funny, if they thought anything about it at all. But for Gore, who obsessively followed Bush's every move and word, such a statement was no laughing matter. After Bush's jeer, Gore decided, once and for all, to keep the best politician in the world from doing any significant campaigning for him.

Clinton was old enough to remember *The Shadow,* the radio show on which Bush's taunt was based. He recognized what Bush and Rove were doing as a form of psychological warfare. "All of this is a head game, you know. All great contests are head games."

• • •

WHETHER AL GORE lost because Bill Clinton was too visible or not visible enough should not concern 2008 presidential candidates as much as the more generic Trade Secrets that Gore disobeyed.

In the end, Gore lost because he let his bad story resonate much more strongly than his good story. George W. Bush won (yes, with some help from the Supreme Court) because his good story struck a chord that rang much louder than the counternarrative.

The main Trade Secrets to be learned from Gore's experience are:

If your traveling press corps is hostile to you and the Old Media has settled on a negative meta-narrative about your candidacy, you cannot make real progress in any part of your campaign until you address those problems.

If the Old Media has settled on a negative narrative about your campaign, the oppositional New Media will produce a giant feedback loop that will reinforce your problem. This will be more likely to happen to the Democratic nominee in 2008 than the Republican.

Of course, Gore's campaign had many other problems that cost him votes besides an ineptitude in dealing with the Old Media and the Freak Show. The vice president had plenty of smart, experienced political advisers helping him. But Gore flung away perhaps his finest weapon by largely rejecting the assistance and advice of the greatest political strategist in the Democratic Party. Meanwhile, the man who would become the forty-third president of the United States kept close at his side the greatest political strategist in the Republican Party.

SECTION III

★ ★ ★ ★ ★

"EVIL GENIUS"

★ ★ ★ ★ ★

WHO IS KARL ROVE?

★ ★ ★ ★ ★

HUDDLED IN A YELLOW PONCHO, seated near the stage but off to the side, Karl Rove was an unobtrusive figure at the William J. Clinton Presidential Library and Museum dedication in November 2004—though hardly an unnoticed one.

Everywhere, people were stealing glimpses of the man President Bush had called "the Architect" of his reelection victory. Later that day, in the hotel lobbies and bars of Little Rock, Democrats giddily were recounting Rove sightings. Even among Washington political professionals, Rove remains an elusive figure, at once ubiquitous and obscure. He is talked about constantly in reference to both his talents and his travails. Decisions in the farthest corners of government confidently are presumed to bear his imprint. Yet, unlike generations of presidential aides and strategists who have made themselves familiar faces in the capital culture, Rove has been a spectral presence. (Rumors of his attendance at dance parties at the Silver Spring, Maryland, home of *Wall Street Journal* reporter John Harwood created buzz in Democratic circles.)

He does not frequently dine at the Palm or other high-profile Washington restaurants, or hold sociable meet-and-greet sessions with members of the rival party. He has not been a regular on the Sunday morning public affairs shows.

But there he was in the flesh at the library opening. For many Clintonites, it was as if they had glimpsed a magenta unicorn.

Rove was treated to a private tour of Clinton's library. Both a naturally and preternaturally curious man, Rove was brimming with questions for the tour guide.

"You're not such a scary guy," the guide observed.

"Yes, I am," Rove replied—no doubt in jest, but in a way that caused a fever of speculation among Democrats when the story of the conversation made the rounds in Little Rock and was written about by Sidney Blumenthal.

After the soggy formal ceremony was a VIP luncheon in a tent next to the new library. There, the top political strategist of the Democratic Party walked over and swooned over the top political strategist of the Republican Party.

"Hey, you did a marvelous job, it was just marvelous what you did," Clinton said to Rove, impressed by the Republican's artistry in beating John Kerry and securing a second term for George W. Bush. The two men had met casually in larger groups before, but this was the first time Rove was showered by Clinton's full attention. "I want to get you down to the library," Clinton continued, inviting him to return for more quality time. "I want to talk politics with you. You just did an incredible job and I'd like to really get together with you, and I think we could have a great conversation."

For all the Oz-like mystique he cultivated, Rove hardly was immune to flattery. Despite avowed sour feelings about Clinton—in conversations the strategist excoriated Clinton, and was contemptuous of how he had conducted his presidency—he was quite pleased to accept this compliment. Later, back at the White House, Rove would regale people with his own telling of the encounter, complete with a credible raspy-voiced impersonation of the forty-second president.

· · ·

CLINTON WAS AS eager for answers as all the other Democrats in Little Rock. *Who is Karl Rove?* And how had Rove managed twice in a row to direct victories over Democrats in elections that Clinton felt certain could have been won—indeed, *would* have been won—if someone named "Clinton" had been at the top of the ticket?

For savvy Democrats, Rove personified what their party lacked. Rove was organized and understood how to unify his party; Democrats were disorganized and fractious. Rove projected strength and moral certitude in his candidates; Democrats could not seem to do either. The Democratic Party in the last few years has identified these as big problems, and has struggled, however ineptly, to fix them; the indirect assistance of a flagging Bush administration has not yet revised the dynamic. Many Democrats have settled on Rove as the prototype for a cure (minus the dinged reputation), and over the course of the Bush presidency have shifted from merely despising him to viewing his abilities with rapt wonderment and envy.

Since the 2002 midterm elections, the mantra "We need our own Karl Rove" has been a battle cry for a Democratic Party crippled during the early George W. Bush years and desperate to replicate the effectiveness and discipline Rove provided to his principal and to his party. Yet among even sophisticated operatives, there is very little understanding of what Rove actually brings to the table beyond being the apotheosis of *tough, relentless, victorious.*

In the collective mind of the liberal Establishment, Rove inevitably is labeled an "evil genius," a phrase that has become a cliché as applied to him. Combining Rove's name with "evil genius" on Nexis produces more than a hundred stories in which the writer or editor succumbed to this hackneyed description. Run the same search on Google and you get tens of thousands of hits.

It seems somehow to console Democrats to think of Rove as evil. But any politician of either party who wishes to avoid Al Gore's fate, or John Kerry's, should be more interested in understanding Rove than denouncing him. Here is the first step: *Separate the adjective from the noun.* They have almost nothing to do with each other.

Is Rove evil? The idea that President Bush's top aide is the product of a demon seed that took root and came to blossom in the Texas Hill Country derives from events early in his life, even before the Colorado-born and Utah-raised Rove found his way to Texas. Rove's first documented "dirty trick"—one to which he admits—came in 1970. The national College Republicans sent him to Illinois to work on the Senate campaign of Republican Ralph Smith. Rove, then just age twenty, stole some stationery from the offices of Smith's Democratic opponent and printed up invitations promising "free beer, free food, girls, and a good time for nothing" to everyone who showed up at the grand opening of the Democrat's headquarters. The invitations were distributed at soup kitchens and rock concerts. The result Rove and his fellow mischief-makers hoped for was exactly what they got. All manner of grubby folk turned out for the Democrat's party, swamping organizers with a crowd twice the size of what they planned for. (Ralph Smith lost the race.)

In 1973, Rove's campaign for national chairman of the College Republicans was hit by new allegations of dirty tricks, based on audiotapes of Rove's training sessions in which he supposedly described how to implement shady campaign tactics. The complaints, apparently circulated by a Rove rival, were investigated by the FBI and the Republican National Committee but never proven. And on it goes through the years. In 1986, Rove was accused of planting a listening device in his own office to create a hubbub during a heated Texas gubernatorial race. There were two theories. One held that Rove hoped Democrats would be blamed for a dirty trick. The other was that Rove wanted to create a diversion in case his candidate performed poorly in an upcoming debate. Later, allegations surfaced that Rove worked hand-in-glove with an Austin-based FBI agent who conducted investigations of the consultant's political foes.

Proponents of the Rove-is-evil thesis regard these musty episodes as the gestation period for a malignancy that metastasized fully during Rove's Washington years. According to this theory, Rove secretly orchestrated the most vicious attacks made against John McCain before the crucial South Carolina Republican primary in 2000. He used his White House perch to manipulate the timing of the confrontation in Iraq to gain partisan advantage in 2002. He casually smeared anyone in his way, as illustrated by the outing of covert CIA official Valerie Plame after her husband, Joseph Wilson, had the audacity to question Bush's rationale for invading Iraq. Rove watched blithely—and no doubt participated behind the scenes—as the Swift Boat Veterans for Truth falsely tarred John Kerry's war record in 2004. He delighted and saw electoral benefits in the worst elements of human nature, exploiting homophobia and paranoia. In short, this view of Rove goes, Bush was elected (despite a reputation as a spoiled playboy and an intellectual lightweight) and then reelected (despite a tenure of policy fiascos at home and abroad) largely because he enjoyed the services of this cynical and cutthroat man.

Rove engaged in apparent deception regarding the CIA leak, although the exact nature of his actions and motives remains murky. But the larger Rove-is-evil indictment has problems. For one, its most damaging counts are mostly unproven. Did Rove really orchestrate the efforts of the Swift Boat Veterans? It is fashionable in the salons of Chevy Chase, Manhattan, Cambridge, and the Westside of Los Angeles to assert this as solid fact, but there is no evidence of it. (And there are plenty of reasons to doubt that Rove would be so foolish as to expose himself and Bush to a potentially campaign-ending controversy if any secret coordination came to light.) The same lack of evidence ruins the anti-Rove conspiracy theories on most every other accumulated charge against him.

Maybe Rove bugged his own office. Maybe he secretly directed slurs

against Texas governor Ann Richards, John McCain, and John Kerry. But reporters and Democrats (and sometimes Republicans) have had every motivation to unearth some actual proof of these rumors, and nothing ever has been
found.

Maybe this means that Rove was as brilliant at covering up his evil as he
was brutal in perpetrating it. Or maybe this means he was so intimidating
that no one dared come forward with testimony against him. But *maybe* does
not seem reason enough to assail a man's record and reputation.

Typical of the standards used to judge Rove was a 2004 *Atlantic Monthly*
article that set out quite clearly to illustrate that Rove's savagery in close campaigns knew no bounds. The article was filled with language about Rove's
"animal ferocity," his "apparent willingness to cross moral and ethical lines,"
his "unscrupulous tactics," and "a willingness to fight in territory where conscience forbids most others." It also contained a recital of Rove's alleged,
well-publicized dirty tricks and some relatively fresh charges about Rove's
suspected tactics in a few Alabama campaigns in the 1990s. But the supporting evidence was flimsy. The two most significant allegations—that Rove
printed attack flyers against his own candidate to spur a backlash and that
he initiated a whisper campaign accusing a Rove opponent of being a
pedophile—were based exclusively on anonymous quotes from "someone
who worked for" Rove and "a former Rove staffer."

Rove is a tough guy. He gets angry at those who cross or disappoint him.
He has spoken so harshly to friends that they have been reduced to tears. He,
though usually a disciplined and self-effacing man, has a boastful, bombastic
streak that sometimes slips its leash and goes on a public romp. He has "used"
national security and other Republican strengths as issues in campaigns (in
the same way that Democrats "use" Social Security and education). In victory
he has appeared remorseless about his give-no-quarter tactics. He has been
merciless in attacking Democrats when they have shown vulnerability, employing polling and every available means of communication with voters. And
sometimes, when cornered or threatened by circumstances, he has attempted
to bully and intimidate journalists or political enemies. Rove has been more
tenacious and more intense than most political strategists. But he has advanced his goals, according to both admiring colleagues and bitter competitors, in much the same way as other political operatives. Rove deserves
unique notice for one reason: He is an exceptionally good political strategist.

Even if one wants to believe that some of Rove's tactics and motives have
been evil, they are mostly irrelevant to the reasons he has been a winner. It is

the noun that is worth studying. While it is not a given that Rove indubitably is a "genius," it sure seemed that way back in November 2004. He was fresh from leading George W. Bush to his fifth consecutive victory (the governorship in 1994, the reelection of 1998, the presidency in 2000, the dazzling Republican performance in the 2002 midterm elections, and the 2004 presidential reelection). Early in 2005, *Time* magazine put Rove's name on a list of the world's "most influential people," including him in the section for "scientists and thinkers." America's most famous Democratic consultant, James Carville, endorsed the choice, calling Rove "the pre-eminent political strategist in the U.S. today."

By November of 2005, the Rove-as-genius thesis was gasping for air. Rove himself was in the crosshairs of a special prosecutor investigating the Valerie Plame leak and the possibility that Rove had lied under oath about his role in the shabby business. Although Rove was cleared in June 2006, the Plame case restructured his public image. Enemies gloated over Rove's multihour forays before the grand jury and his forced nonchalance strolling past clusters of waiting cameras outside the federal courthouse; the press adopted the fresh story line of Rove as potential lawbreaker and dissembler rather than as triumphant architect; and the public perceived him as a man in trouble, destined to watch the next election from the confines of a prison cell. No longer was Rove seen as Bush's ultimate weapon for victory, but as a symbol of the president's arrogant overreaching. What kind of genius finds himself in a fix like this?

It is not yet known where Rove will land on the spectrum between visionary and washout by the end of 2008. It is the 2006 midterm and 2008 presidential elections, nearly as much as the previous ones, that will determine Rove's place on the historical ledger. Perhaps he will be seen as a smart man but also a lucky one, who ran the table for a while, until his luck ran out in 2005. If his luck returns, however, it is possible that Republicans can retain their congressional majorities after the election of 2006 and hold the White House in 2008. In that case, even amid war, bad judgment, and scandal, and the natural tendency of presidencies to draw down power in their closing years, Rove's lifetime ambition of promoting conservative power and conservative goals will live on.

Should that happen, few people in politics of any persuasion—conservative or liberal, angelic or evil—would begrudge Rove his reputation as a genius. With the Plame investigation behind him, and a roster of fiery speeches before him, Rove could emerge as strong as before. Even if it does not happen—if Republicans are routed in the coming elections and Rove's reputation is permanently tainted—we would still argue that sensible political strategists in the years ahead will still want to know WWKD: *What Would Karl Do?*

• • •

KARL CHRISTIAN ROVE was born on Christmas Day in Denver in 1950. His father, Louis Rove, was a mineral geologist whose work caused the family to move often. The second oldest of five children, Karl did not have an especially political upbringing, but even at age nine, he was an ardent Nixon backer in the 1960 election. By his teenage years, he was living in Salt Lake City and attending Olympus High School, where he may not have been cool but he definitely drew notice. Extracurricular life was driven by the debate club—Karl was a ferocious competitor—and the student senate—he became president after running a campaign in which he lampooned the tactics of professional politicians.

His upbringing was not defined by poverty but it did instill in him a sense of the precariousness of economic and social status. Rove was once asked what he was insecure about. "I'm insecure about my own personal finances. Tomorrow it will be the Great Depression. I'm the cheapest guy you've ever met. . . . My grandfather literally . . . worked on a road crew and began selling knives off the back of his pickup truck. My mother grew up in a tar-paper shack in Pueblo, Colorado, where they would literally take the newspaper and flour-paste it onto the wall. I can remember my grandfather and my grandmother talking about . . . selling butcher knives off the back of a pickup truck to little grocery stores in southern Colorado and I remember my grandmother talking about they found a twenty-dollar bill on the road when they were living in Fort Collins and that's what allowed them to start their business. So I'm just a cheap guy."

Rove enrolled at the University of Utah, but his freshman year brought some unhappy surprises at home. On Christmas Day of 1969, Rove's nineteenth birthday, his father walked out, and his parents' marriage ended. Soon after, Rove learned a secret: Louis Rove was not in fact his biological father, and Karl would be in his forties before he met the man who was. As for Karl's mother, Reba, she did not have an easy life. In the early 1980s, she committed suicide. At the time of her death, Karl Rove was newly single, as his first marriage had resulted in divorce.

Domestic dysfunction and tragedy had done nothing to inhibit professional success, however. During his student years, Karl Rove made a name

for himself, at least among a certain circle of junior Republican activists.
First, he became the national executive director of the College Republicans.
Then, in 1973, he ran in a bitterly contested election to be national chairman
of the same group. His campaign had him traveling around the country with
another zealous young partisan named Lee Atwater, who would become famous on the national stage a decade before his friend. The race for chairman
became so heated that the convention at Lake of the Ozarks, Missouri, broke
up amid procedural disputes. Rove and his opponent both claimed victory
and appealed to the Republican National Committee for a resolution. It was
during this phase of the contest that his rivals leaked to the *Washington Post*
a tape in which Rove was heard at a political training session recounting tales
of campaign pranks and mischief. ("GOP Probes Official as Teacher of
Tricks," read the *Post*'s Watergate-era headline.) An RNC investigating committee cleared Rove of wrongdoing, and that summer he was awarded the
chairmanship. It was then that Rove met the man serving as chairman of the
Republican National Committee, a patrician former congressman from Houston named George H. W. Bush. The older fellow took a shine to this self-
confident, if unpolished, youth. Rove certainly was more appealing to a man
like Bush than those insolent, long-haired protesters running wild on so
many college campuses. A few months later, the day before Thanksgiving
1973, Rove was introduced to Bush's eldest son, a jocular, rakish twenty-
seven-year-old who wore an Air National Guard flight jacket. In that initial
encounter, George W. Bush struck Rove as one of the most charismatic people he had ever met.

Rove attended several universities but never graduated; even so, he was
ready for the next phase of his life.

Washington, D.C., would have been the natural place for someone of
Rove's ambitions to settle down. But personal priorities pointed elsewhere.
His first marriage, at age twenty-six, was to Valerie Wainwright, who came
from a socially connected family in Houston. Although they had met in
Washington, she wanted to live in Texas, and so Texas it was. The move was
one more example of how serendipity is the strongest force in life. The marriage failed within a couple of years, but by then Rove was already inextrica-
bly intertwined with Texas politics, and on his way to becoming one of the
most important figures in the modern history of the state. He would play a
central role in changing Texas in less than a generation from a place totally
dominated by Democrats to one totally dominated by Republicans. In 1978,
Rove worked on the gubernatorial campaign of Bill Clements, who became

the first Republican elected governor in Texas in 104 years. Rove moved to Austin to be his deputy chief of staff.

Leaving government, in 1981 he opened Rove + Co., an Austin-based direct mail business. There are two things to keep in mind about this moment. The first is that Texas was then still overwhelmingly Democratic, with the state legislature firmly in Democratic hands. In 1982, every Republican running statewide lost, including Clements in his bid for reelection. To be an ambitious Republican in Texas during this time was almost by definition to be a boat-rocker. Additionally, the notion of making a business out of politics was still relatively unusual. There were small fraternities of people aligned with each party who did it, and everyone in the business pretty much knew everyone else. Things are much different now, with Washington, D.C., and state capitals filled with consultants who become rich by selling their expertise in polling, media strategy, image shaping, and grassroots organizing. Although Rove's business included work for nonprofit organizations and cultural institutions, he was a pioneer in the new industry of politics.

The particular niche of the business in which Rove settled is also noteworthy. Direct mail, while lucrative, is generally considered low on the status ladder of political consulting. Media consulting, as first practiced in the late 1960s and early 1970s by people such as Roger Ailes for the Republicans and Robert Squier for the Democrats, is where the glamour was and where the most ambitious people operated. Rove was the only top-level presidential campaign strategist to come out of the world of mail. He had first learned about direct mail a decade earlier during his College Republican years. Though in time both parties gained expertise in this new medium, it was no coincidence that the early practitioners were mostly conservative Republicans. Innovators like Richard Viguerie, who turned direct mail into a potent tool of the Right in the 1970s, knew that the country was filled with frustrated people eager to hear messages almost never conveyed by traditional methods of political mass communication such as news coverage and paid advertising. The way to reach people was through *targeted* communications that got to them right at their kitchen tables. Through mail, it was possible to say things—attack opponents in harsh language, for instance, or espouse outspokenly conservative ideological views—that would be impolitic in other settings. Indeed, the most effective direct mail tended to be the most provocative. It was a way of escaping the bland conventions and restraints of conventional politics, in which the boundaries were enforced by a liberal news media.

Recall that the essence of Freak Show politics is the incentives it creates *against* moderation and rhetorical restraint and *for* personal attack and ideological combat. These are precisely the incentives that animate the most successful direct mail. No one opens a letter, and decides that very moment to drop everything and write a fund-raising check to Smith after reading that Jones, while basically an honorable man, simply is not as sound on the subject of government procurement reform. People write checks because they decide Smith agrees with them on something they consider urgent and emotional—banning abortion, for instance, or ensuring that it stays legal; supporting gay rights or blocking gay marriage—and that Jones is a dangerous man who is hostile to values they hold dear. Rove came of age learning where the pressure points lay in American politics, those issues that got the Right most excited, and those on which the Left was most vulnerable.

There could hardly be better training for an era in which success comes from defining the opposition as not wrong just on the merits, but morally unacceptable. Rove's sharpest and most memorable speech lines of his White House years (*Republicans have a post-9/11 worldview, and many Democrats have a pre-9/11 worldview*) could well have been lifted straight from a direct mail piece.

Rove had another advantage in this type of politics. Intellectually, Rove could be detached and analytical. Emotionally, he entered any contest with an intensity that could be downright frightening. His wife, Darby Rove, once described this single-minded ferocity to the *New York Times*. "He's learned to lay back a little bit when he and [son] Andrew play chess," she recalled, "but even in croquet he'd be hitting my ball so far I was crying on vacation." When it comes to his job, she observed, "working for Republicans is the organizing principle of his life, at the center of his world, which he tends to divide into friends and foes." She once told her husband, "You see things in black and white."

• • •

ONE THEME OF this book is comparing how Bill Clinton and Karl Rove each have played and won the game of American politics. But the comparison is hobbled by a fundamental difference between them. Clinton is a principal, a man who dominates and is thoroughly comfortable on the public stage. Rove, for all his influence, has always been a staff man, a supporting player who is supposed to spend most of his time behind the scenes. Almost by definition this produces confusion and intrigue. Rove's power has been wielded by indirection. Much of what George W. Bush executes reflects Karl Rove's thinking in ways that neither man can acknowledge publicly. But much of what George W. Bush executes reflects his own thinking and values, in ways that people who are convinced Rove is in control will never accept.

Rove is not "Bush's brain," and Rove cannot claim full credit for his own success in presidential politics. His achievements were inseparable from the unusual, perhaps even unprecedented, relationship between a politician and his most important adviser. Additionally, the bond extends beyond the professional; Bush and Rove can be unself-conscious in describing their mutual affection.

Bush told the *Washington Post* in 1999 that Rove was "a very unique and very smart and very capable person. He is—he's just Karl, and when everybody understands what 'just Karl' means, we all get along."

Frank Bruni of the *New York Times* offered this excellent summation: "When Mr. Rove talks about Mr. Bush, he radiates a regard for him that goes beyond professional obligation or selfish investment in Mr. Bush's fortune. It is more like a crush, both platonic and political and it underscores the oddness of this particular couple: the pale, intense, bookish Mr. Rove and the ruddy, easygoing, folksy Mr. Bush."

Rove once put it as simply as this: "He's my friend, and I love him."

Such a plain utterance does not capture the full complexity of the relationship. Bush and Rove are friends, but an adviser never can be on a totally equal footing with a president. Bush was more likely to unload on Rove than on any other staffer, ripping into him if a public event was poorly organized or if he felt he was being overscheduled. Rove was a staff man, but one with a license to speak to his boss with more directness and familiarity than other White House aides would dare. In 2000 and 2004, it was Rove who pushed a complacent Bush to get up out of his chair and onto the campaign trail when he felt the candidate needed to shake some more hands.

The most successful politicians invariably have someone in whom they can confide. Bill Clinton split the job between two quite disparate people— Dick Morris and Hillary Rodham Clinton. Rove fulfilled both their roles. He was one part Dick Morris, who melded policy and politics into a seamless strategy, and one part Hillary Clinton, who imparted a sense of discipline and direction her husband never could have summoned on his own. Clinton has said he would not have been president without the guidance and support of his wife. He was not being falsely modest. By the same token, it is no slight on George W. Bush to say that it is equally impossible to imagine him becoming president without Karl Rove.

There is one key ingredient to every profitable relationship between a candidate and an adviser: *confidence*. Campaigns are insecure places. So are White Houses. Each day brings newspaper and television reports providing new examples of people who call you a fool or a scoundrel. Often the stories offer telltale signs that some of the hecklers are in your own party or on your own staff, even if they are not quoted by name. Politics is a business in which personal humiliation and career disaster are omnipresent possibilities. The most effective advisers give politicians reassurance that disaster will be averted, or, if not, that recovery is achievable. When in 1995 Clinton looked like he was Jimmy Carter redux, another failed Southern Democratic president, Morris insisted that reelection was a given if Clinton followed the plan.

Clinton's counselors—certainly Morris, and perhaps Hillary Clinton herself—found themselves moving closer in or further out in influence, depending on the moment. George W. Bush's orbits tend not to change. For more than a decade, he and Rove had a fixed relationship, one in which neither man seemed to have questioned the abilities or the trust of the other. Skeptics might note that Bush and Rove, who have appeared to critics and even some supporters as arrogant, might have benefited from occasional moments of self-doubt. But this mutual and reinforcing confidence was at the heart of any success they enjoyed.

Only occasionally did President Bush decide that Rove was getting, or taking, more credit than politicians typically are willing to relinquish to their staff. Laura Bush was more apt to put the pin in Rove's balloon. During an unusually prickly interview with the *New York Times* in which she rapped the media, Mrs. Bush described Rove "as not as powerful as 'the chattering class' believes.

" 'I would say his role is definitely overstated, but he probably loves it,' she said, smiling. 'He's very happy to have his role overstated.' "

• • •

THE FIRST LADY herself may have exaggerated this point. In Rove's case, just as with Dick Morris in his season of power with Bill Clinton, his influence flowed from a critical insight: In a modern White House, it is essential to knock down the traditional wall separating policy from politics. In an earlier era, these two realms were mostly insulated from each other except at election time. The distinction made sense when politics was less pervasive. But such fastidiousness has been rendered obsolete by the Freak Show. Just as news cycles are now twenty-four hours a day, political cycles are 365 days a year. That means there is never a moment when a president is not at risk of losing control of his public image or his political circumstances. The only way to counteract this reality is with a seamless presidency.

In the White House, Bush prudently gave Rove a central role in every matter relating to politics and domestic policy, as well as a supporting role in decisions about the public presentation of national security.

James Carville was very good at crafting campaign messages, possibly better than Rove. But the idea of Carville leading a meeting on welfare policy is comical. It is not ludicrous to think of Rove leading that meeting, and he has led countless such sessions for the Bush administration. Clinton pollster Mark Penn is very good at reading data. But Clinton would not have asked him to assemble a coalition of special interest groups to back a new proposal on the president's legislative agenda. Penn, for one thing, would not necessarily know the names of the right people to call. Rove does know the names, telephone numbers, and e-mail addresses of the right people, and probably would have long-established relationships with them already.

The answer to why Rove is good is that he is smart about a lot of things. This explanation is more than a tautology. It reflects a principal insight about the presidency that will be as true for the forty-fourth president as it has been for the forty-third. Every president needs an adviser (or, if no single evil genius is available, a well-coordinated team of nasty, brainy folks) who has a synoptic view of politics—who understands that in a modern environment every important political challenge is related to other important challenges. Most professions are becoming ever more specialized. In political strategy, this is the age of the generalist.

It is also an age that rewards strategists who are willing to sync up their work schedules with the never-ending news cycle and political threats. Almost everyone in presidential politics at a senior level keeps long hours, but few likely worked harder than Rove did in 2000 and 2004.

• • •

WHEN LAURA BUSH needled Rove in 2004 about his allegedly overstated role, she was right about one thing. His prominence was becoming bad for business—Bush's business and Rove's own. In 1999, Rove was asked about his visibility as a Bush adviser, which even then was on the rise. Would he end up becoming famous? "No," he replied, "and it will become a distinct failure on my part if I do."

Six years later, he was reminded of this quote. His first instinct, as ever, was debate. "Look, this town runs on myths," he said. "I love the things that I get credited or blamed for."

But, no matter the reason, he was now a famous—and notorious—person around the world. Was there anything he could have done to avoid this? "I don't know," Rove responded. But what about his original pledge—that it would be a failure if he became well known?

Rove stopped arguing and acknowledged the point. "I failed," he said.

This so-called failure is one of the great ironies of Rove's story. One of the things he does best is discern the dynamics of the Freak Show. He used this understanding in campaigns that caused both Al Gore and John Kerry to lose complete control of their public images. Halfway through Bush's presidency, however, Rove lost control of his own.

The Freak Show has made Rove the most written about, pictured, lampooned, caricatured, and condemned political adviser in American history. There is no precedent for a White House staff member gaining such an outsized public profile. Rove sat for a television interview for Barbara Walters's Most Fascinating People at the end of 2004, and was deemed most fascinating of all, despite his wary and guarded manner. He beat out the flashy Paris Hilton, the iconic Oprah Winfrey, and the passionate Mel Gibson. *That* is the personification of ultimate fame in early-twenty-first-century America.

After President Bush, Laura Bush, and Vice President Cheney, Rove is the fourth most sought after speaker at GOP fund-raisers. But his persona itself may have swelled Democratic coffers even more so, since his adversaries crammed their fund-raising letters with warnings about his vicious tactics and grand designs for power. He has received regular attention in books, documentaries, cartoons, late-night comedians' jokes, prime-time TV scripts, blogs, and websites. He is the subject of polling questions, cable TV chatter, and magniloquent public attacks.

In the main, the Old Media's coverage of Rove came from the perspective of standard East/West Coast elitism, which considered Rove's outlook on life confounding. Rove's sensibilities reflected his Western ethos, with its anti-Washington, anti-Establishment, free market, pro-gun, pro-faith orientation.

Imagine a Democratic Karl Rove, and how the Old Media would treat him. Rove's campaign colleague Stuart Stevens argued persuasively that a Democrat Rove would be hailed and feted rather than tarred and feathered. "If he worked for a candidate the intelligentsia embraced, Karl would be the toast of every ed board and sought out at every Hamptons dinner party. Because Karl works for a candidate who is not supported by the . . . media elite, and because, most annoyingly to them, he tends to be right and they are wrong, there is a need to paint him as an Evil Genius. . . . When [Democrats engage in] all kinds of things, from manipulating and berating the media to threatening someone who dares oppose their candidate . . . [this] is considered cute and endearing by the media because the assumption is that these are good men doing bad things for a good cause. There's no such assumption for . . . Karl."

• • •

ROVE MAY NEVER have had a fighting chance to be an Old Media darling, but the descent/ascent to notoriety was gradual, and he began to lose control of his image well before he ran afoul of Patrick Fitzgerald's investigation into the Valerie Plame case. Within conservative and Republican circles in the 1980s and 1990s, Rove was a familiar and respected figure, but he was mostly an unknown quantity to "regular" members of the Gang of 500. A handful of political reporters, including Dan Balz of the *Washington Post*, Howard Fineman of *Newsweek*, Wayne Slater of the *Dallas Morning News*, Robert Novak of the *Chicago Sun-Times*, and Fred Barnes of the *New Republic* and the *Weekly Standard*, followed Rove's career, but he lived a life of quiet and lucrative anonymity.

In Washington, he granted only the occasional official interview (although a close reader of newspapers and magazines could divine that there was that long-standing stable of reporters to whom he spoke off the record and on background), and dealt privately with major conservative groups and party fund-raisers.

Rove became enmeshed in several controversies during Bush's inaugural year in the White House, involving his personal finances, his aggressive politicking, and his assertive role in policy fights. Just a month before the September 11 attacks, the *New York Times* went so far as to place Rove at the center of a "can't-anybody-here-play-this-game?" piece, saying he was part of stumbling moves "that are not merely embarrassing but also perilous to Mr. Bush's political standing." Rove had been blamed for alienating Vermont senator Jim Jeffords right out of the Republican Party, giving Democrats control of the Senate. Bush faced a dicey budget situation, and calls for a midcourse correction, not even a year into his first term.

With the September 11 attacks came an across-the-board recalibration. Would Bush and Rove have been able to right things without that horrific intervention? The world will never know.

What is apparent is that Rove led an effort to focus the administration's midterm election planning on the Republican Party's perceived superiority on national security matters. Rove said as much in a now-famous speech to the Republican National Committee in January of 2002. From that moment forward, Rove became the hottest button any Democrat could push to fire up the faithful. After the Republicans defied history and won midterm seats in both the House and the Senate, Rove was given much of the credit, and his critics hated him even more.

In the 2004 Democratic presidential nomination fight, the candidates took advantage of this phenomenon, invoking Rove's name on the campaign trail as the personification of Republican ruthlessness. Each candidate argued that he himself was the only one tough enough to stand up to Rove in the general election. John Kerry assailed Rove's lack of military service. Howard Dean cracked wise about Rovian sabotage when the sound system or lights malfunctioned at Dean's campaign events. None stopped to consider how unprecedented and peculiar it was to attack their opponent's staffer. (It is impossible, for instance, to imagine George W. Bush similarly going after Kerry's campaign manager, Mary Beth Cahill.)

When the Plame case reached a boil after the election, Rove's Washington house was subjected to a media stakeout. That led Associated Press reporter Darlene Superville to stand in front of Rove's "million dollar brick home" and file an entire dispatch on the contents of his garage, as best she could tell from the street. "Can the master of Bush's political planning figure out where to put the ladders, paint cans and cardboard boxes?"

Superville, of course, was only feeding public demand. So was the entrepreneur who began marketing the "Karl Rove NeoCondom." An advertisement promised the "first edition prophylactic . . . embossed with the face of our President's Chief Political Strategist (i.e. 'Bush's Brain')" on the theory that "Some Things Should Never Leak." The World Wide Web is filled with missives, ballads, and odes such as this uncredited haiku:

> *Karl Rove is Satan*
> *Hell is where he longs to be*
> *He is the Dark Lord*

In 2005 and 2006, as Rove hovered on the verge of indictment in Fitzgerald's case, those words came close to describing the consensus view of Rove in the Old Media Establishment. Typical was a 2005 *Boston Globe* editorial that declared, "Over 35 years, he has been a master of dirty tricks, divisiveness, innuendo, manipulation, character assassination, and roiling partisanship."

What happened to Rove and his reputation in the year following his 2004 triumph may, as the *Globe* editorial board certainly believed, be a case of poetic justice—decades' worth of foul chickens finally home to roost. For the Old Media and the Left, Rove's three national election victories in the first half of the decade were faded memories, except to the extent that they showed Rove's force. Instead, he became seen as both cause and symbol of an exhausted and failing presidency.

What a politician thinks about Karl Rove is a matter of individual conscience, to be resolved in the privacy of his or her own focus group. But, regardless of how one feels about Rove's ethics or governing record, there are clear lessons to be drawn from his career for anyone who wants to understand how presidential politics works today.

In the next several sections, we will explore what those lessons are. Each chapter follows a similar path—excursions into Rove's past, illustrations of how those years have influenced his time in Washington, and his Trade Secrets for the 2008 campaign.

Rove Beyond Famous

★ ★ ★ ★ ★

LIKE GEORGE W. Bush, Karl Rove is allergic to admitting failure. But in the case of his stated goal of avoiding fame as a presidential aide, even Rove has acknowledged that his efforts have been a fiasco.

Rove tried to dodge celebrity either by refusing to cooperate with most media profiles or by submitting only grudgingly. He has turned down hundreds of television interviews for every one he accepted, sidestepped being quoted by name, and rarely made himself available to journalists on the record.

And yet he has become the most famous political adviser in American history. Here are some of the more intriguing manifestations:

- Featured as a recurring character on Fox's 2005 animated series *American Dad,* where he was depicted as a cross between *Star Wars*'s Emperor Palpatine and a vampiric fiend, draped in a cowl and attended by wolves and bats.

- Inspired a host of fictional shadowy political advisers and Machiavellian gurus on dramas all over cable TV.

- Cited by a button-eyed teen as the emblem of ambition and political machinations on Fox's youth drama *The O.C.*

- Chosen as the subject of two 2003 biographies, *Boy Genius* and *Bush's Brain,* the latter of which was made into a film.

- Scrutinized in a *Frontline* documentary entitled *The Architect,* which debuted on PBS April 12, 2005.

- Splashed on the covers of *Time* (thrice—"How They Aced Their Midterms," November 18, 2002; "The War over

the Leak," October 13, 2003; and "Rove on the Spot," July 25,
2005) and *Newsweek* ("The World According to Karl Rove,"
July 25, 2005).

• Saluted with affection and irony by the website
ilovekarlrove.com.

• Portrayed in various theater productions, including the 2006
Off-Broadway musical revue *Bush Wars,* in which a performer
sang "Don't Lie Out Loud" to the tune of the Melissa
Manchester ballad "Don't Cry Out Loud," and the 2005 play
Fear Itself: Secrets of the White House, which featured a
slobbering lapdog called "Rover."

• Mentioned by the politically savvy coach of the Boston Celtics,
Glenn "Doc" Rivers, who said, "If you told me right now I
could be the Democratic Karl Rove, I'd have to think about it,"
in March 2005.

• Illustrated in countless political cartoons, drawn in forms
ranging from Satan (of course); to "Benedict Rove"; to a smug
suit casting a Nixonian shadow; to a nimble leather-clad *Matrix*
character temporarily evading a hovering bullet; to a yapping
lapdog (*Aarp! Aarp! Aarp!*); to a growling attack dog (on Bush's
leash); to a shame-faced leaking boy in short pants, water
pooling around his ankles; to a frantic rower in a gushing boat,
surrounded by sharks; to a shackled criminal in prison stripes;
to a vindictive demigod incinerating his enemies; to an all-
powerful puppeteer, strings in hand.

• Teased innumerable times by late-night comics, including Jay
Leno, who joked, "Did you hear about this spy they found
working in the White House? A guy in Vice President Cheney's
security detail was allegedly passing U.S. secrets to foreign
governments. And Karl Rove was furious. He said, 'Leaking
secrets, that's my job.' "

SECTION IV

★ ★ ★ ★ ★

SERIOUS REWARDS

★ ★ ★ ★ ★

IDEAS MATTER

★ ★ ★ ★ ★

"I AM THE LEADING EXPERT on the principle of equidistance in the determination of seaward lateral boundaries," Karl Rove announced to some visitors in a conversation that was supposed to be about politics, but instead turned to a Dutch legal philosopher. "[Hugo] Grotius wrote about this in the 1600s. . . . If you look back through history it turns out that the geographic principle of using equidistance to determine seaward lateral boundaries is the way it's been for four hundred years, a principle that's ultimately been embodied in the Supreme Court cases, embodied in many pieces of legislation designating a U.S. territory's boundaries in the United States, embodied in two vital Supreme Court decisions and upheld in three or four others, and then written into international treaties between nations in 1958 and 1959 and yet we're sitting here . . . [saying] 'okay, how much do you want?' as opposed to saying what is the principle and how do we fairly go about doing this? I'd be happy to explain equidistance to you."

As it happened, one of Rove's assignments in his second-term job as White House deputy chief of staff was to navigate disputes between states over offshore oil drilling. One question he currently was tackling: As Florida does not permit offshore drilling, but neighboring states do, how does one determine which laws govern a particular piece of the continental shelf? It did not take long to exhaust his visitors' interest in this subject. But the point was clear: This was the kind of stuff that filled Rove's days.

Rove established himself as one of the most influential strategists of all time because he was willing and able to plunge into the picayune details of policy issues such as seaward lateral boundaries. But this was more than a West Wing version of Trivial Pursuit. Rove was interested in policy because he was interested in ideas. He was interested in ideas because he knew they are by far the most important force in politics. A New York Times story got Rove exactly wrong, calling him "the ultimate symbol of politics over policy."

Here is one of the most important and counterintuitive Trade Secrets: *The way to be a successful political hack is to be something more than a hack.* "It is because of the ideas we hold," Rove has said in explaining the achievements of the conservative movement and Republican domination of Washington. "A quarter of a century ago, Senator Daniel Patrick Moynihan said the GOP has become the party of ideas. And he wasn't saying that with happiness in his pen. It was true then and it remains true now; we are the party and the movement of ideas. And as [scholar] Richard Weaver wrote, 'Ideas have consequences.'"

The way to win the presidency is to have the most serious notions about what to do after winning. With few exceptions, presidential contests in recent decades have been won by the candidate who thought through most coherently what the country needed at a given moment, and how his presidency would fill that need. It is not necessarily the case that the smarter candidate, or the more administratively competent, always wins. Yet elections tend to be won by candidates who think *historically.* They do not rely only on a slogan, or borrowed policy prescriptions. They have a theory, rooted in authentic experience, about where their party is at a particular moment, and where it should be, and also where the country is at a particular moment, and where it should be.

There is a difference between a policy pamphlet and a political idea. The pamphlet can be cobbled together by hired hands in a week or so of late nights. In 1992, Bob Kerrey put forward a national health care plan—one that had been stitched together shortly before he began his candidacy and one that had no obvious connection to his Senate record, his professed ideological values, or his failure to provide health insurance to the employees at his chain of Nebraska health clubs. A good political idea, on the other hand, must be the culmination of many more minds and much more road-testing, and even then will carry no power except as articulated by people who have cultivated an understanding over time about where it came from and why it matters. Karl Rove understands this. So do George W. Bush and Bill Clinton.

Politics and journalism are overflowing with people who have scant appreciation for the power of ideas. Most reporters, like most operatives, are fascinated by the techniques of politics. Who will raise the most money, hire the hottest consultant, captivate the crowds with the best stump speech? Above all, the interest is in the power players themselves—their personalities and life stories. This leads naturally to the great weakness of most political junkies: a belief that success in politics is ultimately about biography.

Karl Rove understands that politics is ultimately not about biography but about results. "It's about enacting policies that will have an effect for good or for ill on the people of the state and country," Rove said. "It's the performance in office that ultimately determines whether or not the party has the durability to maintain its primacy . . . over time."

Democrats may well be happy to wage the 2006 and 2008 elections as a referendum on Rove's and Bush's performance in office. The Republican mandate did not look so durable in the sixth year of the administration. But the Bush failures that heartened Democrats in 2006 were preceded by significant successes, both in getting elected and in advancing longtime conservative goals. These were strategic triumphs implemented by people who understood ideas, policy, and politics and the way all three are connected.

• • •

ONE OF THE best articles about Bill Clinton's first presidential campaign was written by Sidney Blumenthal, then with the *New Republic*. "Who the hell is Bill Clinton?" Blumenthal asked. He was writing in early 1992, when such a query was still reasonable, a month before the Gennifer Flowers and draft-dodging accusations ended Clinton's obscurity. Blumenthal answered his own question: "If you have to ask, you're not a Democratic honcho. He is one of the best-known people among the party elites. There is probably not a single one among them of even marginal importance who has not made his acquaintance." Blumenthal went on to describe how the Arkansas governor had over the course of the previous two decades "introduced himself to ever-widening circles of party activists, intellectuals, and officials."

Then he coined a brilliant term that helped explain Clinton's promise: "The essential principle of Clinton's agenda—leaner, activist government—is the result of a rethinking of the future of liberalism and the Democratic Party that he and his wife have been part of for years. This long project may be called The Conversation. The Conversation is not about the nuts and bolts of getting elected. It is about why one should get elected and what to do if one is. . . . From the start, Clinton has been part of The Conversation, perhaps having more ties to more of those in it than any other elected Democrat."

From the time Clinton was a teenager—from Boys Nation; through

Georgetown, Oxford, and Yale; then the McGovern campaign; and his Arkansas political career—he collected influential faces in his head and names on index cards, convincing those he met that he was serious about politics *and* ideas.

His most important ideas were not divorced from politics, of course, but nor were they divorced from substance. One reinforced the other. James Carville got lots of credit for the winning strategy in 1992. But Bruce Reed, a boyish-faced expert on welfare reform and author of the campaign policy book *Putting People First,* got too little. And neither Carville nor Reed would have been successful had they not worked for a candidate who needed no tutoring on either politics or policy—or on the cardinal bond between the two.

The notion of Bill Clinton as a student of ideas is not a hard sell. The notion of Karl Rove as a student of ideas *is* a hard sell, even among many Republicans. Had you asked GOP operatives in Washington about Rove in the 1990s, most of them would have said something like this: *Sure, I've known Karl for years, does direct mail down in Texas. He's very good, but he costs a bundle.* Outside a small circle, few thought of him as a participant in the conservative equivalent of The Conversation. But throughout the years when his business was taking flight and his reputation as a political tactician was growing, Rove was busy entering into his own Conversation.

He took subscriptions to conservative publications like *Public Interest* and *Policy Review,* along with more liberal-leaning ones such as the *New Republic,* and hefty reads such as *Foreign Affairs.* He also started going to policy symposiums at places like the American Enterprise Institute in Washington. One such venue was a conference at Stanford University's Hoover Institution in April 1998. The event was organized by Alvin Rabushka, one of the "fathers of the flat tax," who assembled a group of intellectuals, journalists, and political strategists to discuss what it would take to actually change the tax system.

Rove attended the meeting while George W. Bush was in the midst of his reelection campaign for Texas governor, a race Rove believed was going to serve as the launching pad for a presidential run. Rove's Hoover presence reflected his understanding that tax reform was an issue with deep resonance for the conservative movement and the Republican Party. He was there because he knew that ideas matter, and that they would affect Bush's future as much as the quality of his TV ads or the fulfillment of his fund-raising goals. During breaks at the Palo Alto conference, Rove was on the phone to Austin tending to political business. But whenever the next session began he was back in his seat, listening intently, scribbling notes on his pad.

One of Rove's presidential campaign colleagues, ad-maker Stuart Stevens, said that Rove is the rare political operative who "read the briefing books prepared by the propeller-heads." Stevens remarked that it was the equivalent of "finding a fifteen-year-old who actually reads the articles in *Playboy*."

• • •

ONE REPUBLICAN PRESIDENT was never far from the thoughts of Rove and Bush as they began exploring the ideas that would power the 2000 campaign. A piece of conventional wisdom about Ronald Reagan has taken root in the nearly twenty years since his presidency ended and the conservative myth-making machine started to construct his legacy. It is said that Reagan was a success because he was an optimistic man who resisted and ultimately routed the prevailing pessimism of the age. Like most enduring myths, this one is partly true. But also true is that Reagan's movement was propelled by discontent. If ideas are the engines of politics, grievance is the fuel.

The direct mail business gave Rove a superb vantage point for understanding the diverse resentments that had spawned the Reagan Revolution. Reagan resonated with his most fervent supporters not because he was cheerful but because he shared their anger—against taxes; against an overweening federal bureaucracy; against liberal 1960s pieties on race, crime, and poverty; against the notion that the United States should seek accommodation and understanding with its Cold War adversaries, rather than to proudly assert American superiority. In the 1980s, Rove's direct mail appeals had worked their magic on behalf of candidates by stressing the same themes—almost always, though, leavened by a positive message as well (just like the Reagan model).

But Rove and Bush, and many of the most committed activists in the Republican Party, were aware of something else about Ronald Reagan. His rhetoric and reputation were far more conservative than his record.

Reagan signed into law major tax increases; put Sandra Day O'Connor and Anthony Kennedy, accommodationists both, on the Supreme Court; accepted a Social Security commission report that recommended tax increases to shore up the system; created a new cabinet department, and increased the federal workforce.

The list of things Reagan did not accomplish is even more notable. He did not fight to add market incentives to entitlement programs such as welfare, health care, and Social Security. He did not seek to shake up the education establishment or the federal bureaucracy. He did not forcefully challenge the United Nations or other international organizations and agreements. He did not attempt to inject explicit expressions of faith more directly into the town square and government programs. He famously fired the nation's air traffic controllers in a 1981 strike, but did not take on union bosses and trial lawyers, or use every tool at his disposal to weaken liberal special interests or transform the Establishment consensus that prevailed when he arrived in Washington in 1981 and was scarcely less entrenched when he left in 1989. Worst of all, he sometimes ate dinner with the *Washington Post*'s publisher Katharine Graham—and seemed to enjoy it.

In short, Rove believed that there was a vast amount of unfinished business and untapped grievance on the right, waiting for Bush to run on. Rove was certain that George W. Bush, unlike Reagan, would walk the walk. Rove's interest in ideas was not purely academic. He also was interested in ideas as the most critical component of power. He envisioned a Bush presidency that would transform the way Americans viewed government, and that would allow the Republican Party's principles to dominate American politics for decades, just as Democratic principles had dominated for nearly thirty years from the New Deal to the Great Society.

Bush and Rove thought they knew how to fuse the energy of the conservative movement's decades of railing at the liberal Establishment with a broad, positive, and well-defined agenda for conservative change. Grievance may be the greatest source of energy in politics, but it is effective only when harnessed to a proposed solution.

In the late 1990s, Rove believed that there were many conservative solutions out there ready to be planted in the fresh soil of the coming decade. This sensibility flowed from a lifetime of reading serious books; indeed, he probably has worked his way through more weighty volumes than any other political strategist in the country. He had studied and been influenced by such conservative intellectuals as Myron Magnet, Richard John Neuhaus, and John J. DiIulio Jr.

The reissued paperback of Magnet's 1993 book, *The Dream and the Nightmare,* modestly says that it "helped make George W. Bush president." The book is a broad indictment of misguided intentions of 1960s bleeding hearts, and of the libertinism that had been sanctioned by the sexual revolution. The people who paid the greatest price, Magnet asserted, were the supposed beneficiaries of liberalism—those trapped on welfare, mentally ill people liv-

ing on the streets, and African-Americans paralyzed by feelings of victimiza-
tion and entitlement. This was a gloomy portrait, but Magnet came to an optimistic conclusion. By establishing a culture of discipline, morality, and hard
work, and a respect for intact families as the basis of functioning communities, many of the worst social ills would right themselves. Bush himself said
the book "crystallized for me the impact the failed culture of the sixties had
on our values and society. It helped create dependency on government,
undermine family, and eroded values which had stood the test of time and
which are critical if we want a decent and hopeful tomorrow."

Along with Magnet's book, Rove and Bush were inspired by Marvin
Olasky's *The Tragedy of American Compassion,* published in 1992. Olasky
argued that charity without a personal connection and without an emphasis
on spiritual and moral advancement is worthless and, furthermore, downright dangerous. The less fortunate required not just a helping hand but a
firm one—something faith-based institutions were more likely to provide
than an impassive government agency.

It was from books like these, and conversations with their authors, whom
Rove and Bush met with in Austin, that the 2000 campaign's message of
"compassionate conservatism" was crafted. Bush and Rove were drawn to a
focus on the need for God, morality, personal interaction, and judgment over
impersonal bureaucratic solution in government-aided programs. While the
phrase "compassionate conservatism" has been much derided in some quarters, it captured Bush's Texas agenda (juvenile justice, education, and welfare reform) and much of what animated his first run for the White House
(education standards, Social Security personal accounts, and faith-based
programs).

If the notion of Karl Rove as a closet intellectual is a stretch for some, the
image of George W. Bush curled up on the couch reading Marvin Olasky will
strike others as absurd. Even Bush might make fun of the idea. But Bush's
success in 2000 came because he was driven by the combination of grievances and remedies around which he fashioned a platform. He garnered an
inevitable momentum for the GOP nomination because of family connections, and a large lead in fund-raising, but none of this would have happened
had there not been a core plausibility to his candidacy. Bush ran for president
not to avenge his father's defeat eight years earlier or because the party's
heavy hitters told him he could win (although such motivations may have
nudged him forward on his path). He ran chiefly because he wanted to advance ideas that had an authentic connection to his own life experience.

Though from a privileged background, Bush harbored resentments against liberal elites—a carryover from his days at the Andover-Yale-Harvard trifecta of educational boutiques. His contempt for the permissive baby-boomer culture sprang from his own self-described "young and irresponsible" days, in which he engaged in unspecified young and irresponsible conduct. His views of morality and personal behavior also had been greatly influenced by his religious awakening in 1986 and his decision to stop drinking alcohol. His experience as Texas governor had given Bush confidence that he could prosper by challenging the Establishment status quo, taking on teachers unions with his education reforms and trial attorneys with civil litigation reforms. Bush's ideas might be good ones or bad, but he did not get them simply by perusing Rove's briefing book. And Rove did not push those ideas as a mercenary hired to do a job, but because he, too, wanted to advance the policies. Bush, at least, felt the spiritual hunger for higher meaning in his own life, and both men sensed that much of the country was searching for the same thing.

After being exposed to different people and opinions, each arrived "in his own way . . . in the same place," as Bush friend and political adviser Mark McKinnon once observed.

It was a place in which Ronald Reagan's ideas were informed by a radical new energy and aggressiveness that Reagan himself might have found unfamiliar.

· · ·

BUSH, OF COURSE, unlike Reagan, had the distinct advantage of working for most of his presidency with a Republican-controlled Congress. And it was a Capitol Hill majority that shared Bush's vision for a domestic concentration. Most of Rove's planning in the late 1990s was based on that expectation. Everything was transformed by the terrorist attacks of September 11, 2001.

Bush had never been part of the decade-long movement among neoconservative thinkers who had been chomping to challenge Saddam Hussein in Iraq, and more robustly project American power and ideals around the world. To the contrary, he had run in 2000 preaching a humble foreign policy. Even so, his faith in the power of ideas made his embrace of the neoconservative agenda in post-9/11 circumstances an easy transformation. Rove, likewise, quickly saw that policy in the national security realm could be an even more powerful servant of politics than it was in the domestic realm.

Although the wars in Iraq and against terrorism have come to define his presidency, Bush accomplished many of the primary unachieved goals of two generations of Republican politicians: a steadfast "no new taxes" governing philosophy; legal, regulatory, and energy policy reform; a shift in the balance on environmental policy toward business interests; the injection of faith into public life; a move to put the Republican Party back on the offensive on abortion-related issues; the marginalization of labor unions and trial lawyers; and a general unwillingness to accommodate liberal interests. Bush also demanded more accountability from the United Nations; installed more conservative judges on the courts, including confirming two Supreme Court justices; directed grants and other federal largesse away from liberal groups and toward conservative ones; and neutered the bureaucracy.

There were some obvious aberrations in the conservative record of Bush's presidency: massive deficit spending, the largest entitlement expansion in a generation in the Medicare prescription drug benefit, tens of billions of dollars of new spending in agriculture and transportation laws, the near abandonment of school choice, protectionist steel tariffs, and the signing of the McCain-Feingold campaign finance law. Rove justified these deviations by maintaining that the legislative process is imperfect, and arguing that these accommodations all served to keep Bush's overall push for conservative change moving in the right direction. (Sometimes he even defended these measures as conservative in nature, such as allowing Washington to mandate education standards in the states.) For some conservatives, these accommodations have ruined Bush's second term, even his presidency.

• • •

IN ITS OWN way, the backlash illustrated the same principle—ideas matter—being turned against Rove and Bush, rather than working to their advantage. When things went smoothly for them, from 1999 to 2004, it was because ideas and performance worked in concert to produce effective politics. When things went poorly, as in 2005 and into 2006, the opposite was true. Both instances offer the same lesson for 2008 candidates. The election will be decided by voters who care about what a candidate believes, and whether he or she will implement policies that reflect those ideals.

The Trade Secrets of Being President That George W. Bush and Karl Rove Learned from Bill Clinton's Successes (and Failures)

★ ★ ★ ★ ★

- Americans want a president they can respect.

- Get off to a fast start—the first 180 days in the White House are key, and you cannot waste a day being off message.

- Make sure your staff uniformly refers to you in the third person as "the president" and not just by your last name.

- Take advantage of the public's disdain for the media, so you can tell the press no whenever you want to; so you can leave the press pool behind when it suits you; and so your staff can choose to not return their calls.

- Empower your press secretary to turn the daily White House briefing into a nonevent, to suck all the air out of the room with nonanswers and to diminish the chances that unfavorable news will be made.

- Squelch bureaucratic dissent and leaks.

- Lonely electoral victories are lonely—and often ephemeral—so spend political capital helping your down-ballot party candidates get elected.

- Winning reelection is a lot easier if you do not have a nomination challenge.

- If there is a third candidate in the general election, have it be someone more likely to put pressure on, distract, unsettle, and draw votes from your opponent than you. (Ross Perot twice during Bill Clinton's presidential battles; Ralph Nader twice during George W. Bush's.)

- Oprah's show is always a great platform, if she'll have you.

PLAY TO YOUR STRENGTHS
(AND AWAY FROM YOUR WEAKNESSES)

★ ★ ★ ★ ★

RUN TO THE RIGHT in the primaries, Richard Nixon famously advised his fellow Republicans, *then run to the center in the general election.*

Nixon's logic was easy to follow. People who care enough to pay attention to nominating contests are ideologues virtually by definition. But ideology is scary to the middle-of-the-road voters who determine general election outcomes. So shrewd politicians embrace the ideologues when they need them. Then they abandon, or at least back away from, the zealots when the need is gone. It was cold advice, and it had the virtue of applying equally well—swapping left for right—to Democrats. The trick, according to Nixon and a generation of like-minded strategists, was not to become so overcommitted to extreme interests in the primaries and caucuses that it was impossible to wiggle free in the general election. Very simple.

But if Nixon's advice was so simple, how come smart fellows such as Bob Dole, Al Gore, and John Kerry could not use it as a map to victory? The answer is that Nixon was wrong. Or, more accurately, he was right about how to run for president in an earlier era, but his strategy is incompatible with this era. Just as the advent of Freak Show politics changed the dynamics of scandal, so has it changed the dynamics of electoral strategy.

Because of media saturation and vehement interest groups who are always poised to attack from all angles, any candidate who attempts clumsy lurches of the sort Nixon suggested would find his or her contradictions and cynical maneuvers exposed and ridiculed. "Crook" is no longer the most damning insult one can throw at a politician (as Dick Nixon would be happy to learn). It has been supplanted by "phony" (as Kerry was unhappy to learn). Meanwhile, because of the polarization of the electorate, any candidate who tried the patented Nixonian two-step in such an obvious way soon would have few allies either on the excitable fringe or in the sensible center.

These days, even the weakest presidential candidates know that Nixon's advice is obsolete. For that matter, many of their supporters know it, too. In recent years, "electability" has been a critical force in shaping the decisions of primary and caucus voters. Both parties have their absolutists. But just because nomination voters are impassioned does not mean they are stupid. They know a presidential nominee must appeal to general election voters who are more moderate than they are. So they are tolerant, within limits, of candidates who challenge party orthodoxy in the name of victory. But striking this balance when seeking the White House is harder than it looks.

As ever, John Kerry is a case study in how not to do things. On national security, he spent part of his time running for the nomination on a strategy the opposite of Nixon's: He would beat Howard Dean by outflanking him to his right on military and international matters, and convince even dovish Democrats that he was the man most likely to beat Bush. As the antiwar movement gained power, however, Kerry began to lose his nerve. Determined to regain favor with the Democratic base, he voted against an $87 billion funding measure for the Iraq and Afghanistan operations, even though he originally supported both interventions. Apparently believing that ambivalence would be taken as proof of sincerity, he made his claim that he had first voted for the $87 billion before later voting against it—words he would spend the rest of the campaign (and beyond) trying to explain.

On domestic issues, Kerry in fact had a list of past actions and statements that could have formed the basis for an effective and courageous centrist positioning. And for a time, it appeared that he planned to make the case that he was indeed a "different kind of Democrat." Early in his campaign, Kerry insistently (but sporadically) asked reporters to note his previous support for the Gramm-Rudman-Hollings balanced budget measure, a capital gains tax reduction, and free trade agreements, and his past rhetorical openness toward experimenting with school vouchers, reshaping teacher tenure, eliminating the Department of Agriculture, revisiting affirmative action, and raising Medicare premiums for the wealthy. From this patchwork of issues he might have sewn together a coherent thematic argument suggesting his independence from an imperfect Democratic Party.

Kerry was self-consciously aping the Clinton model, but his wobbly level

of commitment to the effort was exemplified by his failure to make an enduring public pitch explaining how these stands defined who he was as a politician and a person. In fairness, Kerry's blunders were no more ungainly than
those of two earlier losers. After seventy-three years as a traditional Midwestern balanced-budget conservative, Bob Dole reinvented himself in 1996
as a tax-cutting supply-sider. In 2000, Al Gore could not decide whether
he preferred navy blue suits or earth tones, or whether he was a consensus-
seeking moderate Democrat or a rip-roaring New Deal populist.

Here were three honorable, serious men who orchestrated their own
humiliation and defeat. There was a unifying theme to all three embarrassments: improvisation. They and their advisers careened from state to state,
from week to week, and from news story to news story, bouncing between
rallying partisans and reassuring general election voters.

Successful candidates of this era—Clinton and George W. Bush—
navigated differently. They had the vision and self-confidence never to take
their eyes off the horizon. They started thinking of the general election years
before the nominating contests. And they never stopped thinking of it no
matter how cold it became in January in New Hampshire, or how hot it got
when the race wended down to the South later on.

This is not to suggest that Clinton and Bush did not sometimes pander to
their partisans. It also is not to say that every time they ran against party
type—as when Clinton called for "ending welfare as we know it," or when
Bush implied that his brand of conservatism was more compassionate than
the one Republicans in Washington offered—they were engaged in crass attempts to capture the center. To the contrary, Bush and Clinton really believed those ideas. What set Clinton and Bush apart was that the expedient
positions and the heartfelt ones were part of a coherent whole. They knew
that the only way to win the presidency was to have a strategy capable of simultaneously winning two races, nomination and general election, without
glaring contradictions between the two.

Building a theory of the case requires three steps. One: Understand the
strengths and weaknesses of your own party. Two: Understand the strengths
and weaknesses of the *other* party. Then work tenaciously to narrow the gap
on the places where the other party does better than your party.

Perhaps this advice seems as simple in its own way as Nixon's did. Following it, however, is surprisingly difficult. By life experience, intellectual habit,
and, most of all, emotional instinct, most partisans do not find it comfortable

or natural to think candidly about the weaknesses of their own side, or the strengths of the other side. Bill Clinton, joined by Hillary Clinton and a succession of advisers, was able to achieve this feat. George W. Bush, with Karl Rove as his indispensable partner, had a similarly rare talent. This ability is the most important political trait Clinton, Bush, and Rove have in common. They tried to understand as much about the other party as they did about their own. It is not a coincidence that Bill Clinton's closest adviser after his wife was Dick Morris, who spent much of his career consulting for Republicans. Nor is it a coincidence that among the top advisers on Bush's team, reporting directly to Rove, were former Democratic operatives such as Matthew Dowd and Mark McKinnon.

One way to tell a strategic political mind from a conventional one is to examine how they read a poll. One should have nothing against polls. Despite the popular taboo against them, studies consistently have shown that poll reading is normal and healthy human behavior. Most aspiring politicians start doing it in their teenage years and continue through adulthood—in some cases several times daily. For poll reading to be more than an exercise in self-gratification, however, it requires *looking at the right questions*. These are not the constantly fluctuating results about which candidate is rising or falling on a given day. The most significant questions are the ones that begin, "Which party do you trust to do a better job on . . ." Fill in the blank: education, terrorism, health care, crime. These numbers do not change overnight. Getting them to change at all is among the hardest tasks in politics.

The burden for a presidential candidate is to rank higher on key issues on which he and his party are weak compared with the opposition. (All of these rules work with female pronouns, too.)

There are several sub-stipulations to this. First, it is not necessary to eliminate the gap completely. A candidate and his party simply need to close the gap to a manageable percentage (say, single digits).

Second, a candidate works within the context and confines of the image of his party, and must worry more about his own number than the party's. In fact, often a candidate can leverage his party's failings with the public to improve his own standing on a given issue.

Third, once a candidate becomes a presidential nominee (and, thus, his party's chief symbol and spokesman), he often is able to lift the party's standing as well.

Some Democrats felt slapped in the face when Clinton singled out his own side for being weak on crime. Yet they were delighted when, over time, their footing with the public on crime improved along with Clinton's. Most of the party's candidates, including 1988 nominee Michael Dukakis, had faced a double-digit deficit on crime. Throughout 1992, Clinton, with his emphasis on the death penalty and community policing, consistently ran even with or even ahead of George H. W. Bush on the issue.

Understanding how a candidate's and a party's relative position can be augmented, and having the discipline to actually do it, is the mark of a winning politician.

• • •

HERE IS ANOTHER mark of winning politicians: They are thieves. When they see a valuable Trade Secret, they steal it. Imitation, it should be noted, is not necessarily intended as flattery, sincere or otherwise.

As Bush and Rove began planning the 2000 presidential campaign, Ronald Reagan may have been the inspiration for much of their governing agenda, but Bill Clinton was, at that time, the greatest influence on their political agenda. No presidential campaign was more aware of where the incumbent president had succeeded and where he had failed than the one operated by Bush and Rove in 2000. By the late 1990s it was impossible to be a serious player in national politics unless one was ready to come to terms with the Clinton legacy.

Clinton loomed large at decade's end because of decisions he had made at the decade's beginning. In 1992, Democrats were strong on the domestic issues—health care, education, worker retraining—which were returning to prominence in the wake of the Cold War. Clinton's insight was to recognize that there was no way to exploit these big opportunities without first surmounting even bigger obstacles. There were many voters who might have seemed to be natural Democratic supporters, but apparently had stopped listening to Democratic politicians. A popular perception, especially among white, rural Americans, that Democrats loved abortion and hated guns was part of a larger problem, a common belief that Democrats intrinsically were hostile to their cultural values.

Clinton understood the Republicans' liabilities and assets just as keenly. He was among the first in either party to realize that a purportedly formidable president, George H. W. Bush, was in fact much more vulnerable than he seemed during the season of triumph and soaring approval ratings that followed the U.S. victory in the first Persian Gulf War. A sluggish economy and widening social divisions had left middle-class voters with deep anxieties to be tapped by a Democrat with the right message. At the same time, Clinton recognized that the electorate still trusted the GOP more on questions of national security, taxes, and law and order. What's more, after occupying the White House for all but four of the previous twenty-four years, Republicans had become the default presidential party in the minds of many voters. This was a powerful psychic hurdle and one that still threatens Democrats running in 2008.

Clinton's improbable victory came about in part because he fully exploited Democratic advantages, with a robustly progressive agenda that included a pledge of securing health insurance for all Americans. Even more crucial, he transcended his party's flaws. Rather than trying to "run left" for the nomination, Bill Clinton began his presidential campaign in 1991 with a series of speeches in which he cast himself as "a different kind of Democrat," one freed from liberal orthodoxies.

On America's role in the world, Clinton was hawkish, outflanking then-President Bush on the right on stopping ethnic cleansing in Bosnia and confronting China on human rights. On abortion, he abandoned the language of pro-choice interest groups by asserting that the procedure should be "safe, legal, and rare." On the poor, he rejected decades of liberal pieties and promised to "end welfare as we know it." He ensured that these phrases would resonate by repeating them over and over. At prominent moments, he blatantly advertised his differences with his own party. He appalled liberals when he flew back to Arkansas from the campaign trail to authorize the execution of a mentally disabled man. He infuriated the Reverend Jesse Jackson by denouncing the racist rantings of rap singer Sister Souljah when speaking to Jackson's Rainbow Coalition. (The episode inspired a new political phrase: A *Sister Souljah moment* is whenever a politician gains political advantage by prominently offending an influential interest group allied with his own party.)

Why did all this work for Bill Clinton? If getting elected president as a Democrat involved nothing more than rousing the enthusiasm of party activists, then Howard Dean might now be commander in chief. If it were as simple as cautioning that the party had grown too liberal for its own good, then America would have its first White House kosher kitchen under a President Joe Lieberman. It worked for Clinton partly because he was a better politician than the rest of the 1992 field—more articulate, more competitive, more exciting. Yet the core of his triumph involved a larger element: Through a combination of intuition and design, Clinton had arrived at an election formula vastly superior to Nixon's outdated recipe.

Clinton knew that, particularly for a nonincumbent, it sometimes is necessary to run against one's own party, even before the nomination is in hand, but doing so effectively requires at least five components:

1. **A large network of personal contacts.** Bill and Hillary Clinton had old friends across a generation of liberal thinkers and interest group leaders, from Robert Reich at Harvard University's Kennedy School of Government to Marian Wright Edelman at the Children's Defense Fund. Some of Clinton's views made liberals uncomfortable, but in the end they tolerated these deviations because many prominent liberal leaders had long, sometimes close, relationships with him.

2. **In line on the Big Stuff.** Hard-core Democrats were confident that Clinton would pursue an activist federal government for such causes as universal health care, and that he would put pro-choice judges on the bench. Being true to the party doctrine on bedrock issues generated some leeway.

3. **Ideas.** By seeming smart and sincere—and by actually *being* smart and sincere—Clinton persuaded many skeptical partisans that his departures from party orthodoxy on such issues as welfare reform reflected new ways of achieving cherished traditional party goals.

4. **A considered plan.** There is no way to pull off a delicate ritual of *simultaneously* defying and reassuring one's most important supporters without careful preparation.

5. **The ultimate incentive.** Even partisans who did not trust Clinton's principles trusted his political instincts. They accepted that his ideological deviations were electorally necessary. Sensing victory after twelve years out of the White House, activists swallowed medicine that would not have gone down well under different circumstances.

· · ·

BUSH AND ROVE plotted their bid for the presidency just as Clinton had eight years earlier, by taking inventory of the strengths and weaknesses of both parties. Virtually every calculation in this exercise confronted them with some version of the same question: *What did they think of Clinton and his record?*

At the personal level, there is no doubt what Bush and Rove thought: They abhorred him. In 1998, the *Washington Post* writers David Broder and Dan Balz traveled to Austin for a private dinner with the Texas governor. Laura Bush was there, and so was Karl Rove, but Bush himself did nearly all the talking. As Bush spoke about his ideas, the reporters noted aloud that many of them sounded quite similar to things that Clinton was saying. Bush

visibly recoiled. As Broder later recalled, "The intensity with which that possibility was rejected gave you a very clear sense about how much of the pain
or the burn of having seen his father lose to Bill Clinton still was there in the
younger George Bush."

That dinner is worth keeping in mind any time you see the latest pictures
of Bill Clinton touring a disaster zone with the forty-first president, or hear
the forty-third president joke about how Clinton is now his surrogate brother.
Perhaps time really has healed the personal resentments between these
families. But it has *not* changed how George W. Bush and his team view the
Clinton presidency. To this day, Clinton's name inspires snorts of derision
from top Bush aides in any situation when they are confident no one is quot-
ing them by name. The problem with Clinton, according to Bush and Rove,
was not merely that his personal character was flawed (as George H. W. Bush
tried to warn in 1992). Just as bad was his political character. The forty-
second president, in the Bush appraisal, was the epitome of a politician who
wanted the office in order to be someone rather than to accomplish something. He frittered away his time as president pursuing "small-ball" policies,
such as asking corporations to donate cell phones to neighborhood watch
groups, rather than pursuing grand visions. He achieved, in the current President Bush's words, "lonely victories," doing little to help other Democrats win
elections, while seeking to protect his own hide. He obsessed about his poll
ratings, without investing his popularity in any consequential goal. The easi-
est way to describe George W. Bush's self-definition as a politician—the way
he imagines himself rather than the way he actually is—is with a negative:
not like Clinton.

Unlike their fellow Republicans in Washington, however, Bush and Rove
knew how to separate personal convictions from political judgment. The Texans recognized that the Republican Party's biggest fault was that conservatives saw something quite different than the rest of the country whenever
they looked at Clinton. Republicans saw a latter-day Caligula, a morally de-
fective man trying to re-create the United States in his image. Most Americans, meanwhile, saw a beguiling composite of strengths and frailties, a man
who could be frustrating at times but on balance did a decent job running the
government. What's more, Clinton had been searingly effective at maximizing this GOP error, casting his opposition as ideological extremists more interested in waging an argument than solving problems. Most troublesome for
Republicans on the brink of another presidential election, Clinton had used

issues like the environment and education to make big strides with upwardly mobile suburban voters whose positions in other areas, like taxes, should have made them natural GOP allies.

Rove was galled by how congressional Republicans kept losing the battle with Clinton. "They have fought a war where their losses were high, their gains were small, and the outcome was never really in doubt," Rove said in an interview in 1999. "It's really ironic: here we are, the conservative party, with conservative ideas, with a Democrat president attempting to co-opt conservative language, and demonizing the Republican Party as extremist."

Rove had an idea of how to win the fight: Stop fighting. "I have no stake in the bitter arguments of the last few years," Bush said in his 2000 nomination acceptance speech. At the same time, Bush did not need to mention Clinton's name to win appreciative nods, even from voters who happened to like the president, for his repeated pledges to "change the tone in Washington" and "restore honor and dignity" to the White House. Bush's challenge was really no different from Al Gore's. He needed to embrace some aspects of the Clinton legacy while repudiating others.

Bush's approach to the Clinton conundrum—"compassionate conservatism"—was a good bit more graceful than Gore's. Advertising himself as "a different kind of Republican," a shameless appropriation of Clinton's own language eight years earlier, Bush worked vigorously to take back the suburban voters who had drifted to the Democratic side.

He abandoned off-putting ideas embraced by fellow conservatives, such as eliminating the federal Department of Education, and downplayed others, such as support for private school vouchers. Instead he touted his No Child Left Behind policy, which expanded the federal role in education. Rather than changing themes and messages from week to week (à la Dole, Gore, Kerry), Bush hewed strictly to his original strategy. He never stopped talking about his education record in Texas and visiting schools around the country. Meanwhile, he looked for other opportunities to soften the hard-edged image of his party. He frequently brought up his support for a "patient's bill of rights" and a new prescription drug benefit for senior citizens under Medicare, both items that had languished in the Republican Congress under Clinton. He even had his own Sister Souljah moment, when he rapped congressional Republicans for trying to "balance the budget on the backs of the poor." In addition to soothing words, Rove and communications director Karen Hughes never forgot the power of reassuring images. There was Bush hanging out with minority youths in Sacramento. There he was kissing a young African-American child, a photo that made the front page of the *New York Times*. By all appearances, it seemed David Broder had been right after all: George W. Bush was running as a Republican Bill Clinton.

All of this was being done in the service of a specific plan. Throughout the 2000 campaign and during the ups and downs of Bush's White House years, no political data made Rove more animated than the numbers that charted Bush's progress, along with the Republican Party's, in narrowing the Democrats' advantage with voters about who was more trusted to handle education. Rove always reminded reporters and Republican audiences that the goal was not necessarily to eliminate his party's disadvantage, but to shrink it so that it did not decide the election or taint Bush's overall image.

Right before the 1996 election, Republican nominee Bob Dole ran thirty-five percentage points behind Bill Clinton when Gallup asked voters about education. In March 2000, just as Bush emerged as the presumptive Republican nominee, his emphasis on education left him only eight percentage points behind Democrat Al Gore. By Election Day, the education gap had disappeared completely, with 45.8 percent of voters saying they trusted Bush more and 44.8 backing Gore.

Bush's feat duplicated Clinton's performance eight years earlier on the crime issue.

· · ·

WHY DID THIS work for Bush? How could a party that until recently had boasted of its rabid anti-Clintonism tolerate a nominee who was running on an Oprah Winfrey platform (and who had appeared on Oprah's show to give the hostess a smooch)? For an answer, please consult numbers one through five in the list above. Bush got away with it because he and Rove knew enough well-connected and influential conservatives to be certain that they could risk some ideological deviations in a party desperate to recover after four years of electoral routs. Elite and rank-and-file conservatives trusted that Bush was unwavering in his support for no new taxes and opposition to abortion. Compassionate conservatism also worked because enough Republicans concluded that some of Bush's ideas, such as updating national education standards, were not retreats so much as new ways of achieving old goals. It worked also because most Republicans, like Rove, were sick of losing to Clinton, and had no desire to repeat the pattern with Gore. If it required copying Clinton to defeat Clintonism, they were prepared to live with it. Above all, Bush's balancing act of reaching out to moderate voters while keeping conservatives in line succeeded because many on the right instinctively realized something that the moderates did not: The notion of George W. Bush as a Clinton clone was nonsense. By the time the Supreme Court decided the outcome of the 2000 presidential race, Bush had proven that he could employ Clinton tactics to achieve goals quite different from anything Bill Clinton had in mind.

The new president's real ambitions soon became obvious. In the opening months of his administration, even before September 11, 2001, Bush did not show deference to the disputed election results with conciliatory gestures, such as appointing a Democrat or two to high-level cabinet posts. He did not try to address unease over the size of his tax cuts by offering to split the difference with his opponents. With very few exceptions, Bush's days of Dick Morris–style triangulation ended with the campaign.

A pause is in order to reflect on why Bush's 2000 Trojan horse campaign fooled so many people. Perhaps the biggest reason is that many journalists are suckers. Bush was effective in dressing his conservative aims in centrist clothing because so many reporters admired the wardrobe.

A minor, though not inconsequential, Trade Secret of the Washington press corps helps explain Bush's success. Notwithstanding forty years of conservative complaints, it is not only liberal bias that shapes the thinking of the typical political reporter. On many issues, there is also a pronounced *centrist* bias.

The mind-set of modern journalism descends from a Progressive Era tradition. The Progressives believed that most policy questions could be solved through rigorous analysis by experts, if only the problems could be divorced from the clamor and irrationality of politics. To the extent most reporters are forced to think about policy ideas at all, they favor those who run against the grain of partisanship. The best way for a Democratic politician to get good Washington press is to announce, Joe Lieberman–style, that the party is too much in the grip of the teachers unions and Hollywood. The best way for a Republican to get good Washington press is to announce that the party has got to move beyond its conservative social agenda and have the "courage" to increase taxes.

In 2008, any candidate pursuing an avowedly ideological agenda—on either the Left or the Right (but particularly the Right)—must be prepared for the scorn of the Old Media commentariat. Any candidate willing to denounce his own party for paying too much attention to the demands of ideologues can expect to bask in the glow of positive press. But the glow may be short-lived, and won't come at all if the denunciation is perceived as too transparently political.

• • •

THOSE 2008 CANDIDATES will be running in the most confusing political landscape of a generation. Just as Bill Clinton hovered over the calculations of every candidate in 2000, George W. Bush will hover over 2008. With Clinton, at least it was easy to distinguish his strengths from his weaknesses.

In Bush's case, those strengths and weaknesses are thoroughly interwoven. His greatest strength is the perception of his steadfastness in protecting national security. His greatest weakness is the perception that his bullheaded-ness and misjudgments over Iraq have undermined national security. Republican candidates will have to decide when to embrace the Bush legacy and when to disown it. Democrats must decide whether a headlong assault on the Bush record will do more damage to themselves or the opposition. Candidates of both parties must decide whether Bush's refusal to govern as a Clinton centrist was the reason he succeeded in 2002 and 2004 or whether it was the reason he encountered so many problems in 2005 and 2006.

A discussion of the differences between the Clinton political model and the Bush model will come at the end of this book. For now, let us simply note that there are two candidates who have a huge advantage in the game of navigating the frailties of their party and the strengths of the opposition. Hillary Clinton and John McCain have spent years considering this problem.

Of course, there is a political eternity between now and the culmination of party nomination battles of the next presidential election. As late as 1990, it would have looked foolish to predict that the Democratic Party would soon nominate for president a candidate who was pro–death penalty, pro–welfare reform, and pro–free trade. Yet fifteen years later, some of Clinton's positions and innovations are themselves the new Democratic orthodoxy, with many of his more centrist stands having been adopted into the formal and informal party platforms. And commentators now squeal with delight whenever a candidate produces a Sister Souljah moment.

While it is difficult to predict *what* issues will work for a Republican or Democratic presidential candidate in this respect in 2008, in the interests of fairness, this chapter will close with some Trade Secret advice to everyone whose name is not "Clinton" or "McCain":

Dear Mssrs. Allen, Edwards, Romney, Warner, et al.:
    Do you really want to be elected president of the United States in 2008?
    Here is what you need to do. Ask your pollster to tell you what issues Americans care most about. (One need not pay for an expensive private

poll to find this out; save some money and do what Karl Rove often does—look at public polling or some "research" from a friendly trade group or business.)

Then ask your pollster, "On which of those top issues is our party significantly less trusted by voters than the other party?"

After you have those answers, send your pollster out of the room and ask yourself some questions:

- *On which of those issues do I have policy ideas that I really care about, and that will likely help close the gap between my party and the other side?*

- *Can I figure out how to take positions on these issues without damaging my fund-raising or interest group support in the nominating process?*

- *Can I credibly convince the elite political reporters and columnists that my heart is in the policies, and that as a matter of pure political strategy I can narrow the gaps?*

- *Am I prepared to do more than one hundred events between now and Election Day 2008 that reinforce the substance and symbolism of my message on each of the chosen issues?*

- *Will the criticisms I level be of my own party alone? A pox on Washington generally or on both parties doesn't cut it. (Note that many of Senator McCain's outspoken positions fit into this latter category.)*

- *Do I realize that these criticisms must be part of a broader thematic critique of how my party has moved to the extreme—not just a scattershot censure?*

- *Do I realize that if I accuse my party of having gone too far to the center, I might mean what I say and it might help me get the nomination, but it will not be a Sister Souljah moment?*

If you cannot answer with a righteous yes to all of those questions, you might as well save your time and effort and endorse John McCain or Hillary Clinton, should they be in the race.

What Bush Knew and When He Knew It

WHILE GEORGE W. BUSH'S AIDES have often taken steps to trick his enemies into "misunderestimating" him, even they would acknowledge that Bush's reputation for unwieldy syntax and stilted mannerisms developed divinely on its own, without staff intervention. They also would acknowledge that, time and again, Bush benefited to a grand degree from the soft bigotry of low expectations.

Bush was able to build up steam for his initial White House run because many Democrats did not take seriously a seemingly inarticulate man who had only recently entered public life, with no obvious experience in national security or federal matters, or any evident ambition for the job.

In fact, Bush had studied virtually every aspect of presidential politics during the heartrending runs of his father, making him a political sophisticate of the highest order. But he purposely concealed this from the public.

Given all the scrutiny he received, how was Bush able to hide what was in his head? Back in the 1990s, Bush was smart enough to realize that no good could come from commenting on his own campaign efforts or about politics in general. Reporters and opponents, he knew, jumped on punditry from any politician. And the public wanted its officeholders to be focused on substance. (Trade Secret: *Do not try to be a serious presidential candidate and talking head at the same time.*)

As Bush's governorship progressed, he became even more knowledgeable about public policy, and thus could speak more authoritatively and fluently, although he used this well-honed skill not to show off, but to deflect unwelcome, off-message questions.

But even if he did not talk like a pol in public very often, Bush had plenty of know-how he utilized in private. He made a few mistakes in his two gubernatorial campaigns, but by 1999 he had amassed an impressive understanding about how presidential politics works. Conversations with him at the end of the previous decade revealed that well before Bush made his first speech as a presidential candidate, he knew an astonishing number of Trade Secrets.

He understood how to structure a campaign operation to breed loyalty, to convey good and bad news, and to have clear lines of authority.

He understood substantially more about how the political media works than did Bill Clinton in his pre-presidential days.

He understood what it takes to motivate local campaign officials and workers to promote his agenda.

He understood how power courses through America's political circulatory system, up from counties and cities, to the statehouses, to Washington, and then back down again.

He understood the level on which most Americans engage with government and with politics (that level would be *low*).

He understood enough to not be afraid of the power that comes with the presidency and he had an idea how to preserve and consolidate that power.

He understood how the bureaucracy tries to stymie the agenda of elected officials, and how to counteract such efforts, by steamrolling over bureaucrats.

He understood how the legislative process works, including how lawmakers who appropriate tax dollars make decisions.

Bush strategist Mark McKinnon witnessed this firsthand. In assessing Bush as a first-time presidential candidate (and exhibiting his own generally rosy opinion of Bush, his longtime work in Democratic politics before he became a Bushman, and his attraction to extended metaphors), McKinnon said,

> George W. Bush was as knowledgeable a candidate as I've encountered in my professional career. He may have dubbed Karl Rove "the Architect," but the President knew even then quite clearly exactly what kind of campaign he wanted to build, what materials he wanted to use, what kind of carpenters he wanted to hire and what he wanted the campaign to look like when it was constructed.

Like a good seasoned campaign professional, he had very clear ideas about what he wanted to say, how he wanted the campaign run and who he wanted to run it.

The President didn't need to be reminded of his firmly held convictions. He sat us down and said, "Here's what I believe in. Here's what I want to say. These are our messages. Now, you go figure out how best to communicate them."

Bush's reservoir of knowledge does not necessarily surge inside the brain of the typical presidential aspirant. Most know far less than they think they do about what is required to run for president and how to do the job itself if they win.

And if you are reading these words and plan to run in 2008, you cannot begin to imagine how far behind you are now compared with where Bush was in 1999. (With the usual exceptions of the Gentleman from Arizona and the Gentlelady from New York, if they make the race.)

SECTION V

* * * * *

PUTTING PEOPLE FIRST

* * * * *

KNOW A LOT OF PEOPLE

★ ★ ★ ★ ★

AT AGE TWENTY-SEVEN, Karl Rove did not know much about stocks. But, as a young newlywed in need of something that resembled an income, he decided it might be time he learned. That is how one day in 1977 he found himself in the office of a Houston brokerage firm, talking to a friend of his wife's family, politely inquiring about career options.

Three decades after the fact, it is nothing short of bizarre to contemplate the most influential political strategist of his era enjoying a career in finance. Even Rove considered it an awkward fit at the time; he already had spent the previous eight years immersed in Republican national politics. In 1977, however, campaign consulting was still in its infancy, and there then seemed to be no plausible way for the young political junkie to make a career of it. Perhaps he might have pulled it off if he lived in Washington, D.C. But Rove lived in Texas.

That choice had been dictated by his first wife, Valerie Wainwright. At the time of their marriage, he was working at a minimally paying job as finance director for the Virginia Republican Party. After their Texas wedding, on the long drive from Houston back to Richmond, Valerie was in tears. The message was clear—the young bride needed to be in Texas near her family. In short order, they returned.

For a while, Rove worked as a staff man for Fred Agnich, a Texas state legislator. But the legislature, like all of Texas politics in the 1970s, was dominated by Democrats. The career opportunities for a young GOP operative were nonexistent. Rove soon concluded it was necessary to step up a notch from his $12,000 annual salary. That meant it was time to let go of politics, grow up, and get a real job. Stockbroker seemed like a real job.

Thirty years later, Rove speculated whimsically where that path might have led: "I'd be a wealthy guy, living in River Oaks," the Beverly Hills of Houston. Perhaps the skills and reputation that shaped his career in politics would have flourished in another field. Imagine a fellow with an unquenchable thirst for price-to-earnings ratios in small-cap tech firms instead of a hunger for voting patterns in exurban Ohio. He would no doubt be beloved by his clients but despised by competing brokers, and trailed by a long line of hazy but unproven stories of market-manipulating schemes and other freebooting exploits.

But as Rove was casting about for options in the financial world, he made a call to a contact of his own for advice, his old Washington mentor from the Republican National Committee, George H. W. Bush. Bush made Rove an unexpected offer. He was assembling a political action committee designed to position him for the Republican presidential nomination in 1980, then three years away. Bush needed someone to serve as its day-to-day manager. The most important part of the job would involve coordinating Bush's trips around the country as he met with influential Republicans and laid the groundwork for the coming campaign. Would Rove be interested? There was no more talk about the brokerage business.

Even in 1977, Rove was a shrewd hire for one reason above all: his Rolodex. His days as the chairman of the College Republicans had required him to travel to some forty states while still in his mid-twenties, and had rewarded him with a seat on the Republican National Committee. He knew hundreds of important political activists nationwide. For the next nineteen months, from May 1977 through December 1978, he would meet hundreds more as he worked for the man who would become the forty-first president a decade later.

Many of the Trade Secrets that explain Rove's success as a political strategist sound simple but in fact are exceedingly difficult to emulate (a common hitch with Trade Secrets of every stripe). Here is another one: *Know a lot of people.*

Rove's Rolodex eventually would be replaced by a Palm Pilot and then by a BlackBerry, but the principle is the same. He knew more people than anyone else in his business. He knew them longer. And they did not live disproportionately in Washington, D.C. Instead, they lived in places that, unlike the nation's capital, cast significant votes in the Electoral College and elected governors and members of Congress. A state judge who happened to be one of the keenest political observers in northwest Ohio? Good guy—befriended him in 1973. The Republican with the deepest pockets in the state of Iowa? Rove met him through Bush in 1978. The attorney general of North Dakota? He'd been a Rove buddy for thirty years. Missouri's leading anti-abortion activist? The country's leading home schooling organizer? Rove knew them, too.

George H. W. Bush saved Rove from a life of stocks and mutual funds. Thirty years later, the Bush family was still reaping the benefits.

• • •

AT BUSH's PAC, Rove had a heady job for a man his age. He was in on the ground floor of a presidential campaign. For all intents and purposes, he *was* the ground floor.

For both the candidate and his staff, the whole venture had an implausible air. Bush barely registered in single digits in presidential polls. The prospective 1980 field was dominated by much bigger names, especially those of former California governor Ronald Reagan and former Texas governor John Connally. Rove's candidate had been a two-term congressman, and had been named to an impressive variety of appointive jobs—ambassador to the United Nations, RNC chairman, CIA director, envoy to China—but currently held no office.

Like Jimmy Carter four years earlier, Bush was basing his campaign almost entirely on the premise that it was possible to leverage personal contacts into a credible national force. Through considerable charm and an exhaustive travel schedule, Bush would tap old friends and make new ones and see where it all led. In 1978 alone, he logged nearly a quarter-million miles in political and business trips. Bush's schedules from these years are preserved at his presidential library in College Station, Texas. Cumulatively, they offer a vivid window into a presidential campaign during its start-up phase. It is an intimate enterprise of commercial airplane flights and cocktail receptions, in which the possibility of crowds and glory is far off in the future and the possibility of empty rooms and humiliation is always close at hand.

But these journeys are worthwhile if the candidate spends the right kind of time with enough of the right kind of people. Assuming the candidate performs well, the single biggest variable in determining success is if the events are set up correctly. And the single biggest variable in determining if these events are set up correctly is if the people setting them up have enough contacts to get good advice about where to go and whom to see. It was a task at which Rove excelled.

David Bates, who was a school friend of Bush's son Jeb and who replaced

Rove on the road starting in August of 1978, recalls that Rove "had a great network even then of people around the country." Rove's friends would be recruited as volunteers, offer advice on which local candidates to meet and which fund-raisers to attend, and explain how to maximize Bush's time on the ground.

Bush's trips varied widely. Sometimes there were stops in New York for speech coaching, or excursions to Washington for think tank meetings and tennis matches with well-connected partners. Then there were the clubby Establishment events that produce the mix-and-mingle moments that can create lifetime ties: a trip to the Super Bowl with Jack Kemp, a stop at the male-bonding nirvana of the Bohemian Grove near San Francisco, and a night at the annual Alfalfa Club dinner in Washington, D.C. The basic itinerary, however, involved the touring staples for any presidential hopeful. Fly into a city; be greeted at the airport by a few supporters; have a briefing on the local lay of the land; do some interviews with a regional reporter or maybe even a curious national reporter; give a political speech to a meeting of an organization or club (so a room does not need to be rented and a crowd does not need to be lured); appear at a fund-raiser for a candidate running in the midterm elections (in order to scratch an itchy back and cultivate the donors for future giving); attend a smaller reception and perhaps a dinner with whichever big shots might be found. When possible, stay in someone's home (to establish a bond and save on hotel costs).

During this period, Rove learned in granular detail how the politics of a given state or community works: who runs the party, who the important journalists are, who has the money. Notes on Bush's schedules read like intelligence reports. On Wednesday, September 13, 1978, Bush attended a press conference at a Des Moines Howard Johnson's, driven there, per his schedule, by "two Shriners." Appearing with him at the press conference were the state's national committeewoman Mary Louise Smith and national committeeman John McDonald, and a local judge named Ted Miller (who was identified on Bush's schedule as "Master of Kadosh, which is the top elected official of the local Scottish Rite," and who had invited Bush to speak to his group of "between 1200 and 1500 males" after the press conference).

Two others listed to attend presumably were less well known to Bush, but important to impress, since they were described in detail in the schedule:

"RALPH BROWN—law partner of John McDonald's, set up press conference, good person to know in Iowa—his friends are in the press."

"MARVIN (MARV) POMERANTZ—You met him at the breakfast on your last Des Moines trip. He is Governor Ray's campaign manager. Very Big Bucks. <u>Very</u> influential in Iowa, a <u>good</u> person to know."

As it turned out, Brown and Pomerantz indeed would be good people for George H. W. Bush to know; they helped him defeat Ronald Reagan in the 1980 Iowa caucuses, a victory that established Bush as formidable enough to earn the spot as Reagan's running mate.

But Brown and Pomerantz also proved to be good people for Karl Rove and another of his clients to know. Both Iowans contributed the maximum allowed to each of George W. Bush's presidential campaigns, with Pomerantz kicking in $5,000 more to the Florida recount effort in 2000. They both also gave to the Republican Party during the years 43 was in office. Though hardly major fund-raisers or national political kingpins, they are the kind of reliable donors and activists whose support is vital to getting a president elected.

Each week brought new travel, and new opportunities for Rove to learn about the politics of a state. Bush went to fund-raisers for members of Congress such as Iowa's Jim Leach, Indiana's Dan Quayle, Florida's Bill Young, and New Jersey's Marge Roukema. He attended events with key groups, such as the American Enterprise Institute, the World Affairs Council, the Detroit Economic Club, the Cato Institute, the Denver Oil and Gas Association, the National Flexible Packaging Institute, and the American Fats and Oils Association (okay, why those last two are key is not entirely evident, but they got on Bush's schedule nonetheless). In Iowa, there was a stop at the Spencer Chamber of Commerce; in New Hampshire, a Nashua Rotary lunch. There were meetings with Dick Cheney, Donald Rumsfeld, Howard Baker, and Don Evans.

Those years with 41 also were Rove's introduction to major-league press relations. There was a drop-by for Bush at the Manhattan apartment of Barbara Walters, and a session with the editors of *Newsweek* described as "Completely OFF THE RECORD." Rove even learned the fine art of the media stiff-arm. "JON MARGOLIS of the CHICAGO TRIBUNE wants to be with you while you are in IOWA," Bush's schedule read. "He will be at all the events and has asked to fly on the plane with you, and/or have some time alone with you. He has been told that the plane is full. You may see him during your rest period or put him on the plane—there is room."

Those months at the Bush PAC were also an introduction into the extended Bush political family. Among the others who worked in the office with Rove was Margaret Tutwiler, who would go on to serve in senior positions in the Reagan and both Bush administrations. The operation was overseen by James A. Baker, the future cabinet secretary and longtime Bush family friend, who took a bigger role in the political operation after he lost his own race for state attorney general in November of 1978. Years later Baker would come to the rescue in 2000, masterfully representing George W. Bush on the ground during the Florida recount. Another person in the office was a young woman named Becky Brady (the granddaughter of Mary Louise Smith, who was also a former national party chairwoman), who like Rove had moved to Texas because of marriage. Twenty-two years later, after her first marriage ended, she was back in her native Iowa, now called Becky Beach. She was tapped in 2000 by Rove to plan the schedule for George W. as he competed in the state's all-important caucuses.

Beach's memories of Rove during the 1970s were of a man who could be serious beyond his years one moment, and a raucous adolescent the next. He loved to strut around Houston, pretending he was one of Steve Martin's "Wild and Crazy Guys." Above all, she remembers an unusual political talent, who knew the history of every state, a man constantly collecting new contacts, always on the telephone, and who seemingly never forgot a name. "He just had it naturally," recalled Beach.

• • •

THEN IT ALL came to an abrupt end. Bush's frenetic travels in 1977 and 1978 were the start of a campaign that vaulted the Bush dynasty, before then a fading enterprise with dying New England roots, onto a permanent place on the national stage. Bush went to the White House with Reagan. The man who had been present at the creation of his campaign stayed in Texas. Rove stayed there during Bush's vice presidential years. And he stayed there during Bush's 1988 presidential campaign, and during the presidency that followed, and during the ill-fated reelection attempt of 1992, holding only marginal roles in these efforts and never joining the inner circle. Like Bill Clinton, Rove had been studying the presidency since boyhood. But twenty years would pass between the first time he played an important role in a presidential campaign and the second.

Three decades later, the precise circumstances of what happened at Bush's Houston headquarters in the winter of 1978 are a mystery. Even at the time, they were subject to conflicting interpretations. What is clear is that this was a bad month for the Bush operation. James Baker lost his bid for state attorney general. Closer to home, young George W. Bush lost his race for Congress from a Midland-area district.

One explanation for Rove's sudden disappearance from the Bush campaign involved his contentious exchanges with a colleague, Jennifer Fitzgerald, who had a close relationship with the Bush family. Some of those working for Bush's PAC recall Rove-Fitzgerald conflicts over rough election night remarks (and their aftermath), as well as classic intra-office turf battles.

Whatever the case, Bush's operation was getting ready to move from Houston to Washington, and Rove claims he made the decision to stay put. If his intention was to sacrifice professional advancement for personal purposes, the bet did not pay off. In 1979, his marriage to Wainwright, which had brought him to Texas and nearly pushed him out of politics, ended suddenly, Rove says, by her choice.

For the next few years, Texas remained Rove's base of operations, first in a top staff job with Republican governor Bill Clements, and then as the founder of his own consulting business, Rove + Co. One can't help but wonder what pangs Rove might have suffered, as he watched old friends such as Lee Atwater become major Washington figures during the Reagan and Bush years. But Rove's success as a strategist today is vitally linked to the fact that he did not go to Washington in the late 1970s and did not follow a conventional path. If he had, he might well have become like most Washington-based consultants—bewitched by the capital's professional and social ladders. Instead, Rove spent nearly thirty years preparing for a successful White House run by taking on without intermission a series of jobs that allowed him to develop political ties to, and a sophisticated understanding of, every state in the union. As a political consultant, Rove did races in about half the fifty states, beyond his Texas base. In his adopted home state, in particular, his relationships with the Republican moneyed class allowed him to pick and choose his candidate clients, who knew that if they hired Rove, they were in effect also acquiring a ready-made list of financial supporters.

With his vast storehouse of acquaintances and friends, whenever a new political challenge comes up, Rove discerns who the right people are to consult. Shake him awake in the middle of the night and ask such thorny questions as "Who would be the strongest candidate to run for governor of Montana next year?" or "What is the exact status of the asbestos legislation on Capitol Hill?" or "Who are the three most important party fund-raisers in Atlanta and who are they supporting in 2008?"—a sleepy Rove likely could supply the answers himself, but if not, he could tell you whom to ask.

It is not that Rove during the years in the Texas political wilderness developed no understanding of Washington. To the contrary, he studied it intently, but as an outsider, not immersed in the city's constant currents of gossip and intrigue. Mary Matalin, another member of the Bush extended political family, described Rove's frequent trips to D.C. in the years before George W.'s White House run, when he would gather together small groups of people, speak briefly, sit back, listen, and take notes. Matalin said he focused so intently on the ideas being presented that those in attendance "really want[ed] to say something" useful, allowing Rove to "collect threads, collect threads, and all of a sudden he [had] a tapestry."

In the 2000 campaign, Rove aimed to revive a strategy Ronald Reagan had employed successfully in his 1976 effort. He wanted to enlist volunteers at the state and local level throughout the nation who would "wander around the countryside" talking up George W. Bush. Rove told the governor, "They'll be moving around on your behalf. They won't be costing us money. They'll be there before we get staff put in place. They've got connections." This cadre of volunteers, which included politicians and expert operatives from the Reagan, George H. W. Bush, and Dole campaigns, functioned as one of Bush's unmatched weapons of the 2000 campaign. The volunteers gave their time to fund-raising, but also to less glamorous pursuits, such as advancing and staging events and serving as surrogates at minor gatherings. Rove drew on his own longtime relationships, and conferred with veterans of past campaigns, ascertained who was clever and skillful and easy to work with, and brought them on board.

Says Mary Matalin about Rove's design: "It was all very mechanical. . . . No one had ever done it before. . . . Who would think that in a population of this size you could do . . . what amounted to a pyramid scheme. . . . There was no presumption that Bush was the guy. . . . Bush had to deliver the goods, but Karl got the right people there."

RELATIONSHIPS, NOT TRANSACTIONS

★ ★ ★ ★ ★

IN THE HEAT OF A PRESIDENTIAL CAMPAIGN, thousands of person-to-person interactions take place during an average day—e-mails, phone calls, meetings, requests, behests, debates, favors, and accommodations. These interactions can be based on a businesslike exchange of goods and services and a precise accounting of accrued debts. Or, they can spring from a personal relationship, steeped in warmth, history, trust, and the shared expectation of achieving mutual goals, both in the short term and the long.

Relationships work better than transactions. Guess who understood this Trade Secret?

At the time Karl Rove was working for George H. W. Bush's nascent presidential campaign in 1978, a man who would become one of his other Texas mentors was making a run for governor. Bill Clements was trying to become the first Republican elected to that office in more than one hundred years. Clements had a business background, as did many of his senior advisers, and as Rove later recalled, his campaign was filled with "managerial types" who tended to think in terms of reaching objectives through the right organizational chart, as they had in their successful careers in the military or Texas old-boy business networks. These advisers taught the young Rove something. They considered the ultimate currency of politics to be the real human beings inside an organization, and focused on maximizing this asset.

Also on the ballot that year was John Tower, the state's first Republican United States senator since Reconstruction, who was seeking a fourth term. Both Clements and Tower were expecting close races in what was still largely a Democratic state. They believed victory in an off-year election required a massive turnout operation, driven in part by phone bank calls to targeted voters. In the end, both won, but by fewer than twenty thousand votes out of several million cast.

Despite the closeness of the races, or more likely, because of it, Rove asserts, it then became gospel in Texas Republican politics that winning major statewide races required huge numbers of volunteers to staff exhaustive phone-banking efforts and other grassroots activity. After the two '78 races, Rove explained, "This then becomes the practice and habit in Texas for the thereafter. If you're running for U.S. senator or governor and you don't have fifty-some-odd phone banks and a hundred thousand volunteers, you're thought to be a pathetic candidate. And as a result you move from being transactional to being relational."

While certain aspects of successful campaigns are planned in a clinical, antiseptic fashion, the most important building blocks come from finding the best people and convincing them to join the cause. The questions in Texas were simple and specific. " 'Who is the best person in Lubbock to be your phone bank director?' " Rove recalled campaigns asking. " 'Who is the best person in the River Oaks phone bank to be the shift captain in the evening?' I mean that's all what it gets to be about and a campaign gets built around that maintenance, encouragement of and development of those [relationships]." Even campaign money, sometimes called "the mother's milk of American politics," was most easily accumulated when a campaign first built up a network of individual relationships, inspiring people to give and raise financial contributions, to feel personally invested in the outcome.

Concentrating on the personal is relatively simple when a political organization is small, with a few employees, perhaps all located in one office. In a small campaign, most everyone knows the candidate, giving staff members a connection to something larger than themselves. But as campaigns grow to the scale necessary to win a competitive election, maintaining that dynamic of reciprocity becomes a challenge. The demands of attending to the various organizations and individuals who want a piece of the campaign grow exponentially over time, while the number of staff members (and volunteers) grows only geometrically.

There is simply no way for even the best intentioned and well-organized campaign (and every campaign is disorganized) to return all its telephone calls, provide enough surrogate speakers to fulfill each request, or substantively consider and respond to every absentminded professor or think tanker who sends in a novel theory for how to win the race. But a campaign that is built around human contact, rather than formal exchanges (such as: *Our teachers union will endorse you if you oppose merit pay*) puts a premium on responsiveness and indulgence, in order to build a community of shared interests and collective enterprise.

The way to get bigger and stronger at the same time is to rely on your old friends for as much help as they can give, and to treat people you meet along the way as new friends, and then, before long, as if they were old friends, too. In other words: Winning politics should be about relationships, not transactions. All of George W. Bush's campaigns managed by Rove were run this way because both men understood how effective a personal approach can be.

Among Rove's intellectual and practical interests was the challenge of directing organizations so they grow without outgrowing the enthusiasm and intimacy that inspire people to join up in the first place. His knowledge was informed by sources beyond his professional experience. He had conversations with management experts, and he had book learning. Rove, from his earliest years, read, absorbed, and applied lessons from serious books on a range of issues having nothing to do with campaign tactics.

In the early 1970s, Rove developed a passion for the work of fabled management consultant Peter Drucker, whose oeuvre he credited with shaping his sense of the importance of centering campaign and governmental contacts on relationships. Drucker's work also was influential in the growth of many of the nation's mega-churches, whose pastors, Rove noticed, adopted the "relationships, not transactions" model to maintain their identities while they continued to grow bigger and bigger. Indeed, two of the Republican Party's institutional pillars during Rove's career were Big Business and churches, particularly the evangelical mega-churches. These groups also served as organizational role models for how to build large successful campaigns.

As Rove understood, the churches were able to use their members (or "customers") as "marketeers" to help add even more parishioners. That served as an archetype of the Rove-led efforts in Texas and nationwide to build the Republican Party. And, of course, Rove and Bush benefited from the increasing strength of the churches, many of whose members were devoted supporters of the administration's efforts.

Rove cited an article by Malcolm Gladwell to illustrate the importance of the "relationships" Trade Secret. In the *New Yorker,* Gladwell wrote about pastor Rick Warren, the author of *The Purpose-Driven Life,* who, interestingly, was also a student of Drucker. Warren's Saddleback Church has been built up over twenty-five years from nothing to tens of thousands of members in one of the largest congregations in the United States, in part by emphasizing kinship:

"Churches, like any large voluntary organization, have at their core a contradiction," wrote Gladwell.

> In order to attract newcomers, they must have low barriers to entry. They must be unintimidating, friendly, and compatible with the culture they are a part of. . . . They need to give their followers a sense of community—and community, exclusivity, a distinct identity are all, inevitably, casualties of growth. As an economist would say, the bigger an organization becomes, the greater a free-rider problem it has. If I go to a church with five hundred members, in a magnificent cathedral, with spectacular services and music, why should I volunteer or donate any substantial share of my money? What kind of peer pressure is there in a congregation that large? If the barriers to entry become too low—and the ties among members become increasingly tenuous—then a church as it grows bigger becomes weaker. . . . One solution to the problem is simply not to grow, and, historically, churches have sacrificed size for community. But there is another approach: to create a church out of a network of lots of little church cells—exclusive, tightly knit groups of six or seven who meet in one another's homes during the week to worship and pray.

Beyond Drucker, Rove said that the Progressive historian Robert Wiebe, the conservative thinker Michael Novak, and a fellow by the name of Alexis de Tocqueville ("Those that despise people will never get the best out of others and themselves") all influenced his thinking on the imperative of the relationship model.

· · ·

WITH EACH IMPORTANT constituency—the "bundlers" (fund-raisers who gather up checks from their friends and business associates and deliver them in bulk to campaigns), the donors, the Washington wise guys, the volunteers, the activists, the think tankers, the members of Congress, the party consultants, even the media—the Bush campaigns established the terms of interaction that were based on the "relationships, not transactions" structure.

In the normal transactional model, a campaign takes what it needs (money, advice, ideas, endorsements, labor, good press clips) and gives back in return only the bare minimum of acceptable compensation.

The special benefits the Bush campaign could bestow on supporters were unusual access and the latest information. Early political devotees were brought to Austin to meet with Bush in the intimate setting of the Governor's Mansion. Big bundlers were invited to ranch barbecues. Issues seminars were held with the candidate. And information—political strategy, the latest polling, the juiciest insider gossip—was dished out in private briefings and exclusive e-mails. As a package, all this represented a degree of personal attention beyond what most campaigns give their supporters. Even the wealthiest and most successful people appreciate these gestures and are flattered to be considered part of the team.

Rove had helped Bush construct this kind of human daisy chain in Texas for the gubernatorial campaigns, leading to a smashing turnout and rout in Bush's 1998 reelection. Supporters from outside Texas would ask what they could do to help besides give money, and the campaign invited them to come to the state for the final few weeks before Election Day, stay at a Motel 6, and join the fun at a local Republican phone bank.

When Bush and Rove shifted to the presidential arena, however, they discovered several things. First, the Republican Party had no such warm and fuzzy network on the national level. Second, even with the record-breaking sums of money Bush was raising, there was never enough cash to accomplish all the tasks Rove thought were necessary to win. But Rove *was* pleasantly surprised at the extent to which the campaign was able to employ its relationships standard and to engage its *old* old friends and its *new* old friends in helping the campaign. Bush advisers such as Don Evans and Jack Oliver turned the members of the campaign's finance squad into political field hands after they were done raising cash, and they showed great gusto for rolling up their sleeves, going door-to-door, or making phone calls. Instead of allowing the vast size of the operation to let the emphasis on relationships fall by the wayside, the campaign valued it even more.

One of the more clever and counterintuitive ways in which the Bush campaign's 1999 and 2000 dealings with its donors relied on relationships was the catering service at its fund-raising events. Normally, people who give the maximum contribution to a presidential campaign are invited to a plush room for a sumptuous, seated, multi-course dinner that can cost around $150 per person. Instead, at many of their premium fund-raisers, the Bush campaign served inexpensive finger food, like pretzels and hot dogs, even to its fattest fat-cat crowds. Rather than complain, the donors appreciated playing their part in the bargain. Most of them had access to extravagant dinners all the time. They were investing in Bush not because they wanted to eat a fussy meal in a hotel banquet room, but because they wanted him to win. Standing with a hot dog in hand as the bigwigs in the room around them cheerfully did the same, donors could perceive (and taste) their dollars going to good use.

The Bush team continued this philosophy even after securing the Oval Office. In the 2002 midterm election campaign, the political operation helped to raise a remarkable amount of money for the Republican Party and its candidates. A trio of aspirants got special attention. The real focus of the cycle was winning back control of the Senate, which the Republicans had lost when Vermont's Jim Jeffords, claiming he was alienated by Bush's policies and actions, bolted the party to become an independent who caucused with the Democrats. The Three Amigos (as they predictably became known)— Senate candidates John Thune of South Dakota, Norm Coleman of Minnesota, and Jim Talent of Missouri—all faced tough races. None was well known nationally, and none was from any of the mega-states (such as Florida, Texas, California, New York, or Illinois) that dominate fund-raising.

But the Bush campaign was able to reach out to its financial supporters all over the country and say, in effect, "Make our friends your friends." A special fund-raising committee called the "Road to 51" was set up for the Amigos. When Rove's colleagues Ken Mehlman and Jack Oliver made it clear to the money types that these three candidates were a key part of the plan to achieve their shared goal of winning back control of the Senate, the funders got the message. The Amigos did a road show, hitting big cities, in which they consistently raised serious money. It was not necessary for Bush or, in many cases, even a prominent member of his political team to be in attendance; the clear communication between Bush World and its donors about how important these races were to the White House dispelled any doubts.

Rove had calculated that winning two of the three races would almost certainly mean winning back the Senate. Coleman and Talent won, Thune narrowly lost. The Republicans got the majority back.

The White House followed the same method in 2004, setting up another joint committee to which Bush donors could contribute, with the money then distributed by formula to about a dozen Republican Senate races. That allowed eventually victorious candidates such as Mel Martinez of Florida, Richard Burr of North Carolina, and David Vitter of Louisiana to raise hundreds of thousands of dollars without breaking a sweat. This time, the team was so well oiled that the Bush "family" sometimes donated to the cause without an actual fund-raising event. Calls were made. Checks were written. And the party increased its hold on the Senate.

· · ·

FOR A 2008 presidential campaign, what is required to mimic the Bush-Rove model on "relationships, not transactions"? First off, you need a candidate whose personality and ideas attract a crowd, and one who can apply charm and a sense of familiarity.

But such an effort also requires the intellectual agreement and coordinated dedication to make the model work—a commitment from the campaign manager, the finance chair, the political staff, and the scheduler. Finally, the campaign leadership has to make it clear to everyone on the team that relationships will define the way they deal with the world. All that is easier said than done; it is a lot of work.

Most of the special dealings of the Bush operation and other practitioners of this school are not visible to the media eye; indeed, the very nature of the bonds inspires and requires intimate interaction. But disarming fellowship is not limited to big donors and power players. Journalists, too, seek some up-close and personal attention. Democrats and press critics who have complained about the relatively soft coverage that Bush got in his first presidential campaign groused as he dispensed jaunty nicknames and amiable teasing to the reporters who covered him.

An underappreciated reason for Bush's favorable press, however, was that his campaign cannily dealt with journalists on the basis of relationships, not transactions. They were strong and smart when handling the press by almost any standard, but certainly compared with most Republican presidential campaigns. So, attention, 2008 candidates: Make your campaign all about relationships. Be nice to your donors, cater to your political supporters, stroke your volunteers, but, above all else, *return our phone calls.*

KARL ROVE IN YOUR MAILBOX

★ ★ ★ ★ ★

IN 1976, twenty-six-year-old college dropout Karl Rove became a professor. The Republican Party was still in a shambles in the wake of Nixon's Watergate scandal. Trying desperately to help its candidates recover, the Republican National Committee began something called Campaign Management College. Aspiring politicos from around the country flew to Washington to sit through training sessions at the Twin Bridges Marriott, just across the Potomac River from the capital. These seminars were led by a young operative named Joe Gaylord, who recently had been running the Iowa Republican Party and later would move on to become the chief strategist for Newt Gingrich. In those days, Gaylord recalled, his job was something like a "game show host," trying to keep seminar participants from getting bored while also trying to impart some kind of useful knowledge. One of the most popular speakers at his college was Karl Rove, who was always full of entertaining patter and practical advice.

Rove's subject could not have been more pedestrian: how to publish effective brochures. A black-and-white pamphlet, he told his audiences, can be more powerful because that conveys the authority of a newspaper article; a blue-and-white layout may look snazzy but will strike many voters as "sleazy." He held forth on such questions as how to display a leaflet's text ("the copy") and how much "white space" to leave at the margins.

There was no doubt Rove knew what he was talking about, although it would be five more years before he would turn to direct mail as a full-time career. But it may not be apparent how the minutiae he was sharing with a passel of campaign managers back in the Disco Era has any connection to his helping the most conservative president of modern times win successive elections a quarter-century later. In fact, the two are linked by a long if circuitous line.

Take a moment to think of the leading successful political operatives of our day. Prior to Rove, the most famous such Republican was Lee Atwater. The Democrats tend to be better known, which is not a coincidence; Democrats spend more time trying to become better known. Celebrity Democratic operatives include James Carville, Paul Begala, Bob Shrum, and the late Robert Squier. What each of these strategists had in common is that they came out of the world of media. Their specialties were television ads and press relations, or crafting strategies to use both to help frame a candidate's campaign message. Before Rove, the idea that a presidential campaign strategist could emerge from the world of brochures and direct mail would have been regarded as peculiar—like hiring a plumber to design a house. By the late 1980s, Rove had expanded his portfolio to include general campaign strategy, but he had not abandoned the insights he learned during the beginning of his career.

Rove's mastery of technology was one part of his success. But mastering the *means* by which you reach voters does not amount to much if you do not know how to get their attention or what to say once you have it. In an age of digital politics, campaigning is being redefined by the infinite new potentialities of e-mail and the World Wide Web. The closest thing to the Web in the pre–Internet Age was . . . direct mail.

At the most conceptual level, the two mediums have important similarities. Unlike television or radio, for instance, in which the message is boiled down to thirty, or maybe sixty seconds, both the Web and direct mail have ample room to craft lengthy arguments. Both depend on a creative combination of text, graphics, and photos. And both produce at least the illusion that the target of the political communication is an active participant. Watching a television ad is a passive experience; the target may be simultaneously eating chips, paying bills, or hollering at the children. Reading a piece of mail, like clicking around a website, requires engagement. In both cases, the engagement is designed to produce a specific reaction (*Send a message to Ted Kennedy and the liberal media by contributing now!*).

The most important similarity is more profound, and even more applicable to the challenge of winning the presidency in an age of media fragmentation. It is a big country. Many of the people who live here feel disconnected

from politics. From an early age, Rove learned that successful political communication creates intimacy where none existed before. When the message
hit home, the results were tangible.

• • •

ONE OF THE MOST concrete pieces of evidence amassed during Rove's career
can be found by visiting room 2109 of the Rayburn House Office Building. Back in 1984, Joe Barton was an earnest man of thirty-five who had a
strong desire to go to Congress and negligible prospects of actually getting
there. Today, although little known to the general public, the Texan is one of
the most powerful people in Washington. He serves as the chairman of the
House Energy and Commerce Committee, with jurisdiction over interstate
and foreign commerce, including energy, telecommunications, and health
care.

It is possible that, had Joe Barton not hired Rove twenty-two years ago
when launching his political career with a run for a seat in the United States
House of Representatives, he would not be where he is today. Without Rove,
Barton unquestionably would not have won that first race.

Barton had some reasonable credentials in 1984. He was a successful energy consultant who had served a short stint in the prestigious White House
Fellows program in the Reagan administration. But these calling cards were
not enough to draw much notice in a sprawling district that stretched across
a broad swatch of central Texas, including pieces of the Dallas and Houston
metropolitan areas. An operative at the National Republican Campaign
Committee in Washington recommended that Barton hire a Washington
strategist named Bob Weed, who managed a number of House races.

When Barton contacted him, Weed gave some advice free of charge: Forget the race, it is unwinnable. When Barton persisted, Weed offered him a
deal. He would take on Barton as a client, though only on the side with no
expectations that the candidate would get much of his time. There was one
other stipulation: Barton should also hire his friend, a fellow down in Austin
named Rove, who did direct mail. It seemed apparent, Barton later recalled,
that they had some kind of arrangement in which each steered business the
other's way.

Weed and Rove both made clear that the underdog candidate was not a
charity case. "They were both very fiduciary," recalled Barton. "They both
wanted to be paid on time, and they wanted to be paid up front." Once that
was established, Rove got to work. He sat Barton down in front of a tape
recorder and told him to start talking.

The significance of this session should not be underappreciated. The reason most campaigns seem artificial is that they are. Consultants take what they understand to be the winning national message of a given year and package a version of it with every client they have, whether the candidate is trying to win in Dallas or Duluth, and often with little regard for what the candidate has done or believed in the past. Rove wanted to know who Barton really was and why he truly wanted to be elected to Congress. If they were to construct a winning message, it had to start with words that sounded natural coming out of Barton's mouth.

Politics is full of bluster because it is full of imponderables. In most cases, no one can say for sure what caused a race to be decided one way and not the other. One reason Barton's election echoed in Rove's career is that it is one of those instances where there really is no doubt why Barton won.

He was one of four candidates in the Republican primary. His main opponent, Max Hoyt, heavily outspent Barton. What's more, Hoyt started out considerably better known, since he came from a county north of Houston that was far more populous than Barton's neck of the district. Given the large media markets, television advertising was prohibitively expensive; even radio was not much of an option. In-the-flesh candidate campaigning across the vast district was necessary, but highly inefficient.

That left Barton with only one principal means of communicating with voters: direct mail. And it left only one explanation when Barton won the Republican nomination (after a primary battle, a runoff, and a bitterly contested recount that Barton won by a scant ten votes). In the general election that followed, Barton did not cut it quite so close, winning with 57 percent of the vote in a campaign that again was waged mostly through the mail. Twenty-two years later, Barton readily acknowledged that he won the election because of Karl Rove's letters. "It's the one thing we did which touched everyone who voted in the Republican primary. And my mail was better than theirs."

What Rove did that year for Barton was to seize a big and wide-open Texas district and make it small. In the nomination contest, he took an unknown person and made him familiar—in an overwhelmingly appealing way. There were photos of a pleasant-looking man with his wife and three young children. Although direct mail often can be scorchingly negative, the first mailings had little to say about Barton's GOP opponents. Instead, they were all about Barton himself. "Elect the Proven Cost Cutter," read the mailing. The text told the tale of a man "Educated to Lead" with his degree from Texas

A&M, "With Roots in Texas" and "Committed to His Community." Those catchphrases stood out in sharp relief, but they were embedded in copious amounts of text. The mailings contained hundreds of well-chosen words about the candidate and his message, as opposed to the few dozen or so that might be uttered in a typical thirty-second television ad. For the values of this particular district, there was nothing not to like about Joe Barton as presented at length and with great style by Karl Rove.

Later, in the general election, there was slightly rougher stuff, the kind of thing for which both direct mail in general and Rove in particular got their reputation. Barton's Democratic opponent, Dan Kubiak, also was presented by Rove as a familiar figure—but in an overwhelmingly negative way. Barton's mailings scored "Kubiak's Record as a Professional Politician: Eight offices and 15 campaigns in 15 years." Once Kubiak had been quoted in the newspaper speaking about the "constant strain" of his former job in the state legislature. Barton's mailings featured a picture of Kubiak with a caustic caption: "Any job—as long as it pays well and isn't a strain." There was even a picture of a man standing by the highway with a homemade sign that said "ANY Public Office—Austin or Washington, D.C." That reflected another Rove fetish: Find something your opponent has said that will stick in the minds of the voters and define him or her in negative terms. Then repeat it over and over. (As in: *I actually voted for the $87 billion before I voted against it.*)

The cornerstone of Barton's general election campaign was a four-page letter blasted across the district. Four pages seemed like a lot to the candidate. *Couldn't it be shorter?* he asked. Rove replied that voters *liked* long letters. In any event, Rove had plenty for Barton to say about his positions. And he was not about to let that old Kubiak newspaper quote go gently into the night: "The Texas Legislature meets for six months every two years, but that was too much of a strain for Kubiak! How can he expect to do a good job in the Congress that meets almost all the time?" The sixth district was historically Democratic, but the mailing argued that Kubiak was not Texas's kind of Democrat: "Kubiak may try to sound conservative, but a man who attacks Reagan-Gramm economic policies and supports a repeal of the third year of the 25% Reagan-Gramm tax cut is a big-spending, high-taxing liberal, no matter how he tries to hide it." There were references linking the Democrat to "Tip O'Neill and the spend and splurge crowd" in Congress, not to mention the "Union Bosses in Washington or New York or Cleveland." It was all there: alliteration, humor, insult, and partisan invective.

And it worked. No one who has made it this far in this book should have to guess what happened to Kubiak: *He lost control of his public image.* This hapless figure—who, after all, "Once Compared Phil Gramm to Hitler"—has a small place in history as a man who served as target practice for the guy who later shot down John Kerry.

• • •

THROUGH THAT DECADE and into the next, Rove + Co. would write and mail many millions of letters that usually fell into one of two types—some to solicit contributions and others to try to persuade voters to cast their ballots for (or against) a candidate or cause. Both types relied on the same insight that grievance is what makes the political world go round. A stack of yellowed Rove + Co. letters is a virtual anthology of conservative resentments from the 1980s and 1990s—decades when Republicans were generally in the ascendancy but their partisans still felt besieged by the secular, tax-addicted, criminal-coddling Left.

The letters show how disciplined Rove was in employing proven methods from race to race. As with his work for Joe Barton, the prose was nearly always crisp, clear, and conversational. The tone shifted naturally between optimistic and foreboding. Nearly every one of the letters played off the basic us-versus-them mentality that motivates partisans of all types.

Inevitably, the letters catered to a recipient's vanity, in particular the notion that his or her state had exceptional character—as in "Illinois values" or "Nebraska values." Iowans were flattered as "the best people in the nation."

And always there were villains. Sometimes they included familiar types, such as trial lawyers, "ultra-liberals," and unions. Sometimes the villain was no less menacing for being unnamed: "they." A September 30, 1993, fundraising letter for Utah senator Orrin Hatch's reelection made repeated reference to "they"—the diverse enemies of the conservative movement—and evinced a sense that the recipient was part of a brave band of warriors holding liberal interests at bay. "They are aided by friends in the national media— fellow elitists who think it's their right to smear and break those who dare to disagree with their prevailing Liberal orthodoxy," the letter declared.

A 1995 letter soliciting new members for the Independent Cattlemen's Association sounded a dire alarm: "Our future is in danger. Our heritage and way of life are under attack. Consider just some of the obstacles being put in our way: the golden cheeked warbler . . . the coastal management plan . . . federal wetlands policy . . . outrageous environmental laws. The people who oppose our industry are constantly finding new ways to attack our livelihood."

A 1998 letter from the Citizens for Nebraska's Future was part of an effort to pass a ballot measure limiting taxes. Written in the informal tone of one neighbor chatting with another, the piece began:

Dear Ms. Vanderslice,

The Vanderslice family lives on a budget. So should state and local government, don't you think?

A 1998 fund-raising letter for Iowa gubernatorial candidate Jim Ross Lightfoot darkly cautioned about one Democrat: "Newspapers say he set up a slush fund to 'pump a couple hundred thousand dollars' into the Governor's race." And it described Iowa's Tom Vilsack (the state's longtime governor, whom John Kerry considered as a running mate in 2004 and is a potential 2008 presidential contender) as "an ultra-liberal trial lawyer with an anti-business, pro-tax record in the Iowa Senate."

In a 1988 fund-raising letter for Pennsylvania senator John Heinz, Rove demonstrated that he could demonize pretty much anyone for tactical advantage, even his fellow Lone Star Staters. Signed by Heinz, the letter warned ominously that Democrats would stop at nothing to beat him: "A Houston, Texas oilman heads their fund-raising." (There's nothing scarier, really, than a Houston oilman, except, perhaps, a labor boss from Cleveland.)

But the messages were not always negative. An August 4, 1995, "Dear Friend" fund-raising letter for the just elected Governor George W. Bush struck a softer tone: "I campaigned on issues, not personalities, spending 14 months telling Texans what was in my heart and listening to them."

Over the years, Rove has spoken rarely about his craft in public. In a 1985 interview with the *Austin Business Journal,* he said he was not offended by the term "junk mail" ("if you're not interested in it, you consider it junk"), and claimed that data from the Direct Marketing Association showed that people preferred to be added to lists, rather than deleted from them, by a ratio of about three to one. He described his business as a mix of art and science ("It's an art in that there's no easy answer—it's whatever it takes to get the job done. But it's a science in that you can quantify it all"), and emphasized the importance of being patient and spending resources on the front end for a big payoff down the road. As he explained, "The idea is to build a list of names so that you are making money on the process with the realization that it is in subsequent months or years when you really make your high net dollars."

In Rove's case, the payoff definitely came. But he remained a bit sensitive that his early work had been misunderstood. In an interview, Rove said the common assumption that his career had been about the triumph of "narrow-casted," negative messages—speaking to small slices of the electorate with carefully targeted appeals—was often exaggerated. The targeted messages, he said, worked only to the extent they could be braided into a larger and more unifying one. "Direct mail caused me to think about themes and messages that could knit people together," Rove said. "Your object was to get 50 percent plus one and you might have had to have different messages to talk to different groups, but they were not messages at odds with each other."

• • •

EVERY CAMPAIGN CYCLE of recent years has seen the emergence of a new way of communicating with voters. Clinton's 1992 victory showed the ascendancy of chat broadcasts such as *The Arsenio Hall Show,* just as 2004 showed the ascendancy of websites as a political tool. There is no way to know what new twist will arrive in 2008.

It is worth noting, however, that over the course of his career the two Trade Secrets of Rove-style political communication remained consistent, even as the favored means of communicating have changed. These two principles are as valid for a Democrat as they have been for a Republican.

The first one is: *Narrow the distance between politician and voter.* Rove used direct mail in 1984 to introduce Barton to his wide-ranging district and turn him into a reassuring figure even to people who did not know him. By 2004, new tools performed a similar task. There was the Bush-Cheney campaign's list of 7.5 million e-mail supporters, who got regular updates from the campaign. And there were the hundreds of thousands of campaign volunteers, who phoned and visited their neighbors to carry the Bush message forward. The principle was the same: Political communication should be intimate.

The second principle flows directly from the first: *Create communities of like-minded people.* The way to create these communities is through appeals that couple a positive message (*Bush and Barton are like us*) with a negative one (*Kubiak and Kerry are not like us*). So unlike us, in fact, that voters concluded they were unacceptable as leaders.

COMITY IS PRETTY

★ ★ ★ ★ ★

PRESIDENTIAL CAMPAIGNS ARE SNAKE PITS. They typically are filled with men and women who are insecure, turf-conscious, and competitive. The senior levels of almost every campaign include people who think they are smart and most of their colleagues are stupid. Who will aggressively pursue power, fame, influence, and access to the candidate at the expense of their associates. Who will shamelessly lie, steal credit, and pass blame, even if it hurts the feelings and careers of co-workers they pretend to esteem.

People who work in presidential campaigns, and the journalists who cover them, spend an enormous amount of time recounting such conflicts in minute detail. There is no greater source of inefficiency or negative press coverage than these in-house battles.

Bush's two presidential campaigns were notable because almost none of their negative energy was directed inward onto internal rivalries. In both 2000 and 2004, Bush's opponents wasted time and psychic energy grappling with the problem that many of their advisers could not stand one another. To be sure, there was some sniping within Bush's campaigns, but, by every account, there was decidedly less. The Bush campaign was a snake pit with very little hissing.

This may be a hard point to digest. The strategic mastermind of these campaigns was a man with perhaps the most serpentine reputation in American politics. Yet both of the presidential campaigns overseen by Karl Rove were staffed with people who were courteous to one another; who were inclined to air their disagreements face-to-face rather than through anonymous carping in the media; who recognized collegiality as a core campaign asset; and who strove to maintain harmony even when pure self-interest would have dictated otherwise. Bush himself insisted that his staff live by these rules, in contrast to the every-man-for-himself ethos of his father's operations.

In Bill Clinton's two presidential campaigns, the most important staff members were easily identified by the faction to which they belonged or the enemies they shared. In Clinton's 1992 campaign, for instance, there was a camp including pollster Stan Greenberg and strategist James Carville, which often clashed with Hillary Clinton friend Susan Thomases, Arkansan Betsey Wright, and campaign chairman Mickey Kantor. They squabbled over policy decisions, campaign spending, and candidate scheduling, and sometimes went running to the press to hash out their differences and score points. In 1996, Dick Morris and his tight band of allies regularly warred with longtime Clinton aide Harold Ickes and many of the original 1992 political strategists.

There certainly were personality clashes on Bush's team. Reporters easily could guess what Rove really thought of Bush adviser Karen Hughes. But that's just the point—one would have to guess. Almost no news stories appeared from either 2000 or 2004 detailing disputes over tactics, policy, or personality within the Bush campaign, and the incidents of spiteful blind quotes were equally rare.

One reason for this was Bush's own insistence that campaign dissension stay private. But, more important, there were fewer such quarrels and, when they did occur, they lacked venom. There was more back-slapping than back-stabbing, and far less of the intrigue that characterizes most presidential efforts and administrations of both parties. This was a huge competitive advantage. And it perhaps demonstrates just how ruthless the Bush people were—they were willing to be nice in pursuit of victory.

• • •

THIS CHAPTER'S COUNTERINTUITIVE Trade Secret: *Being nice helps you win presidential campaigns.* Alas, it is necessary to explain why hiring nice people to work in a not-nice world contributes to winning. Kind people are less likely to hurt each other's feelings. They are more likely to support each other during the moments of stress that arise frequently in the heat of a campaign. They are more likely to focus on the work at hand and not get caught up in petty bickering. They are more likely to contribute to a healthy, stable office environment.

In politics as in life, it is easier to get through the workday productively if you don't have to spend time deflecting legions of enemies, inside and outside the tent. Ask your typical senior White House adviser or campaign operative (or network or newspaper political correspondent) what chunk of his or her day is spent fighting off internal foes, and a truthful answer will yield an alarmingly high percentage.

If in-house civility provides a campaign with a competitive advantage, the question becomes: Is Rove amiable enough to take advantage of this Trade Secret?

At first glance, the evidence would suggest no. Over the years, in talks with scores of Democrats, most assert acidly that not only is Rove *not* nice, but that he's evil incarnate. And many Republicans close to Rove will, if pressed, offer up the following terms to describe him: *controlling, demanding,* and *unforgiving.*

Even Rove himself, when addressing this aspect of his reputation several years ago, was equivocal. Is it important to him, he was asked, that people on his staff think he treats them well?

"No," he answered, bluntly. "It's important that *I* think I treat them well. . . . [T]ry as you might, you're just not going to make everybody happy. . . . I'm demanding. . . . I'm not always, I think, understanding of people who can't keep up. . . . I don't think I've got arrogance, but I move at a very fast pace, and sometimes that rubs people the wrong way."

Case closed. Such a person cannot be nice.

On the other hand, some who know Rove best almost uniformly believe he is a nice person. His campaign colleague Stuart Stevens declared, "Karl is the kind of guy who does a ton of little things for people—the guy who takes interns to lunch who don't have money, buys ice cream for everybody in a campaign, calls when you or a loved one is sick. Gore Vidal says to be interesting, you have to be interested. Karl is interested in all kinds of things, including other people. My wife maintains that it's a good thing most people don't know what an incredibly kind, loving guy he is or it would ruin his image."

In the mold of the two Presidents Bush, Rove values the importance of the personal gesture—the handwritten letter, the thoughtful phone call, the mention from the podium—to grease the skids of party politics and human relations. Throughout his busy White House years, Rove continued his practice of regularly penning notes of appreciation, congratulations, and condolence. He has been known to write thank-you notes in response to thank-you notes. Even as he grew richer, more powerful, and more experienced, Rove never abandoned the hard-nosed but good-guy behavior that contributed to his triumphs.

To be sure, a handful of Republicans have been his publicly sworn adversaries. But if you consider the number of enemies the typical White House official, party activist, or political consultant incurs, having just a handful might well be considered one of Rove's top career achievements.

Because Rove thought of geniality as an effective campaign tool, he tended to surround himself with people for whom affability was second nature. There have been some notable exceptions (and you know who you are). Not everyone who has worked for Rove is sweet, and not everyone who has worked for other campaigns is sour. But person for person, the Bush-Rove operations visibly aimed for politeness and warmth.

As Bush strategist Mark McKinnon recalled, the two presidential campaigns were largely "friction free and absent competing agendas. . . . It was kind of shocking in a good way." He added, "I've worked city council races where there was more back-biting. I never had to look over my shoulder about who was coming after me."

Bush deserved a lot of the credit, McKinnon said. "There is a particular culture" in Bush World of collegiality. During the 2000 campaign, the candidate told his top staff, "Always return each other's calls first," because, as Bush himself wrote in his campaign book *A Charge to Keep,* he "felt it would foster good communications" and "make sure . . . [his] senior people would seek one another's advice and guidance."

Requiring comity was part of the way Bush and Rove minimized the kind of top-level conflicts that have bedeviled every presidency and presidential campaign of the modern era—and, possibly, since the advent of politics. Thus, unequivocally a Trade Secret: *Be kind to those on your team and ensure they are kind to each other.*

And a potential Trade Secret corollary: *Being kind to those on your own team allows you to conserve your brutish tendencies to destroy political adversaries.*

SECTION VI

★ ★ ★ ★ ★

THE EFFECTIVE EXECUTIVE

★ ★ ★ ★ ★

RENAISSANCE, MAN

★ ★ ★ ★ ★

MARK MCKINNON ONCE WAS PRESSED to explain why exactly he thought Karl Rove was an effective political strategist. He responded with a tale from early in Bush's first presidential campaign.

It was in 1999, months before the first primaries, on a campaign plane headed from Texas to California. Most of the campaign staff was killing time as they jetted over the West, wandering up and down the aisles, chatting with colleagues. Rove stayed in his seat, furiously typing on his laptop. By the end of the three-and-a-half-hour flight, he had written three sets of user manuals: one for the campaign's state chairmen, one for county coordinators, one for local precinct leaders. Each was filled with detailed explanations of the specific roles in the larger strategy of the operation. In a couple of hours, McKinnon marveled, the job was done; the manuals needed merely to be printed before being distributed around the country. In other campaigns, the same thing might have taken a couple of weeks—one meeting to assign the task, a couple of days for a staffer to compose a draft, another few days to circulate the draft, another meeting to declare the draft inadequate, followed by time spent on a revised draft and another meeting.

So there you have it, McKinnon said, a man and his laptop, the virtuoso at work.

As action adventures go, McKinnon's story is a bit underwhelming. There would be more dramatic scenes if this were a book about the world's best shark photographers, or urban demolition teams, or champion snowboarders. Political consulting is made up of an accumulation of quotidian tasks, none of them visibly dramatic. Who can lead a more productive meeting! Or quickly tap out the e-mail that precisely clarifies what a campaign should be doing six months from now! In its way, that airplane flight illuminates what may be the most important thing to understand about why Rove has won elections: He is expert at a variety of things.

The Renaissance Man dimension to Rove's abilities is another by-product of his remaining in Texas to build his career rather than going to Washington as a young man. At Rove + Co., he tended to dominate the state campaigns he ran in Texas and elsewhere around the country, in ways that would not have been possible had he made presidential consulting his full-time job earlier in life. Whether he was hired to oversee an entire campaign or just provide direct mail services, his interests gave him increasing authority and on-the-job training. The result was that, by the late 1990s, he had experience in nearly every aspect of campaigns: policy, communications, press, scheduling, advertising, direct mail, polling, research, opposition research, field organizing, fund-raising, budgeting, event planning, political and legislative strategy, campaign law, crisis management, personnel, constituent group outreach, grassroots organizing, and volunteer coordination. Some of those jobs he had performed full-time at one point or another in his career. Others he learned by working as a general strategist and studying the facets of an operation as it was under way.

It is as if the CEO of an airline not only knows how to run the company and brief the shareholders, but also how to pilot the planes, service the engines, man the control tower, offload the baggage, pass out the peanuts, and collect the five dollars for the headsets.

· · ·

ROVE'S CELEBRATED ABILITY to hold two conversations simultaneously, one by phone and another by e-mail, was not merely a personality tic. It was representative of a set of skills that was well suited to the changing nature of presidential politics.

The point is worth repeating: For campaign strategists, this is the age of generalization. In most fields—science, medicine, economics—specialization is the order of the day. Deeper knowledge and ever more narrow expertise is required to gain mastery over ever more complex subjects. In politics, however, the historical currents are flowing in the opposite direction.

There were once clear boundaries among campaign occupations. Media experts made the ads. Press operatives calculated how to coax favorable news coverage from reporters. Pollsters tried to figure out what voters thought. Field organizers worried about voter turnout. The drones in the policy shop sequestered themselves, writing issue papers that went unread by many others in the campaign.

In recent elections, all these lines have blurred. The most effective campaigns have knocked down traditional campaign walls, creating demand for people who know a little about a lot, with a special premium on those rare souls who know a lot about a lot. Like so many of the other political trends discussed on these pages, this change is rooted in the historical forces transforming modern media, which have altered human communication. As politics is mostly about communication, the organization of campaigns and the skills required to win elections have mutated as well.

In the previous generation, the dominance of the Old Media, in particular, the huge audiences for a tiny number of television networks, meant that two factors by far were the most important in a presidential campaign. One was the paid advertisements on the stations affiliated with these networks. The other was the campaign coverage of network news divisions. If these things were going well, the other parts of the campaign did not matter so much. The power of mass media was fearsome, but for political strategists it made life simple: They had a captive audience in front of the tube. These days, the audience is hardly captive. It is wildly liberated; widely dispersed, easily distracted, sharply savvy. What's more, people have enough sources of information, and enough exposure to the bluster and baloney of political advertising, to be highly skeptical about the messages they receive.

Television spots still count in presidential politics, but they have lost all novelty. As Ken Mehlman has said, "In a world with a wealth of information there is a poverty of attention." Ads work best when they are coordinated with the other parts of a campaign, with each element reinforcing the other. An effective ad amplifies a message a voter is already prone to believe based on what he or she has learned from news coverage (*Know something about the press*). The message will be even more believable if it is repeated and deepened with materials delivered on the front doorstep or at soccer practice by a neighborhood volunteer (*Know something about campaign brochures and fieldwork*). And the messages in all these forums will resonate only if they are linked in some plausible way to ideas and proposals that are actually emerging from the candidate's mouth (*Know something about speechwriting and policy*). In this new environment, as Bill Clinton and Dick Morris showed in 1996, it is folly to insulate the policy shop from the polling operation, or the speechwriting division, or the ad-makers. All must operate in unison. And they will do so far more effectively if the person at the top of the operation has synoptic vision—the ability to see how each part of a campaign fits into the larger whole.

When the Bush campaign held meetings to discuss turnout in key states, Rove would chair them, often demonstrating detailed knowledge of federal programs in specific regions of a state and how various local controversies might affect voting patterns. When Matthew Dowd, Bush's polling coordinator, would return with new numbers, Rove did not have to nod his head in feigned understanding of what the data signified. When ad-maker McKinnon brought back his latest spot, Rove did not have to take his word about whether the commercial was any good.

In most cases, Rove would be intimately involved in creating the ad before it was shot. On July 26, 2004, the day that John Kerry's nominating convention began in Boston, Rove once again was busy at his keyboard. This time he was spinning out thoughts—something less than orders but more than suggestions—for the filming of a series of ads. The spots were to feature the President and First Lady Laura Bush talking, as though conversing with an off-camera interviewer. In the old days, it was standard to dress up political commercials as "news-style" interviews. In the age of *Survivor* and other programs, however, they seemed more like reality TV confessionals, complete with a calculated combination of dewy eyes, knowing smiles, and jut-jawed resolve. The memo Rove sent to McKinnon and a group of top Bush advisers at 10:26 that evening was titled "Ideas For Filming President and Mrs. Bush." He noted, "Attached are catch phrases and questions to help the president frame his thoughts on issues we will touch on in spots." What followed was seven full pages of sculpted language and talking points on a range of issues such as education, health care, taxes, and terrorism. Rove's suggestions were a combination of what he knew the Bushes wanted to say and what the American people wanted to hear. "On Social Security, we want to talk about strengthening—not modernizing—or reform. . . . The President should talk about what was going through his head the day he toured [New York's] Ground Zero and met with victim's families. Arlene Howard, the fireman who lost a brother [in the September 11 attacks], the workers at Ground Zero. . . . To the extent he is comfortable discussing. . . . Now that his girls have graduated from college, describe the world he wants them to live and prosper in. . . . The First Lady will want to be prepared to talk about the President: How he makes decisions, his thoughtfulness, consideration, and empathy. . . . Gathering dangers—why we had to deal with Iraq."

Rove was comfortable giving marching orders of this kind in part because

he had been doing it for years. Stuart Stevens observed: "One of Karl's qualities that does, I believe, put him into genius rank—and yes, I'm totally
serious—is his ability to focus on little things and big things at the same
time, and focus on the next five minutes and the next five months simultaneously. It's fairly stunning." Stevens recalled an incident from Bill Webster's
campaign for Missouri governor in 1992. Over lunch, Stevens asked Rove for
advice about television spots. "He thought about it for a beat or two," Stevens
said, "then just laid out the whole campaign. 'I'd start with welfare reform to
nail down the base but do it in a different way, not straight conservative, "welfare is bad." Have smarter policy. Then . . .' He just went through the whole
campaign. I was scribbling notes like crazy.

"About six months later, when the television campaign was starting,
[Rove] called and said, 'I've been thinking about the sequence we talked
about and maybe you should think about . . .' It was like he was picking up
the conversation from the day before. And his point was that we should sequence spots differently in the Kansas City media market where there had
been a huge court fight over funding of schools. 'I'd think about having Bill
talk directly about what he has done as AG as the first spot . . .' That's one of
Karl's favorite lines. 'I'd think about . . .' Since 99% of the time, he's dead on,
most people would say, 'Look, do this or that.' Karl has a different manner. He
gives you room to disagree or discuss. 'I'd think about . . .' "

● ● ●

OTHER TOP STRATEGISTS have many strengths. James Baker, with whom
Rove worked on George H. W. Bush's PAC, was also a multitalented political
strategist, who served Reagan and Bush in a variety of government and campaign jobs. But Baker was more of a big-picture guy, who did not always
get his hands dirty with the details of a campaign. The other most influential
and successful presidential campaign advisers of the modern era—Lee Atwater, James Carville, and Dick Morris—had responsibilities that were limited compared with Rove's. Notably, these three all had to battle for turf,
status, and control within the campaigns they ran (as did Baker). Under
Bush, Rove's authority was understood and rarely challenged.

After Josh Bolten took over as Bush's chief of staff in spring of 2006, during a second term shake-up, Rove's portfolio was reduced. He no longer was
in charge of supervising the White House policy formation process. It was
the first time in Rove's association with Bush that he was publicly forced to
relinquish power. Rove's critics in both parties and many in the press cast his
diminished responsibilities as a dressing down and a component of Bush's

efforts to revive his presidency. Rove's defenders insisted the change was intended to free him up to engage in long-range planning, including for the midterm elections. As a practical matter, it was clear he still enjoyed wide-roaming influence over domestic policy, congressional relations, and any-thing relating to Bush's political fortunes. Yet the reassignment gave the impression of a negative verdict on his performance in the year following the 2004 reelection.

Back in 1999, Rove's end of the bargain was that he was supposed to wear his authority lightly, at least in public. Pressed then for an on-the-record de-scription of what his role would be in Bush's upcoming presidential cam-paign, Rove made a rare departure from his customary stance and spoke about what he did in specific ways, undraped by ritual disclaimers that his role was overblown, that it was a big team, that he was just one of many, and, in any event, that Bush himself was calling all the important shots. He began by saying simply, "I'm the strategist."

But then he continued, allowing the breadth of his responsibilities to un-furl: "I work with the political division and work on message. Supervise the media guys and the pollsters who focus on message. I do have a unique posi-tion, I readily admit. I'm a division director. . . . I have a brief that allows me to sort of be involved in other people's business so I have to be very conscious of how I do that and why I do that. . . . I'm involved with research, I'm in-volved with policy, and I'm involved in press. I do all the fund-raising mail for the campaign. I'm doing all the voter contact mail for the campaign. I chair the message meeting, which talks about what it is we want to say and where we want to say it. I'm deeply involved in setting out the schedule. I brain-storm about the [advertising] scripts. So I've got the ability because of my po-sition and because of my brief with him to do this, I've just got to be careful to do it in a way that I don't unnecessarily irritate my colleagues."

• • •

ROVE SOMETIMES DID IRRITATE his colleagues, though whether this was nec-essary or not is open to debate. Moreover, there were obvious perils to the amount of power Bush invested in him. In 2005 and 2006, as Bush's second term began with a succession of painful stumbles, there was an increas-ing din of not-for-attribution muttering from colleagues about Rove's White House style. Some believe he meddled in the work of others, particularly when his influence increased with the departure of Karen Hughes and Con-doleezza Rice from the White House to the State Department. Some believe that his judgment faltered, as he spread himself too thin and became preoccupied with his own legal problems in the Valerie Plame leak case. Bush has spent much of his second term with low approval ratings, and under such parlous circumstances, it hardly can be presumed that the president bene-fited from the advice of an all-knowing ambidextrous sage.

Certainly, the next president would want to think twice about following the governing style that Bush and Rove fashioned in the White House.

But whether to install your campaign adviser in the West Wing is a deci-sion that belongs only to people who actually win the presidency. The record in elections at least seems clear—the way to win is to have a strategist who knows how to shift from one subject to another, with equal expertise.

MACHINE POLITICS

★ ★ ★ ★ ★

AT AGE THIRTY-ONE, Karl Rove was a man in love. A quarter-century later, he still struck a wistful tone when describing the object of his affections. She was temperamental, prone to breakdowns. And she didn't come cheap. Rove paid a quarter-million dollars for his cherished first Hewlett-Packard computer. The compatible laser printers cost another hundred grand apiece. Within a few years, these bulky contraptions would seem primitive. But at the time, the technology was wonderfully exotic, and even more wonderfully effective. The computers and printers worked in tandem to send out fundraising and "voter contact" materials that were personalized, with the recipient's name sprinkled throughout the appeal. Or they could be used to print absentee ballots with everything filled out—for a straight Republican ticket—so that all a person had to do was sign his name and return the postage-paid envelope.

This equipment was an audacious purchase for the young founder of a brand-new business in early 1982. But Rove had the money. The people who joined him as investors in Rove + Co. believed that, when it came to start-ups, flying first-class was better than coach, and that it was preferable to have too much capital than too little. (Nor did they ever have occasion to regret their investment. Rove was fond of boasting that when he finally bought his partners out, a dozen years later, they received 100 percent annual return on their original money.) The Hewlett-Packard mainframe was nearly as big as an office desk, and in rapid succession Rove bought more of them, along with several HP desktop computers. When the desktops broke down, Rove took them for repair to a young college dropout named Michael Dell, whose little walk-up shop on Austin's Guadalupe Street near the University of Texas campus was more humble than the multibillion-dollar computer empire he would go on to build. Tending to the mainframes was a bigger challenge. Eventually, Hewlett-Packard had a service technician assigned solely to Rove + Co. By the mid-1980s, however, HP began losing some of its edge. As more of the computing power moved to desktops, Rove became an Apple Macintosh man, at the time the new thing.

For most of his career, Rove was a man in search of technology's new, new thing, in Michael Lewis's phrase. He was among the very first people to use e-mail in the 1980s. At the advent of the Internet, when only Al Gore (and a few other people) knew about the Information Superhighway, he registered the domain name www.rove.com. He was compulsively multitasking long before that word became a cliché, and recent years did not tame his addiction. His BlackBerry and mobile phone allowed him to carry on multiple conversations during meetings and, at least once, while giving a speech to the Manhattan Institute.

This facility with the instruments of the Digital Age was more than a hobby. There are lots of people in politics who share Rove's fascination with gadgetry. But there are very few who have harnessed that interest to a larger awareness of the way that technology has changed the nature of political communication. There is a direct connection between that hulking HP in Rove's Austin office and the election-night surprise that greeted John Kerry in 2004, when the most effective voter turnout in the history of the Democratic Party was surpassed by an even more effective GOP turnout operation, the latter planned in Rove's White House office and executed by his subordinates at the Republican National Committee, at the Bush-Cheney reelection headquarters, and by allied groups throughout the country.

Rove spent a career living by this Trade Secret: *The way to win elections is to be first in adapting new technology, and putting that technology at the center of your political strategy.* This may sound prosaic, but there is no way to overstate its relevance to Rove's success. His campaigns always had the most advanced gizmos. And he used them in ways that made the basic transaction of politics—persuading individual voters to act one way and not another—more efficient and more productive.

No Democrat we know would dispute this. This scarcely proves the proposition, of course. Politics is filled with envy. Perhaps the most common belief among all breeds of partisans is that their side has better ideas but the other side has better skills. The opposition always is more proficient in the pursuit of power. One person who believes this is Hillary Clinton. For years, she has complained privately about the Republicans' technological superiority. In this case, envy is based on reality. When it comes to technology, the Democrats' bark has always been worse than their byte.

With no significant interruptions, this Republican advantage has prevailed for decades. The Republican National Committee typically has been a full election cycle ahead of the Democratic National Committee in technologically driven tasks, such as collecting and mining data on names, addresses, e-mails, and issue preferences. Every DNC chairman in recent years has taken office promising to end this imbalance. So far none has done it. Meanwhile, for thirty years, Rove's career was emblematic of—and in recent years was a driving cause of—the GOP's technological edge.

This advantage has historical logic. Republicans are more nimble in embracing technology for the same reason they are more adept at the new politics of the Freak Show. Conservatives were at a disadvantage in the old order, so they had more incentive to abandon it. Conservatives prospered when they could escape mass media and speak in more targeted fashion to their sympathizers. This was true of direct mail in the late 1970s and early 1980s, talk radio in the late 1980s and early 1990s, and the ascent of the Internet and blog culture in the late 1990s and early part of this decade.

Rove naturally had a conservative's sympathy for technology as a tool to communicate without going through the Old Media filter. His direct mail experience also gave him another critical insight: Politics is won and lost at the margins. Successful operatives obsess about small percentages. Technology gives one mastery over those small percentages. Before faxes became commonplace, and years before e-mail, Rove was insisting that his clients install Quip machines—a sort of private telegram service—so that the proposed copy for his mailings could be shared back and forth. This was quicker and cheaper than using overnight mail delivery. He was also an early user of modems—very, very slow modems—to transmit large amounts of data. A mailing list might begin transmitting at 11:00 P.M. and not be finished until six the next morning. Nevertheless, that put him a day ahead of the competition. In one space of his brain, Rove calculated the accumulation of all those marginal advantages gained through the finest equipment.

By using computer programs to organize his mailing lists, likewise, he might find that a planned mailing of 100,000 could be trimmed to 93,000, by identifying people who had moved out of a district or state. (Even more important was finding the new people who had moved in.) Additionally, overhauling the lists so that they included nine-digit ZIP codes was a worthwhile expense, since it saved money later on postal rates. These were seemingly small things, hardly glamorous, but in Rove's line of work they were the difference between a profitable business and a struggling one (and often between winning elections and losing them). Over time, Rove's business went from billing about $8 million a year with twenty-two employees to billing $22 million a year with eighteen employees.

Those early years also gave Rove an appreciation of another insight: Data is cumulative. What you learn in this election cycle will be invaluable in the next one. In 1999, Rove reflected on the technology that had shaped his career. "The power of the computer is marvelous," he rhapsodized, "and the cost of computer power is small, and you can over time build files that have lots of information on them about people's past preferences, and prejudices, and living patterns."

All this, in Rove's mind, had vast implications for how power is distributed in a society. He became a student of the impact of the personal computer, which he believed was almost by definition an instrument that favored conservatives: "I mean you are sitting there with a little laptop that has more computing power on your lap than the Manhattan Project had in all of its far-flung apparatus. Suddenly, you have a sense of power. You can find things, move things, manipulate things, the way the computer allows people to do it. It gives you a sense of your relevance and your power and your influence, and diminishes that of all big things, whether it's a big company, a big union, or big government."

To stay current with the direct mail business and other campaign crafts, Rove for years pored over such specialty publications as *Advertising Age* and *Communication Arts*. He speaks with obvious enthusiasm whenever recounting how he solved a problem, made a buck, or won a race through the clever marriage of art (his campaign's message) and science (the latest technological advancements).

Rove's interest in the power of technology, needless to say, was not strictly intellectual. Twice during the Bush years, his understanding of the way technology can be bonded to political strategy has changed history.

The first time was in 2002. This was the year of the "72-Hour Project," the name Rove and his team gave to an intricately orchestrated effort to turn out Republican voters in the last three days before the congressional midterm elections. The 72-Hour Project had its origins in Bush's close call of 2000. Rove had expected Bush to achieve a comfortable victory of perhaps a few percentage points. Needless to say, that did not happen. Bush's defeat in the popular vote spawned a two-year effort by Rove to understand what had gone wrong and to make sure it did not occur again. Part of the diagnosis was that religious conservatives, regarded as one of the vital organs of the Republican base, did not come to the polls in numbers nearly as robust as Rove had projected. There were different explanations. Among the most common was that the revelation, late in the campaign, that Bush had been charged with drunk driving in the 1970s, had left this constituency cool. Whatever the reason, the result highlighted a disparity between the parties. Democrats had what Republican operatives called a mechanical turnout model. Labor unions and African-American churches tended to push Democrats to the polls regardless of who was on the ballot or what was on the news. Republicans, by contrast, had a *motivational* model: GOP-leaning voters turned out only if they were turned on. Rove's aim was to power the traditional motivation effort with a technological system that could be virtually guaranteed to produce votes on Election Day.

That is exactly what he did in 2002. But first he had to defy some old assumptions. Until recent years, voter turnout has been a clumsy exercise. Fieldworkers devoted most of their efforts to neighborhoods that voted overwhelmingly for their own party. To go into neighborhoods where political preferences were more balanced was inefficient, and it risked energizing the opposition's voters as much as one's own. What is more, in the era of mass media, fieldwork was considered the rump end of the political horse—like direct mail, not as glamorous as communications and advertising strategy. Rove had two insights. The first was that the voter-targeting tools he had used in direct mail could be employed in new ways. He did not have to guess which houses in a given neighborhood were Republican or Democratic. Databases made it possible to know with increasing precision behind which doors lived potential supporters. The second insight was that, as mass media was becoming fragmented, political fieldwork was poised to enjoy a revival. The 72-Hour Project involved massing thousands of volunteers to drive the Republican vote. Since television commercials were no longer as effective as they were a few years before, the most valuable voter communication was from one neighbor to another, or from one church member to a fellow parishioner. The 72-Hour Project's intensive research on an assortment of 2001 off-year campaigns showed this type of human contact was decisive in turning out the vote.

From start to finish, Republicans spent an estimated $200 million on the 72-Hour Project in 2002. It was worth it. Democrats were routed on Election

Day. Bush's popularity and his standing on national security issues, just a year after 9/11, were still then quite high. Nonetheless, every historical trend indicated that a president's party should *lose* ground in Congress during the midterm elections; with two exceptions, that had been the case the previous 126 years. Instead, Republicans picked up seats in both chambers, winning back control of the Senate and expanding their margin in the House. To Rove's great satisfaction, the party also won seats in the state legislatures.

By 2004, there was no way Democrats would be caught napping on the importance of voter turnout. The party that year decided that the way to beat Rove was to emulate him. With an emphasis on employing the most up-to-date equipment, it set out to build its own turnout operation on behalf of John Kerry. The Democratic Party was aided by ostensibly independent groups, such as America Coming Together, funded by organized labor and liberal tycoons like Peter Lewis and George Soros. In Ohio and other states, the party and ACT sent hundreds of paid workers, armed with Palm Pilots, out on the streets to recruit and register Democratic voters. The idea was to gather data in the field, then get it back to a central location for processing and analysis. The original goal in Ohio was to ensure that Kerry received 2.6 million votes, a figure presumed to be large enough to win the state's twenty electoral votes. In the end, Kerry polled 2.7 million votes in Ohio, 600,000 more than Gore got four years earlier. The only problem: Bush received more than 2.8 million votes. Once again, in Ohio and elsewhere, the Republican machine supervised by Rove proved superior. Once again, technological facility was a major reason.

Bush's campaign invested millions mining commercial databases. Combined with the campaign's own polling, the data illuminated the electorate like never before. Some of what Rove and his team learned was predictable. Republican voters were more likely to watch Fox News than were Democrats, and more likely to drink beer or bourbon than brandy. But who knew that homes with caller ID were more likely to be Republican dwellings, or that people who liked to gamble leaned Democratic? This information was dissected and processed until the campaign had arrived at thirty-two different categories of voters, each with its own signatures, including income levels and preferences in television shows and magazine subscriptions. Different categories had different "anger points," be they late-term abortions or out-of-control legal awards. Such elaborate profiling allowed the campaign to speak to voters, through mail, phone banks, or neighborhood door knocking, with tailored messages. An electorate of 120 million people, sprawled across a continental nation, no longer looked like a giant mass of humanity. The Bush campaign instead saw specific individuals, living at specific addresses, who could be coaxed to the polls with specific appeals. This was an unprecedented advance. The hard-to-please Democratic team of Begala and Carville wrote of the Bush campaign's targeting of receptive voters that it's hard "to overstate how remarkable this accomplishment is."

Bush's presidential campaigns gained advantage through technology in countless other ways, such as trading rough-cut versions of campaign commercials on the Internet among staff members and then distributing final versions electronically to television stations, allowing rapid changing of the ad "traffic" to respond to circumstances. Beyond voters, they also built communities through e-mail and the Internet to inspire and provide incentives to donors, volunteers, and election workers.

These achievements were not exclusively Rove's. But they bore his imprimatur at every turn. One thing successful political operatives do is infuse an entire campaign with their values. In Little Rock in 1992, everyone from the interns to Bill Clinton himself had adopted James Carville's ethic about the importance of rapid response: Never, ever let an accusation go unanswered. In the Bush political world, a generation of young operatives is now schooled in Rove's view of technology.

Most of Rove's candidates, including and especially Bush, have been well funded, and spent as needed on technology. But money can't (necessarily) buy you the right machines or give you the experience to deploy them in the most effective way. In the end, for all his mechanical expertise, Rove understood above all that the impersonal 0s and 1s must be put into service to inform, organize, and inspire actual human beings.

During the summer and fall of 2003, when Howard Dean's campaign was flying high, Dean's team invested in some fairly advanced voter outreach tools focused on people as well (including creative ways to build crowds, promote events through the website meetup.com, and raise money). In fact, an incalculably large portion of Dean's success was based on the creative use of technology to engender human communities at the grassroots level. The focus was, quite smartly, on the Internet. Every campaign in the next presidential election will have a World Wide Web strategy, and perceive the Internet as a way to raise money and contact voters. But gaining technological advantage means more than that, as Rove demonstrated.

What will be the right tools to use in the 2008 campaign? Less than a year from now, the senior campaign staff of the next president of the United

States will have to make some capital expenditure choices about what to invest in to win first a party nomination and then the general election. Most certainly, there will not be much of anything on their shopping list with the physical bulk of Karl Rove's vintage early 1980s Hewlett-Packard. But the choices likely will be just as fateful. George Bush was confident his 2000 campaign was being orchestrated by someone who would make sure he had the best of everything. For the 2008 candidates, the process starts not with the acquisition of hardware, but when the politician says to the prospective manager, *What technology do we need to win this race?*

MAKE YOURSELF THE CENTER
OF THE INFORMATION UNIVERSE

★ ★ ★ ★ ★

IN 1973, a young man named Bob Cupp met a young woman named Libby Cochran during a long drive from Ohio to Missouri via Indiana.

In 2004, George W. Bush secured a second term in the presidency by beating John Kerry by 118,599 votes in Ohio.

These two facts, separated by thirty-one years, are related. Cupp's road trip and Bush's victory in Ohio mark points on a long path, winding but continuous, of friendship, politics, and serendipity that mattered more than a little in 2004. The common element is Karl Rove.

Before the explanation, a question: What was a president of the United States doing in Lima, Ohio, on April 24, 2003? Ohio, of course, has long been a key presidential battleground state. But Lima has not previously been an important field in that battle. It is the seat of reliably Republican Allen County, a small town of just 40,000 people (comedienne Phyllis Diller and former 20/20 television anchor Hugh Downs were both natives). There are no big cities nearby. Even the medium-sized ones are a haul—Toledo is a ninety-minute drive to the north, Dayton a ninety-minute drive to the south.

Bush was in Lima because Rove thought it was a good idea. Much of this book is about communication, the new ways in which politicians reach voters and wage arguments in a frenzied age. But part of effective communication is a matter of information, specifically, the information that will answer two questions: *What people are willing even to consider listening to a particular candidate? Where can these people be reached?*

Candidates in 2008 who wish to emulate Rove's record of success must find a strategist who will follow this Trade Secret: *Be at the center of the information universe.*

• • •

EVERYONE KNOWS A person who is at the center of his or her own particular information universe. Such people are routinely the first ones at the office or in the neighborhood to hear some interesting piece of news. They are always online, and always respond quickly to e-mails. They are fun to talk to. When you give them a piece of information, the appreciation is profuse and genuine, and the reward is usually a juicy tidbit in exchange. After a while, they do not have to work as hard to get information. The pipelines flow on their own, from a network of information feeders. Ask such a person the all-purpose question in an information-soaked society, *What's going on?* and they invariably have a worthwhile reply.

Rove is one of these people, only his universe is unusually large and the stakes of his information are highly consequential. In politics, *What's going on?* (or, if it is a James Carville query, *Wazgoanun?*) is at all times the most important question. A campaign will stand or fall on its ability to learn and react to new developments. Rove's status at the center of the information universe was a derivative of two other Trade Secrets discussed elsewhere in these pages. Rove was at the center in part because of his wide circle (*Know a Lot of People*) and because he used technology, e-mail most of all, to maximize his productivity (*Machine Politics*). In combination, they allowed him to make a virtual science of determining which of the countless people encountered during his three and a half decades in politics were worth cultivating and would provide him with the best knowledge. This group serves as a personal intelligence network, part early warning system, part idea generator, and part political force-multiplier.

One of the few articles written about this aspect of Rove's career was by *Washington Post* writers Thomas B. Edsall and Dana Milbank. The story detailed how Rove—"methodically and ambitiously"—built a "web of contacts" around Washington and around the country to keep himself in the loop. The article listed an astonishing inventory of politicians, operatives, special interest leaders, and conservative academics with whom Rove stayed in frequent contact. There were some obvious names in Rove's constellation, like the ubiquitous anti-tax advocate and conservative power broker Grover Norquist. Likewise, Dirk Van Dongen, the politically attuned president of the National Association of Wholesaler-Distributors. But there were many more surprising ones, such as California interior designer Katie Boyd. And, much to the puzzlement of political Washington, the article noted that Donna Brazile—the woman who ran Al Gore's presidential campaign—also trades notes with Rove. Republican pollster Ed Goeas, one of the regulars in Rove's Rolodex, likened these contacts to a "radar system" constantly probing for information, trying to learn "what's sticking and what's not sticking."

Years after it ran, the piece still plainly bugged Rove when it came up in conversation. The irritation was not that that his private network had been exposed. His complaint was that the article suggested that Rove's core group was about 150 people. Actually, he noted, it was far greater than that; there were many names that Edsall and Milbank would have no way of discovering.

One of the names they did not know about was Bob Cupp. A 1973 graduate of Ohio Northern University, Cupp's relationship with Rove dated back to Rove's bid to be national College Republican chairman at the Lake of the Ozarks convention in 1973. (A lesson in Rovology: If you come across a Republican who seems to love or hate Rove with special intensity, and has harbored these feelings for more than the past eight years, chances are there will be a Lake of the Ozarks angle.)

"He was the Ohio College Republican chairman in 1973," recalled Rove, "and came to the convention in Lake of the Ozarks to vote for me and has been my friend ever since. In fact, on the way to the convention we asked him if he'd do us a big favor. We'd lined up the Indiana vote, a little girl named Libby, and we asked him if he would take a detour and pick her up and drive her down to Lake of the Ozarks. So he went by Ball State and Muncie and picked her up and drove her to the convention with a carful of other College Republicans. And . . . they've been married for 30 years."

With their bond established in such a personal way, Rove and Cupp stayed in touch through the years. Cupp became a state senator, and then an Ohio state judge. Rove appreciated his friend as someone who knew the score in Ohio, especially when it came to the politics of northwest Ohio. So he paid attention early in 2003 when Cupp got in touch and urged that Bush start courting the rural precincts of his part of the state. Rove viewed Cupp as a friendly purveyor of reliable information, so Cupp's suggestion moved to the top of the metaphorical pile of advice that people who run presidential campaigns get all the time.

Bush was popular in northwest Ohio, Cupp said; the campaign should try to capitalize on that. But most presidential candidates did not campaign in these small towns. There were far too few votes to be found in such places. Rove, however, believed that maximizing Republican votes in already GOP-leaning areas like Allen County offered the best chance to offset what promised to be record Democratic turnout in Cleveland and the other urban areas of northeastern Ohio. So Bush went to Lima. He appeared at the Lima Army Tank Plant, talked about taxes, and the war in Iraq (which still supplied a good applause line on the stump). As Cupp predicted, the reaction was ecstatic.

The Bush campaign, of course, did not base its Ohio strategy on the e-mailed hunches of some old friend of Karl Rove. The campaign began with extensive analysis on the data from previous Ohio elections (from elsewhere in the information universe). Cupp's recommendation carried weight only after campaign officials determined it was borne out by the numbers. In 2002, incumbent Republican governor Bob Taft had performed especially well in northwest Ohio. That suggested there was a Republican vein to be mined, with the right approach.

Still, the seed was planted by Cupp's early proposal. As research and data reinforced the idea, Rove drew on his trust in Cupp's judgment to keep pushing forward an Ohio strategy that emphasized an aggressive effort in the northwest.

Bush never stopped mining. All through 2003 and 2004, he traveled by Air Force One and bus caravan into places that had not seen a president in decades, if ever. There may have been fewer voters in these locales, but they were paying more attention. In a small media market, a presidential visit would generate news for days—in advance of the event, live television coverage of the event, and stories for days afterward reprising the event. In larger cities like Cleveland or Columbus, by contrast, Bush and Kerry became such familiar presences that voters and journalists alike grew blasé. Each trip would get a story in the next day's paper, and that was about it. Meanwhile, those small towns add up if you stop in enough of them, as Bush and his surrogates did constantly for two years.

Traditional political wisdom holds that Democrats win in Ohio if they rack up big victory margins in their stronghold Cuyahoga County, home of Cleveland, and also eke out a majority in Franklin County, home of Columbus and traditionally a major swing area for statewide elections. Kerry did both—and a lot more.

But Bush's margins in western Ohio were part of a winning plan. Around the state, Bush in 2004 increased his percentage of the vote over 2000 in virtually every rural county. Of the ten counties where vote performance increased the most, seven of them were in western Ohio. Democrats were stunned that boosting the vote in places like Mercer, Shelby, and Van Wert counties—all near Lima—was enough to offset Kerry's powerful performance in the urban areas. But Bob Cupp was not surprised.

SECTION VII

★ ★ ★ ★ ★

LEAVE NOTHING
TO CHANCE

★ ★ ★ ★ ★

DAILY PLANNER

★ ★ ★ ★ ★

PERCHED ON A STOOL at the counter of Madden's Family Restaurant in Derry, New Hampshire, in June of 1999, Karl Rove seemed more like a local businessman catching a cup of coffee than a man in charge of a presidential campaign. Although his friend and boss, George W. Bush, had entered the restaurant and was working the crowd, Rove remained in his seat talking. The governor of Texas was on the third leg of his very first trip as a presidential candidate and was enjoying the heady rush of irrefutable success. The tour had begun briskly in Iowa, moved to Kennebunkport, Maine, for a classic Bush campaign photo op (George and George and Barbara and Laura, oceanside at the gracious family compound), and ended up, naturally, in New Hampshire. Everything, including this diner grip-and-grin, was being chronicled by a media horde far larger than any recent presidential press corps.

Under the circumstances, one might have expected Rove to concentrate exclusively on the candidate he had spent years preparing to launch, or on the minute-to-minute dynamics that drive most fledgling presidential efforts. Instead, Rove was poised on his stool, explaining with fierce conviction to a reporter the macro-strategy of the Bush campaign. Spirited and confident, he detailed how Bush not only was going to win the Republican nomination, but also how he was going to be positioned to emerge in the spring of 2000 as a powerful general election candidate. Although Rove clearly was holding back some of his cards, it was obvious this was stuff that the strategist had thought through thoroughly, and for a long time.

Between joking with the waitress and entering into his Palm Pilot the name and phone number of a would-be supporter he met in the diner, Rove outlined his own "four primaries" which he envisioned Bush tackling over the following months. Separate from the actual voting, Rove identified these conceptual contests as the primaries of money, reassurance, substance, and party leadership.

Rove appeared distinctly unimpressed with the other Republican presidential contenders. He viewed the four primaries as a way for Bush to introduce himself to the American people, establish himself with the Chattering Class, and prepare for what would inevitably be a tough general election fight. Along the way, of course, Bush would secure his party's nomination. Not a mortal lock or a foregone conclusion, in Rove's telling, but just one of many details that had been carefully mapped out.

Almost immediately after Bob Dole's loss in the 1996 presidential race, the Republican Party began looking for the anti-Dole: someone charismatic, from outside Washington, modern, likable, and a great political athlete. Bush's poll numbers, name identification, record in Texas, and fund-raising strength made him an accidental front-runner without lifting a gubernatorial finger. But before too long, Rove knew, a more purposeful effort would have to be launched.

Rove's master plan first was laid out privately in a PowerPoint presentation he wrote in early 1999, while Bush was still committed to remaining planted in Texas until the end of the state legislative session. Rove had composed countless elaborate memos and sketched out schemes during that period, but this document was particularly high-concept.

First, Bush had to win what Rove called the money primary. The conventional wisdom at the time stated that any serious candidate would require $20 to $25 million to compete effectively for the nomination. Rove surveyed the field, examined the inherent fund-raising strengths Bush possessed as a big-state governor and son of a former president, and decided that, with the exception of multimillionaire Steve Forbes, Bush would conquer the money primary without difficulty. Eventually, his expectations in this realm were mightily surpassed. In one of Rove's few miscalculations of the campaign that had a happy ending for his candidate, Bush proved himself to be the preeminent political fund-raiser in the nation's history.

The second contest Rove envisioned was the reassurance primary. Voters in Iowa, New Hampshire, South Carolina, California, and other crucial early voting states, many of whom had never met Bush, nor heard him give a speech, had nonetheless watched as their Republican leaders made pilgrimages to Austin and promptly signed on as supporters of the campaign. Bush's familial credentials and adulatory press clips no doubt served as effective calling cards; yet Rove knew the key was for Bush personally to shake as many hands as possible, appear in cogent on-message photo ops, and send the word to voters that he could be trusted. Bush already boasted unprecedented poll numbers; now he had to back them up by giving voters a sense of who he was, why he wanted to be president, and, as Bush himself liked to say, what was in his heart.

The original President Bush had been trounced in 1992, and left office with many disgruntled party members muttering damning critiques. Yet his reputation, and, along with it, the "Bush Brand," had been burnished during the Clinton years, when disapproving Republicans witnessed the White House overtaken by unchecked staffers, a troublesome Democratic agenda, and personal scandal. Memories of George H. W. Bush's refined demeanor and gilded ties to the idealized Reagan years trumped the recollection of his awkward defeat and his failure to win many conservative victories. All that, Rove believed, would reassure voters of different types. There were plenty of ways to parade the newcomer, and Rove envisioned Bush trying just about every one of them.

The third primary was that of substance, which would come only after Bush had completed the reassurance phase. Reporters clamored for detailed answers to policy questions even before Bush officially entered the race, but Rove knew that in due course Bush would deliver a series of complex policy speeches (three on education, one each on social services, foreign policy, and defense). Although it became conventional wisdom that Bush was not specific on issues, these speeches—particularly those on education and defense—were more definitive and substantive than typical campaign fare. They were based on consultations with some of the leading policy experts in the party, with whom Bush spent hours and whose credentials and experience conferred on the candidate a sense of seriousness in the eyes of many members of the Gang of 500. Those reporters who cared to ask were given background briefings and abundant supporting material, coinciding with the speeches.

The final primary was the battle for the party leadership. Bush began the contest with a sizable base among the country's Republican governors, but throughout the year, he swept up an array of weighty endorsements, often backed by meaningful voter turnout potential, of the kind that even Bush's father had not secured as a sitting vice president in 1988. The dominance of the leadership primary was nearly as great a triumph for Bush as his supremacy in the money primary.

There were bumps and twists and spins along the path to the Republican nomination, including Bush's inability to name the leaders of Chechnya, India, and Pakistan during an on-camera interview with a television reporter; persistent questions and halting answers about past drug use; some fallout when he dodged a debate with his rivals in New Hampshire; and, most significantly, when he lost that state's supposedly decisive primary to Senator John McCain by a staggering 19 percentage points.

In retrospect, however, Bush's win was relatively easy as such things go. The dynamics of contested party nomination fights demand that the front-runner be brought down to earth at least once. But after every stumble, the candidate recovered. Much of the credit for that goes to Bush's skills, as well as to the strong staff he had assembled.

But the careful preparation of the campaign's chief strategist was also critical. The formal launch of Bush's effort had gotten off to a later start than Rove would have liked, but years of plotting ultimately paid off. Bush deserves credit for this as well; he insisted on early and comprehensive planning to create a first-class operation and ensure extensive flexibility. But Rove's execution far exceeded these instructions. Without question, Bush did the delegating and Rove did the strategizing. Asked once what Bush would say if asked about the theory of the "four primaries," Rove replied after just a beat, "He'd say, 'That's Karl's bullshit stuff.'"

• • •

ALL HALF-DECENT PRESIDENTIAL campaign strategists have a concrete sense of what goals must be achieved to win a given election. They also have an idea of how to achieve those goals. But there is a smaller subset of strategists who, at the beginning of a campaign, think through every specific step required to win.

The major elements of such plans include the timing of the candidate's various pre-announcement announcements, exploratory committee announcements, and formal announcements; group and individual endorsements; candidate and major surrogate travel; personnel; fund-raising targets; week-by-week message emphasis; major policy speeches; advertising schedules; debates; the calendar of primaries and caucuses; and convention scheduling.

Rove is of course within the most elite group whose campaign planning includes this level of detail. But the Trade Secret in this chapter is not *Advance planning is a good idea.* That might be a trifle obvious.

Rather, there is a cluster of key Trade Secrets that allowed Rove to develop and execute his long-range plans. In 2008, these sub-Secrets will be important to replicate. According to the model employed by Rove and his Bush colleagues, they include:

• *Get agreement from the candidate, the candidate's family, and senior campaign officials that planning is indisputably good and that good plans, once developed, should be followed.*

In the topsy-turvy world of presidential campaigns, strategists are under enormous pressure to change course on a dime in reaction to external events. Most campaigns are unable to resist such pressures, which come from a variety of sources: the candidate himself; factions within his senior staff; the candidate's precocious (or petulant) child; the candidate's well-meaning (or meddlesome) spouse; the candidate's enthusiastic (or unruly) sibling; unforeseen news events; or, most commonly, attacks from the other side. The statement "Daddy, the consultants don't know what they are doing" is not reason enough to alter strategy. Sometimes, as Rove demonstrated, circumstances dictate making a deviation from the master plan, but only rarely, only in as limited a manner as necessary, and only in a way that preserves every possible inch of the original blueprint.

• *Hire senior campaign strategists who also believe in planning and empower them to do a good job, so you will not eventually feel compelled to fire them.*

The success Bush achieved based on Rove's construct for his initial presidential campaign would have been forgotten had the candidate done what even many of his staffers assumed he would do and dismissed the bunch of them after his New Hampshire primary loss to John McCain. Instead, Bush kept his team together, including Rove, and they stayed the course, adhering to, with a few adjustments, the roadmap that Rove had drawn in Austin.

• *Develop strategy with input from all the campaign's major players, so everyone has a stake in success.*

At the beginning of both the 2000 and 2004 efforts, after soliciting recommendations from a range of sources, Rove presented to Bush and his colleagues thematic and scheduling overviews of how the campaigns would unfold from beginning to end. At points along the way, senior officials were convened to review where they stood on budgeting, advertising, debates, and other major issues. These meetings were important occasions to provide updates, but they were just that—updates about how the original plan, which they all had endorsed, was rolling along.

  • *Campaign planning should be driven by the rationale of the candidacy, with the schedule geared to communicating the rationale—not to the mechanics of who travels where when.*

Too often, campaigns let the intense burden of logistics, interest group demands, or hidebound tradition dictate their movements. Sometimes these factors need to be considered, but they should not drive decisions. In 2000, the Bush campaign emphasized putting the candidate in front of the right voters and conveying his motivation for wanting the job.

Bush took the White House for many reasons. But the contrast between Bush and the opposition in terms of making a plan and sticking to it was pronounced, and maybe determinative.

• • •

AL GORE MADE numerous errors in his campaign for the presidency, but the failure to start planning early enough was not one of them. In fact, even before Gore and Bill Clinton were reelected in 1996, the vice president's politically minded staff was mapping out a 2000 run.

When campaigning for his own ticket and for other Democrats around the country in 1996, Gore followed a strategic design in which he collected chits, built ties to interest groups, and got quality time in states vital to his future. Having helped secure another term for Clinton, Gore's team was thinking about how to use their remaining time in the White House to position their man for his own presidency.

So almost immediately after the reelection, Gore's political advisers put together a memo entitled "Long Range Planning" that laid out the tasks they felt needed to be accomplished before the first formal battles of Iowa and New Hampshire, three years hence.

The final product was anchored by a fifty-two-page overview dated April 18, 1997, that was described as "the beginning of a plan designed to put you in the strongest possible position should you decide to run for President." Along with the core document, Gore was given a thick binder of original research, a series of practical decisions that needed his immediate attention, and copies of early planning memos from past Democratic campaigns.

In retrospect, the advice distilled into these documents was pretty darn good. Much of it echoed exactly the lessons that the Bush campaign had gleaned from studying previous elections. Almost every factor that ultimately contributed to Gore's failure to take the White House in 2000 after eight years of peace and prosperity was identified right away by the Gore staff as a problem he needed to surmount in order to win.

But despite the clear detection of these land mines, Gore ignored the Trade Secrets that could have saved him and that allowed Bush's campaign to plow forward on schedule at almost every stage. Naturally, the Democrat's campaign followed some of the plan set forth in the memo, but even a casual observer of Gore's 2000 effort, first against Bill Bradley in the nomination battle and then in the general election against George W. Bush, would notice more than a missed stitch or two.

Among the advice Gore got:

- Presidential campaigns failed when staffers "were poorly coordinated, they undercut each other's decisions, and no one knew who was 'in charge.'" (*Ask any of Gore's multiple campaign chairs, managers, spokespeople, and five pollsters how he did on this score.*)

- Campaigns won when "four or five trusted advisors were given a great deal of responsibility over campaign operations." (*See above. Also: Look up the definition of "trusted."*)

- The core campaign team "should be experienced, empowered to make decisions, trusted by you, and able to get along with one another." (*Some members of the Gore campaign did not trust or get along with the empowered Naomi Wolf, the feminist author who secretly gave Gore colorful advice about his wardrobe and masculine bearing before her role was exposed.*)

- "Past campaigns teach us two important lessons about message: (1) if you run, you must have a message about why people should elect you President of the United States, and (2) it must be integrated into all you do. . . . We need to make sure that our scheduling choices are as driven by message—what we are saying to whom and who will hear it—as they are driven by the policy demands of being Vice President and the political demands of visiting key states." (*Gore's awkward straining as he tried to find positions on the return of Cuban child-icon Elián González to his homeland and the proposed release of oil from the Strategic Petroleum Reserve to help alleviate high gas prices did not provide a decisive message of leadership.*)

• "In a contested primary, you cannot get to the general without winning the base vote constituencies in the early primaries, but we must never let a primary strategy undercut our ability to win the moderate votes who would matter in a general election." (*Gore's proposal to require a pro-gays-in-the-military litmus test for members of the Joint Chiefs of Staff certainly didn't help beat Bush.*)

• "Answer the question: What is a Gore Democrat?" (*The world still waits.*)

• "By June of 1997, have in place a program for regular, casual, intensive contact with members of the press . . . to insure that they continue to see the relaxed and open side of you. . . . Such meetings are an important part of restoring the good will between you and the press." (*This one is too silly to warrant a comment, except to say that Gore's formerly positive relationship with the media was a disaster throughout his presidential bid, with the word "stiff" competing for space with the word "phony."*)

• "Every effort must be made to resist talking insider baseball with reporters." (*We blame ourselves.*)

• "By December 1997, review proposals for a possible book [that] would be a Gore Manifesto for the 21st Century." (*OK: Gore probably should be glad he didn't put out something called a "Gore Manifesto."*)

• Rebuild political standing in Tennessee as a " 'home town' favorite," because people there seemed to consider "you now more of a Vice President of the United States than a guy who comes from their state." (*Apparently, on Election Day 2000, Tennesseans still felt that way when they handed their electoral votes to George W. Bush.*)

Most of the staffers Gore hired and fired during his long campaign would agree that these best-laid plans were not executed. As Bush political operative Terry Nelson said about the difference between campaigns that just make plans and campaigns that actually follow them: "Unless there is a system, where you . . . follow up, it's just a thought, and at the end of the day a thought doesn't win a campaign."

• • •

AT THE BUSH campaign, there was a more systematic approach: Draw a roadmap and then actually follow it. For the 2000 campaign, the "four primaries" was just one element of Rove's overall vision. Even before Bush gave the green light to begin plotting out how a run would work, Rove produced documents that eventually were made part of presentations to Bush and his other senior advisers.

Rove constantly back-timed from Election Day, using calendars filled with every detail of what needed to get done (in what sequence and when). Like his colleagues in the campaign, Rove seemed to be hurtling from meeting to meeting, loaded down with hourly and daily tasks and responsibilities. Unlike them, he was able to think about every aspect of campaign preparation as well. Rove's colleagues recalled a few decisive moments in both 2000 and 2004 in which he unfurled intricately detailed blueprints that spelled out the course the campaign would take.

In the early summer of 1999, one of Rove's *aha!* moments had the appearance of being ad hoc. Gathered in the concrete-walled conference room in the offices of Maverick Media, the Bush advertising team, Rove and his colleagues were meeting to outline some initial ideas for the campaign's message. The session began first thing in the morning and was supposed to include substantial give-and-take. Mark McKinnon, who had worked on Bush's advertising in his 1998 gubernatorial reelection effort, made an opening ten-minute presentation.

Rove listened quietly and then took the floor after McKinnon was done. He drew by hand with an ink marker on an easel-mounted pad a list of some themes and strategies for Bush to run with, giving his colleagues a forty-five-minute lecture. As he spoke, Rove wrote:

1. PHILO/NEW LEADERSHIP/DIGNITY/CHARACTER/ RESP.

2. COMP. CONSERVATISM/DREAM FOR EVERYONE

3. FAITH BASED/RALLY ARMIES OF COMPASSION

4. PROSPERITY PURPOSE
   (ECO. BRIDGE)

   5. EDUCATION—HIGH STANDARDS, RESULTS

   6. STRENGTH FOR UNCERTAIN WORLD

   7. SUCCESSFUL GOV/NEW KIND OF LEADER

   8. GENERAL REPLY

   9. SPECIFIC REPLIES—TAXES, ETC.

  10. MOMENTUM/3RD PARTY

  11. ASKING FOR ORDER

As he sketched out his diagram, Rove drew arrows from item 7 to item 1, and from item 4 to item 2.

Translated, the chart read:

   1. Bush would present himself as a candidate with a distinctive philosophy, who was not part of the failed Washington Republican leadership of the 1990s or someone who reflected a Clintonian lack of "responsibility."

   2. Bush's campaign would center on a series of optimistic inclusive signature phrases ("compassionate conservatism," "new kind of leader").

   3. The injection of faith and religious institutions into the delivery of services to the needy would appeal to spiritual conservatives, with crossover appeal to many traditionally Democratic groups.

   4. Economic growth proposals would be injected with both a higher meaning and a sense of universal applicability.

   5. Bush would make education policy a centerpiece of his campaign, undermining the Democrats' dominance of the issue by stressing national standards.

   6. Even before 9/11, for Bush's first campaign, Rove branded a phrase that foreshadowed the focus of his reelection, with an emphasis on the Republicans' traditional strong suit: "strength for an uncertain world."

   7. Bush's Texas record of legislative accomplishment through

bipartisan cooperation would appeal to an electorate interested in changing the tone in Washington.

8. On many of the peripheral attacks that came Bush's way, the campaign would avoid getting into specifics, rising above the fray with general answers.

9. But on issues near and dear to the hearts of voters, the campaign would be ready with on-point responses.

10. Bush would build momentum by gaining the validation of endorsements from people and groups cast as independent of the campaign.

11. "Asking for order" was an odd Texas way of expressing one of Bush's own personal Trade Secrets. A voter had once told him that he had not cast his ballot for Bush in his 1978 House race because the candidate had never explicitly asked for his support. So Bush resolved to ask regularly and directly.

There was nothing purely original in what Rove proposed to his colleagues. In fact, that was the strength of his presentation. In a short list, he had synthesized Bush's message from his gubernatorial days, along with the national arguments and rationale he had started to tease out. If you look at the major moments of Bush's campaign—his announcement speech, his convention acceptance speech, his advertising, and his debate performances—all of them reflected the themes that Rove summarized that day on his chart.

The meeting had been scheduled to go several hours, through lunch. It ended as soon as Rove had finished speaking.

• • •

STARTING IN LATE 1997, Rove had begun researching ballot access and other election issues, caucusing with major party players, attending Republican and national governors meetings, and burning up phone lines and modems out of Austin. For Bush's gubernatorial reelection in 1998, Rove initiated an intense grassroots appeal to voters of all parties and demographics to win as large a share of the vote, overall and from specific groups, as he could. The outcome was never in doubt against Bush's weak Democratic opponent, Garry Mauro, but Rove knew Bush's attractiveness as a national candidate would be enhanced if he demonstrated wide support from women, Hispanics, and African-Americans. He also arranged the campaign so Bush would

emerge with an issues mandate (on education, taxes, crime, and welfare reform) and a reputation as a politician with an agenda. Finally, he knew Bush
would need a national fund-raising base to run for president, so he moved the
candidate around the country—New York, Boston, Greenwich, Kansas City,
St. Louis, Los Angeles, San Francisco, Washington, and Denver—to raise
funds, but also to build up a lush donor list of more than twenty thousand
names.

Bush's trips produced something besides money. "What it generated,"
Rove explained, "was a huge steady stream of people saying we want to
come talk to you about running for president." Indeed, groups of movers and
shakers began arriving in Texas to offer their support.

Rove organized trips to Austin for clusters of fund-raisers and then politicians, groups that eventually reached thirty-five people at a time. Rove handled the logistics of escorting groups to Austin ("I was the tour director," he
joked), while Bush worked his charm on the eager visitors, usually in the Governor's Mansion. Bush managed to squeeze in only a few of these gatherings
before his reelection, but they began in earnest immediately in late 1998.

Bush, although ostensibly still undecided about entering the presidential race, empowered Rove, Joe Allbaugh, his campaign manager, and Karen
Hughes, his communications director, to do whatever was necessary to keep
the option alive. While Allbaugh and Hughes mainly were occupied with
running the governor's office and preparing for the second term, Rove was
working virtually full-time to put together a turnkey presidential-campaign-
in-waiting.

Finally, in January, around the time of his second inauguration, Bush gave
the go-ahead for Rove to look seriously at how a presidential operation would
be structured. Rove spent the end of '98 and the beginning of '99 engaged in
concrete nuts-and-bolts planning, somewhat complicated by Bush's commitment to remain at home until the legislative session ended on May 31. One
of Bush's top volunteer recruits, veteran Republican lawyer Ben Ginsberg,
advised Rove on what steps could be taken without Bush having a formal
campaign.

Finally, on March 2, 1999, Bush officially announced his decision to form
an exploratory committee, for which Rove conceived one of the most successful events of the 2000 presidential cycle, and a paradigm for a campaign
kickoff. On March 7, a Sunday afternoon, a large delegation of national
media gathered in Austin at the Convention Center to watch as Bush was

praised by the ten members of his exploratory committee. The committee members were not chosen casually. In order to utilize the megaphone of what was sure to be major national media attention, and to demonstrate the breadth of Bush's support throughout the party and the country, Rove assembled a geographically diverse group that spanned the breadth of the Republican Party: three women, two African-Americans, a Hispanic, some pro-choicers, and members of the Establishment. With staging from Karen Hughes, the event drew huge press coverage. The *New York Times* the next day ran a front-page photo of Bush surrounded by the faces of minorities and women, with the headline "Bush Tests Presidential Run with a Flourish." In his accompanying story, political reporter Richard Berke described Bush's "grand pageant of political might," as the new candidate flaunted his "different kind of Republican" emphasis.

The event also signified the kickoff of Bush's full-blown fund-raising effort. From the day Bush announced the exploratory committee, the astonishing capacity of the campaign and the candidate to attract money was manifested each day in the number of checks that poured in. Rove did a huge first direct mail solicitation, and commented, "We knew virtually the moment the money started coming in. . . . We had a lot of people around the country who were revved up." Rove would get spreadsheets faxed to him daily showing the totals, and it was soon clear that the goal of $25 million for the year was far too modest. The campaign raised a breathtaking $7.6 million in twenty-three days from a standing start without Bush attending a single fund-raising event.

A human face was put on the effort on March 20, when the core group of Bush's financial supporters in Texas gathered in Austin's Palmer Auditorium for a finance meeting. The attendance of eight hundred people would have constituted a very successful turnout for the other candidates had it been a fund-raiser, but for Bush, it was a chance for his home state backers to get competitive about who was going to raise the most for the campaign in the coming year. The event was for serious money people. Rove remembered: "I've never seen anything like it in my life. . . . Now the price of admission is, you've got to agree to raise and give a total of $10,000. So you've got 800 people in that room. That's $8 million that those people" represented.

For all this success resulting from careful plotting and scant competition from a weak field of candidates, there were a few times Bush and his campaign were tested, bringing into question their readiness for big-time national politics. Senator McCain's shellacking of Bush in the New Hampshire primary had some old Washington hands doubting Rove's competence, both for his original scenario and for his capacity to adapt to changing circumstances.

But Bush stuck by Rove and his whole team, and in short order they dispatched McCain and the rest of the field. Yes, Bush was the son of a president, but Rove had leveraged many advantages and leapfrogged over other candidates with more national political experience. All according to plan.

• • •

FOUR YEARS LATER, in the more formal setting of the White House, Rove had moved from marker on paper to a DVD. It was February of 2004, and most of Bush's crew had a bit of whiplash adjusting from their long-held assumption that Howard Dean would be their opponent to the prospect of facing John Kerry. Although Rove had shared the expectation of Dean's nomination with his colleagues, he also had made certain that the research, thematics, and strategy were ready in case Kerry somehow pulled it out. Dean's campaign collapsed in December and January, and Kerry was the one.

The Bush campaign had decided that no matter whom the president faced, the major themes would be "strength," "trust," and "values," along with "steady leadership in times of change," harking back to 1999's scrawled "strength for an uncertain world."

Against Dean, the contrast was going to be "steady" versus "unsteady." The research on Kerry suggested a different contrast: "steady" versus "inconsistent." But there was much to be agreed upon regarding how to approach Kerry and, now that there was a de facto Democratic nominee, regarding how Bush should gear up the more public and explicit portions of his own campaign.

So on a weekday at 11:00 A.M. in the White House's Yellow Room, it was time to roll out the big ideas for the approval of President and Mrs. Bush, Vice President Cheney, Chief of Staff Andy Card, Communications Director Dan Bartlett, and a handful of others. After some technical difficulties, Mark McKinnon screened rough-cut versions of the proposed initial five television advertisements, which Rove had already approved. There was a bit of discussion about them. *Was the mention of the weak economy too negative?* some wondered. Without much ado, the group accepted about 85 percent of the text and look of the ads.

Now it was Rove's turn. He loaded up his DVD, the culmination of years of thought about how to get a conservative Republican president named "Bush" reelected. That process had started before George W. Bush even took office in 2001. Now Rove presented an integration of themes, sequencing, free and earned media, and schedules for the Bushes and the Cheneys, all laid out month by month straight through Election Day.

Rove's presentation, which lasted just short of an hour, was a tour de force. Many of those present looked at one another, stunned by the level of sophistication and amount of work involved, even by Rove standards.

When he was done, the room sat in silence as the president asked a few questions, mostly about scheduling. Eventually, 80 to 90 percent of what Rove laid out that February day was enacted as part of Bush's successful re-election race.

• • •

THE CAMPAIGN'S SENIORMOST officials met every few months to keep tabs on how Rove's strategy was being carried out. At one of the first meetings of the so-called G9 high command, featuring the campaign's nine top advisers, in early 2004, they reviewed a series of PowerPoint slides laying out their fundamental goals. Two things stood out about that presentation. First, the campaign put an explicit emphasis on the virtue of organization. Among their "Underlying Principles" were "state-of-the-art campaign" and "leverage economies of scale." They wanted a "seamless campaign from spring through election day" that would be the "best organized presidential campaign" ever.

The other striking quality was the degree to which the campaign met its objectives, from its "Message Phasing" (*March–May: Define Kerry and key issues. June–July: POTUS world leader, Kerry on defense. Post–Democratic Convention: Progress vs. Pessimism. Fall: Choice on WOT [war on terror], economy, values*) to its tactics, political goals, and deployment of resources.

The ground game—the work of the field operatives and volunteers in the states—was devised from the lessons learned from 2001 onward, as Rove's operation conducted test after test to determine what worked and what did not. The vaunted 72-Hour Program produced a plan for not just the last three days before Election Day, but an overall design intended to get all the parts in place in time for a strong push at the end that would match the Democratic-friendly AFL-CIO unions and other liberal groups in their mechanical turnout.

• • •

IT IS IMPOSSIBLE to measure with precision how much planning Rove and his colleagues did in their two presidential campaigns compared with other modern efforts. But there is no doubt that the nation's first MBA president insisted upon organized campaigns, and that in both cases he got them, allowing him to win two elections he arguably should have lost.

Ask senior officials in most presidential campaigns "What are you doing next week?" and the honest (and actual) response will be "Next week? We don't know what we are doing the day after tomorrow." Bob Dole famously and frantically looked at maps of the United States on his presidential campaign plane, making midair decisions about where to fly next to try to pull out a victory, according to writer Richard Ben Cramer.

Of course, the Bush campaigns, even the more organized 2004 version, did plenty of last-minute scheduling and other deviations from Rove's original vision, as events demanded. But the early overviews guided Bush's campaigns, informed by experience, and years of American history.

Have the Electoral College on the Brain

★ ★ ★ ★ ★

UNLESS THE 2008 PRESIDENTIAL ELECTION is an Electoral College blowout, the chances are the outcome again will be determined by a handful of states in the Great Lakes–Mississippi River region (Ohio, Michigan, Iowa, Wisconsin, Missouri, Minnesota), the near West and Southwest (Arizona, New Mexico, Colorado, Nevada), Pennsylvania, and Florida.

In a competitive election, the Republican nominee will take the solid South and the Plains states, while the Northeast and West Coast states will go for the Democrat. Forty-seven states, plus the District of Columbia, voted for the same party in 2004 as in 2000. Unless one party nominates a candidate who is pure poison or a candidate who is a true powerhouse, it is difficult to imagine even a dozen of those states being dislodged from their current Red/Blue slotting.

Whether the battlefield ends up being this small or not, presidential campaign strategists who take their eyes off the finish line of 270 electoral votes for even a moment are fools. In crafting a candidate's message, schedule, endorsements, hiring, paid and earned media strategy, and policy rollouts—in every decision a campaign makes—nothing should ever preempt the compulsory sole emphasis on reaching that magic number.

On the stump, many politicians rhapsodize about how America is similar from place to place: how the good people of Arizona have a lot in common with the good people of Ohio, for instance. It is an old and often effective way to simultaneously pander to the locals by demonstrating that you understand their daily lives and principles, and establish you have the right sensibility to unite the country into one friendly, values-laden entity.

But most candidates and strategists don't think beyond the throw-away line to ponder the more important point. For the purposes of winning the presidency, knowing what is *different* about Arizona and Ohio is far more important than knowing how they are *similar.* Karl Rove and Bill Clinton recognized that each state has distinctive po-litical rhythms and rules informed by unique cultural, economic, and administrative histories.

And if you are someone who has been dreaming about winning the White House from your earliest days on earth, each state is like a puzzle piece on a child's map of America, with the number of elec-toral votes stamped in big digits right beneath the state's name. Spend your life mastering the Trade Secret of what makes Ohio dis-tinctly Ohio and you have a better shot at winning its electoral votes when the time comes.

That means considering and understanding every state's econ-omy, history, legislative balance, media, interest groups, dominant personalities, demography, and political trend lines.

And it means knowing about each state's culture and traditions in ways that do not at first glance seem strictly political. *How big a deal is the state fair? What about the annual pumpkin festival? Which local sports teams are more a way of life than a casual pastime? What do they grow, what do they manufacture, and what do they export?*

Show Karl Rove a map of any electorally vital state, and he will sweep his hand over it, pointing out the regions and pockets from which a Republican majority can be drawn. So "this part" of New Mexico "right here" is "Little Texas," with a populace indistinguish-able from the voters who put Bush in the Governor's Mansion. And "that part" of Minnesota is filled with people who own guns and snowmobiles, whose cultural affinity with Al Gore or John Kerry would be *de minimis.* Come within a certain percentage of the Democrat in "these suburban areas" of Pennsylvania and you "can't lose" the state's electoral votes. Easy as an America-shaped pie.

Attention, 2008 candidates and campaign strategists. Once you are appropriately focused on the overall attitude required to win in-dividual states (which subsequently will allow you to win the overall country), you are ready for some additional Electoral College Trade Secrets:

- Today, right now, bookmark on your Web browser a site that has an "Electoral College Calculator" and play with different combinations day and night. Practice, practice, practice, until the answer to the question "What states do you have to win if you lose Michigan, Pennsylvania, and Iowa?" is as automatic as the answer to the question "What is 5 + 5?"

- A candidate's announcement speech should reflect not just what motivates the person to seek the highest office in the land, but (not coincidentally) what the general election message will be. Go back and read what Bill Clinton and George W. Bush said in their respective announcement and convention speeches, and you will see clarity and continuity prompted by an obsession with the Electoral College. John Kerry's announcement speech was written and rewritten based on competing drafts from rival campaign factions and based on short-term pressures applied by Howard Dean's then-front-running effort.

- As early as you can, move as many potential battleground states as possible from "toss-up" or "leaning" your way to "solid" in your favor. This will allow you to save your resources, especially the two most important—candidate time and paid media. The Bush campaign did this with West Virginia, Missouri, and Arizona in 2004, and it made a big difference.

- Have an expansive view of what states are in play, with an eye on changing demographics and recent voting patterns.

- Look at states that recently have been won by the other party at the presidential level but which feature sitting governors of your party. Ask yourself (a) if you can replicate the kind of winning message that worked for those governors, and (b) if those governors have formidable political machines that they will put in service to your cause.

- Find ways to draw media attention simultaneously in multiple battleground states for a single event or trip. The Clinton-Gore 1992 bus trips drew blanket coverage in several states at once, with local media turning every stop into a three-day story

(*They're coming! They're here! There they go!*). Al Gore did the same thing with a boat trip in 2000. George W. Bush and John Kerry borrowed the bus idea in 2004 for trips through the Midwest. Dangling "exclusive" in-bus or on-boat candidate and spouse interviews in front of local television stations is a surefire way to garner even more coverage.

• While stretching the Electoral College playing field as much as you reasonably can, do not waste resources in states that are indisputably out of reach. Bill Clinton's romanticized attachment to the mango ice cream at San Antonio's Menger Hotel from his days working on George McGovern's Texas campaign somehow convinced him he could win the state in 1992, and he spent time and money there on a lost cause. The Bush campaign wasted millions in 2000 trying to win California.

• Do not let the candidate overreact to one poll (or one well-meaning, woozily optimistic friend) suggesting a singularly elusive state is somehow suddenly winnable.

• Hire as your battleground state campaign managers people who (1) the candidate and the national chief strategist respect and trust implicitly; (2) have managed past winning presidential campaigns in that state, or at least in one of comparable size; (3) have strong working relationships with the senior elected state officials from your party; and, (4) for 2008, were born before the Beatles broke up or man walked on the moon.

• Micro-target negative messages to battleground states in which your opponent's well-liked national positions are unpopular. Many of Al Gore's 2000 stands on guns, tobacco, and the environment were widely endorsed nationally, but were a toxic mix in West Virginia. The Bush campaign made certain that the state's voters were bombarded with communication laying out Gore's views, without having to make those assaults part of its national message.

• Know the visages, names, frailties, vanities, and career histories of each state's three most influential newspaper and wire service reporters. If the state has full-time television political reporters, memorize their stats, too, plus how they prefer to be addressed at press conferences.

• If you are the Republican nominee, have a detailed plan on how you are going to minimize the public whining of your California financial and political supporters while limiting the resources you spend there.

• Win your home state.

KNOW MUCH ABOUT HISTORY

★ ★ ★ ★ ★

KARL ROVE KNOWS his American political history and drew on its lessons to win the White House. Everyone in politics retains concepts from previous campaigns, but mostly from the recent past, and not systematically. Perhaps they remember how things were done during their last two or three assignments, and the successes and mistakes of their party's latest presidential efforts. More organized strategists make time before a campaign heats up to solicit the views of "old hands"—grizzled political veterans who provide ad hoc tips. But an average campaign strategist is too busy putting out daily fires, too distracted protecting turf, and too dismissive of the power of the past to pay history much mind.

Starting in the late 1990s, Rove regularly grilled his party's most experienced presidential campaign strategists, trolling for data to advance Bush's cause. People such as Reagan adviser Michael Deaver gave advice on the full range of tactics and strategy. More distinctive, however, was Rove's use of formal historical models. As an intellectual matter, he is fascinated by history. As a practical matter, he wrings from the past lessons about how to achieve his goals, from the thematic to the operational.

Some of Rove's historical preoccupations are well known, such as his curious fixation on the similarities between William McKinley's 1896 presidential campaign of change and Bush's 2000 effort, and the concerted attempt to avoid repeating the mistakes that did in George H. W. Bush's reelection bid. But while these examples may be the most familiar, they are far from the only cases Rove studied while managing W's presidential portfolio.

Other modern presidential campaigns of both parties commissioned studies (such as research for Vice President Gore on how former incumbent second bananas tried to avoid slipping on the peel), but rarely with the same an-alytical rigor. In Bush's presidential races, every relevant aspect was spelled out far in advance, all with specific targets and deadlines, based on detailed studies of how prior campaigns had handled matters such as announce-ments, fund-raising, endorsements, advertising, policy development, and an-ticipated voter turnout. Not only did the studies enable the Bush team to avoid the mistakes made by predecessors, but they provided a steady flow of talking points, to defend against critics, or to brag about how well Bush was doing compared with previous candidates.

Most campaigns fly blind without this kind of research, and then scram-ble when they absolutely need it to produce some slapdash report a couple of dollars short and a news cycle late. The studies so valuable to Rove are considered a luxury by most campaigns, if they think about them at all. Op-eratives worry there is never enough time in the pressure cooker of campaign life, and that precious, ever-draining supplies of funds, personnel, and time should be spent only on the most crucial, immediate needs.

Rove was careful, though, not to over-learn the lessons of the past. Each campaign and each political fight is different, he knew, and one must pick and choose wisely from the available and appropriate examples.

While Florida's electoral votes were still being fought over in November of 2000, Bush strategist Matthew Dowd worked with a team of young volunteers to put together a report on the history of the start of the terms of presidents back through John F. Kennedy. How much did they travel, both domestically and overseas? How many policy initiatives did they launch? How many ex-ecutive orders did they sign? How many news conferences did they hold? What kind of speeches did they deliver? The report was given the simple title "First 100 Days" and consisted of individual write-ups for each president ranging from seven to ten pages.

From that analysis, completed on December 8 of 2000, and other work, Rove developed a series of insights, including a vitally important one. The concept of "the first 100 days" had become the conventional measuring stick for the Chattering Class, based on Franklin Roosevelt's remarkable begin-ning. But in fact, modern presidents largely had used the first few months of their terms to adjust to the rigors of the office and tee up policy proposals.

Rove knew that in the instant-gratification media culture in which Bush would operate, there would be a strenuous effort (particularly from the Left and possibly from the press) to stall Bush's presidency before it got off the ground by suggesting that any early setbacks foreshadowed doom (and to assert once more that Bush was not the rightfully elected president). So, before Bush even took office, Rove began pointing out that, in reality, the burst of initial legislative accomplishment for presidents typically took place over 180 days or so. He pushed this finding on reporters to try to effectively double the length of Bush's honeymoon period. Proving Rove's claim, the two signature domestic achievements of Bush's first year—his $1.3 billion tax cut and the No Child Left Behind law—both occurred after the 100-day mark, and only after protracted legislative and public battles.

Even as Rove was using lessons from the past to inform the first term of Bush's presidency, he was setting up a system to advance the president's re-election.

In 2001, Rove formed a team of professors to produce historical studies and then matched the scholars up with Republican National Committee officials to discuss the results and their potential applications. Led by Daron Shaw of the University of Texas (who had worked with the Bush campaign in 2000 as the director of election studies, examining historical data on the Electoral College and vote number targets), the group was made up of that rarest of commodities—academics who were willing to help Bush get re-elected.

Participants included the University of Maryland's James Gimpel (who was awarded a "gold medal" for finding the time to attend all of the group's meetings), James Campbell of SUNY-Buffalo, John Petrocik of the University of Missouri, Brian Gaines of the University of Illinois, William Mayer of Northeastern University, Wendy Cho of Northwestern University, and David Brady and Morris Fiorina of Stanford.

Known as the "Academic Advisory Committee," the group put together a briefing book for each meeting with short memos and carefully selected data. The RNC officials also outlined their thoughts in advance and the two sides engaged in a freewheeling back-and-forth. As follow-up, the AAC offered suggestions and critiques of what the campaign officials had presented. And some members of the RNC prompted ad hoc conversations with professors who had presented data relevant to their specific responsibilities. The essence of the project—marrying the academic with the practical—was achieved regularly, in tasks such as Gimpel's work analyzing and geo-coding voter lists (which, as all readers are aware, means using historical voting records to map the longitude and latitude of voters' homes in order to figure out how to reach them through door knocking, billboards, signs, or other communication).

The group formally convened for the first time at the Washington Hilton on November 3, 2001, to discuss "Modeling Congressional Elections, Targeting Voters in Midterms, Issues and Traits, Elections, Public Opinion and the Use of Force."

In March of 2002, the group debated "What have previous midterm elections been about?" and "What is 2002 likely to be about?" In August of that year, the topics were "Targeting and Mobilization, Subgroup Outreach, State-by-State variation." In September, it was "Reaction to the RNC's 72 Hour Plan." After the successful midterms, in December, they asked the question "Is it still a 49% nation?" followed up with "Where do the Democrats go from here?" and explored "Geographic Targeting and battlegrounds for 2004."

Rove got another research project under way in the summer of 2002, when Dowd made some discreet visits to presidential libraries to get a fuller picture of the manner and timing of decisions made by preceding campaigns. Dowd put together several binders of material after stops at the Ford, Reagan, and Bush 41 presidential libraries, along with the James A. Baker III Institute for Public Policy at Rice University, which housed the papers of 41's former top strategist.

Dowd ended up compiling books that went to Rove, White House Chief of Staff Andy Card, and President Bush in the late summer of 2002, as well as to campaign manager Ken Mehlman a little later.

Dowd investigated how previous reelection campaigns had been run (badly) and saw that there was constant friction between the White House staffs and the campaign teams. Both Reagan's relatively easy 1984 saunter to another term and Bush's ill-fated 1992 stumble to defeat were characterized by intramural fights over scheduling, message, policy, personality, power, and dueling conceptions of competence.

Dowd's caution to Rove and his colleagues was clear. What was needed was a system that would minimize conflict, miscommunication, and overlapping boundaries. So on May 30, 2003, as Bush was establishing his formal reelection campaign, Card issued to the full White House staff what became known as the "pipeline" memo. It was short and sweet, and the money paragraphs were clear:

> Campaign-related communication between the White House and the reelect campaign and the Republican National Committee (RNC) will be coordinated through the Office of the Senior Advisor or me.

Israel Hernandez is the White House liaison to the re-election campaign responsible for coordinating the Bush-Cheney '04 campaign scheduling of the President, the Vice President, the First Lady, Mrs. Cheney,
and other Administration figures. Note, however, that the actual scheduling of the President will continue to be the responsibility of the White
House Scheduling Office, as approved by me. Susan Ralston is the
White House liaison to the re-election campaign for other campaign-related
communication between the White House and the campaign. Campaign-
related communication with the Bush-Cheney '04 campaign and/or the
RNC **must** be coordinated through either Israel or Susan or authorized by
Senior Advisor Karl Rove or me [muscular emphasis in original].

Ken Mehlman, who was announced as Bush's campaign manager in the
same memo, had reached clear agreement with Rove that the campaign
would be better off if Mehlman had autonomy over day-to-day operations, including personnel, another lesson learned from the past. There were, of
course, some violations of both the "pipeline" memo and Mehlman's understanding, but far less than might be expected. The players at the top of both
organizations were very familiar with the experiences of their predecessors
and were determined not to repeat old errors.

Based on Dowd's research, the key to victory was a coordinated communications strategy, limited points of contact between the campaign and the
White House, and a set meeting structure between a small number of senior
officials of both entities. That insight led to regular sessions of the G9,
including Cheney, Card, Rove, Mehlman, Commerce Secretary Don Evans,
Karen Hughes, campaign chairman Marc Racicot, RNC chairman Ed Gillespie, and the campaign's treasurer, David Herndon. Other officials, such as
Dan Bartlett, the campaign's finance chairman Mercer Reynolds, and experts
in areas such as polling, budgeting, messaging, and political organizing,
would sometimes be present as well.

Although there will be no incumbent running in 2008, for the candidates,
the lessons are clear. *Study the past—with actual studies.* (And use Karl Rove's
versions, if you can get ahold of them.)

CONTROL FREAK

★ ★ ★ ★ ★

ONE OF THE OLDEST TRADE SECRETS in politics is: *Don't worry about what you can't control.*

But many political operatives have trouble telling the difference between what can't be controlled and what can be. Rove may be a control freak, but even he has been able to recognize when an outcome is impervious to his influence. Still, he is always looking to gain advantage by broadening the definition of what is malleable—or, at least, what is subject to meaningful manipulation.

Presidential campaign strategists have so much responsibility over so many daily issues that it may be tempting to ignore anything extraneous or beyond easy reach. But Rove and his team worked aggressively in 2000, 2002, and 2004 to control the political environment on any matter that might have an impact on Bush's future, such as ballot propositions and amendments, candidate recruitment, and state redistricting. It is impossible to determine which of these efforts had the greatest bearing on the eventual results. But close elections are won on the margins, so even the most marginal concerns were worth the trouble.

If Bob Cupp's suggestion that the president campaign for reelection early and often in the northwest part of his state helped George W. Bush win Ohio (and thus a second term), the decision to encourage Florida's Republican leadership to put a constitutional amendment requiring minors to notify their parents before getting an abortion helped win the Sunshine State and the White House that year, too.

At the time, Florida was one of the few states in the union without a parental consent or notification abortion requirement for minors. With

Florida's legislature dominated by Republicans and the president's brother Jeb in the governor's office, pro-life groups were agitating for a constitutional amendment.

Early on, the Bush campaign had conducted careful research for each of the battleground states to determine the specific process by which different types of provisions could qualify for the November ballot. After the virtual electoral tie in 2000, the Bush campaign's attitude was that whatever might even slightly enhance Republican prospects in a battleground state was worth trying.

Florida, of course, was a special case. As the Bush campaign's political director Terry Nelson recalled, "Our mindset was anything that could help us in Florida we needed to do. Even a marginal impact in Florida could be decisive," given the handful of votes separating Bush from Gore (or was it Gore from Bush?) in 2000.

Nelson, like Rove, was someone who held an expansive view of what could be influenced, but he had seen a lot of campaigns "filled with great thoughts about these kinds of things"—but without follow-through. Nelson felt the prospect of Florida voters casting ballots on parental notification was clearly in Bush's interest. It would inspire the conservative base of the Republican Party to turn out to vote. The campaign believed that the great motivator in Florida, as elsewhere, would be the presidential race. But, with their eyes on boosting every advantage, Nelson and his colleagues applied two tests to Florida's electorate and the abortion measure: *What is motivating people to get out to vote? Does this make Election Day more important to targeted voters than it otherwise would be?*

Ken Mehlman shared Nelson's instincts that the abortion measure's presence on the November ballot would help their reelection campaign. In one of Mehlman's many conversations with Governor Bush about the right strategy for winning the state, they discussed how Republican legislative leaders were interested in gaining the three-fifths majority required in each chamber to put an amendment on the ballot. The two men agreed that the move would almost certainly help President Bush win and they encouraged House Speaker Johnnie Byrd and Senate President Jim King to persist.

Starting in the fall of 2003, Heath Thompson, the Bush campaign's Southern regional political director, began the first of what would be a couple of dozen conversations with Jeb Bush's political advisers and the key players in the legislature to make sure everyone was in sync. No "strong-arming" was required, Thompson says. The campaign simply needed to make sure that "the message was delivered."

For a time, a few unrelated personality clashes, the normal complexities of the legislative calendar, and minor differences between the Florida House and Senate over how to word the amendment seemed to imperil the measure's passage. So the campaign "ran back through the Rolodex" to deal with some "grumbling about who was holding it up, but then everyone got it."

"At key moments," Thompson recalled, "the right people needed to be touched," and reminded of the campaign's view: "This sure would be good for the team and the President's party if you all could work this out. This was a priority for folks to work this out. Set aside the politics for the larger good."

The campaign's concerns were allayed when, at last, in April 2004, the state Senate, with just one Democratic vote and unanimous Republican support, passed the measure 27 to 13. As the legislative session was winding down, the Florida House worked late on a Friday night and, along straight party lines, passed the law putting the amendment on the ballot 93 to 24, all with Governor Jeb Bush's publicly declared support.

It was at least a three-fer for conservative groups, which were fired up by having the measure on the ballot. Anti-abortion forces were energized. But so were parents' rights advocates and organizations opposing judicial activism (Florida's Supreme Court had invalidated two previous laws on the matter).

Right-wing interest groups celebrated the state's chance to vote on the amendment. The statement from the Center for Reclaiming America for Christ was typical: "As Florida Right to Life cheered the passage of the bill, the usual suspects were already hard at work condemning the decision. The ACLU, NOW, and Planned Parenthood all spewed their anti-life vitriol, standing true to form."

Thompson said, "It helped unite conservatives early in the process . . . because there were some mutual goals" between the groups and the campaign.

The pro-amendment groups engaged in grassroots activism to turn out voters to cast ballots in favor of the provision, and, in many cases, for Bush as well.

The Bush campaign gained new appreciation for just how powerful an issue the amendment was when it discovered that Florida's prized Cuban-American voters seemed more worried about minors having abortions without parental notification than they were about Fidel Castro. According to Mehlman, the campaign conducted focus groups with voters in the Little

Havana section of Miami when researching its home-stretch strategy. The Bush researchers asked about some of John Kerry's past statements regarding Castro, including some presented as typical Kerry flip-flopping. They also raised questions about Kerry's position against parental notification requirements. To the surprise of Mehlman and his colleagues, the assembled voters were more exercised about Kerry's position on abortion than they were about any vacillating stance on Castro.

From that analysis the campaign and the party recognized the potential statewide potency of the amendment, and they crafted language for use in various forms of voter contact. There were multiple mailings, mass telephone calls, and radio advertising—some of which was targeted at the Hispanic community. Successful political campaigns require passion, and the parental consent issue gave the Bush side an emotional hook with which to grab voters.

On Election Day, the measure passed with 65 percent of the vote, while Bush won the state 52 percent to 47 percent. Thompson had no doubt that some of the groups supporting the measure used their focus and energy to make certain that their members came out to vote. In a campaign whose premise was to achieve a better-than-usual turnout among its partisans, he believed that the amendment got more Republicans to the polls.

Would the amendment have been on the ballot without the Bush campaign's encouragement? Perhaps. Would the Republicans have won the state's critical electoral votes without the turnout help they received from the measure's supporters and their own passionate invocations of the provision? Maybe. But Rove never had to answer those questions, and he did not have to worry about the alternatives because he got what he wanted when the legislature acted.

In other cases, as with the Florida amendment, after Rove made the determination that it was in Bush's interest for a measure to qualify for the ballot (through voter signatures, legislative action, or some combination of the two), allies were instructed, sometimes discreetly, to proceed. Resources may not have been devoted officially to the ventures, but Rove never lacked for comrades to provide the necessary funding to ensure that his wishes were honored.

Throughout his career, Rove's detailed and updated knowledge of the political climate, state laws, moneyed interest groups, grassroots power brokers, and electorate of each state allowed him to evaluate what ballot measures might channel voter turnout. Rove knew which actions and down-ballot races had the potential to swell polls in his favor (or against), and he marshaled resources to shape the most advantageous overall environment for his needs.

The anti–gay marriage provisions on various battleground-state ballots in 2004 are another example. Rove was well aware of what was being done by interest groups and local politicos to get the ballot measures qualified in as many battleground states as possible. And he was well aware that the issue was an emotional and energizing one for many voters across the country.

The White House was determined to get the anti–gay marriage measures qualified in states targeted by Rove and Mehlman, without picking up any backlash or baggage that might come from moderate voters or the Old Media. Once the invisible hand of helpful allies met the requirements in each selected state, Rove could count on interest group efforts to reach out to like-minded voters. The Bush-Cheney campaign, along with the national and state Republican Party, therefore, could use the laundered issue as part of their targeted voter contact pitches. It would carry the same kind of emotional impact (with the base and some swing voters, too) as the Florida abortion amendment.

On Election Day, there was wide majority support in all eleven states that voted on the issue, including in the battleground states of Arkansas, Michigan, Ohio, and Oregon.

Candidate recruitment was another area in which Rove long assumed an unusually activist posture. Such intercession requires a slightly different set of cold-eyed calculations than ballot measures. All White House political operations engage in candidate recruitment, but Rove's team always was systematic and aggressive. Rove believed in finding the most electable, acceptable Republican to win any given seat.

Rove learned this lesson well in Texas, when helping to change the state from a Democratic stronghold to a Republican one. The Trade Secret was simple: *Find a candidate who is a match for the constituency and the times.*

By applying this rule in Texas, Rove earned the unwarranted reputation with some conservatives for being either unprincipled or liberal. But when Rove maneuvered to get a more moderate Republican into a race, he did it in order to win as many seats as possible for his party. Having strong candidates on the ballot with Bush also could produce "reverse coattails" in which the candidates' popularity and voter turnout operations could enhance Bush's chances of impelling party-line-voting Republicans to the polls.

Rove was not reluctant to use carrots and sticks to clear a primary field for a favored choice, or to confront a potentially weak candidate with one he considered stronger. There were a few notable cases in which Rove's perceived use of mob-style tactics to effectively designate the Republican nominee surfaced in the media. In fact, Republicans say, those published reports represent only a fraction of the times Rove employed brutally firm-but-quiet (or at least private) persuasion to get his picks on the ballot.

Rove has always had a keen interest in using his recruiting leverage in races for open seats and against vulnerable Democratic incumbents. But he paid special attention to opponents whose elimination would further Bush's specific political and governing goals.

For Bush and Rove, the sweetest and most illuminating example was the 2004 contest between Republican John Thune and then Senate Minority Leader Tom Daschle of South Dakota. Daschle had become the greatest obstacle to Bush's legislative agenda through his use of parliamentary maneuvers in the Senate. He was a high-profile opponent of the White House. And the White House wanted him gone.

Bush's political team took a clinical and comprehensive view of the race from the very beginning, seeing significance beyond just the office in question. They had an appreciation for the practical, symbolic, and psychological damage a Daschle loss would have on the Democratic Party. Thune was at the time a lobbyist, having left Congress and his House seat after narrowly losing a race for the Senate against South Dakota's other Democratic senator, Tim Johnson, in 2002 (Thune had been one of the Three Amigo Senate candidates promoted by the White House that year). Rove and others convinced Thune to make another run, promising fund-raising and other assistance and assuring him that Bush's coattails would make the difference. Overcoming initial reluctance, Thune entered the race, and his eventual victory over Daschle was for Bush Republicans nearly as satisfying as the president's own reelection.

Rove took a similarly vigorous stance on other inside-baseball political battles that directly influenced Bush's standing or the future balance of political power in the United States. These included state redistricting fights, debate rules, public statements made by "independent" interest groups, and the placement of favorable opinion pieces in newspapers.

As with many Rove Trade Secrets, replicating this one requires more than following the formula, since one cannot quantify or define precisely what can be controlled. But there are some things in politics that can be measured.

METRICS

★ ★ ★ ★ ★

AMONG ALL THE SERIOUS PEOPLE involved in waging the battle for the White House in 2004, there was always an expectation that the whole bloody thing would come down to which side could register the most new voters in the battleground states.

The announcement speeches, the fights over consultants, the debates, the television ads, and the negative attacks might have gotten more attention. But everyone on both sides (the well-oiled Bush machine, the squeaky Democratic National Committee, and the chafing Kerry campaign) understood that the way to win was to increase the number of potential voters *before* Election Day, which in turn would increase the number of votes *on* Election Day.

Getting favorably disposed new voters registered and measuring the rate of progress in signing them up is part art and part science. Using a combination of campaign numbers and state-by-state data, both sides attempted to monitor how they were doing throughout the election cycle.

From Karl Rove's perspective, the imperative was clear. Bush had lost the popular vote against Al Gore, starkly illustrating the realities of the 50-50 nation. In sketching out reelection, Rove and his colleagues had convinced Bush that 2004 was going to be a "base" election. That meant that the normal presidential year emphasis on appealing to so-called swing voters would share strategic space with a Bush Politics attempt to inspire a large turnout of citizens already deeply inclined to vote for Bush.

In a conservative country, during a time of war, under a president sporting a record partially defined by an attempt to move the country so far rightward he induced intense polarization, it seemed like a smart, if somewhat unorthodox, decision. What the plan required was a concerted effort to enlist new recruits—potential voters who, for whatever reason, were not yet registered to cast ballots in November 2004.

Rove, Ken Mehlman, and Republican National Committee chairman Ed Gillespie approached this challenge the way they tackled every important political detail that could affect George W. Bush's life: with comprehensive organization and a wary eye on the opposition.

Publicly, Rove, Mehlman, and Gillespie expressed no doubt that they would win the registration war, boasting of their vast network of volunteers, the intensity of support President Bush's leadership inspired, and their smarter-than-the-average-bear focus on those people most likely to register and vote, such as upwardly mobile professionals who had moved from one community to another between elections and had not found time on their own to reregister (what with being worried about locating a new church, a good school for the kids, and the closest Starbucks).

A heavy investment in consumer and other micro-targeting data gave the Republicans confidence that they were building a system in which registration was only the first step of a process that would culminate in an actual vote cast for Bush. The Democratic efforts, they thought, were too scattershot and bound to appeal mainly to people who ultimately would never make it to the polls.

Privately, however, the members of the Bush team were concerned when they saw that the Democratic Party's characteristic disorganization was being supplemented by the well-funded efforts of labor unions and by so-called 527s, independent groups whose spending to influence the outcome of elections is largely unregulated. These groups were savvy, focusing on using portable digital technology to locate and register battleground-state voters likely to be highly motivated to get Bush out of the White House.

Mehlman, similar to Rove in so many ways as a tactician, closely monitored both Democratic and Republican voter registration even before he moved from his job as White House political director to Bush campaign manager in the late spring of 2003. Both Rove and Mehlman insisted on the strict use of metrics, their term for measuring every aspect of the campaign's performance that was susceptible to quantification. For voter registration (and a parallel effort for absentee ballot programs in states that permitted them), there were objectives for each state, county, and precinct.

While it can be artificial to apply measurable numbers to certain elements of the chaos of the political process, both Rove and Mehlman were drawn to benchmarks and goals. They recognized that instilling discipline and motivation in workers down the hierarchy is best accomplished by giving them specific instructions and achievable targets, yielded from a rational plan.

Partly in reaction to the blundering Bush 41 reelection bid in 1992, which was unusually haphazard for an incumbent's operation, and partly due to the shared sensibilities of George W. Bush, Rove, Mehlman, and the other senior leaders of the reelection campaign, registering voters for a victory in 2004 was accomplished with precise calibration. As Mehlman said in early 2004, "On a grass-roots and regional basis, this campaign is already underway," boasting of "local committees named; voter registration drives launched; millions of supporters signed up; websites and e-mail systems humming."

But just a few months before Election Day, Mehlman's public bravado was hiding some real concern. Rove had delegated to him the job of ensuring that the campaign establish registration targets and then meet them. The campaign had set goals for outputs starting in May 2003, and for the first year or so the carefully calculated program was going well. But in May and June of 2004, things changed. Their progress, as measured month to month and week to week, began to recede. In some key states, including the keyest of all, Ohio and Florida, the Democrats were producing substantial gains in signing up new pro-Kerry voters. Mehlman was in constant direct contact with operatives in the states, both because he was a Class A neurotic and because he believed interaction with national headquarters helped to inspire the troops on the ground. His sources offered reassurance. But the numbers, *the metrics,* suggested real problems.

Mehlman was not interested in reaching abstract goals. You are not guaranteed a victory just because "you can run a five-minute mile" if "the other guy can run a four-minute mile," Mehlman said. He was getting cheery monthly and then biweekly reports back from the field suggesting his operatives were meeting all of their quotas. But Mehlman also began seeing regular data demonstrating that the other side was doing better than expected in some critical states—better, in fact, than Mehlman's troops. He brought in his deputies and said he felt like a Soviet leader being given inflated "tractor production numbers."

Mimicking a Communist functionary, Mehlman would tease his sanguine staffers by parroting, "Mr. General Secretary, tractor production is up 400 percent in the Soviet Union!" Mehlman was joking, but his point was serious. The data told the story. The Bush campaign had a big problem.

Rather than just pat everyone on the back and encourage them to improve, Mehlman ordered changes. Although the Bush campaign had taken chauvinistic pride in its use of unpaid, local volunteers to perform such tasks as voter registration (compared with their opposition's use of paid staffers), Mehlman's team ordered the hiring of more workers to step up the effort, with additional compensated employees overseeing the activities of the volunteers. The campaign also acquired fresh lists of potential registrants, to expand their target pool. And they supplemented their door-to-door efforts with new direct mail pitches promoting voter registration.

At the same time, the Bush campaign comforted itself with the reminder that not all new registrants are created equal. The Democrats' efforts, they believed, were not based on a true metrics model, because there was little quality control. They were signing up lots of people, but there were indications that many were not new voters, or would not actually make it to the polls come Election Day. And the out-of-state paid workers who were handling the sign-ups would have difficulty forging a sustainable connection to those registering.

Bush and Rove did not micromanage Mehlman's efforts, but they did reinforce his natural inclination to use metrics. Both men preferred to set broad parameters for their deputies, and leave it to them to figure out how to achieve what was expected, as long as they got results and held responsible those who failed.

In fund-raising, the Bush campaign had two critical insights about the 2004 environment that expanded on their 2000 experience. First, there was a whole new crop of potential donors and bundlers, many with New Economy wealth, who were anxious to enter the world of big-time presidential fund-raising. These people were aggressive and competitive. The second insight was that both these new money types, as well as the more established ones, could be pitted against each other in a series of quantifiable contests to raise money for Bush and the Republican Party, complete with fastidiously assembled data and a system of rewards for those who performed.

Every fund-raising event the campaign organized had a specific overall target, the sum of the efforts of each individual working on that event. The perks associated with the fund-raisers were doled out based not on tradition but merit. "The old model," Mehlman explained, "is to say, 'Let's have a fundraiser and let's let the guy Mr. Big Dog who's always been the one because in 1984 Reagan stayed at his house, he's the guy that always introduces the president, let him introduce the president this time.'" Instead, the campaign gave positions of prominence and responsibility to those who actually brought in the most money.

Another area in which the campaign demanded not just measured results but the *right* measured results was press coverage. Mehlman did not care how many press releases were sent out; he wanted to see metrics that showed how much actual news coverage—the outputs that mattered—was garnered by those press releases. How many minutes on the local and national news were allotted to their candidate's ideas? How many headlines focused on the Republicans' message of the previous day? How many inches of text were printed in the newspapers?

Mehlman believed that so-called earned media was one of the areas most likely to be analyzed by "motion" instead of "progress." He said of his campaign communications staff, "Communicators are wonderful people. . . . Their strength is the clever line, the shape. Communicators by definition are good at shaping things. They're good at tone. They're not necessarily metrics-oriented people. And so when we first come up with it a lot of people are like 'We're not doing this, this is bullshit.' And the answer is 'Yes, you are because otherwise you have no idea if it's actually sticking. It could just be a lot of stuff that's not sticking, that's not connecting with people.' "

But the most important Trade Secret about metrics from the 2004 Bush campaign came before the massive efforts to register voters, raise money, or earn media coverage. Perhaps Mehlman's most profound insight about metrics, one shared by Rove, is the importance of maintaining personal contact with operatives at the local level—those people assigned to attain the goals. Mehlman had been field director for Bush's first presidential campaign in 2000, and he knew that the most common source of tension between the national headquarters and the politicians and workers in the states was resentment that "Austin" was telling people what to do without a real clue about local conditions.

So in his early days setting up the campaign, Mehlman made time to travel to the battleground states and meet with the senior elected officials, the people who had run the 2000 campaign, the top state strategists, the grassroots activists, and the resident consultants to review the 2000 and 2002 cycles and to get their input about what it would take to win the state in 2004. This gave everyone a stake in the process and the numbers.

Those discussions allowed the campaign to establish the benchmarks they expected for each state, county, and precinct in terms of voter registration, absentee ballots, and volunteer recruitment. In the 2000 campaign, if things were going badly in a particular state, Mehlman said, Austin would demand answers, and the locals would either deny that the sky was falling or claim it was the fault of the national staff. That did not happen in 2004, Mehlman explained, because "if you agree up front on the metrics, if you agree that we're going to determine how you're doing based on [metrics] and they all agree up front and you don't achieve it, it's not Washington telling you what to do, it's the goal hasn't been met."

The Kerry campaign, meanwhile, was staffed by some of the most sophisticated vote counters and targeters in the Democratic Party, such as Michael Whouley and Jill Alper. In many battleground states, they met their targets for the number of votes they thought they would need to win, in some cases far exceeding Al Gore's 2000 vote totals. The Democrats were stunned when on Election Day it turned out that their models were trumped by the Republican design. Bush's reelection was not necessarily a numerical certainty, but the Trade Secret here is elementary: *Do the math.*

MASTERING
THE FREAK SHOW

INTRODUCTION

* * * * *

THE DIE IS CAST: The next presidential election will take place in a Freak Show environment more virulent than anything Bill Clinton and George W. Bush ever faced. With sixteen straight years of polarizing presidents, new bloggers and websites popping up daily, a poisoned tone in Washington, unshackled interest groups, campaign finance laws that help channel money toward shadowy sources, fewer moderates in Congress, and the further decline of the Old Media's commitment to serious news coverage—with all that, plus a wide-open race with no incumbent president or vice president running, the 2008 election is sure to be one in which nearly every hand reaching for the brass ring will be wearing brass knuckles.

Currently, there are no institutional, technological, or individual factors that suggest a reversal of the dynamics that have created and maintained the Freak Show. To the contrary, all of these forces will continue to *expand* the incentives for extreme behavior in 2008.

George W. Bush has inspired more anger and polarized ire than any recent president, including Richard Nixon. By the end of his time in office, Nixon had virtually no supporters left. Bush, even at his low points, continued to excite intense loyalty among his partisans.

For all the negative energy that has swirled around him, Bush, until recently, rarely was a Freak Show victim. His controversies in the main were about his *policies;* he was mostly immune to the *personal* vivisection of the sort that Bill Clinton, Al Gore, and John Kerry all suffered. During his first term, Bush effectively managed the Old Media, exploiting its weaknesses, and minimizing its power over his presidency, mainly in ways that were painful for the press to acknowledge. The New Media, meanwhile, was more often his friend than his foe. He proved that it was possible for a politician to keep the Freak Show's snarling anger chained, and increase the odds that its fangs would be embedded in an opponent's throat rather than his own.

By the sixth year of his administration, Bush had lost this advantage. He and Rove were still able to use the Freak Show to define their opponents in short-term battles, but the overall narrative of his administration turned negative, dictated by the rising left-wing elements of the Freak Show, a somewhat emboldened Old Media, and, most of all, the consequences of Bush's own mistakes, involving the Iraq war, the mishandling of Katrina, and the deterioration of the uniform support of his base. The majority of Americans, according to polls, had become dissatisfied with his presidency in ways he could not control.

The unraveling of Bush's mastery of the Freak Show should not obscure the Trade Secrets of his five-year run of success, when much of the public viewed Bush on his own terms, seeing the same rugged, relaxed persona he brought with him to the White House, strengthened after 9/11 and guided by the same ideas, ideals, and agenda. He did not become a full-blown caricature. His private life never became the stuff of gossipy speculation.

This was a powerful achievement for the man who replaced Bill Clinton. There were some simple explanations. One way Bush avoided his predecessor's problems was by not inviting them directly into the Oval Office. Bush also benefited from the conservative-favoring bias of the Freak Show discussed earlier in the book. But his relative success at image control was also the result of some specific decisions he and Karl Rove made at the outset. They looked at the Clinton experience—how his presidency had been knocked about by the media and by the Washington political culture generally—and decided: *This will not happen to us.*

From 1999 onward, Bush's political operation purposefully implemented a series of Trade Secrets to insulate him from the most destructive currents of modern politics. Bush's strategy for keeping control of his public image while causing opponents to lose control of their own flowed from complex conceptions he shared with Rove and other advisers about how the modern media operated. Like other aspects of the Bush political legacy, their record in this realm was mixed. The Bush media strategy was of a piece with what we have called Bush Politics, an approach based on stigmatizing opponents and inflaming the passions of supporters. Bush Politics succeeded powerfully during the congressional elections of 2002 and the presidential reelection of 2004. But on the brink of another congressional election in 2006, the White

House was beset with problems, which included hostile media relations and lowered credibility with the public, at least in part the result of Bush Politics.

But what about Bush's original success? Every 2008 presidential candidate faces two immediate real-world questions. Did Rove's Trade Secrets for taming the Freak Show serve Bush well? And, if so, can they be copied, in whole or in part, and put in the service of another politician?

The practical answers to those questions to some extent depend on whether a candidate is a Republican or a Democrat, and whether a candidate plans to practice the Clinton Politics of consensus or the Bush Politics of dramatic change. But all candidates face roughly the same reality, one that does not necessarily serve the public interest. Surveying how Bill Clinton and George W. Bush each handled the Freak Show, a smart and realistic person considering a try for the Oval Office would think:

> As I see it, I have a choice. Do I think the Freak Show was managed better by the first president of this insane new era or by the second? Neither Clinton nor Bush avoided the Washington wars, but Bush at least consistently had a plan to deal with the Freak Show, and Clinton initially did not, and I have found that in life "having a plan" is better than "not having a plan."

Besides the changed media landscape that favored conservatives, there were other reasons Bush was not at first consumed by the Freak Show: his family pedigree, including a mother who had become an iconic and protective figure; his wife's popularity and political savvy; his innate shrewdness; and his willful restoration of the dignity and prerogatives of the office, helped along by 9/11. But most of all, Bush made smart strategic and tactical choices, executed in conjunction with his like-minded subordinates, who shared his worldview about the Freak Show, the Old Media, and executive power. First and foremost in this group: Dick Cheney and Karl Rove.

Cheney said this new arena was unruly but more fair:

> I don't worry about that aspect of negative commentary and so forth. And I guess maybe I've been in the business a long time. I can remember leaving here after the '92 election and we'd been riding high for twelve years but then we got beat. And I went home to Wyoming—initially Jackson Hole and [later a move to] Dallas. . . . During those years you had Rush Limbaugh, whose audience built and he sort of kept the [conservative] network, if you will, tied together out here with millions of people every day

who tuned in to hear Rush. During this period of time you had the development of cable networks and . . . a lot more stuff out there, opportunities,
media outlets especially broadcast and cable business, and it's not that
they're all on the right by any means, they aren't. But that there are just a
lot more opportunities; it undermined the [Old Media] monopoly.

The Bush political operation's mastery of the Freak Show was not absolute
but it played a major role in its 2000, 2002, and 2004 election triumphs.
Rove's umbrella Trade Secret was to use the Freak Show to create favorable
conditions for his side across every dimension of policy and media. In addition to maximizing the potential of the New Media, this required aggressively
moving to delegitimize and control the Old Media; promoting a shared stake
in success with political allies; insulating their side from Freak Show attacks;
and using the Freak Show to devastate opponents. In addition, Bush's Old
Media and political standing would have been even worse in his second term
were it not for Rove's techniques for manipulating the Freak Show. In the
next three chapters, we break down how Rove and his colleagues used these
methods.

UNDERSTAND AND CONTROL THE OLD MEDIA

★ ★ ★ ★ ★

IF YOU UNDERESTIMATE how intently George W. Bush watched his father's presidency, and how seared he was by the experience of a single term that ended badly, you will fail to understand the nation's forty-third president. The younger Bush shared a close bond with his father and harbored animosity toward those he thought contributed to the 1992 defeat. But he also made a systematic study of the older man's errors and learned many important lessons before he began his own run for president. This certainly included what he thought about the political press.

Some of his most famous early flashes of public anger were directed at journalists who had written harsh things about his father (such as Margaret Warner, the *Newsweek* reporter who authored the famous "Fighting the Wimp Factor" magazine cover). His basic attitude about Old Media journalists was that they were an Eastern elite, liberally biased against Republicans; they were scandal- and process-obsessed; and they were most easily neutralized by a courtship consisting of clubby nicknames, controlled candidate access, and daily dog-and-pony shows. So when he became a presidential candidate, George W. Bush shrewdly hid his fury; he understood that as long as the Old Media held substantial power in the electoral process, it was not in a candidate's interest to challenge its members directly.

Bush and his political team determined to live a double life during the 2000 campaign. In private, they shared much of Richard Nixon's critique of the Old Media; while in public, they were all about doling out pet names ("What's up, Poncho?"), harmlessly chatting on the campaign plane ("Hey, Glen, how did the Red Sox do last night?"), and staging fun-to-cover choreographed events (Bush tosses a football around with teenagers!). There were occasional naked bursts of their true feelings ("There's Adam Clymer—major league asshole—from the *New York Times*," Bush said into a microphone he did not know was live. "Oh, yeah, he is, big time," replied Dick Cheney.). But mostly the campaign followed Bush's disciplined lead.

Bush and his staff did not let their view of the media become a great internal psychodrama (unlike Nixon and Clinton). They simply dealt with reality. One truth they understood was that the Old Media, particularly the television networks, continued to have considerable influence over the information the public learned about the candidates. The Old Media might be losing viewers and readers, but it remained the most efficient way to reach tens of millions of voters. (The rise of the New Media notwithstanding, this still will be the case in the 2008 campaign.)

While Karen Hughes and others were formally in charge of Bush's communications operation, Rove always played a central role in those elements of press relations that concerned the Freak Show. In 1999, Rove was like Bush: possessed of a traditional conservative view of the left-leaning bias of the Old Media; dogged in looking for ways to get a chosen message before the voters without going through a hostile filter; and eminently knowledgeable about the press and the pressures it imposed on political campaigns.

By November of 1999, Rove said he already believed that the media was "more interested in covering . . . [campaigns] as a sports contest than it is as a high-minded political debate. . . . [T]here is an incentive in the current process that forces campaigns inexorably into a focus on . . . gaffes, attacks, scandal, process, and polling."

Six years later, Rove reflected on how much the media landscape had changed from the time of Ronald Reagan's reelection in 1984 through Bush's second run in 2004. Recalling a conversation he had with Reagan image-maker Michael Deaver, Rove said it was like "talking to a guy who was from the Stone Age. Because he would say, 'we had one [photo opportunity] picture, you know one message [a day]. . . . And I thought, 'God-dang, think about all the content demand that there is [now], and all the competitive pressures.' "

Rove knew how important it was for candidates to keep the press as favorably disposed toward them as possible. So he mostly followed an adaptation of the Trade Secret from *Bambi* (and John McCain): *If you can't say something nice about the press, don't say anything at all.*

Rove rarely briefed campaign or White House reporters formally or made himself available to the traveling press on Air Force One or in media filing centers on the road. Still, despite his low profile and routine avoidance of most reporters, he understood how they operated. He shared the view that many reporters were ignorant of history, easily intimidated, often lazy, and overly susceptible to an assured argument from a powerful source in a position to know what he or she is talking about.

Rove was fully aware of how to control the press during campaign season. Even in the fractious realm of presidential politics, Rove's usual emphasis on avoiding discord in the midst of a race (whenever possible) extended to media relations. Rove followed simple rules for dealing with political journalists, even if he usually delegated the tasks: Be accessible, be prepared, and give them something to cover. In the White House, except during Bush's reelection process, of course, responsiveness and accessibility were a low priority, to put it mildly, for Rove and his colleagues, although former Fox News commentator Tony Snow was hired as press secretary in May 2006 in part to alleviate ill will.

Rove was a believer in creating the *appearance* of candidate access, such as Bush's visits to the back of the campaign plane in 1999 and 2000, and his frequent short question-and-answer sessions during photo opportunities in his first term. In his second term, in the face of sinking poll numbers and diminished Freak Show effectiveness, Bush began to make himself more accessible through an increased number of press conferences and supplemental private meetings with select White House reporters.

In 2000, the team took advantage of controlled contact and Bush's discipline (along with the press's lack of discipline and Al Gore's lack of political skill) to avoid giving specific answers regarding the details of Bush's Social Security plans, tax cuts, or military record. This was useful in getting Bush elected.

• • •

TWICE AFTER COMING to Washington, Rove delivered public speeches on the role of the press. For these occasions, Rove set aside the predictable conservative critique of liberal media bias. Instead he focused on a more academic assessment, making arguments that Bill Clinton would have no trouble endorsing. Both Clinton and Rove have praised the 1993 book *Out of Order,* by Harvard professor Thomas Patterson. Patterson argued that the press had failed to serve the public interest in American presidential campaigns by emphasizing tactics, strategy, and horse race story lines over substance. Rove clearly concurred, but he couched his criticism in softer language. "These are indeed remarkable, challenging and historic times," Rove told the American Society of Newspaper Editors in 2003. "Such times demand the best of us. That is true for those of us serving in government, and it is certainly true for all of you serving in the media. As a member of a Republican administration, it may surprise you to learn that I have confidence in both institutions."

In March of 2005, with Bush safely reelected, Rove gave a speech at Washington College in Maryland in which he focused on the press as a polarizing force. It was a scholarly and meticulous dissection of the Freak Show, particularly how its ethos has taken over the Old Media under pressure from the New Media. The press, he contended, is drawn to conflict: "They cover it, they encourage it, they provoke it, and once it occurs they high-mindedly condemn it. . . . They lament how polarized and uncivil and unserious our politics has become."

As Rove explained it, four things caused this acidic polarization in the media: "an explosion in the channels of communication"; "an even larger increase in the demand for content by those channels"; "the competitive pressures these two factors create for working journalists"; and "the oppositional attitude of the press."

Rove described the pervasive impact of the Internet, along with wire services, cable TV channels, AM talk radio, and other forms of the Old and New Media. These outlets treated news as a far more perishable product than they had in the past, in which "a cult of the new" led reporters and their editors to move constantly "to the next big thing" with the desire to "get it first" outweighing the need to "get it right."

In the aftermath of Vietnam and Watergate, Rove stated, "the press underwent a transformation in attitude. Reporters now see their role less as discovering the facts and fair-mindedly reporting the truth and more as having been put on this earth to afflict the comfortable—to be a constant thorn in the side of those who are in power, whether they are Republican or Democrat."

Rove made many valid points in these speeches, but it is unlikely that he expected the Old Media would take heed, elevate its performance, and improve its reputation. The evidence suggests that Bush and Rove *welcomed* these shortcomings, and hastened the diminution of the press's public standing.

Once in the White House, Bush authorized Rove and his associates to empower and take advantage of more friendly media and protect his Republican administration from the depredations of the Old Media. Hardball tactics included secretly paying conservative commentators such as Armstrong

Williams to spread their message; distributing government-produced video press releases in the style of television news pieces, blurring the line between journalism and propaganda; and singling out by name reporters and news organizations for condemnation, with Bush, Cheney, and top administration officials personally offering stinging commentary. A major component of this enterprise was predicated on further undermining the status of White House reporters and the political press in general.

Bush's political team was certain that the behavior of the press corps at the televised daily briefing was reinforcing the impression that journalists "don't represent the public any more than other people do," as Andy Card once said. In fact, many Bush Republicans believed that reporters were less representative of the public than most any other group, and looked for opportunities to make that point to their base and to a wider, sympathetic audience.

As Pulitzer Prize–winning *Los Angeles Times* media critic David Shaw wrote in 2005:

To the Bush administration, journalists are not surrogates for the American people; they're just another annoying group of lobbyists, special-interest pleaders seeking not the information necessary for citizens to make intelligent decisions but only the journalists' own ego-gratification, career advancement and ideological advantage.

Shaw also wrote, channeling Rove and other Bush strategists:

The way things have been going lately, the media may decertify itself. Just look at any of the recent public opinion surveys showing a steady decline in public confidence in the media. The media have already done far more to damage their own credibility than anything the White House has done or could do.

The cast of recent journalistic felons is by now too familiar to require yet another roll call, but their serial fabrications and plagiarism clearly betrayed their colleagues, their profession and our society. . . .

The last time I checked, President Bush didn't dictate wall-to-wall coverage of Michael Jackson, Martha Stewart, Scott Peterson and Chandra Levy.

Dick Cheney, too, has weighed in on the remade media landscape—in his view, at once more substantive and more Freakish, with the Old Media monopoly shattered.

I think it's one of the things about the New Media if you will, I think they present a tough challenge to the traditional press because they are more content-oriented. And a lot of what has gone on in the past in terms of traditional coverage of the White House, you guys love campaigns and you love covering campaigns and it's great to be in New Hampshire two years before the primary up there at the Wayfarer Inn at the bar, throwing them down with [longtime *Baltimore Sun* reporter] Jack Germond, talking about what happened back here in the '80 primary. That's just sort of a natural function I think from a lot of people who cover the White House, we're political junkies or we wouldn't be in the business we're in.

But I do think that a lot of the—sometimes it's pretty trashy, but a lot of the discussion and debate on all the shows that are out there now gives you more time for substance. If you go on Fox News—the Brit Hume show in the evening—you've got a panel at the end of it. It's got a guy like [Charles] Krauthammer on there, or [Fred] Barnes and [Morton] Kondracke, and it's a great part of the show. And it's substance-oriented, oftentimes. Or you'll have an issue on there that may take ten minutes on a story. You never see CBS or ABC or NBC on the evening news do ten minutes on a story. And again I say sometimes it's pretty trashy, sometimes it's about, you know, the kids locked in the car trunk . . . there's a lot of trash that goes out there as well too. But I guess I'd put the proposition that there's more time and opportunity for policy discussions and debate than there used to be.

· · ·

WHILE THE WHITE House's attempt to create reality by proclamation may have been troubling, the Old Media's inability to respond to this effort and vindicate its own standards was even more disturbing.

Bush's first two press secretaries, Ari Fleischer and Scott McClellan, seem to have been instructed never to make news from the podium at the White House daily briefings except on the rare occasions when an attack was needed. At a morning session (known as "the gaggle") with reporters early in Bush's first term, Fleischer's responses to a series of questions delineated quite nicely the limits of subjects he would address. Asked about something that had gone wrong the previous day, Fleischer demurred, saying the matter was in the past and the administration preferred to look forward. A bit later, a reporter inquired about some ongoing Middle East negotiations; Fleischer said that since the talks were in progress, he wanted to wait to comment until the issues were resolved. Toward the end of the session, the press secretary was asked about an upcoming event. No, Fleischer would have no comment on this either, since he did not want to speculate about impending or hypothetical matters. So it was pretty clear: Fleischer was available to comment about everything, except topics pertaining to the past, present, and future. Bill Clinton's press secretaries quaintly thought they worked for both the president of the United States *and* the American people. Fleischer and McClellan did not operate with any such mixed loyalties. Instead, they were part of a concerted effort to break the Freak Show dynamics that swamped the Clinton White House by employing Trade Secrets as coldly uncompromising as they were obvious. The appointment of Tony Snow was an implicit acknowledgment by the administration that perhaps they had gone too far.

Bush Politics thrives on finding the weaknesses in the opposition and hammering on them unrelentingly while energizing allies, who get turned on by the sight of the hammer going up and down and the sound it makes on impact. Rove and his colleagues inherited a weakening Old Media press corps and they used Bush Politics to further alter the dynamic and establish more favorable conditions, which prevailed until things soured after the 2004 reelection, when these same Trade Secrets stopped working and backfired with a vengeance:

- *Break through to the base by speaking to Old Media allies, such as conservative columnists Fred Barnes and Bob Novak, and to receptive New Media.*

- *Break the spirit of the Old Media by not returning its telephone calls, by putting reporters on notice when they exhibit independence of action or thought, and by refusing to respond to most questions with real answers.*

- *Break the back of the Old Media by allowing its members to flail away at the daily briefings.*

- *Break the code of the Old Media by taking advantage of its institutional weaknesses, general disorganization, and less experienced members.*

- *Then break the rules that every modern president has followed and do not give a rip about the approbation of a Washington Establishment anchored by the media.*

The Bush administration's leading lights could have been honored every night at one fashionable Georgetown salon or another if they had wished. But Rove said he spent his time worrying about Georgetown, Texas (population 36,462), rather than about the tony Washington neighborhood of the same name, an easy jog from the White House. Why take or return the telephone calls from the *Washington Post*'s beat reporter when nothing in your psychic, cultural, or tactical universe compels you to do so? Rove and his colleagues recognized that the real power lay in their hands, and that media gibes were rarely more than mere nuisance.

As Cheney chuckled wryly, "I tune in to Imus most mornings when I'm shaving and I can recall the day . . . he's talking about somebody called 'pork chop,' and I always remember that—he's talking about me. I'm pork chop. And I laughed like hell. But I also think, you know, when you start your day watching Imus there isn't anything that can be said about you during the day that's as bad as what you can hear first thing in the morning when you've got Imus on at six o'clock."

Al Gore and John Kerry insisted they felt the same nonchalance as Bush and Cheney toward the ridicule of Imus and others. But their visceral and tactical reactions to such needling belied their claims.

• • •

GEORGE BUSH'S FIRST formal trip as a presidential candidate in 1999 was dubbed by the Bush staff the "Great Expectations" tour; they commemorated the event with star-shaped yellow rubber toys printed with the phrase "Squeeze to lower expectations," which they handed out to members of the traveling press. Contributing to the cheery tone, Bush chummily joked with the reporters over his airplane's public address system. This convivial beginning created a set of expectations for the Old Media upon Bush's election. The new administration, it seemed reasonable to assume, would be an accessible bunch, understanding of journalists' professional needs and respectful of their special role in the system.

Nothing could have been further from the truth. It quickly became apparent that its only priority was limiting the traditional press corps's capacity to do it harm, making available only a highly scripted and not particularly well-informed press office. Under Bill Clinton and most of his recent predecessors, White House reporters for major news outlets could expect to speak on a daily basis to senior presidential advisers, even to those who were not part of the formal press operation.

The Bush administration seemed not to care about keeping these channels open. The exception appeared to be for journalists from conservative-sympathizing outlets like Fox News or the *Washington Times,* or for avowedly ideological organs like the *Weekly Standard* magazine. Some reporters for major newspapers covered the Bush White House for years and spoke to Rove rarely, if at all, or never once met Andy Card, who served as chief of staff for more than half a decade. While this kind of purposeful indifference was the norm, occasionally the Bush team projected a more menacing air. Officials sometimes pointedly told reporters who asked tough questions at the daily briefings that such queries were being duly noted by top presidential advisers. In a few instances, reporters who were deemed especially hostile were cut off from virtually all contact with White House officials.

The Bush administration's emphasis on control manifested itself in small ways as well. In previous administrations, it used to be that after reporters finished conducting interviews at the Old Executive Office Building across the street from the main White House building, they could exit unescorted. This made it possible to wander about and poke their heads into the offices of other officials they knew or bump into sources by chance on their way back to the press room. The Bush White House insisted that reporters be escorted by minders at all times.

This suspicious mood predated the September 11, 2001, attacks; afterward, the limitations on information became even more severe. Faced with this challenge to their professional status, many Old Media reporters went through something akin to the classic stages of grief: denial, anger, bargaining, depression, and, for all but the most determined and conscientious journalists, sullen acceptance. For White House reporters, there were no expectations (great or otherwise) about gaining access to or information from government officials. And that is precisely the way Bush, Cheney, and Rove wanted it to be.

The substantial vacuum created by the weakening of the Old Media, caused by its own shabby actions, historical trends, and the maneuvers of the semi-invisible hand of the Bush administration, was filled by the New Media. Its multitudinous new outlets gave Bush and Rove the means to reach like-minded individuals. But even they could not supply all the necessary content themselves, nor could they win political battles without significant help. In the election wars of the Freak Show era, highly motivated and intensely involved troops are required for victory. So George W. Bush and Karl Rove set out to build their army.

RALLY THE BASE

* * * * *

The Freak Show's incentives favor attack over restraint and sensation over substance. They favor moralistic and personal judgments (*My opponent is corrupt and unworthy*) over detached and impersonal ones (*We disagree over whether the top tax rate should be 33 percent or 39 percent*). The pervasiveness of these incentives is something that a president or serious presidential candidate faces every single day. The political opposition and the media (both Old and New) are filled with men and women who prosper by doing damage to personal reputations. No candidate can be considered serious without an understanding of Freak Show incentives and a strategy for dealing with them.

Bill Clinton's strategy was to try to rise above the Freak Show; to make himself so popular that he could survive the attacks of his enemies.

George W. Bush's strategy has had a different emphasis. He has tried to counter the Freak Show's incentives for his destruction by making sure that there are plenty of people with equally powerful incentives for his success. The critical cog in that strategy for Bush was Karl Rove.

Starting with the 2000 election, nearly every member of the Republican coalition thought of himself or herself as a "Bush Republican." (The only significant exceptions were people in the camp of Senator John McCain.) The corporate lobbyists on K Street, the Capitol Hill party leadership and rank and file, the major fund-raisers, the ideologically driven interest groups, the think tankers and academics, the religious grass roots, the state and local elected officials, and ordinary GOP voters all came to think of Bush's success as central to their own.

This did not happen by chance. America's two dominant political parties are big tents, filled with diverse and fractious members who are exceedingly difficult to unify over the course of a campaign, let alone a presidential term. Bush's coalition was created by a careful cultivation of interest group leaders, often attended to by Rove personally. It was sustained by a rigid code of expectation that members stay on the reservation, also enforced by Rove.

When Democrats talked about the Bush presidency, they always asked several questions that fell into what might be called the "I just don't get it" category. Chief among them: Why did Freak Show attacks on Al Gore and John Kerry always seem to hit their mark and cause terrible damage, while Freak Show attacks on George W. Bush—on his National Guard service, business deals, or his 1970s drinking and presumed drug use—always seemed to bounce off harmlessly? In the 1990s, even many Democrats supported investigations into Bill Clinton's Whitewater imbroglio and other uproars, but Republicans in Congress, with one exception (the bungled early response to Hurricane Katrina), were not willing to use their congressional subpoena power to investigate Bush administration controversies. How did the Republican coalition, which included Big Business leaders eager for less intrusive government and anti-abortion activists eager for more intrusive government, manage to stay unified while the diverse Democratic coalition always threatened to splinter? Most of all, when Democrats looked at Bush during his first term, they saw a politician who appeared to them manifestly unworthy of the office he held, and wondered: *How can he still be so popular with so many in his own party? What is it with these people?*

The answer in every case was that Bush and Rove had implemented a political strategy in which the different parts of the Republican base all perceived their own self-interest and Bush's self-interest as being squarely the same. Bill Clinton habitually perceived his self-interest to require detaching from his party's base. With few exceptions, Bush's answer to every challenge was: *Rally the base!*

There is a price to be paid for such a strategy. Bush's success at base rallying was probably the main reason he failed at his stated goal of "changing the tone" in Washington. Far from working hard to change the tone, Bush and Rove approached partisan anger and mistrust as great weapons in polarized America. On the other hand, the us-versus-them brand of politics left them acutely vulnerable when support among "us"—Bush's conservative backers—began to cool, as it did in 2005 and 2006.

That caveat, though, hardly diminishes the Bush-Rove election achievements. Rarely has a presidential candidate enjoyed such unalloyed support from his own party as Bush did in 2000, 2002, and 2004. For five years, the

Bush White House enjoyed a degree of campaign and policy coordination with the Republican National Committee, the congressional campaign committees, and the party's Capitol Hill leadership unmatched in modern times. Any candidate from each party in 2008 would do well to understand the approach that produced such a united and energized team.

· · ·

GEORGE W. BUSH's initial national success, it is worth emphasizing, started because, in 1999, he was selling merchandise that Republicans wanted to buy. Inexplicable as it may be to Democrats, Bush's biography, his personal style, and his religiosity all made him singularly appealing to conservatives. This is a simple fact but an essential one. As Rove once said of his boss, "He comes from good stock, he seems like a good fellow."

But Bush's personality was not enough. Rove also employed his own years of experience with the party and the conservative movement; his ability to stay in touch through technology with an incalculable number of people; his emphasis on personal relationships; and his careful planning to keep Bush's supporters informed, on board, and on message (including at meetings and on cable television and talk radio).

As Rove's longtime friend Richard Land, the leader of the conservative evangelical Southern Baptist Convention, said, reflecting the views of many conservative leaders, "There's no question this is the most receptive White House to our concerns and to our perspective of any White House that I've dealt with, and I've dealt with every White House from Reagan on. . . . In this administration, they call us, and they say, 'What is your take on this? How does your group feel about this?' "

In 2004, Paul Weyrich, a mainstay of the conservative movement, remarked about Rove, "I'd send him an e-mail at 5 o'clock Sunday morning and would have an answer by 7:30. He never failed to respond, even when he was on Air Force One. I got swifter answers from him than I do from my own staff." That level of outreach was the norm for the Bush political operation for years, in good times and bad.

Many of the groups that make up today's conservative coalition did not exist in their current form, or even at all, back in 1980. Nevertheless, the breadth and sturdiness of Ronald Reagan's support among such groups was inferior to what Bush had gathered around him at a parallel time in his first presidential run. Reagan generally is considered the gold standard in this respect, but Bush's support was actually greater.

Throughout his first term and into his second, public opinion polls showed Republican support for Bush regularly around 90 percent among self-identified members of his party. Surveys also suggested support from Democrats in some cases to be below 10 percent. These two facts were not unrelated, but, considering the base-focused emphasis that is the essence of Bush Politics, the gap did not necessarily matter.

Republican elites were well aware of Bush's level of support within the party and understood its implications. The president's standing could be used to help win grassroots support, pass elements of the conservative legislative agenda, raise money, and challenge the Old Media and the liberal Establishment. The unity Bush inspired, and the motivation that unity gave lobbyists, donors, activists, and others, were the most valuable commodities in American politics for the first term of his presidency.

• • •

As BUSH ENTERED the national stage for his first White House run, Rove made certain that conservatives were animated and intrigued by the candidate's strengths, and aware that only a conservative movement exhibiting unity and discipline could prevent Al Gore from extending the Clinton years.

Back in 1981, just after Reagan took office, Weyrich described his expectations for the new executive: "Personally, I tend to doubt that the New Right will have a part in the Reagan administration. . . . We tend to be very controversial." No figure of any stature in the conservative movement said anything like that publicly in May of 2000 about Bush; rather, the leaders were openly sanguine about the presumptive Republican nominee. Allied by their hunger to win back the White House and their general belief in Bush, conservatives all signed on with donations, endorsements, and votes at levels that were formidable and determinative of Bush's success.

One of Rove's skills was knowing how to capture the vitality of his party's right-wing base, without that energy spooking the center. (Note the difficulty that Democrats have had matching this minuet, with groups such as MoveOn.org seen by some in their party as embarrassing and extreme albatrosses.) Longtime conservative coalition members such as the National Rifle Association were integrated into Bush's national political machine, but Rove taught them the wisdom of another Trade Secret: *Private strokes and public policy results are better than public strokes and no results.*

Throughout his own two campaigns and during legislative fights, Bush seldom appeared publicly with or talked about the NRA, the Christian

Coalition, or other controversial organizations committed to his election and agenda, but the groups devoted millions of dollars and countless volunteer hours to make sure their shared goals were achieved. Only someone who systematically read every word Bush uttered would catch him alluding to these organizations. But almost without exception, those groups got what they wanted from the White House, including frequent private reassurances and thanks from Rove and his colleagues. Despite some 2000 rhetoric about mandatory gun safety measures, Bush did not veer from an absolutist Second Amendment stance in the White House. And as president, he signed numerous executive orders favored by the pro-life community. Yet in public he hardly ever discussed such positions.

Unlike his immediate Republican predecessors, of course, Bush's party retained control of both chambers of Congress for most of his presidency, with working margins wide enough to pass much of his agenda, but slim enough to require an uncommon degree of party cohesion. This challenge—of keeping a diverse congressional party unified—was mirrored in the wider electorate. Bush delivered a broad message to the whole country and to the coalition, while Rove used targeted and private communication to ensure that members with special concerns got the kind of singular assurances they required to stay in the tent.

This is one of the many places where Rove's background in the language and narrowcasting principles of direct mail had wider applicability. Rove would identify elected officials who held necessary votes but were not particularly inclined to cast them in the president's favor, contact them individually, and promise that their concerns would be met in future legislation, if they would just vote appropriately on the upcoming bill. This happened time and again with must-pass legislation. Working through the Republican congressional leadership and in one-on-one confidential conversations, Rove and Bush kept the party unified on vote after vote. Many moderate Republicans held their tongues about, for instance, environmental policies they did not like, while many fiscal conservatives voted for the expensive Medicare prescription drug benefit.

Moreover, Rove engineered disciplined support for the entire agenda and the 2002 midterms by making a sometimes explicit, sometimes implicit bargain with the full coalition. Basically, in for a dime, in for a dollar. If you wanted the benefits of membership—having other coalition members work for your special agenda items, sharing in the success of the administration overall, not getting yelled at by Rove on the phone—you had to play by the rules, and Rule Number One from the beginning was: *Support Bush, Bush's candidates, and the full Bush agenda.*

Did the heads of the Washington offices of the major business groups care about partial birth abortion? Did Second Amendment advocates get hepped up over No Child Left Behind? Sometimes yes, sometimes no. Occasionally coalition members surpassed mere lack of interest in a Bush item to outright opposition, but the rules set down by the Bush apparatus largely inhibited individuals or group coalition members from open disagreement.

This is also the governing model of the weekly Wednesday Meeting run in Washington by Rove ally Grover Norquist. The Meeting is made up of representatives from nearly every important conservative interest group. Those present do indeed agree on many issues; however, potential fissures naturally arise. For instance, should the federal government tighten control of the border and deport non-U.S. citizens, or allow American employers continued access to cheap labor from Mexico? Or, on the question of sexual content on the Internet, should the free market prevail, or should the government impose regulating standards? The rules of the Wednesday Meeting call for placing the highest emphasis on racking up as many conservative wins as possible, and that means minimizing differences for the good of the cause.

To this day, despite the publicity the Meeting has received, liberals have no system that comes close to it in building tribal cohesion and in putting as many oars in the water as possible to row in tandem. Norquist speaks with both humor and intensity about "our team" versus "their team," and hosts prominent representatives of the Bush administration, who brief the crowd and listen to feedback. Even so, the no-nonsense nature of the Meeting allows for collaboration with the enemy; the members are considered so influential and effective that in recent years both Al Gore and George Soros have crossed the divide to address the group.

During Bush's first term, his administration supported several measures that challenged conservative principles, such as the prescription drug benefit, prompting quiet grumbling from true believers about the president's purity. Bush made these policy decisions for tactical reasons or out of genuine belief, but such aberrations usually were carried out with the long-term political success of the party and the movement in mind.

Meanwhile, premium Bush-Rove attention was bestowed on every significant element of the conservative coalition for years, and paid off most of the time with the shock troops necessary to whip up the base in defense of Bush and his issues, or in opposition to Bush's foes. In 1999, Rove originally conceived of a broad message of limited taxation, less regulation, legal reform, and "family values," along with a narrowcasted message of pro-life, pro-guns, and other conservative staples to hold the coalition together. After September 11, 2001, the war on terrorism superseded all those elements. But the principle for Rove was the same: Keeping Bush's Republican support sky-high using a combination of personality and policies.

· · ·

WHERE THE FREAK Show was concerned, Rove knew the rally-the-base approach required more than giving partisans someone to love. It also required giving them someone to loathe.

With the exception of the CIA leak investigation, the biggest moments of public attention Rove received grew out of remarks he delivered excoriating Democrats. Once again, it serves to examine two key Rove speeches, this time with a special emphasis on the timing. One was given a year into Bush's first term and the other just after his reelection; both inspired media uproars. Not coincidentally, the speeches focused on national security, the issue on which the Democrats were the most vulnerable.

Whatever else one thinks about Rove's methods and motives, these presentations serve as models for how a presidential campaign machine gets its base emotionally stoked to fight the battles on which Freak Show politics thrives.

The first came when Rove appeared at the Republican National Committee meeting in Austin on January 18, 2002. It was a triumphal homecoming for a man who had worked at or with the Republican National Committee his entire career. Now it was *his* committee. He controlled every major decision, and the RNC was gathering in his adopted hometown to plan for the midterms in which his accumulated vision of how to win elections would be tested like never before on a national scale. Speaking to the most committed Republicans in the country in a modest meeting room at Austin's shabby Hyatt, Rove laid out his game plan.

Everything else he said that day was overshadowed by one relatively brief section of his talk. Later, Rove claimed he considered those particular comments unremarkable. But the assembled national media and the Democrats who subsequently heard his words recounted latched on to them, and they would be replayed, repeated, and twisted for literally years afterward. Few times in American history have the observations of a presidential adviser stirred up such controversy or boasted such a long shelf life.

The *New York Times*'s Rick Berke (who over the years has made regular cameos in media-driven Rove brouhahas) wrote this lead for the next day's paper from Austin:

> Karl Rove, President Bush's chief political adviser, sought today to turn the war into partisan advantage, telling Republicans gathered here that the administration's handling of terrorism could be an important theme for the party to trumpet in the November midterm elections. . . . "Americans trust the Republicans to do a better job of keeping our communities and our families safe," Mr. Rove said in a luncheon address at the winter meeting of the Republican National Committee. "We can also go to the country on this issue because they trust the Republican Party to do a better job of protecting and strengthening America's military might and thereby protecting America."

Much of the Gang of 500 instantly condemned Rove for saying this. His sound bite appeared on the network newscasts, and Democrats went into high dudgeon. His image as a bullying, say-anything political hit man was amplified overnight.

And yet, consider the counterargument. Rove offered a perfectly standard and acceptable line of reasoning in Austin. It was an election year. Rove was speaking to a political committee. National security and the war on terror were two of the biggest political issues facing the country and were certain to be on voters' minds come Election Day. And what he said was a matter of irrefutable fact—every piece of available data suggested that Rove's party was more trusted to defend America than the Democrats.

Still, the notion that Rove was "politicizing the war," as Democratic National Committee chair Terry McAuliffe charged, quickly became conventional wisdom. The never understated McAuliffe jacked matters up several notches by deeming Rove's words "nothing short of despicable." The hyped-up press and the angry Democrats believed that asserting a public perception of confidence in the Republican Party on a matter of national importance (particularly one involving national security) amounted to "politicizing." To Rove, what he said amounted to acknowledging the jumbo elephant in the room. Under attack from all the usual suspects, Rove did not back down, the White House did not back down, and the story line was set: Republicans planned to improperly "use" national security as an issue in the elections.

Now, when it came time to execute that strategy in the 2002 election overall and in a few particular races, Republicans engaged in some tactics that were rough indeed. And quite routinely, the Democrats and the press would link those efforts to Rove's words from January. For the first time since before the September 11 attacks, Rove was at the center of the storm, and he did not seem to mind. He might have felt especially satisfied after his party won the next two elections in large part because of the perceived disparity between the two parties on national security. The image of strength unified and energized Republican activists and won the votes of some independents. Whatever Rove's true intentions, the credit for the Republicans' smashing success in the 2002 midterm elections goes to the elevation of national security as a primary focus, prominently stoked by Rove's speech to the RNC, and the reaction to it of his rivals.

When Rove was asked in March of 2002 by Charlie Rose if his Austin statements had been a mistake because Democrats had jumped all over him, he insisted it was the Democrats who had erred:

> I thought it was a mistake, frankly, because it just drew more attention to something that is a simple fact. Every public opinion poll shows that if you ask the American people who is better on the issue of national defense, who's stronger and willing to, you know, do the right things on national defense, they give the Republicans a big advantage, just like they do the Democrats on the issue of, say, the environment, give them big advantages.

Years later, he said, "I didn't think I'd said something all that provocative. I was sort of amused by it because it struck me, well, they're just simply repeating my argument, which was good."

In the summer of 2005, in the midst of the CIA leak controversy, Rove again chose a highly visible, partisan audience to argue the parties' relative strengths on national security. By now, Rove was an extraordinarily well-known figure, with newsmagazine covers, biographical documentaries, and late-night comedian jokes on his Freak Show résumé. Any pretense of national unity about the war in Iraq (or anything else, really) was long gone. George W. Bush was facing declining national support for the war and his re-election was a mixed blessing. On the one hand, he was securely returned to the White House; on the other hand, there was no visible electoral enemy or obvious point of contrast to elevate Bush, flaws and all, above the fray.

So on that night, June 22, 2005, at the Sheraton in Manhattan, Rove gave an unambiguously confrontational speech to a dinner of the Conservative Party of New York. After a litany of differences between conservatives and liberals on domestic issues, Rove lit up the board with some of the toughest public rhetoric ever spoken by any Bush White House official:

> Perhaps the most important difference between conservatives and liberals can be found in the area of national security. Conservatives saw the savagery of 9/11 and the attacks and prepared for war; liberals saw the savagery of the 9/11 attacks and wanted to prepare indictments and offer therapy and understanding for our attackers. In the wake of 9/11, conservatives believed it was time to unleash the might and power of the United States military against the Taliban; in the wake of 9/11, liberals believed it was time to . . . submit a petition. I am not joking. Submitting a petition is precisely what MoveOn.org did. It was a petition imploring the powers that be to "use moderation and restraint in responding to the . . . terrorist attacks against the United States."
>
> I don't know about you, but moderation and restraint is not what I felt as I watched the Twin Towers crumble to the earth; a side of the Pentagon destroyed; and almost 3,000 of our fellow citizens perish in flames and rubble.
>
> Moderation and restraint is not what I felt—and moderation and restraint is not what was called for. It was a moment to summon our national will—and to brandish steel.
>
> MoveOn.org, Michael Moore and Howard Dean may not have agreed with this, but the American people did.
>
> Conservatives saw what happened to us on 9/11 and said: we will defeat our enemies. Liberals saw what happened to us and said: we must understand our enemies. Conservatives see the United States as a great nation engaged in a noble cause; liberals see the United States and they see . . . Nazi concentration camps, Soviet gulags, and the killing fields of Cambodia.
>
> Has there been a more revealing moment this year than when Democratic Senator Richard Durbin, speaking on the Senate floor, compared what Americans had done to prisoners in our control at Guantánamo Bay with what was done by Hitler, Stalin and Pol Pot—three of the most brutal and malevolent figures in the 20th century?

Let me put this in fairly simple terms: Al Jazeera now broadcasts to the region the words of Senator Durbin, certainly putting America's men and women in uniform in greater danger. No more needs to be said about the motives of liberals.

Unlike the Austin speech, the New York address was arguably demagogic and sure to incite controversy. Although some lines of the text cited specific people, others referred more generally to "liberals," when, in fact, the vast majority of Democrats had backed Bush wholeheartedly in the wake of September 11, did not excuse or offer explanations for the perpetrators of those attacks, and supported military action against Afghanistan. Many, too, had endorsed giving the president the authority to invade Iraq. This was the discourse of a man who understood his audience, but not someone with any apparent interest in "changing the tone" in politics.

When it was suggested to Rove months later that he must have known his comments in New York would be considered provocative, he retorted that Democrats had foolishly overreacted to his words, just as they had in Austin:

> I didn't think it would be treated that provocatively because I was very narrow in my definition of who I was attacking. . . . I named my targets, MoveOn and Howard Dean and Durbin. So I'm very narrow in my context. . . . If they had said nothing that speech would have come and gone without attention, but when they all went out there and said, "By God, he's attacking my patriotism, I supported [military action against] Afghanistan," I mean it reinforced "Okay, well, you're against Iraq and you're not willing to discipline the MoveOns and the Howard Deans and the Durbins, you're just not."
>
> And if they had just simply said "interesting speech to the Conservative Party" [that would have ended the discussion]. . . . What would really have been something is . . . if somebody had stepped up and said, "I have said something about MoveOn.org and the extremes on the left." Taken the Clinton approach, "I'm cleansing the party, we've had a Sister Souljah moment when it comes to the defeatist wing of the Democratic Party and by God I'm there."
>
> It was a timely topic. . . . I was deliberately precise because . . . to me one of the great problems in America today is the decline of bipartisanship in foreign policy, which I understand is not as possible on security questions in the aftermath of the Vietnam war.

Before the Vietnam war the fight, frankly, was within the Republican Party over bipartisanship because you had the isolationist wing, which was against the internationalism of Truman and Roosevelt and suspicious of Eisenhower, so that was the battle.

Now we see the battle over bipartisanship to be found within the Democratic Party where the defeatist—apply whatever label you want on it—but the Left of the Democratic Party is very much out of tune with a bipartisan consensus.

So Rove claimed his remarks were meant merely to highlight significant divisions within the opposition. But the speech actually had a cohesive effect on the Democratic Party, which was once again united in its condemnation of Rove. That led to a comparable reaction from Republicans, who always became more unified in the face of group attacks on *their* president, and who could feel energized about the muscular national security posture of the Bush White House and how it promised to unsettle Democrats. For the second time, Rove personally had set off a charged dialogue about whether or not the opposition party was weak on defense, the issue terrain most favorable to his boss.

Rove, speaking on behalf of the president, validated the stock Washington joke that Bush's claim to be a "uniter not a divider" proved true because he united the Democratic Party. This time, Rove united the Democrats, and, in doing so, the Republican Party even more so.

• • •

ROVE MAY HAVE helped unite each party internally, but like George W. Bush, he never was able to bring both parties together in a bipartisan union. (And also like Bush, Rove did not seem to care.) Yet even without universal adoration, through three national election victories, and domestic policy achievements, they rarely lacked for surrogates to deliver hard-line talking points; for the capacity to win close congressional votes with Republican support; for the ability to rouse tens of thousands of die-hard volunteers to work on their behalf; or for the power to prompt more voters to cast approbatory ballots than ever before in a presidential election. They erected a model for electoral victory based on the party faithful.

As the conservative writer Rich Lowry pointed out, Bush's 2004 campaign "built a grassroots force that, had it been marshaled on behalf of a liberal, would be celebrated as a great 'people's army.' " Keeping this "people's army" together often required more than just celebrating Bush and conservative ideas, of course. Never forgetting the movement's roots in the politics of grievance, Bush and Rove also relied on well-chosen enemies such as Al Gore, Tom Daschle, John Kerry, Hollywood, Howard Dean, Michael Moore, and Hillary Clinton to provide energy and concord.

If their achievement appears easy—an example just waiting for others to follow—it is important to recall that one Democrat already has tried to replicate it. In 2003, former Vermont governor Howard Dean and his supporters thought that they had duplicated Bush's base-rallying achievement with the Internet-driven enthusiasm he engendered around the country during his presidential campaign. The Dean machine can be forgiven somewhat for the miscalculation. The former Vermont governor drew some of the largest crowds in modern American history in the year before a presidential election—rallies attended by thousands of people, backed up by a rabid online community of tens of thousands more and millions of dollars in campaign contributions. But Dean's campaign made two errors.

First, they failed to realize that in a country of three hundred million people, *tens of thousands* of engaged fans is not enough to win a national election. And, second, Dean's backers and staff were naive about the real-world imperatives of Freak Show politics. When Dean started to be attacked by rivals, suffering hits that were compounded by his own verbal gaffes on the campaign trail, he needed forces to defend him, and they were nowhere to be found.

His campaign manager resigned. Some of his supporters criticized his advertising strategy and his temperament. Former United States senator John Durkin, a New Hampshire Democrat, withdrew his endorsement on the eve of his state's primary, after Dean's weak third-place finish in Iowa and his famous caucus night scream. In the primary, Dean got fewer than 58,000 votes, lagging dismally behind John Kerry by more than 25,000. Instead of rallying and making Dean stronger, his former backers abandoned him and made him weaker, until he was forced to drop out of the race.

The Deaniacs *appeared* to have been mobilized, but they were not personally or ideologically invested in their candidate's success the way Bush's forces were invested in his goals and achievements four years before. As Dean's Democratic rivals, the Republican Party, and the Old Media begin firing away at the former Vermont governor, some of the most lethal shots were volleyed from liberals, engaged in a new-fashioned fragging. "I liked Dean, but he didn't look too presidential. He looked like a maniac," Kevin Burke, a retired computer engineer who had been for Dean, told the *Los An-*

geles Times. Even the activists who put their blame elsewhere failed to stay energized and coordinated enough to come to his rescue.

Candidates in 2008, be forewarned. If you animate forces who do not feel a strong enough bond to you, the mob that had your back can become the mob at your door. Bush himself got a taste of this reality after rousing ire with his aborted nomination of Harriet Miers to the Supreme Court, his administration's failed effort to allow a company owned by Dubai to operate some United States ports, and his push for immigration reform. Conservatives revolted in the wake of these moves, teaching Rove and Bush a Trade Secret they had not confronted before in the White House: *There is a thin line between rallying the base and being trampled by the horde.*

The Language Karl Rove Uses
to Describe Democrats

★ ★ ★ ★ ★

(A/K/A LABELS THAT WHITE HOUSE OFFICIALS, Bush-Cheney strategists, Republican National Committee staffers, Republican members of Congress, and surrogates with talking points use to describe Al Gore, John Kerry, and all other prominent Democrats on the national stage. To the 2008 Democratic nominee, this means you, so toughen that hide and remember: *Names* can *hurt you*.)

1. *desperate*

2. *out of the mainstream*

3. *willing to say or do anything to get elected*

4. *out of touch*

5. *wild-eyed*

6. *extreme*

7. *purely political*

8. *old*

9. *tired*

10. *unrepresentative of the people who elected them*

11. *sharing the sensibilities of Hollywood elites*

12. *obstructionist*

13. *out of ideas*

14. *more interested in partisan politics than in solving problems for the American people*

15. *liberal*

16. *captive to the Democrat Party's special interests*

17. *appealing to the Michael Moore, Howard Dean, MoveOn wing of the Democrat Party*

18. *loser*

19. *weak*

20. *negative [irony not included]*

TRANSCENDENCY, TRANSPARENCY, AND DESTRUCTION

★ ★ ★ ★ ★

ARMED WITH HIS DOCTORATES in Old Media Practices and Base Rallying, Rove recognized that both areas of expertise were required to achieve the twin goals of defending Bush against the Freak Show and exploiting it to destroy his opponents.

Rove's performance in insulating Bush from damage during his two presidential campaigns was not flawless. But he demonstrated a greater awareness of what needed to be done than those competing against him.

Nearly every presidential candidate, in contrast to Bush and Rove in 2000, makes the same faulty assumptions: *I have run for office in a tough political state many times. I have served as governor/senator/whatever for years. Perhaps I've even run for president before. The biggest newspaper in my state has done stacks of investigative stories about my past, digging into my finances, my war record, and my family. I have been picked at, prodded, probed, and fully vetted in the public arena.*

This mind-set leads White House aspirants to believe that everything about their history that possibly might hurt them already has been revealed, or is so well hidden or of little consequence that it will not be exposed during the presidential campaign process.

Gore and Kerry proved just how misguided this expectation is. Gore had been the son of a scrutinized senator; an elected congressman and senator from a swing state; Bill Clinton's running mate, vetted by a squadron of lawyers and research teams; and a candidate for national office three times. Kerry had been a man in the national spotlight since he was in his twenties; a prosecutor, a lieutenant governor, and a senator from a politically punishing state with a hyper-aggressive press corps; and, as a possible running mate to Gore, vetted by a squadron of lawyers and research teams.

This means that no one (NO ONE!) is immune to this Trade Secret: *The fight for every presidential nomination and every general election campaign dredges up past votes, quotes, actions, and inactions from everyone who runs for president, no matter what rough-and-tumble political scrutiny they previously have endured.*

Attention, those of you who are war heroes; former first ladies of small Southern states and large nations; current senators; regular targets of the *New York Post;* and past presidential candidates, even those who beat Karl Rove's boss by 19 percentage points in a New Hampshire primary—this means you, too.

Bush might have been the son of a former president; a previous candidate for Congress; and the two-term governor of Texas, but in 1999 Rove knew that his candidate was far from immune. Bush's most glaring vulnerabilities were his self-described "young and irresponsible" bachelor days, including his admitted drinking and rumored drug use; his semi-cushy Vietnam-era service in a coveted Texas Air National Guard slot; his business record, which included a mix of apparent failures, questionable federal regulation, and sweetheart deals; and his governing performance in Texas, with debates about his achievements on issues such as health care, the environment, and education.

From a practical point of view, the smartest thing Bush, Rove, and communications adviser Karen Hughes did to insulate the candidate from Freak Show damage was to put Dan Bartlett in charge of mastering Bush's record on all these matters and responding to press questions about them.

Bartlett, who would go on to serve as a top adviser in the Bush White House, was at the time a young aide to Hughes and Rove who had worked closely with Bush for a number of years. He had handled many of the same concerns during Bush's two runs for governor, and was familiar with Bush's record in office from working in his administration. While he never was formally designated as the person charged with keeping scandal at bay, this history made him the obvious choice for the job. Bartlett collected documents, financial records, and oral history on a rolling basis beginning in late 1993 and ramped it up again in both 1997 and 1999. He spent time gathering data in Midland (Bush's boyhood home) and Arlington, Texas (where the Bush-owned Texas Rangers played). He spent hours talking to Bush's accountant and his lawyers, as well as to various National Guard officials.

Because speed and expertise were required to protect Bush's public image, Bartlett was in effect always on call. Within twenty minutes of proposing marriage on the Fourth of July in 1999 to the woman who would become his wife, Bartlett was summoned to the telephone to answer press inquiries about Bush's investment portfolio. He interrupted his honeymoon in the spring of 2000 to address another story about Bush's past.

While Bartlett made himself accessible to the press, the key to his effectiveness was that Bush made himself accessible to Bartlett whenever controversies arose. Bartlett had another big advantage. He was not afraid to ask Bush about sensitive matters. The value of being able to speak freely in this context cannot be overstated. Bush is by nature an early riser, and when he hit the campaign trail in earnest, he would call Bartlett first thing in the morning from the road to check in. Bartlett frequently used the opportunity, weekly or more often when the circumstances dictated, to verify personal details from the source. Bartlett claimed nothing was put off limits about Bush's Guard records, business dealings, or other matters of controversy. "I didn't have a candidate who was wrestling about his past," Bartlett said.

Even in areas involving Bush's "young and irresponsible" days, Bartlett was able to confront his boss with every piece of innuendo that floated his way. Bush remembered the names of plenty of people from his past, and on at least one occasion referred Bartlett to an ex-girlfriend to provide corroboration.

For Old Media journalists, there was no ambiguity. If you had a question about Bush's biography, Bartlett was the one-stop-shopping place to go. And he generally was responsive, returning reporters' calls, inviting them for Austin sit-downs to go over documents, and creating the appearance of being helpful. Actually, he often *was* helpful. And this clear channel in turn was helpful to Rove and the Bush campaign, since it meant that Bartlett was continually updated on percolating Democratic tips, ongoing reporting, and impending television and print stories.

This reciprocal exchange of information stands in contrast to typical campaign proceedings. Normally, there is a clumsy tussle during which the campaign staff tries to chase down and tie up the facts before the media or political opponents swoop. This almost always ends in partial or total failure. Few candidates, defensive and prickly as they tend to be, are willing to submit to the intrusion of allowing even their most trusted employees and closest supporters to poke around in their business. And a shortage of lucid and complete information always makes the press suspicious.

Additionally, having Bartlett as the single point man removed some of the uncertainty and tension that inevitably accompanies these biographical controversies. On the Clinton, Gore, and Kerry campaigns, in comparison, different officials were (somewhat) responsible for different aspects of their candidates' records. These unfortunate souls were usually inaccessible, unaware of relevant data and documents, and diffident about pressing their candidate for more details. Thus, negative stories were allowed to inflate without interference, blowing up instead of blowing over. Bush and Bartlett took the necessary steps to shape controversial stories and deter the press from filling a vacuum of confusion with a feeding frenzy.

After Bush was safely reelected, Rove said that the strategy in the first campaign amounted to what he called "T2"—*transcend and transparency.* Rove believed that Bush could avoid getting drawn into a discussion of his own personal life if he stayed away from directly criticizing Bill Clinton's peccadilloes, a game plan that was executed with great success. Rove maintained that their efforts at transparency included getting out every National Guard and business record they could find, while drawing a line on questions about drug use. The uproar that greeted the last-minute disclosure of Bush's 1977 drunk driving arrest—one skeleton that deliberately was left in the closet—was proof, said Rove, that a goal of transparency was the "right strategy."

That Bush agreed to this approach was to his benefit, particularly since the more common pattern followed by modern presidential candidates is as careless as it is dangerous. 2008 hopefuls: Ignore these Trade Secrets if you want to guarantee your past will dominate your present and ruin your future as you run for president:

- *Assign someone as early as possible to create a dossier on your life.*

- *Choose for the above task someone you trust, who is media-savvy, and who is not unduly intimidated by you.*

- *Choose just one person. One. Not a group, a handful, or a pair—one.*

- *Direct your financial advisers, lawyers, family members, business associates, and friends to cooperate with your self-generated background check.*

- *Have all your facts in a row for rapid response when a story breaks.*

- *Do not, should the first wave of stories about an aspect of your past cause only minor damage, assume the matter has run its course and won't come back up again.*

Most of the Clinton-era carnivals were prolonged and amplified by the forty-second president himself, who was famous for dodging and weaving, to'ing and fro'ing, dissembling and evading, and dribbling out sometimes contradictory explanations for embarrassing stories. Beyond Gore and Kerry, there is a long list of serious people who have run for president in the Freak Show era and seen their chances for their party's nomination diminished or eliminated by a failure to have the facts at the ready and a plan to mold the press coverage. Who can forget (besides history, most readers, and, perhaps, the candidates themselves) Lamar Alexander's cozy business deals, Bill Bradley's medical records, and Howard Dean's outspoken statements on a Canadian public affairs show about the flaws of the Iowa caucus process? At the time, all these episodes were serious distractions to candidates who had assumed their personal virtue was beyond reproach.

The use of previous controversial actions and comments to shape the public image of presidential candidates poses a grave threat to any campaign. But for a variety of reasons—the complexities of human psychology and the simple reality of pervasive disorganization that afflicts campaigns—most candidates neglect to protect themselves from this danger.

Rove, Bartlett, and their team recognized that the way to avoid being turned into a main course in the Freak Show buffet was to know all the facts and act decisively when Bush's reputation was challenged. But there *were* exceptions. In three instances, Bartlett's efforts were less than comprehensive. Each situation was slightly different. In the case of the National Guard, Bartlett said he searched for every document he could get his hands on during the 2000 campaign, but was given bad information about what records might exist in different places. His failure to put together a complete dossier allowed the issue to reappear in the 2004 election.

In the case of Bush's alleged past drug use, a decision was made to not answer specific questions, although Bartlett had private conversations with Bush to assess his level of vulnerability.

And in late 1998 or early 1999, Bartlett was informed by Karen Hughes with Bush's permission that he had been arrested for drunk driving in Maine in 1976. Bartlett was told that very few people knew of the incident, and that the candidate already had decided not to reveal the story publicly, in order, he said, to avoid setting a bad example for young people such as his daughters.

In 2006, Bartlett acknowledged, "Everybody understood the vulnerabilities" of not disclosing the drunk driving event themselves, but it was emphasized that "the decision was made" and final. In retrospect, Rove believed the exposure of Bush's arrest in the last week of the campaign ultimately did more damage than any other revelation about the candidate's history.

• • •

ON THE ISSUE of past narcotics use, Bartlett was mute and Bush was defiant. To this day, the world does not know the basics regarding Bush and illegal drugs: *How much, if any? What kind? When?* After several presidential cycles in which it had become de rigueur for baby-boomer candidates to sheepishly acknowledge smoking marijuana (and, in all but one known case, admit to inhaling as part of the process), Bush drew a line in the sand. "I've told the American people—all I'm going to tell them—is that I made mistakes years ago. And I've learned from those mistakes," he said to NBC News's David Bloom in August of 1999, in what was his typical mantra.

Bush maintained his staunch position with the explanation that talking about drug use of any kind also would set a bad example for his twins and other young people. This stance was daring and required a steadfast commitment. Eventually, in the back-and-forth of the campaign, Bush felt compelled to assert somewhat indirectly that he had not used any illegal drugs since at least 1974, but he was never more specific than that. For a time, the issue faded from the campaign debate, except in the leftist-most regions of the Internet.

Is Bush's refusal to answer selectively about particular aspects of his past a Trade Secret worth borrowing in 2008? It certainly flouted the conventional wisdom of the Gang of 500 that there were certain questions a candidate could not decline to answer, mostly a series of "have you ever" queries. Once the press corps decides an adamant evasion is an unacceptable breach of the rules, a candidate normally is subjected to the same questions over and over until a responsive answer is forthcoming (often delivered in a super-hyped interview on a Sunday morning show or in the prime-time hour). Bush resolved he would not play along and had the fortitude and discipline to pull it off.

Note to 2008 candidates: Don't try this Trade Secret at home—or on the campaign trail—unless you have a good portion of Bush's self-confidence and capacity to intimidate the press through some combination of well-timed swagger, charm, teasing, bullying, condescension, nastiness, sociability, and anger. *Transcendence* is a Trade Secret that works only when accompanied by those innate traits, and not everyone has them.

By contrast, there are unambiguous lessons in the way the Bush campaign handled the most prominent attempt to do him damage based on his alleged past drug use. In October of 1999, a major publishing house, St. Martin's, released a book called *Fortunate Son: George W. Bush and the Making of an American President* by J. H. Hatfield. The book charged that in 1972 Bush had been arrested for cocaine possession, and that the matter had been wiped off his record through family connections.

The book's allegations about Bush were promoted on the *Drudge Report* and on the website *Salon,* whose senior vice president defended its coverage with a perfect New Media Freak Show quote: "*Salon,* and the Internet generally, aren't really interested in the corporate-gatekeeper mode of deciding about stories. When a major publisher releases a book . . . we're going to be all over it. On the Internet, you get the information out there and your readers help you evaluate it."

Having been willingly infected by New Media reports, a few Old Media newspapers felt free to run stories, especially after Bush publicly denied the charges and his father called the claims "mindless garbage" and a "vicious lie."

But shortly after the book's publication, it was revealed that Hatfield was a felon who had been convicted a decade earlier for attempting to kill a man with a car bomb. (Yes, *wow.*) Wackily, Hatfield denied his past, claiming it was a case of mistaken identity. (*Wow,* again.)

After Hatfield's history was exposed, St. Martin's withdrew the book (although it remained on sale in some stores, and an upstart publisher later reissued it). Under the rules of the Freak Show, Hatfield had a documentary made about him, which was released in 2003, two years after he committed suicide.

The Trade Secrets of how the Bush campaign staff handled the Hatfield attack are pretty straightforward. Obviously, their job was made easier by the uncorroborated nature of the allegations, not to mention the checkered past of the author. But Bartlett and his colleagues set the pattern for how Bush was protected throughout his two presidential campaigns and during his first term in the White House. First, because they were always plugged in, they knew about the book's allegations early on, well before publication, so they could respond in real time.

Second, they seized on the weakest link—Hatfield's shady saga and unusual résumé—to undermine the allegations. The Bush team used Hatfield's previous quickie books about *Star Trek* and *Star Wars* to denounce *Fortunate Son* as "science fiction" even before they learned about his criminal record.

They quietly urged Old Media organizations to stay away from the story and not to book Hatfield on their television shows.

And, third, they effectively balled up the Hatfield episode and hurled it at the media and political opponents whenever anyone attempted to bring up comparable allegations. This effectively deterred reporters from looking further into the question of drug use—however unrelated to the charges in *Fortunate Son*. Best of all, the effective components of this strategy had no expiration date.

It was a textbook study in how damage control, usually thought of as a defensive exercise, can be most effective when a campaign goes on the offensive. *Those old charges? They are just more wild accusations from* [INSERT NAME OF NEW ACCUSER HERE] *that have no more credibility than when J. H. Hatfield launched his discredited attacks. The voters have made up their minds about these old stories.*

$$\bullet \ \bullet \ \bullet$$

ANOTHER FAMILIAR ITEM popped up again in Bush's second campaign. It was September of 2004, when renewed questions about how Bush got into and out of the Texas Air National Guard moved from simmer to boil in the Freak Show. That the story had returned, with some new details, shows that no one is ever fully immune from his or her past becoming a factor during a presidential campaign—even an incumbent candidate. An interesting life leaves tracks.

George W. Bush during his reelection faced new and more intense queries about his National Guard service than he had in his Texas campaigns and in the 2000 race. How and why the Democrats and most of the national press did not make this a prominent issue during Bush's first run is a curiosity. For a variety of reasons, Bush's Vietnam-era history had produced a spark but not a fire. The result was that his political team never had all the elements of the story nailed down, leaving reasonable questions about certain aspects of Bush's Guard service primed to ignite in 2004.

The surfacing of a couple of new facts and government documents during the reelection campaign caused a furor. After the Associated Press filed a Freedom of Information Act request, the Pentagon in early September 2004 was forced to express regret that it had not found additional records of Bush's training in previous searches. At the same time, a newly formed Texas-based group with the pointed name "Texans for Truth" began a limited television advertising campaign questioning Bush's credibility. One advertisement, self-consciously mimicking the style of the anti-Kerry Swift Boat Veterans for Truth commercials, featured a former Air National Guardsman on camera challenging Bush's account of his service.

Democrats, exasperated by the focus on Kerry's Vietnam history, were delighted to see the puzzles about Bush's military experience gain some traction, and they launched a public relations effort based on the Creedence Clearwater Revival song "Fortunate Son" to raise additional questions about Bush's story. (The echo of the title of Hatfield's book was, as far as is known, an unintended irony.)

As with the drug allegations in Bush's first run, the matter appeared to be building momentum. The press had been resistant for a variety of reasons to Democratic efforts to raise the story, but eventually began to pay attention. It is difficult in retrospect to assess whether the noise posed a serious threat to Bush's control over his public image, but the Democrats were reasonable to think the story had potential. After the publication of the Associated Press account and some newspaper pieces with fresh information, "there was significant media interest in it and it seemed to be gaining currency," said Howard Wolfson, the strategist who directed the "Fortunate Son" effort for the Democratic National Committee, which was launched in early September.

To the Bush campaign's improbable rescue came not the ghost of the late, ill-fated J. H. Hatfield, but a producer for CBS News's *60 Minutes II* named Mary Mapes. Working with Dan Rather, Mapes produced a story for the show's September 8 edition on Bush's Guard record that was based on documents easily discredited as forgeries, by both right-leaning websites and some organs of the Old Media. Discombobulated and enraged by the collapse of the story, one Democratic member of Congress claimed—without a shred of proof—that Karl Rove somehow tricked CBS into doing the story to inoculate Bush. That accusation went nowhere, and Bush's enemies dropped most efforts to make hay out of the matter. Although there was no logical reason that CBS's error should have led other news organizations to abandon legitimate avenues of inquiry about the Guard, "the media lost interest in it," Wolfson said. "We were pushing a rock up a hill to get anyone interested in it. The media felt like the story itself had lost credibility." The fortunate trio Bush, Rove, and Bartlett must have felt an invigorating sense of déjà vu.

CBS helped the Bush campaign by dragging out the process by which it acknowledged the story was flawed, defending its myriad errors for days on the air before eventually commissioning a lengthy report about the whole catastrophe and firing several of those involved. Mapes, among those let go, wrote a book in which she took the position that the onus fell on her critics to prove that the documents were fakes, rather than on her to prove their authenticity. Dan Rather, as longtime target of conservative attacks, Mapes, and CBS News became effective base-riling staples in Republican talking points for the rest of the campaign.

It is tempting to suggest that the Trade Secret deriving from the Hatfield and Mapes episodes is *Being lucky is better than being good,* but in both situations, the Bush campaign was more than just lucky. They initially deflected the drug and Guard stories with a strategy intended to tamp down the questions, if not kill them outright. But when faced with (read: *blessed with*) accusers who could be so easily discredited, they pounced. In both cases, the stories had migrated from the Internet to the Old Media, which validated them somewhat as credible. Once the accusers were exposed, the Old Media felt guilty, the Democrats backed off, and the stories died. For many voters, meanwhile, the blunderings of the press appeared to overshadow suggestions of problematic behavior from the candidate.

So the Trade Secrets: *Bide your time. Strike when an accuser susceptible to being discredited puts forth a potentially dangerous charge. More in sadness than in anger denounce the accuser and the accusation, fusing them together in the public mind. Condemn all future similar accusations and accusers by painting them with the same broad brush and declaring that the voters have already made up their minds about these old stories. Other would-be accusers, regardless of the issue, witness what befalls those who attack the candidate and they are deterred from coming forward.*

Not every presidential candidate, however, understands these rules. Simple human charity makes us wish there was another example we could cite, rather than beat up again on John Kerry. And yet: The Kerry campaign's inability to transcend or subdue the Swift Boat Veterans for Truth illustrates the contrast between the Bush-Rove method of handling attacks and the less effective efforts of a less effective campaign.

Certainly, going on the offense against the Swifties would have been a dicey proposition for Kerry. But it is safe to say that if Bush were being hassled by Jerome R. Corsi, the co-author of *Unfit for Command,* the Swift Boat group's anti-Kerry book, Rove would have fought back immediately. As innumerable liberal blogs announced, Corsi apparently had a history of controversial statements, including posting derogatory remarks about Islam ("a worthless, dangerous Satanic religion"), about Catholicism ("boy buggering in both Islam and Catholicism is okay with the Pope as long as it isn't reported by the liberal press"), and about various leading Democrats on the FreeRepublic website. According to the *New York Observer* and other sources, Corsi admitted the postings were his, but said, "I always considered them a joke."

The Kerry campaign and its allies tried to discredit Corsi, but their efforts were made in a typically haphazard and undisciplined manner. Rove and Bartlett would have tied someone as combustible as Corsi around the neck of every person who made any negative suggestion whatsoever about their candidate. The Democrats failed to do so, and the Swift Boat Veterans' charges separated Kerry from control of his public image, splintering Kerry's confidence and the confidence of the voters and denying him any political advantage from his war record. J. H. Hatfield and Mary Mapes, on the other hand, might as well have been working for Dan Bartlett.

• • •

MOST OF THE techniques used to deal with the Hatfield book were not available to the Bush campaign when the existence of the candidate's prior drunk driving arrest surfaced on November 2, 2000, just four days before the election. The story broke in the press while Bush was at a campaign rally in Wisconsin. After finishing up the event, he admitted that in September 1976, he was pulled over and arrested for failing a sobriety test, with a blood alcohol level of 0.10, after drinking a few beers at a local bar and driving back to the family's Kennebunkport compound. His seventeen-year-old sister Dorothy was in the car, along with Australian tennis player John Newcombe and Newcombe's wife. The event occurred a year before Bush's marriage to Laura Welch and a decade before he became a teetotaler. Bush pleaded guilty to misdemeanor driving under the influence, paid a $150 fine, and had his license temporarily suspended in the state of Maine.

At his Wisconsin press conference, Bush declared, "I told the people I made mistakes in the past, and this is a mistake I made in the past. . . . I'm the first to say that what I did was wrong and I think the people of America will understand." He added of his twins, "I didn't want to talk about this in front of my daughters. I didn't want them drinking and driving. It was a decision I made." His attitude was straightforward and stoic. "I'm not proud of that. I've often times said that years ago I made some mistakes; I occasionally drank too much. I did on that night. I was pulled over. I admitted to the policeman that I had been drinking. I paid the fine. I regretted that it happened. I learned my lesson."

Bush may have appeared composed as he relied on his inherent reservoir of poise, but his normally unflappable campaign team was flapping mightily. They highlighted the Democratic ties of some of those involved in releasing the information, but as few Bush staffers had been made aware of the arrest, they were uncharacteristically unprepared, which created greater chaos than Rove operations normally allow. Because Bush had put the topic off-limits, the campaign did not have all the specifics and documentation at its fingertips when the news broke, and the classic scramble that ensued set off a Freak Show frenzy.

Bartlett, clued in only to the rough outline of the incident, never confirmed the detailed particulars with Bush. The story's varied ramifications combined with its election-eve surprise disclosure threw Bartlett's operation off balance. The Democrats, meanwhile, let the Freak Show do the work, and denied promoting the story. Bush himself asked, "Why now? . . . I've got my suspicions," while Gore spokesman Chris Lehane merely offered the prim: "This is just not something the Gore campaign is involved with in any shape, way or form. It's not something we would engage in."

On the campaign trail, Hughes was besieged by reporters, who asked her to clarify Bush's 1998 assertion that he had never been arrested after 1968. She tossed around an all-purpose quote from Bush—"I do not have a perfect record as a youth"—and was subjected to rolled eyes and raised eyebrows from reporters. A column in the *New York Post* called her response "Clintonian." All in all, the four-day drunk driving frenzy became tangled in the midst of the usual pre-election turmoil, but was shortly thereafter supplanted by the unprecedented madness of the election-night Bush-Gore tie. Still, without hard evidence, Rove blamed Bush's failure to win the popular vote on the negative publicity that the incident created.

• • •

DESPITE THE OCCASIONAL dramatic flare-ups, as noted earlier, Rove for the most part was able to use the Freak Show as an offensive weapon. He came into both presidential campaigns with a few other vital, hard-edged election Trade Secrets up his sleeve.

Democrats remain convinced that Rove was behind the big money that funded television ads intended to help Bush in 2000 and 2004. There were the infamous commercials financed by the Wyly brothers of Texas blasting John McCain during the 2000 nomination fight, as well as the efforts of the Swift Boat Veterans for Truth impugning John Kerry in 2004 (with some of the money coming from other Texans). Rove's foes took as an article of faith that he pulled the strings to get that money flowing and targeted.

Such coordination would have been illegal in most cases and politically explosive in every instance, but no one has proven that Rove was mixed up in these efforts. Even so, Rove's place as Bush's top strategist surely encouraged the spending of outside groups. Rove's well-cultivated infrastructure (with its sprawling political ties) meant that there always were rich people in his orbit willing to lend a hand. And Rove's history of acceptance of the rough-and-tumble of politics gave major donors confidence that they would not be crossing him or his ethos by contributing to those outside groups. Contrary to being punished for getting involved in this way, the contributors could be certain that Bush and Rove would know who gave what, and that they were helpful in a critical way at a crucial time. (Although many Bush aides still claim those Wyly brothers commercials ended up backfiring and helping McCain.)

• • •

ONE OF THE BIGGEST mistakes the Democratic Party made during Bush's rise to national power was its failure to use his 1998 reelection race in Texas as an opportunity to bloody him. Bush's overmatched opponent that year was the Clintons' old friend Garry Mauro, who had been the state's land commissioner. Bill Clinton, Hillary Clinton, and Al Gore among them did more than a dozen events for Mauro, including fund-raisers.

There was never much of a chance that Bush would lose the governorship, but there was great awareness that he intended to use the race to demonstrate his political strength, including the ability to appeal to nonwhite and female voters. He already was seen as the Republican front-runner for the 2000 presidential nomination and a force to be reckoned with. But Democrats passed up the opportunity to use the race to define Bush on their terms, before he established his positive public image with a wider circle, including the national media and the Gang of 500.

Had Al Gore had his own Karl Rove in his life back then, you can be sure that a coordinated effort would have taken place to try to expose Bush's vulnerabilities throughout 1998. Gore, as his party's front-runner, had a sufficient number of political advisers and enough influence at the Democratic National Committee to get this process moving.

Just based on the facts known now, there was plenty with which to work. The DNC could have found those government documents proving Bush had been arrested for drunk driving. There were those obtainable papers and witnesses raising issues with his military service.

There were unresolved questions about an old Securities and Exchange

Commission investigation into a Bush stock sale, plus concerns about the profit he made from his ownership share in the Texas Rangers baseball team.

More broadly, another potential area of inquiry was Bush's gubernatorial record on basic issues such as education, health care, the environment, and social services. Democrats friendly to Gore could have organized a bus tour of national and state leaders to highlight the poorer areas that were not thriving in George Bush's state.

Or they could have meticulously collected every comment Bush had ever made, from newspaper clippings, local television interviews, and transcripts. From this research, they could have issued press releases through the Texas Democratic Party or the Mauro campaign, trying to trap the incumbent in contradictions, or show him making controversial statements, such as in support of Social Security's partial privatization during his failed 1978 campaign for the House of Representatives.

Many of these matters became problematic in one or both of Bush's presidential campaigns. The Texas media prodded around them a bit, but state news organizations lacked the resources and institutional mission to stir up serious trouble for Bush. Here is a Trade Secret known to everyone on the inside and few on the outside: *A very large number of "investigative" stories in newspapers and on television news are the result of specific, detailed, and virtually gift-wrapped tips from the political opponents of the subjects of the stories.*

If the people on Gore's team were waiting for the local media to dig this stuff up, rather than find it themselves and throw it over the transom of the *Dallas Morning News* or some other Lone Star news organization, they made a big mistake.

There were also cheap and gimmicky (but effective) things they could have done, too, such as making a gag video spooling examples of Bush's tongue-tied speaking style.

Even a well-organized and aggressive effort would not have caused Bush to lose the race, but it would surely have made at least a dent in the sterling public image he had firmly in his grasp after he won reelection in Texas with an astonishing 69 percent of the vote, including impressive support from Democrats, women, and nonwhites, all without breaking a sweat or going negative on his overmatched opponent.

Contrast this Democratic failure with the organized and relentless Rove-directed efforts to rough up everyone who might emerge as the Democratic presidential nominee in 2004. The Republican National Committee methodically collected past statements and video of all the possible candidates, stored them systematically, and put out pungent press releases to begin the process of separating people like Al Gore, Dick Gephardt, John Edwards, and John Kerry from their public images.

Another Rove Trade Secret is *Figure out what gets under the skin of your opponents, and press those hot buttons as often as you can.* Bush and Cheney largely have been immune to this kind of thing because nothing much needles them. Even when barbs hit home, they rarely show it publicly. Their confidence and ostensible lack of insecurity gave them a who-the-heck-cares attitude during both presidential campaigns. Gore and Kerry, on the other hand, and their allies, were easy to rattle.

The formula was pretty simple (although not so simple that the Democrats figured it out). Bait the opposition into talking about something that made them insecure, which the Democrats would invariably do in a way that evinced anger and emotion. That would guarantee press coverage, which would be a winner for the Republicans for two reasons. First, it would feature the Democrat being angry and emotional (two things the American people disdain in their leaders). Second, the discussion would center on terrain that by Republican design was an area of weakness for the Democrats. The Bush campaign was able to produce this effect over and over with an ease that prompted both amazement and amusement in its war room, where strategist Steve Schmidt presided over a staff whose assignment was to make Kerry's life miserable.

A textbook example occurred in the 2004 campaign. The Republicans knew that the Democrats still were deeply upset that national security allegations were used to beat incumbent Georgia senator Max Cleland in 2002. Cleland was a Vietnam veteran and triple amputee who was ousted in a harsh campaign by Republican Saxby Chambliss, with the help of a television commercial linking Cleland to Osama bin Laden and Saddam Hussein and accusations that the Democrat was weak on national security.

For John Kerry and his allies, the idea that a veteran could be defeated with such a charge by a party led by two men who avoided seeing combat in Vietnam was more than they could bear. And the Bush campaign was well aware of this lingering indignation. So in 2004, as often as they could, the Republicans trotted out Chambliss, by then a sitting United States senator and eager surrogate, to make national security attacks on Kerry in the media. The Pavlovian response from the Democrats was as automatic as it was predictable. Their reactions invariably produced an extended debate on terrorism and defense matters in which the Democrats appeared emotional and agitated and the Republicans appeared calm and strong.

. . .

WHILE THE REPUBLICAN Party's convention was under way in New York in August 2004, John Kerry defied the wishes of his campaign advisers when he decided that he just had to try out his spiffy new windsurfing equipment in the cobalt ocean of upscale Nantucket. His downtime activity produced a moment nearly as significant as his I-actually-voted-for-it-before-I-voted-against-it sound bite. Sequentially, the Bush campaign demonstrated their mastery of two Freak Show Trade Secrets. First: *Patience pays*. Second: *Video rules*.

Bush's media team knew immediately that the footage of Kerry skimming the waves in his vibrant outfit was potential fodder for a television advertisement. But they also knew there was no reason to hurry out a commercial, when the video was getting free play on news and entertainment programs. Jay Leno quipped that the episode showed even Kerry's "hobby depends on which way the wind blows." David Letterman scoffed that "John Kerry spent yesterday windsurfing—because when you're in a statistical dead heat you just want to kick back and relax."

The typical grumbling within the Kerry campaign started, with unnamed officials complaining to the media that the candidate had committed yet another unforced error that was harming his image.

On September 12, Mark McKinnon sent an e-mail to Rove, laying out his sense of the gift of the Brahmin:

From: Mark McKinnon
Date: Sun, 12 Sep 2004 12:05 PM
To: Karl Rove
Subject: Iconic Image

I had a feeling when I saw it that the Kerry windsurfing images might become a huge deal.
It clearly has. Even his own supporters have been sniping about it anonymously in the press.
It was clearly a HUGE mistake.
It is a lasting image that says so much about what people dislike about Kerry.
Elite, out of touch, disconnected, arrogant.
Much like Dukakis in the tank.
I think we ought to consider a spot on this. Not one we necessarily put points behind. Like the Ailes tank spot on Dukakis.
Would serve to create further internal friction in their camp. . . .
Anyway, we're going to carve around on something for you to look at.

Rove agreed:

From: Karl Rove
Date: Sun, 12 Sep 2004 12:56:30 -0400
To: Mark McKinnon
Subject: Re: Iconic Image

I like it, provided it's in the right context—like a flip flop thing (when the wind changes, kerry changes more than just directions while windsurfing—like that only crisp and on target)

The Bush campaign made an ad, but initially determined to hold it until the eve of the first presidential debate on September 30, to sow more discord among Kerry's team, frame the debate around the flip-flopping theme, and, perhaps, rattle Kerry himself. Instead, on the 22nd, the campaign released its ad. They changed their schedule in part because an allied group, the Progress for America Voter Fund, began running its own flip-flop windsurfing ad (but without the actual video), and in part because Kerry began making a forceful and effective attack on Bush's Iraq record. Even on the new schedule, the Bush team still waited a full three weeks before striking, and as a result, benefited from free media, keen timing, and the subtle advantages of psychological warfare.

Some of Kerry's advisers considered the ad one of the most devastating of the entire campaign.

• • •

So, TO REVIEW Rove's all-important Trade Secrets for mastering the Freak Show:

- *Understand the motivations, practices, and weaknesses of the Old Media.*

- *Get your base supporters invested in your success and poised to be foot soldiers in the Freak Show wars.*

- *Speed can be addictive, so maintain control of your tempo and timing.*

- *Defend against all charges and attack the chargers, especially when you can discredit them.*

- *Know the facts about your own candidate's past.*

• *Know the facts about your opponent's past.*

• *Befriend rich people and skilled operatives prepared to run advertisements, send direct mail, and make robo-calls attacking your opponents.*

• *It is never too early to define a potential opponent in negative terms.*

• *Use surrogates that drive the enemy batty.*

The last two men to win the Democratic Party nomination for president of the United States did not understand these basic rules. The woman who might be the party's next nominee already has shown that she not only understands them, but knows how to use them.

Laura Bush
The Second First Lady of the Freak Show Era

★ ★ ★ ★ ★

ONLY TWO WOMEN HAVE HELD THE TITLE "First Lady of the United States" during the Freak Show era. Measured strictly by popularity, the second one, Laura Bush, has been significantly more successful than the first, Hillary Clinton.

Mrs. Bush has maintained her public virtue even with some biographical elements (furtive cigarette smoking, pro-choice views that clash with her husband's, and a teenage car accident that killed a friend) that surely would haunt Hillary Clinton were they a part of her political résumé.

Laura Bush, indeed, is one of the most popular modern first ladies. She has been every bit as nonpolarizing in the White House as Hillary Clinton was polarizing.

Whenever President Bush got in trouble during the 2004 race, his advisers knew that they could deploy his wife in any region of the country or before any group, her austere charm serving as a balm on whatever ailed the reelection campaign. She appeared regularly in his television commercials. Mrs. Bush was not a secret weapon but a powerful one.

Even when President Bush's job approval ratings dropped, the first lady sustained her favorable status with the American people. Not coincidentally, she demonstrated a near-complete immunity to Freak Show attacks.

In the extended Bush 43 political family, there is no accomplishment more impressive than this one. More than George W. Bush's three against-the-odds national election victories, more than his staggering fund-raising totals, Laura Bush's likely completion of eight years in the White House without generating even a ripple of polarization is a feat worth studying.

How has Mrs. Bush managed this? She is very pretty, but in a pleasant, unthreatening way. She defers to her husband, but does not appear spineless. She has no manifest sense of humor, but seems willing to make and take a joke. She has no competing career of her own, but has held jobs—indeed, the most reassuring jobs imaginable: teacher, librarian, storyteller-to-small-children. She has produced attractive daughters, but has distanced herself with cool efficiency from their sometimes wild ways. She is a traditional first lady, but spices things up with a few modern touches (her famously daring *Desperate Housewives* speech to the White House Correspondents' Association dinner in 2005, her nonmatronly charisma, her stolen cigarettes, and her subtle acknowledgment that she and 43 have a *good* marriage).

Speculation and reporting about the behind-the-scenes dynamics of the Bushes' relationship are virtually nonexistent, particularly in comparison to the endless supposition about what goes on between the Clintons. The Bushes joke innocuously about their marriage in public, but always using the same stock themes and anecdotes. The handful of friends, family members, and aides who have insight into their union exhibit so much code-of-silence discipline that the political press corps for the most part has given up trying to break new ground. To even close observers in this gossipy media age, the "Bushie" rapport remains indecipherable from afar, making conjecture futile.

But—let's face it—to paraphrase a famous political metaphor once applied to her father-in-law: Laura Bush started out as first lady already on third base, thanks to the contrast with Hillary Clinton.

In Laura Bush's cosmically successful tour of duty are Trade Secrets for how the next married aspirants to and occupants of the White House can deal with the Freak Show. First, it is indeed possible for a post-Clinton first lady to play no formal role in policy or in lightning-rod areas such as congressional relations. Second, a strong spouse can be a huge asset in protecting a presidential candidate and president from the Freak Show. And, third, the best defense against the Freak Show is a perfect blend of accommodating sweetness and chilly intimidation.

SECTION IX

★ ★ ★ ★ ★

HILLARY CLINTON, THE FREAK SHOW, AND THE PRESIDENCY

★ ★ ★ ★ ★

What Hillary Clinton and Karl Rove Know About the Way to Win the White House in 2008

★ ★ ★ ★ ★

- Long before the campaign gets under way, hire someone who is tough, fearless, assertive, discreet, and of unquestioned competence to do opposition research—on yourself.

- It's never too early to have your allies say negative things about the people who might someday run against you; strangle challengers in the crib.

- In polarized America, base voters care greatly about general election electability, so from the beginning of your nomination campaign, find ways to convey that you can win 270 electoral votes.

- If you have a relative who has been president, determine how to leverage the upside and limit the downside.

- Co-opt your opponent's strengths. For example, if your rival has a positive image as a reformer, you should cast yourself as "a reformer with results."

- Run with the same message in the nomination fight that you plan to run with in the general election.

- Relentlessly sell long-term and short-term narratives about your life that reflect your personal biography and political agenda.

- Figure out what the press and public like about you (note: the press won't like much of anything about you, unless your last name is McCain) and emphasize the events and statements that exhibit those positive traits.

• Figure out what the press and public don't like about you and minimize the number of events and statements that exhibit those negative traits.

• When you are attacked, respond to the accusations that are false and overreaching, so you can avoid responding to the accusations that are true.

• Be ready to answer the incessant and inevitable media questions about controversial topics with an immaculate version of the exact same rehearsed response, every time.

• But don't seem *too* rehearsed.

• Reporters are not your friends; steel yourself against illusions to the contrary.

• You can't know too many rich people.

• You can't have too much staff loyalty.

• Senior staff friction inevitably will occur within your campaign; keep it in the family and out of the press.

• Compile a mental enemies list of people who have crossed you. Never write it down. Make sure people are afraid to be added to the list, and even more afraid when they are on it.

• Never lose control of your public image.

INTRODUCTION

★ ★ ★ ★ ★

As HILLARY CLINTON KNOWS TOO WELL, she has a special relationship with the Freak Show.

No politician, not even her husband, has suffered as many of its mean-spirited attacks or served as such an all-purpose instrument for filling its airtime and Internet space. No other potential 2008 candidate's chances would hinge so decisively on the ability to manage its destructive forces. That is her special burden.

But she also has a special advantage: No other figure in public life knows more of the Trade Secrets required to tame the Freak Show and limit its ability to destroy reputations.

In the 1990s, Hillary Clinton lost control of her public image almost entirely. Today, no Democratic officeholder has a deeper understanding of how the Freak Show works, especially the ways it benefits conservatives, or has built a more sophisticated operation to serve as both a shield and as a weapon.

Clinton has gone from being the greatest casualty of the Freak Show to being its greatest survivor, poised to reenter the White House as president of the United States, should she choose to run in 2008.

Hillary Clinton continues to be attacked regularly by the Freak Show. Although her standing in the Senate has deterred some of the particularly scurrilous attacks that pierced her in the past, she has replaced Edward Kennedy and Bill Clinton as the leading *bête noire* of the Right. Her enemies have powerful financial and political incentives to make her the iconic face of the Democratic Party. The language used about her on the Internet, in books, in fund-raising appeals, on talk radio, and on television is pervasive and personal enough to make a shock jock blush. Though such attacks still seem to wound her, for the most part, confidants say, she has learned to detach herself emotionally from them. She is a warrior who is realistic about the political violence she would encounter in a presidential campaign.

Hillary Clinton closely watched how the Right usurped the public images of Al Gore and John Kerry. One can be certain that if she became a presidential candidate she would head off any assaults directed at her in the same fashion she has done in her Senate years. "If there is one thing that I have learned in my years in politics," Clinton wrote in a March 2005 fund-raising pitch, "it's that you can't let the opposition set the terms of the debate."

In another solicitation in November of 2005, Clinton declared, "As Karl Rove wrote in an e-mail to a New York Republican one year ago, 'We have to do something about her.' Well, I'm going to do something about that."

As part of an effort to win back the White House and to ensure that her party does not keep losing the Freak Show war, Clinton has used her clout to demand change from the powers that make up the Democratic Party—her congressional colleagues, the interest groups, the campaign committees, the left-leaning portion of the New Media. She has brought both insight and zeal to this cause because many of the attitudinal and institutional weaknesses that left her so vulnerable to the Freak Show in the 1990s are identical to the weaknesses that caused her party to lose the last three national elections and allowed Bush to win his major legislative victories. Clinton regularly has pushed her Senate Democratic colleagues to fashion a tougher and more consistent approach to framing a public message. She has mused longingly of how liberals must build "an infrastructure" of think tanks and advocacy groups to match the ideological and communications apparatus that conservatives spent decades building. Clinton has spoken approvingly of such groups as the Center for American Progress (designed to be a liberal counterpart to the Heritage Foundation) and Media Matters (devoted to condemning journalism that allegedly favors conservatives). Although Clinton usually guards her fund-raising network vigorously, she has urged some of her wealthy allies to support these groups as a long-term investment in reviving progressive politics.

This effort remains a work in progress, and Clinton's advisers are concerned that the party's bulwark still will be inferior to the conservative and Republican armory during the fight for the White House in 2008.

In building up the capacity to defend herself and attack her adversaries, the Hillary Clinton of the twenty-first century is a different person from the one America first met and dissected in the 1990s. These days, she has her public image firmly in hand. Rove attributed this change to Clinton gaining her own platform and political post for the first time after decades as her husband's satellite. "She got a position where she could actually do things and shape her own destiny," Rove said. "It's one thing to be the spouse of the president where his actions and the actions of his staff and his cabinet are going to shape largely how you're perceived, and another one if you're able to shape your own perceptions."

In the 1990s, Hillary Clinton exhibited five factors that make someone susceptible to the Freak Show.

1. A determined set of enemies who have their daggers drawn.

2. Biographical and professional vulnerabilities.

3. A public persona that makes enemies see red and personal facts seem hazardous.

4. The scent of a helpless loser in the Freak Show wars.

5. Little or no infrastructure in place to protect from attacks.

Beginning with her Senate race and continuing through her career in Congress, Hillary Clinton has systematically worked to eliminate these factors from her life. With rare exceptions, she projects an image that is less inflammatory and more stateswomanlike. She has built around her an infrastructure that protects her with quiet efficiency, but with ferocity when necessary. Her team has learned to target both existing and potential opponents. Like Karl Rove, Hillary Clinton knows that playing offense is better than playing defense.

As she has carefully built a record of professional success as a senator, author, advocate, fund-raiser, and politician, she has gone from being a consistent loser to becoming one of the paramount political winners in American politics. Clinton's formidable standing has created a far easier path to Senate reelection than anyone might have predicted.

Clinton based many of her 2000 Senate campaign's organizing principles on lessons learned from her husband's political mistakes. During her Senate term, she and her advisers borrowed some strategies of Bush and Rove, most notably their Trade Secrets for dealing with the Old Media, budding ene-

mies, and anticipated attacks. Hillary Clinton obviously dislikes Bush's policy goals, but she appreciates some of the methods he has used to achieve
them.

When the Freak Show controlled her image, Clinton was painted as *an
arrogant, power-hungry, corrupt, harsh, hypocritical liberal.* These days, even
many detractors grudgingly accept the alternative picture presented by her
biggest fans: *a competent, thoughtful, hardworking, determined, principled
role model.*

If and when Clinton runs for president, she will bring many advantages to
the task. She is already her party's best-known figure, and is the most prolific
fund-raiser in politics besides George W. Bush. She is popular with large segments of the electoral pillars of her party, including women, labor unions,
African-Americans, Hispanics, and gays and lesbians. Like her husband, she
has been part of the Democratic Party's national Conversation for more than
three decades. She has close ties to the elected officials, policy experts, activists, consultants, and political operatives who are needed to run for president. She has been traveling to key early nominating states such as Iowa and
New Hampshire for years and, more recently, has been hosting important activists from those states at her Washington home.

She knows about the importance of not giving up when conditions look
dire in a presidential campaign; about the necessity of projecting optimism;
about the consequence of appearing strong and consistent in message and
policies; about the relevance of reading a poll correctly; about the reasons national security and homeland security are critical to the job of president;
about the imperative of addressing perceived flaws with alacrity; about the
thought processes of values voters; about keeping a keen focus on the Electoral College; and about why it is vital to reflect on the strengths and weaknesses of both parties when formulating a campaign platform. In other
words, Hillary Clinton has mastered most of her husband's Trade Secrets and
has learned the way to win. By no means is she the natural politician that Bill
Clinton is. But that is exactly the point. Most of the principles in this book
can be applied by anyone who has intelligence and discipline, and Hillary
Clinton possesses both in abundance. Nor is Bill Clinton the only politician
from whom she has learned.

She also knows many of the Trade Secrets of George W. Bush and Karl
Rove and *their* way to win—the importance of embracing ideas, of knowing
a lot of people, of building a campaign on relationships and not transactions,
of initiating voter contact, of bringing in talented people and the best tech-

nology, of having a campaign team that gets along, of planning with precision, of learning from history, and of ensuring accountability for results.

In these ways Hillary Clinton is substantially more familiar with the lessons of the past two decades of American political life than any other potential 2008 presidential candidate. Still, there are three big questions about Clinton's chances to become president. *Will the country elect a woman? What will the specifics of her rationale and policy agenda be? And, above all else, can she survive the Freak Show at the presidential level?*

The "woman," "rationale," and "policy" questions will be taken up later when we look at Hillary Clinton's overall prospects as a presidential candidate.

The topic of the next three chapters is the most imperative—Hillary Clinton's evolving relationship with the Freak Show. Her understanding and performance have improved immeasurably. She has learned a lot of applicable Trade Secrets. But *coming a long way* does not always mean *coming far enough*.

LOSING TO THE FREAK SHOW

$\bigstar \quad \bigstar \quad \bigstar \quad \bigstar$

THERE ARE A THOUSAND WAYS to tell the story of what happened to Hillary Clinton in the 1990s (two thousand of which have already been written). The simplest and most complete explanation is that she failed utterly to comprehend the media and political environment in which she operated. Had she purposely tried to spend her husband's administration warping her own persona and dividing the nation, she could not have done any better—that is to say, any worse.

In retrospect, the overall narrative of Hillary Clinton's adult life suggests she was destined for a date with self-destruction. The 1970s and 1980s were the Rodham Years, in which, after earning an impressive set of diplomas, she married and hitched her fate to a man whose political ambitions were tethered to a Southern culture that forced her reluctantly to change her name, her hair, her glasses, and her demeanor. She soon was familiar with the many sacrifices a feminist first lady had to make to be considered an asset. She had to give a lot of tours of the Arkansas Governor's Mansion, appear at innumerable teas and galas, and attend the annual KATV bridal fair.

Arkansas had its own early version of the Freak Show, which most certainly enveloped Hillary Clinton, but it did not keep her from practicing law (at the Rose Law Firm, whose work would later prove controversial); from making lucrative investments (in ultimately suspect cattle futures); from serving on corporate boards (for hefty compensation from companies including Wal-Mart); from investing in real estate (with partners who had business before the state); and from staying in a marriage to a man who caused her pain (just how much was not clear). Mrs. Clinton's exposure to the national political and media worlds during her Rodham Years gave her the impression that her biography and her past would not become any more problematic in the White House than it had been in Arkansas.

In the 1990s, she made most of the same blunders as her husband, without the advantages of his political skills and with the disadvantages of being a woman in a sexist society. A quote Hillary Clinton uttered before her husband won the White House helps explain the clouded mind-set she brought to Washington. In the midst of the 1992 campaign, she created an uproar by saying she was not content to stay home serving cookies and tea rather than pursue an independent career: "I have tried the best way that I know how to be as careful as possible. Now, in hindsight, I suppose people can say 'You should have done this, you should have done that.' I didn't presume that anybody would presume anything other than that I was trying to do the right thing all the way down the line."

When Hillary Clinton arrived in Washington, of course, no such presumptions were made, and she spent the 1990s answering for both the actions of her Rodham Years and the new transgressions, real and imagined, that she committed in the Clinton years. The 1992 campaign had braced both Clintons for how savage the attacks against them would be, even if they underestimated the shifts taking place in the political-media culture and the resulting impact on their chances at political success.

Their victory, coming after so much turbulence, left the Clintons with two sentiments. One was anger, at what they considered the crudeness and irresponsibility of the Old Media. The other was exaggerated confidence in their cleverness and their capacity, with the power of the White House platform, to create their own narrative. The campaign had been wild, but by its end the Clintons believed they had battled and routed their Republican enemies, a rotating cast of unsavory characters from their past, and a scandal-obsessed press corps. Safely inside the White House and with the vast resources of the presidency at their command, they imagined the future would be about governing.

But the Clintons never stopped caring about the opinions of the Old Media and the Washington Establishment. They continued to surround themselves with starstruck, ambitious advisers who angled for invitations to glamorous parties and glitzy events. They could not refrain from scrutinizing and overreacting to the editorials in the *New York Times*. And many of the Clintons' aides, cabinet members, friends, and administration leaders had worldviews that were defined and sustained, without ambivalence or irony, by the reality represented by the Washington culture and what they considered the "mainstream" media.

Years later, Bill Clinton explained that many members of his party had become conditioned to seeing the Old Media as an ally in the search for truth and justice.

"We're all that way," he said, "and I think part of it is we grew up in the '60s and the press led us against the war and the press led us on civil rights and the press led us into Watergate. . . . Those of us of a certain age at least grew up with this almost . . . unrealistic set of expectations."

This attitude meant that bad press wounded the Clintons more deeply than their conservative counterparts, who expected journalists to be adversarial. So the Clintons came to power with two contradictory goals: to isolate the news media and to win editorial validation for the ambitious policy agenda they intended to pursue. By trying to achieve both goals at once, they achieved neither.

Even the most formulaic interactions with the media were carried out in a mood of brittle distrust. The new president waited two months until after his inauguration to have a press conference with the White House regulars, and instead gave numerous one-on-one interviews to local reporters. When journalists who covered the administration full-time complained that the president was not following the pattern of past administrations, Clinton officials proudly and defiantly announced that this was exactly the point. Breaking precedent, officials for a time shut down reporters' access to the upper area of the West Wing where the press secretary's office was located, sealing a path previously traveled with routine informality. In March 1993, when the Clintons fired the White House travel office staff, a unit responsible for organizing official presidential trip arrangements for the media, it seemed they were on track to shake things up.

In general, the Clinton White House of early 1993 had a strategy for handling the Old Media and the capital's Establishment similar to the one that would be employed by the Bush White House eight years later: *Change the balance of power to limit the influence, access, and standing of the Old Media. Look for New Media ways to communicate with the public. Don't give the Washington Establishment whatever it wants simply because of its entrenched status. Resist disclosing documents and revealing facts. Oppose congressional and independent investigations of your past actions. Defend yourself on the merits against attacks as best you can.*

But those Trade Secrets did not work for Bill and Hillary Clinton because the couple failed to implement them correctly or thoroughly, and failed to appreciate the amount of political support and self-confidence that would be required. They charged ahead heedlessly, certain that the power of the office and their crusading energy would enable them to trample long-standing Beltway rules of conduct.

They looked for New Media opportunities to limit the power of the Old Media, and relied on the president's unique political charm and personal magnetism. As Bill Clinton famously teased reporters in 1993, "You know why I can stiff you on the press conferences? Because Larry King liberated me by giving me to the American people directly," illustrating Freud's observation that all jokes reflect the true feelings of the joker.

But the Clintons overestimated the burgeoning influence of the New Media (and badly underestimated the extent to which the majority of New Media outlets were right-leaning and hostile). Having engaged a battle with the Old Media, they soon retreated in the face of controversies. They brought Gang of 500 mascot David Gergen into the White House for damage control and bitterly handed over documents to independent counsels, congressional committees, and reporters.

In the end, the Clinton White House ended up with the worst of all worlds. They infuriated the Old Media and the Washington power structure, setting them on an eight-year track of mistrust, hostility, and investigations, without building up an alternative power structure that could sustain them.

The Clintons tested their Trade Secrets, but paid a price for fumbling them. Upon taking office, the Bush administration honed and executed a slightly revised version of the same list:

You can't simultaneously care about what the Old Media and the Washington Establishment think while you are blowing them up and blowing them off. You can't take away the perks and prerogatives of the Old Media and the Washington Establishment if they are powerful enough to resist. You can't sidestep the Old Media if you don't have the infrastructure in place to get out your message. Ignore the criticism that will arise if you refuse to disclose documents or reveal facts. Without exception, do whatever it takes to halt every congressional or independent investigation of your past actions. While defending yourself on the merits from attacks as best you can, go on the offense by using fast and aggressive research to discredit your accusers. Repeat the mantra "that is an old story the public has decided it doesn't care about" in response to any controversy that the press or political enemies throw at you.

After eight years in office, Bill Clinton's administration was aware of the hard-line version of this set of Trade Secrets, but his team failed to implement them consistently. By contrast, Hillary Clinton's Senate campaign and subsequent congressional operation exercised the correct rules dutifully, in part because the Old Media was substantially weaker than it was in 1993, but also because of calculated manipulation. The Hillary Clinton team has been further encouraged in this endeavor by observing how efficiently the Trade Secrets worked for President Bush.

• • •

HILLARY CLINTON MAY have had an extended crash course in politics during her decades in nonelective public life, but her remarkable success in the Senate is the product of internalizing the paramount Trade Secret: *If you don't protect yourself from the Freak Show and stay in control of your public image, nothing else matters.* Whatever one thinks of her or her prominent role as campaign spouse, the attacks to which she was subjected once her husband launched his presidential bid were unprecedented in the modern era.

As Mrs. Clinton was being introduced to the world beyond Arkansas, keen conservative strategists believed that she could be used to undermine her husband's chances if the public perceived her as the epitome of a shrill, menacing extremist who wanted to inculcate into American society a radical 1960s sensibility. Prominent Republicans spent the spring and summer of 1992 endorsing this notion and making sure it was widely disseminated.

Richard Nixon told *Time* magazine, "Barbara Bush plays the piano so she doesn't drown out George's violin. Hillary pounds the piano so hard that Bill can't be heard. You want a wife who's intelligent, but not too intelligent."

At the Republican convention in Houston in August of 1992, there was a coordinated offensive against Hillary Clinton. Marilyn Quayle, the wife of the incumbent vice president, delivered an oblique but artful censure of Hillary Clinton as a member of the "counterculture."

And Pat Buchanan, given a prime speaking slot despite his well-publicized nomination challenge to George H. W. Bush, laid into Mrs. Clinton with his typical understatement:

Elect me, and you get two for the price of one, Mr. Clinton says of his lawyer-spouse. And what does Hillary believe? Well, Hillary believes that 12-year-olds should have a right to sue their parents, and she has compared marriage as an institution to slavery—and life on an Indian reservation.

Well, speak for yourself, Hillary.

Friends, this is radical feminism. The agenda Clinton & Clinton would impose on America—abortion on demand, a litmus test for the Supreme Court, homosexual rights, discrimination against religious schools, women in combat—that's change, all right. But it is not the kind of change America wants. It is not the kind of change America needs. And it is not the kind of change we can tolerate in a nation that we still call God's country.

• • •

THE DEFINITION OF tolerance notwithstanding, after the election Hillary Clinton was given a bit of a honeymoon during her initial few months in the White House. In the very first week of the new administration, her husband announced that she would head his monumental health care reform effort. She was made "Person of the Week" by ABC News's *World News Tonight with Peter Jennings,* and received messages of encouragement in some Old Media editorials. Friendly words were dispensed from several congressional Republicans who were impressed by her intelligence and visible command of public policy.

Then the honeymoon was over. Problems of all sorts began to erupt, ranging from her role in the firing of the White House travel office staff to the costs of her haircuts to the speculation surrounding the death of her former law partner, the White House lawyer Vince Foster.

The outcome of her health care effort tipped the balance against her. On September 28, 1993, Clinton began marathon testimony on Capitol Hill about the state of the administration's legislative proposal. It was by most accounts an impressive performance heartily praised by members of Congress from both parties. But during her encore appearance the following day, the first lady had a singular colloquy with Republican congressman Dick Armey of Texas, who said to the first lady of the United States, "I have been told about your charm and wit, and let me say the reports on your charm are overstated and the reports on your wit are understated." The insult became emblematic of the Clinton-era Freak Show and exhibited the dramatically different rules by which conservatives dealt with Hillary Clinton.

• • •

ILL-NATURED TEASING may have amused the Freak Show, but the Clinton health care plan suffered a classic capital demise, prolonged and contentious. And it was this legislative failure that defined Hillary Clinton's Freak Show image, along with the relentless investigations that plagued the administration, particularly the tortured multi-act drama of the Monica Lewinsky scandal. Other story lines contributed as well, but those stood out in cementing Clinton for her opponents (and many others) as an *arrogant, power-hungry, corrupt, harsh, hypocritical liberal.*

After the health care bill effectively died in September of 1994, Hillary Clinton never again took on such an assignment. She instead lent her time and influence to a wide range of smaller projects and did not allow herself to be identified with a major expansion of government.

But throughout her remaining days in the White House, Republican chair Ken Mehlman argued, Clinton's public image for many Americans was "the health care woman, the woman who was going to take away your health care and put you in jail if you try to get your own health care. Bad image."

"Hillary Care" became one of the dirtiest phrases in politics, signifying a radical, convoluted, and intrusive big-government program. Whenever possible, Hillary Clinton would kid about what she had learned from the experience—she become a rhetorical devotee of incrementalism—but the tarnish lingered.

The other defining negative story line was a ceaseless one that transfixed the Old and New Media alike. This was the parade of personal Clinton chronicles, including Whitewater, Troopergate, her Pink Press Conference, her lost-and-found billing records, her cattle futures profits, and her grand jury appearance.

Despite this constant barrage of controversy, after the fiasco of health care, she kept up a full schedule of a conventional first lady—or, at least, of a conventional modern one. She started a newspaper column in 1995 and published several books, including *It Takes a Village* in 1996. She traveled internationally, giving a powerful speech on human rights in China and becoming one of the most admired women on the planet (if not by everyone in her home country). She appeared at formal social functions and on the covers of dozens of women's magazines, from *Good Housekeeping* to *Vogue*.

As Bill Clinton said, "She just kept doing things," such as work on early child development, veterans' medical care, and historic preservation. "I think that's what you have to do," he says. "When they try to demonize you, you just have to let people see a different picture every day and pretty soon the old definition doesn't work anymore."

These activities may not have been undertaken explicitly to remake her image, but they generated goodwill in some quarters and, for a few years, gave Clinton the kind of nonpartisan platform she always had envisioned the first lady's office to be. Then, in late January 1998, the ultimate Clinton scandal, and the high/low point in the history of the Freak Show, hit with maximum force, in the form of "Miss Lewinsky."

• • •

THREE WEEKS AFTER the story of her husband's affair with Monica Lewinsky broke, Hillary Clinton was struggling to regain her footing. She had made her famous morning television appearance on January 27, during which she denounced the "vast, right-wing conspiracy" she insisted was out to destroy her husband's presidency. She had maintained a brave face and withstood countless excruciating and humiliating media stories. On February 11, 1998, the intense swirl of special prosecutor Ken Starr's investigation was dominating Washington.

But the Clinton who generated the headlines that day was the first lady, who held what amounted to a press conference about the Lewinsky matter. Although public opinion polls were showing approval for the job her husband was doing as president, February 11 obviously was not an ideal time for Mrs. Clinton to face journalists. But the first lady had an important event planned, and she was not changing her schedule. It was supposed to be a casual meeting with the press. But by the end, Hillary Clinton had delivered an early and unvarnished appraisal of how the Freak Show was threatening her husband's presidency and civil society more generally.

The setting was the White House's Map Room, famous as the ground floor area from which Franklin Delano Roosevelt monitored Allied progress in World War II by studying maps charting the latest military developments. During the Clinton years, the windowless room earned a reputation as a sort of Freak Show Chamber. It was where Bill Clinton and Al Gore conferred with their campaign team in the spring of 1996 to sketch out the reelection campaign's budget—the plan that called for massive fund-raising accomplished in part by holding controversial coffee sessions with big donors, many of which were held in the very same Map Room. It also was where Bill Clinton would sit for his under-oath confrontation with Ken Starr on August 17, 1998, with a live video feed sent to the grand jurors a few blocks away at the federal courthouse.

That February day, in the Map Room, Hillary Clinton had gathered a select group of reporters (with no television cameras present) to discuss the

White House's Millennium Council project, a series of historical and cultural events meant to commemorate the impending milestone of the year 2000. After a lengthy presentation from Mrs. Clinton and a few other speakers, reporters asked just two questions about the Millennium Council before Helen Thomas of United Press International changed the direction with a brusquely elegant transition: "Mrs. Clinton, how do you think the President is bearing up under the present current history and headlines?" Clinton semi-pretended to answer by focusing on her husband's then ongoing face-off with Saddam Hussein.

The next question was equally elliptical and euphemistic ("Are you surprised, gratified perhaps, at the public response to this situation?"). The first lady used the opportunity to talk about the administration's record on deficit reduction, welfare reform, crime, and education, and about her husband's "constant optimism, his good humor in the face of extraordinary challenges and obstacles, his willingness to continue to reach out and work with people." She added, "I think that it's an inspiration to me."

When another reporter returned to the topic of Iraq, Clinton sounded like she was fully focused on the threat of another Gulf war, rather than invoking a national security crisis to divert attention from a personal one: "I think what's driving . . . everyone who is reluctantly but firmly taking this stand against Saddam Hussein is that we know, based on the U.N. inspections, that he has continued his research and development of biological and chemical weapons. We know he is without conscience and has used such weapons against his own people. And for whatever perverse psychological reasons, he seems intent upon this standoff with the larger world community over our efforts to try to protect not only existing human beings, but future generations from this kind of warfare."

So there you have Hillary Clinton's potential 2008 presidential platform: a celebration of the domestic conditions of the 1990s along with tough talk on Iraq, all in one press conference. The reporters, meanwhile, proceeded with their delicate inquisition (the word "Lewinsky" was never uttered in the session), with one journalist noting that in the Internet Age of eternal recall and limitless space, "you could say something and you can't take it back." Clinton was asked if "this new media is necessarily an entirely good thing." She replied,

> We're going to have to really think hard, and I think that every time technology makes an advance—when you move to the railroad, or you move to

the cotton gin, or you move to the automobile, or the airplane, and now certainly as you move to the computer and increasing accessibility and instantaneous information on the computer, we are all going to have to rethink how we deal with this, because there are always competing values.

As exciting as these new developments are, there are a number of serious issues without any kind of editing function or gate-keeping function. What does it mean to have the right to defend your reputation, or to respond to what someone says? There used to be this old saying that the lie can be halfway around the world before the truth gets its boots on. Well, today, the lie can be twice around the world before the truth gets out of bed to find its boots. I mean, it is just beyond imagination what can be disseminated. So I think we're going to have to really worry about this. . . . It can be done to anybody, and it can get an audience, and it can create a falsehood about somebody. And certainly it's multiplied many times over if you happen to be in public life.

I don't have any clue about what we're going to do legally, regulatorily, technologically—I don't have a clue. But I do think we always have to keep competing interests in balance. I'm a big pro-balance person. That's why I love the Founders—checks and balances; accountable power. Anytime an individual or an institution or an invention leaps so far out ahead of that balance and throws a system, whatever it might be—political, economic, technological—out of balance, you've got a problem, because then it can lead to the oppression of people's rights, it can lead to the manipulation of information, it can lead to all kinds of bad outcomes which we have seen historically. So we're going to have to deal with that. . . . We've got to see whether our existing laws protect people's right of privacy, protect them against defamation. And if they can, how do you do that when you can press a button and you can't take it back. So I think we have to tread carefully.

Shortly after offering that commentary, Hillary Clinton concluded one of her most significant on-the-record press events as first lady. The ensuing news coverage centered on her dogged support for her husband and her prediction that the controversy engulfing the White House would "slowly dissipate over time."

Little was made in the moment of her comments about the New Media. For years afterward, however, observers, including Matt Drudge, would seize on her Map Room remarks to suggest she favored censorship of the Internet. Drudge posted parts of the transcript on his site with the preface: "Obviously irritated, but not mentioning the DRUDGE REPORT by name, Mrs. Clinton touched on possible regulation of Internet news reports."

For her part, Mrs. Clinton soldiered on, even as she dealt with Starr's continuing investigation, impeachment, Paula Jones, and multitudinous Freak Show manifestations.

Later that year, in November, New York senator Daniel Patrick Moynihan announced his intention to retire at the end of his term in 2000, and speculation began almost immediately that Hillary Clinton would run for the seat. As the rumors and conjecture whipped up yet another frenzy, Clinton continued to perform her duties as first lady, including her work on the Millennium Council, whose official theme was about to become her own: "honor the past, imagine the future."

CHALLENGING THE FREAK SHOW

★ ★ ★ ★ ★

FOR HILLARY CLINTON, running for the Senate in 2000 was not nearly as grueling as living in the White House. Her first campaign for public office nonetheless provided a bumpy transition from battered symbol to respected member of Congress.

On balance, the strategy developed on her first Senate campaign was just right—an effective break from the practices that had failed her in the 1990s. The approach also was strikingly similar to what Bush and Rove simultaneously were doing in their pursuit of the presidency.

The 2000 Senate campaign had the potential to be a Freak Show classic. Indeed, most political reporters nationally and in New York were expecting a carnival—and her adversaries did their best to wheel in the rides and the shooting gallery. But Clinton proved just how much she had learned over the previous eight years about navigating such challenges. She emerged from the process with both a victory and greater control of her public image. Her approach rested on five Trade Secrets.

First, *Freak Show attacks represent the greatest threat to political health, and maximum force and speed must be used to repel them.*

Second, *Frequent and well-distributed talking points are vital for the candidate, the staff, and surrogates.*

Third, *Focus must be kept on the weak links in the assaults made on you, to discredit the overall attacks, the attackers of the moment, and (preemptively) any future attacks or attackers.*

Fourth, *Reporters are not your friends and do not have your best interests at heart.* Clinton learned this (amply) in the 1990s, but some of her advisers had to be made to understand this reality and adjust their behavior accordingly. A reporter with a shared background, philosophy, and child care issues would not necessarily sacrifice a big scoop or career advancement for the benefit of a chummy campaign operative.

And, fifth, *Not all journalists are created equal, and therefore should not be treated equally.* Clinton's campaign effectively divided the press into groups, each requiring separate rules: The local media outside New York City (essential to deal with, symbolically vital, and mostly safe); the local media inside New York City (essential to deal with at certain times, symbolically vital, and somewhat safe if handled correctly); the national media (essential to avoid, but unneccesary to discredit); and book writers (essential to avoid, and often essential to discredit).

Clinton's team understood that they had additional challenges when mounting their effort to reclaim her image. The two biggest hurdles for most Senate candidates—earning name recognition and raising money—were not problems for Hillary Clinton. But there were lofty nationwide expectations about how she would perform, intense scrutiny of her every move, legions of enemies from all over the country, and persistent questions about why someone from Illinois and Arkansas should represent New York in Washington.

• • •

THE MOST INSPIRED move of Clinton's Senate campaign was to organize her assiduous travel throughout New York around "listening tours" in which she would make stops at schools, community centers, businesses, and neighborhood events. She would mingle with citizens from all walks of life from across the state and engage in detailed conversations about their problems. The advantages of this format were many.

First, it addressed the carpetbagger issue; Clinton wanted to represent people from a state in which she had never lived, but she used the events to convince prospective voters that she understood their concerns. Second, it took the edge off Clinton's image as imperious, engrossed as she was in the respectful act of "listening" to what the Gang of 500 calls "real people." Third, it routinely kept Clinton away from the national press corps, which could not complain that she was neglecting to answer questions, even if they could not ask the questions themselves.

Fourth, it organized Clinton's campaign days around an appearance of substance, emphasizing her greatest strength and (occasionally) shaming reporters into writing stories about actual policy, as well as framing the race as a referendum on issues important to the voters of New York, rather than as a referendum on Hillary Clinton "the controversial first lady." And fifth, Hillary Clinton's star power and personal attention, when directed one-on-one (or even one-on-twenty), was powerful enough to secure the votes of a good number of people who met and spoke with her, even if they had not initially been inclined to cast their ballots her way.

Her spokesman, Howard Wolfson, repeated the same on-message quote: "Over the next months, Mrs. Clinton will travel throughout the state meeting with New Yorkers in small groups and listening to them discuss the issues that concern them the most." Candidate Clinton came primed and ready. She supplemented her vast knowledge of national policy with tutorials on the local matters and personalities of every New York town and county. Her diligence earned her points with many New Yorkers and credit from reporters around the state.

At first it appeared that Clinton's path to the Senate might be blocked by the formidable New York City mayor Rudy Giuliani, whose fund-raising capacity and statewide fame roughly matched her own. But after being an official candidate for just three months, during which he had great success raising campaign money but also problems of his own with the Freak Show, which feasted on his mercurial personality and the convoluted details of his marital breakup, Giuliani withdrew from the race, disclosing that he was undergoing treatment for prostate cancer. It is impossible to say what would have happened if Giuliani had ended up being Clinton's general election opponent. Perhaps he would have won and halted her electoral career right then and there.

Replacing the magnetic Giuliani was the mostly untested Rick Lazio, a Long Island congressman who proved to be an anemic foe. For a time, that seemed not necessarily to matter, since Hillary Clinton was also in effect running against her family's past, her new home state's tabloid media culture, and a national conservative movement determined to stop her. She was always favored to win in Democratic-leaning New York, but the polls stayed close and the race was unprecedented and, thus, unpredictable.

Bill Clinton loomed over the race from start to finish. Behind the scenes, he gave his wife and her campaign plenty of advice. But in public, the campaign generally played down his role, from its slogan on the campaign's posters (the surname-free "Hillary"), to her announcement event (at which he did not speak), to her television commercials (in which he was a nonfactor).

Bill Clinton's presence was felt indirectly through two of his advisers. Pollster Mark Penn and media adviser Mandy Grunwald, along with Wolfson, were charged with protecting and projecting Hillary Clinton's image. All three had plenty of experience in New York's special strain of politics and understood the unique challenges their client would face.

No American city's journalists cover statewide political campaigns as aggressively and exhaustively as the New York City press corps. The daily level of scrutiny was predictably intense, turning events that would be inconsequential in any other Senate campaign into long-running dramas that dominated the news for days or even weeks. There was the question of the authenticity, duration, and strength of Clinton's passion for the New York Yankees; a *Talk* magazine story in which she explained her husband's infidelity with references to his traumatic childhood and Christian theology; her shifting position on her husband's leniency plan for some members of the Puerto Rican terrorist group, FALN, a hot-button issue in a city with a large population from the commonwealth; a controversial embrace she shared in 1999 with Suha Arafat, the wife of Palestinian leader Yasser Arafat; Clinton's failure to tip a waitress after a complimentary meal; and many, many more. The Freak Show cast these developments as revealing of her less appealing traits, or as leadership tests that she could not possibly pass. When it came to the constant barrage of petty or pointed stories, no matter what she and her campaign did to try to limit the damage, it appeared that they had some adverse impact on her reputation.

Taking advantage of the widespread negative energy, Giuliani and then Lazio set up massive fund-raising operations, drawing contributions from across the country. Together, they raised a total of nearly $63 million. Anti–Hillary Clinton interest groups promised a heavily funded effort to defeat the first lady, threatening to derail her campaign with tens of millions of dollars in advertising and voter contact of their own. Yet the money raised by the groups was, for the most part, negligible, and many organizations floundered or failed to follow through on their promised effort.

One group that did launch an attack was the Emergency Committee to Stop Hillary Rodham Clinton, headed by prominent conservative figures such as Ed Meese, Alan Keyes, Lyn Nofziger, Ernest Istook, Bob Dornan, and Morton Blackwell. One of their direct mail letters spewed "Wherever Hillary goes, corruption, crime and cover-up follow." The Republican Party of New York attempted to link Clinton to Mideast terrorism. In some ways, Clinton benefited from these operations, using their menace to generate contributions from her own supporters.

But the main event was Clinton versus Lazio, and on that front things were plenty intense. One of the Republican's last television advertisements showed an unattractive picture of an angry Hillary Clinton, while the announcer's voice-over said, "Hillary Clinton: You can always trust her to do what's right—for Hillary Clinton." The rhetoric from both campaigns was sharp, with allegations about who was less concerned about breast cancer and about terrorists. But the feckless Lazio and his allied political groups posed less of a challenge to Clinton's campaign than attacks coming from the media Freak Show.

• • •

As with George W. Bush's presidential campaign that same year, it was the old-fashioned hardbound book that most tested the skills of the Clinton campaign in protecting her public image. Two separate volumes, published seven months apart, measured Clinton's ability to defend herself.

Around the time that rumblings began in earnest over a possible Senate run, best-selling author Gail Sheehy, famous for the 1970s baby-boomer manual *Passages,* was publicizing her fifteen-thousand-word piece for the February 1999 issue of *Vanity Fair.* More than twenty glossy pages were filled with breathy analysis of the Clinton marriage and speculation about everything from the president's paternity to the first lady's ability to disengage from humiliating rumors and be shielded from unpleasant topics ("no sex, no late-night talk-show gibes, no facts about the scandal that might distress or distract her" found their way to her ears).

Sheehy had trekked from Little Rock to Martha's Vineyard, interviewing such diverse subjects as Dick Morris; his wife, Eileen McGann; Hillary Clinton's mother, Dorothy Rodham; and Clintonite Betsey Wright, who claimed "Hillary Clinton is probably the only person in America you could tell a cigar joke to and she wouldn't get it." Shortly after *Vanity Fair* released excerpts in early January, Sheehy's agent revealed that a book deal based on an expanded version was imminent. That same week Carl Bernstein, of Woodward and Bernstein fame, announced he had agreed to write a book on Mrs. Clinton. Bernstein said he would give the book "the thorough research it deserves." (Thorough, indeed: The work had yet to materialize well into Clinton's Senate reelection.)

Anticipatory publicity about Sheehy's forthcoming book was folded into the six months of speculation about the first lady's post–White House options. Sheehy had talked with, by her count, hundreds of people (with the exception of Mrs. Clinton herself, who had not cooperated with the author since speaking with her for a notorious 1992 *Vanity Fair* piece).

Hillary's Choice was launched in November 1999 with a massive media blitz. The revelations within, however, were deemed insipid, with psychobabble wisps about Hillary Rodham's early life and a purple portrayal of a marriage based on passion, jealousy, hurt, and addiction. None of the disclosures was particularly harmful, but the overall representation threatened to distract New York voters from the precise public image Hillary Clinton was laboring to whittle and buff.

Clinton's advisers recognized the threat and soon settled on what they believed was the most sensible response: a thorough campaign to discredit Sheehy. Central to this effort was Howard Wolfson, who familiarized himself with the text, showed up at Sheehy's public events, and became as visible a television presence as Sheehy herself, manipulating the coverage in his candidate's favor. The heart of the strategy, à la Rove and Bartlett, was to find the factual errors in the book and use them to hammer away at Sheehy's own credibility.

First, the Clinton team responded to the handful of new allegations, such as a story that a young Hillary Rodham might have smoked pot with a college boyfriend, with terse denials and curt conviction. Instead of bothering with an elaborate defense, they concentrated on the book's numerous sloppy errors (many of which were, as far as Hillary Clinton's reputation was concerned, totally innocuous). Sheehy had not helped her cause. After one postponement for more research, the book had been rushed out to coincide with Clinton's anticipated candidacy announcement, and was riddled with inaccuracies and apparent misquotes.

The *Washington Post's* "Reliable Source" column, with some help from the nascent Clinton campaign, took to publishing a regular feature, "Gail's Goof Corner," which highlighted "psychobiographer" Sheehy's mistakes. The column catalogued the confusion over nicknames; famous facts (the context of Al Haig's memorable remark "I'm in control here"); interview subjects (lobbyist Tony Podesta told the *Post* that not only had his personal information been misrepresented, but "Sheehy once made an appointment to interview me and then she canceled it"); and assorted Clintonites (citing Sheehy's dig at onetime White House Chief of Staff Mack McLarty that "It is worth noting that his marriage, to a woman smarter than he, did not survive," the *Post* retorted, "It may be worth noting—but it ain't so. The McLartys have stayed happily married for three decades").

When Sheehy appeared on *Larry King Live* to promote the book, she was followed by Wolfson, who took issue with, among other things, the assertion that Hugh Rodham had been absent from his daughter's college graduation. (Wolfson: "There's a piece of the book where it talks about the relationship that Hillary had with her father and describes it as fraught and it was tension filled as a result of the fact that Hillary's father didn't go to her graduation at Wellesley, and makes a whole big deal of this. The fact is that Hillary's father was at her graduation at Wellesley. So I think that's the kind of thing we find in the book." Larry King: "You mean that's totally incorrect?" Wolfson: "That's correct—totally incorrect.")

After the show, Wolfson and Sheehy quarreled in the CNN green room, and Sheehy subsequently complained to the *New York Daily News,* "I feel mousetrapped. . . . They wanted me to be wrong so they could discredit the book." Wolfson responded, "This is the 'dog ate my homework' excuse. I don't work for Gail Sheehy. I'm not her fact-checker. The onus is on her to get things right. That is the burden that any biographer bears, and in this case she failed."

In addition to the errors, Sheehy's oeuvre as a baby-boomer pundit prompted critics and columnists to regard the new tome with dyspeptic disdain. Reviewers mocked the ham-handed therapeutic ponderings and attempts at analysis, and brushed aside the assortment of intimate details about the Clinton marriage as old news.

Sheehy did not handle the criticism calmly. She sent letters to the various publications that had trashed her book, penning such grievances as "The White House spin and smear machine is making an effort to fog up the warm reception to my book." As the *New York Daily News*'s Tom DeFrank wrote, "Unfortunately for Sheehy, she's made it easy for the Clintonistas . . . the book has a number of inexcusable wrongos." Sheehy fumed, "My book will survive. My larger concern is that this White House spin machine is still able to divide good journalists against one another. This only further tarnishes us as a watchdog of government in the eyes of a jaded public. When will we learn?"

Within days after its release, few were assessing the actual content of Sheehy's book. Talking heads discussed an incident early in Sheehy's career in which the subject of her profile had turned out to be a composite rather than a real person. There was additional chatter citing *Passages* as evidence of her pop culture superficiality. Sheehy was pilloried for her inability to get Hillary Clinton to agree to be interviewed. And many of the book's factual flaws were entertaining enough on their own to sustain a few minutes each on cable TV, further devaluing Sheehy's standing.

By December 1999, the book had been pushed out of the campaign dialogue, after appearing on the *New York Times* best-seller list only one week. Clinton's campaign had effectively shifted the attention of the Old Media and much of the Freak Show from Hillary Clinton's past to Sheehy's credibility and reputation. And they were able to do it by highlighting factual errors that were in most cases fairly insignificant or peripheral to Sheehy's central thesis and themes.

The lessons from this episode for Clinton and for any 2008 presidential candidates:

- *Go on the offensive against anyone who threatens you and exploit any weakness, great or small.*

- *In the Freak Show, you can get journalists to attack other journalists and do your bidding, if you give them the ammunition.*

- *Whenever possible, retaliate against your attackers using a spokesperson or surrogate, rather than the principal, to keep the boss above the fray.*

• • •

THE COMBINATION OF Sheehy's errors and the Clinton campaign's assertive work shielded the candidate from any real harm. In July of 2000, however, another book presented a greater challenge. With Rudy Giuliani safely out of the competition and the shimmering promise of the New York Senate seat within sight, the Clinton team was thrown off balance by accusations of an anti-Semitic vulgarity allegedly once uttered by Mrs. Clinton—a potentially disastrous charge to a candidate running in liberal, ethnic New York.

Jerry Oppenheimer, a former *National Enquirer* reporter, published *State of a Union: Inside the Complex Marriage of Bill and Hillary Clinton.* The Freak Show dined on the excerpts about the couple's alleged hot Yale sex life, cold adulterous marriage, and assorted sexual predilections. But the biggest stir concerned a claim, supposedly backed by three sources, that, in 1974, after Bill Clinton lost his bid for Congress to a Republican incumbent, Hillary Rodham called her husband's campaign manager, Paul Fray, a "f——ing Jew b——d." Matt Drudge broke the media embargo on July 14, four days before the book's release. He announced the news with his signature flashing red light and a headline warning, "**Contains Graphic Description.**" Pop psychology was one thing; staying in a troubled marriage, throwing a few hissy fits, or even exhibiting acute ambition were unappealing but relatively minor offenses. Potential evidence of religious prejudice was a major crisis.

Some of Hillary Clinton's best media strategists were Jewish and they tried to solve the problem. The campaign staffers had two big challenges. First, they did not have all the facts necessary to immediately rebut the allegation. More problematic was that some people felt it was at least *possible* that the charge was true. The stark specificity of the tale coupled with the continuing controversy over Clinton's cordial moment with Suha Arafat catapulted the story to premier Freak Show status.

The varied manifestations of Hillary Clinton's scorching temper were hashed about in the New York media, by those who knew her now and when. Her friends and allies hotly insisted Mrs. Clinton was incapable of bigoted thoughts, let alone words. As for her critics, while few accused her of outright anti-Semitism, some speculated that an angry flare-up might release offensive slurs. A Clinton spokesperson offered the blanket statement, "New Yorkers will be subjected to a lot of trash about Hillary over the next several months. We are confident that they will be able to see this for what it is."

But the charge was so serious that dramatic steps had to be taken. The two-pronged strategy was to issue strong denials, while trotting out earnest surrogates to testify to Clinton's lack of anti-Semitism.

On July 16, Hillary Clinton, with Bill Clinton by her side (and Jewish congresswoman Nita Lowey on hand as well), gave a press conference on the lawn of her Chappaqua, New York, home. With welling eyes, the candidate avowed, "I want to state unequivocally that it never happened and very clearly point out that it goes against my entire life. In the past I may have called someone a name, but I never used ethnic, racial, anti-Semitic, bigoted, discriminatory, prejudiced accusations against anybody. I've never done it. I've never thought it. So why people are accusing me of this is certainly beyond my understanding." She admitted her decision to address the allegation came after "a lot of difficult conversations" with her advisers. The media reviews of this appearance raised the question of why her reaction was so extreme, if indeed she was telling the truth. Clinton, therefore, violated the Trade Secret *Never let them see you sweat (or cry, for that matter).*

President Clinton was, for a change, front and center, issuing a statement defending his wife: "It's unfortunate that people would try to exploit false charges like this in an election rather than look at what she has done for her entire life." That he was in the midst of Mideast peace talks at Camp David did not go unnoticed.

As the story played out (with various tweaked versions of the original tale popping up in the press), aides continued to bash it with defiance. Wolfson told the *Daily News*, "It is clearly designed to divide the Jewish community. We are confident that New Yorkers will see it for the garbage it is."

Over the next couple of days, Hillary Clinton was defended by a wide range of politicians. In one event, Senators Chuck Schumer, Joe Lieberman, Frank Lautenberg, Barbara Boxer, and Representatives Nita Lowey, Eliot Engel, Jerrold Nadler, and Anthony Weiner held a joint press conference in Washington to offer their unqualified support. Senator Schumer was heartfelt: "I have known Hillary Clinton now for eight years, and she does not have an anti-Semitic thought, an anti-Semitic bone in her body."

Clinton opponents sheltered her, too, sort of. Rudy Giuliani gave a press conference at City Hall saying, "I really don't care what she said 26 years ago. . . . I'm willing to accept her at her word . . . I can't imagine that a single voter is going to care about what she said or did 26 years ago." Presidential candidate George W. Bush told Larry King, "I hope she doesn't get elected. I'm for Rick Lazio. But I just cannot believe that, you know, the politics of dredging up something that somebody alleges somebody said 26 years ago as relevant. I don't think Mrs. Clinton is anti-Semitic. I mean, I don't know her but this is not right for somebody to dredge up some quote." His wife, Laura Bush, added, "This is an example of exactly what I think I don't like about politics."

Lazio himself hedged, "This is sort of a 'he said, they said' situation. Three people say Mrs. Clinton said one thing. Mrs. Clinton is saying that she did not say it. I don't know who to believe, quite frankly. And I think one of the things that's disappointing about this is that New Yorkers don't know who to believe." A few other Republicans continued to circulate the charges and call for an apology. The media seemed somewhat uncomfortable with the character of the story, particularly since it lacked sufficient new details to move it forward. Polls, meanwhile, suggested that the majority of New Yorkers (Jews among them) disbelieved the allegations, or at least would not be influenced by them come November.

The coverage evaporated by the end of July. Barely a dozen additional stories appeared anywhere in print for the remainder of the campaign.

The lessons from this episode: *The most difficult Freak Show attacks to refute are those that involve proving a negative.*

Always be prepared, and don't let your emotions get the better of you.

• • •

EVEN THOUGH CLINTON seemed to be running as much against her Freak Show image and herself as she was against Rick Lazio, in the real world, only Lazio actually could beat her, by getting a majority of the vote. The best way to stop that from happening was, of course, to make him lose control of his public image.

Using the Rove technique of unremitting and disciplined labeling, Clinton's media advisers made Rick Lazio into a "Newt Gingrich clone" and, after he physically advanced on Hillary Clinton during a televised debate, they branded him "menacing." Her spokespeople invoked these descriptions about their opponent whenever possible.

Those characterizations had a discernible impact on Lazio's public image, but the Clinton campaign kept at it. They wanted to add a few more unattractive adjectives to the litany. In a New York election, one can hardly do better than "hypocrite" and "anti-Israel," two of the charges that Clinton herself had faced.

Lazio continued to push the Suha Arafat controversy, linking it with what he argued were Mrs. Clinton's pro-Palestinian actions, such as accepting and then returning campaign contributions from a Muslim group hostile to Israel, and, by hugging Mrs. Arafat, effectively condemning Israel for using poison gas. During a debate, he went so far as to say, "When you cavort with terrorists, with people that pronounce that violence and murder can be used as a tool to achieve political ends, you give them credibility."

But Lazio himself had traveled with Bill Clinton as part of a delegation to the Mideast in late 1998, and had met with none other than Suha Arafat's husband, Yasser. A picture of the New York congressman and the Palestinian leader showed the two men beaming and enthusiastically shaking hands. Luckily for the Democratic Senate nominee from New York, a copy of the picture existed in the official files of the White House that was still run by her husband.

The campaign had known about the picture for some time, but kept mum until September 10, 2000, when the photograph conveniently found its way onto the pages of the *New York Post* (the paper said the photo had "surfaced"). The *Post* received the picture just one day after Lazio criticized President

Clinton for shaking hands with Fidel Castro at a United Nations event. At the time, some public opinion polls were showing a tight race, with Jewish New Yorkers a key swing voting bloc. The accompanying story said that the White House had agreed to release the picture to the *Post* after the paper was tipped off by a Democratic congressman from California close to the Clintons, but not known to be particularly close to the *Post*.

The White House press secretary, Joe Lockhart, took responsibility for releasing the photo, after Lazio criticized Bill Clinton's conduct with the comment "I think we send the wrong message when we embrace—whether it's Mrs. Arafat or Fidel Castro. . . . I would not have shook Fidel Castro's hand. . . . Obviously he's been a threat to American security in the past. I don't know what there is to shake his hand about, to tell you the truth."

When faced with the glaring photographic evidence, a sputtering Lazio contended, "It wasn't a kiss. It wasn't a hug. It wasn't a call for Palestinian statehood. . . . This is typical of this White House; they're willing to do anything in order to win this campaign." He reiterated, "I would not shake Fidel Castro's hand. I think he's been a terrorist. . . . [Arafat] is a person who we're involved in peace negotiations with."

Wolfson mused, "I wonder if Mr. Lazio knows how to say 'hypocrite' in Arabic. . . . He should stop the hypocrisy and start coming clean with New Yorkers."

Hillary Clinton was so anxious to highlight the Lazio-Arafat photo-op the day of its publication that her campaign summoned reporters out of a church service they were covering to hear her talk about it. Of the picture's release, Hillary Clinton commented, "You'll have to ask the White House about that," but added, "You know, we need to make sure that people in New York have all the information to cast an informed vote about what's in New York's best interest, and I think that someone who says one thing and does another—consistently, as he has—should be held accountable for that."

The following evening, Mrs. Clinton and her husband serendipitously attended a dinner sponsored by the World Jewish Congress, where the first lady was honored for her work on Holocaust reparations.

The incriminating photograph became a staple of the campaign's final six weeks, during which time strategists for both sides continued to believe that the Jewish vote could determine the outcome. All of New York became familiar with the image. Giuliani told reporters, "I'm a little confounded by it. . . . I don't particularly like to shake hands with murderers," adding the equally damning opinion that perhaps Lazio "doesn't have the background and understanding of Arafat that I do." The Clinton campaign rolled out an ad with former New York City mayor Ed Koch holding the photo aloft, yelling, "Rick, stop with the sleaze already!"

The lessons from this episode for Clinton and for any 2008 presidential candidates:

- *They pull a knife, you pull a gun.*

- *A picture is worth more than a thousand votes.*

- *Timing is everything and patience is a virtue (see "Transcendency, Transparency, and Destruction" for the Karl Rove version).*

- *If you can get your campaign opponent's most prominent supporter to attack your opponent on a critical issue right before the election, that is a good thing. If the attack involves both national security and hypocrisy, that is a great thing.*

And, finally, a Gotham City–style Trade Secret summarizing the whole dustup from Brooklyn Democratic assemblyman Dov Hikind:

- *Before you throw stones at someone, make sure everything is kosher with you.*

Despite the threat of Giuliani, the intensity of the attacks against her, the books, the battle over the Jewish vote, and the flap over whether she was or was not really a longtime Yankee fan, Clinton beat Lazio handily, with 55 percent of the vote. She would have to wait six weeks before finding out if a Democrat or a Republican would replace her husband in the White House.

MASTERING THE SENATE, AND THE FREAK SHOW

★ ★ ★ ★ ★

DURING HER FIRST TERM as a United States senator, Hillary Clinton gained solid control of her public image. She manifested as much political aptitude as any other member of the Senate or, indeed, as any figure in American politics today. Quietly, Clinton demonstrated an ability to assemble coalitions, work with interest groups, and shepherd legislation through the intricate processes of Capitol Hill. More visibly, she has become one of the Democratic Party's most effective advocates and strategists.

Before she was formally sworn in, Clinton still was displaying the techniques she learned as a candidate. At her freshman orientation in December 2000, Clinton made it clear she did not want any "special treatment" despite her first-lady-to-senator transformation and her conspicuous Secret Service protection. "There are a lot of reasons why you, especially as a beginning senator, have to sit back and learn," she said. "And there is a lot I have to learn here. . . . I'm on another 'listening tour.' "

The listening continued even after she took office. Out of the public eye, Clinton consulted widely with senators past and present, congressional experts, and policy mavens to determine whom to hire for her staff, how to get off to a fast (if low-key) start, and how to avoid mistakes.

Clinton secured her base within the Senate by being surpassingly solicitous of her new colleagues, paying particular attention to the chamber's Old Bulls. Senators of both parties were perceptibly flattered by her deference and began to sheathe their long knives. To use the standard Senate metaphor, they had expected her to be a "show horse," but she established right away that she intended to be a "work horse."

Despite her fame and the power of her populous, wealthy state, Clinton methodically focused on the pursuit of legislating, committee business, and constituent service, rather than grandstanding on television, with interest groups, and on the Senate floor. She hired staffers who uniformly were considered professional, competent, substantive, and hardworking. They also evinced a consistent record of not leaking or talking on any basis to reporters in a manner deleterious to Clinton's interests.

Regarding ethics and constituent service, the senator knew that any controversies in her office or in her campaign had the potential to explode, so she dictated who was hired and how they comported themselves.

Clinton realized the importance of building an efficient organization to respond to citizens from all over the state seeking help with such concerns as lost Social Security checks, Medicare questions, and immigration problems. Groups representing various New York constituencies, like the elderly, have given Clinton's office universally high marks for responding to their needs.

Elite constituents have been conscientiously tended to as well, regardless of party affiliation. At once representative and remarkable is the case of New York banker Jeffrey Volk. A former Nixon White House aide, Reagan adviser, and George W. Bush donor, Volk was stuck in New Orleans after Hurricane Katrina hit in August 2005.

Unable to reach anyone from the White House or the Federal Emergency Management Agency to help him get back to New York, Volk telephoned Senator Clinton's office and quickly was routed to a caseworker who stayed in contact with him throughout his ordeal until he was safely evacuated.

Upon his return home, a grateful Volk met with Senator Clinton to thank her. The lifelong conservative ended up co-hosting a fund-raiser for her 2006 Senate campaign and said he "probably would" support her for president if she runs in 2008.

A number of the state's other prominent Republicans have helped fill Clinton's campaign bank account as well, out of gratitude for her assistance obtaining government help or legislation specifically for them, or out of appreciation for her overall work as a senator.

Like Bush during his governorship, Clinton has not been content to appeal only to her ideological, geographical, and partisan bases. She has toiled in the rural, suburban, and more conservative parts of New York, just as Bush appealed to women and voters in the nonwhite areas and big cities of Texas. Both Bush and Clinton knew that improving their standing outside their core supporters even to a small degree gave them exponentially greater political strength and put their opponents on the defensive.

Clinton has gotten extra credit for showing up in remote communities that have not always received attention from federal elected officials. She has tirelessly promoted improvements for special economic, education, health care, and other needs in these areas, winning widespread support from local officials, community activists, and business leaders, prominent Republicans among them. One of her biggest image problems from 2000—that of a carpetbagger—has been neutralized by her consideration to, and continued frequent travel throughout, New York state.

Although New York is dominated by Democratic politicians and voters, during Clinton's time in office, there have been a number of prominent Republicans, including the state's governor, George Pataki; New York City's two mayors, Rudy Giuliani and Mike Bloomberg; and important members of the congressional delegation. Clinton was less in need of public acclaim than the typical politician, so she was able to let New York's Republican House members and state officials get the kind of visibility they craved when undertaking projects with her.

As part of an array of subtle public signals of deference, she almost always let her Republican colleagues take the microphone first at joint press conferences. Working together on matters of special interest, such as 9/11 funding issues and homeland security, Clinton built a bond with many New York Republicans that deterred them from collaborating with interest groups intent on attacking her personally.

• • •

CLINTON'S INTERACTIONS WITH New York's Republican public officials dovetailed with her outreach to Republicans in Washington. She co-sponsored legislation and engaged in advocacy efforts with nearly every conservative member of the Senate and with other prominent Republicans. Most notably, she blunted the memory of her health care fiasco by participating in health care events with former House Speaker Newt Gingrich, and through her many bipartisan legislative initiatives on the same topic. Her bills in this area have been incremental and market-oriented, a clever way to rebuild her bona fides on the issue without exposing herself to more "Hillary Care" razzing.

In the polarized Senate, where members uniting across the aisle on Hill business, or even casually fraternizing with the opposition, have become uncommon, Hillary Clinton has engaged in bipartisan collaboration as much as any of her colleagues. And she has not just teamed up with Republican moderates. Many of her alliances have been with Congress's most conservative members.

Clinton was an original co-sponsor with Robert Bennett of Utah of the Flag Protection Act of 2005; she advocated research into the effects on children of certain computer games, television programs, and Internet sites with Sam Brownback of Kansas and Rick Santorum of Pennsylvania; she and Judd Gregg of New Hampshire co-wrote a bill to safeguard radioactive materials from terrorists; she proposed a provision with Mitch McConnell of Kentucky to offer assistance to businesses in Kosovo; and she worked on preventing a shortage of flu vaccines with Pat Roberts of Kansas.

She also teamed up with Conrad Burns of Montana to co-chair a caucus focused on improving the response times to 911 emergency calls; tried to increase benefits for the children of deceased soldiers with John Thune of South Dakota; joined Trent Lott of Mississippi in promoting Federal Emergency Management Agency projects; worked on health care information technology reform with Bill Frist of Tennessee; and traveled to Alaska, Iraq, and other international locations on official trips with John McCain of Arizona.

One of the Senate's most conservative members, James Inhofe of Oklahoma, who was as virulent an opponent of Bill Clinton in the 1990s as any member of Congress, said, "I would have guessed I would have been the last person in the world who would feel at all friendly with Hillary given all the problems I had with her and her husband during their years in the White House. But I would say we're now even friends."

Representative Thomas M. Reynolds of Buffalo, the extremely partisan Republican congressman who once highlighted Hillary Clinton's carpet-bagger image by calling her "a tourist who has lost her way," told the *New York Times* in March of 2005, "I like Senator Clinton. I've found that when she says she will take on a job with me, she does it."

Clinton even co-authored a February 2003 op-ed article in *USA Today* with then–Texas congressman Tom DeLay, a leader of the effort to impeach Bill Clinton in 1998 and a mainstay of the conservative movement for over two decades. The piece was about their shared interest in foster care reform and a movie screening they were hosting together.

Clinton also forged a relationship with former New York Republican senator Alfonse D'Amato, who played a key role in the congressional Whitewater investigations. She frequently has broken bread at lunch in New York City with the man once known as "Senator Pothole." He has applauded her for emulating his aggressive maneuvers to secure federal funds for New York and his tireless constituent service, both of which contributed to his nickname.

In May 2005, a *New York Observer* editorial, reflecting the sentiments of the considerable portion of the Gang of 500 who live on the island of Manhattan (and of many in the nation's capital, where the bulk of the 500 reside), declared that "Hillary Clinton looks like a winner," saying she had undergone "one of the most impressive acts of public transformation in memory."

To be sure, plenty of Washington Republicans still make private unkind remarks about Clinton, or joke at her expense. There are Republican members of Congress who collegially shower praise on her by day (referring to her as "my distinguished colleague") and then stoke the Freak Show against her at night by appearing on cable television news programs armed with hostile comments; speaking to interest groups at banquets, where the biggest applause lines are found in rancorous tirades about the Gentlelady from New York and her fearsome plans for the nation; telling tales at cocktail parties; or dropping antagonistic blind quotes in the next day's papers. But they all have come to respect her work ethic, her command of the facts, and her toughness.

Attacks on Clinton are less prevalent and less virulent than they would have been without her determined courtship of her Republican colleagues. The same is true of the business leaders, lobbyists, and public interest types to whom she has reached out. And of course, the recent warm relations between the Bushes and the Clintons, with 41 and 42 touring the world on behalf of tsunami victims and those devastated by Katrina, have indirectly reformed her image even more and made it harder to cast aspersions.

This effectively has cleaved the more Establishment portions of the right-leaning Freak Show from the reactionary talk radio hosts, bloggers, and extreme opinion peddlers who have incentives to harass her. Their assaults have been diluted by Clinton's successful disarmament of many of her former Beltway and New York foes. It even is not as easy as it used to be for partisan provocateur Don Imus to bait Republican senators appearing on his radio program into making colorful wisecracks about Clinton. Republican members of Congress are now more likely to choose Howard Dean, House Minority Leader Nancy Pelosi, Senate Democratic leader Harry Reid, or some other Democrat as their rhetorical incarnation of liberal immorality.

There is still a great deal written about Hillary Clinton (on the Web and in direct mail) and said about her (on talk radio and television) that is harsh and personal. But Establishment Republicans now feel circumscribed in what they can say about her, and where they can say it.

• • •

IT WAS IMPOSSIBLE for Clinton to keep a low profile during her first Senate campaign, with an extensive press corps and an adversarial Republican Party following her every move. But senators (even ones who used to live in the White House) can go on vacation, shop, dine at restaurants, and attend all sorts of political events without attracting any notice from the media or their enemies. Press requests to cover Clinton's fund-raisers in private homes or travel with her on political and official trips routinely are refused, and there has been no uproar, in part because her staff cites precedent from other senators and the Bush operation. So with little difficulty, Clinton minimized the capacity of the Old and New Media to interfere unduly with her schedule or her image.

Like Bush, Hillary Clinton realized that she rarely needs to give the national media access in order to advance her agenda. She stays on good terms with reporters and news organizations as required, but turns down most interview requests. Clinton generally agrees to interviews only when done jointly with a Republican (with whom she is on a trip or partnering on an issue of shared interest), or pegged to some major news or occasion (a major Bush administration controversy, say, or the anniversary of September 11). Both types of situations reduce the chance that she will be asked any off-message or unfriendly questions.

While limiting the access of the national press, Clinton assiduously courts the local New York media, with conference call briefings, a daily flood of press releases, and the occasional tête-à-tête. She does not usually bestow Bush-style nicknames, but she turns heads (and perhaps curries favor) with her liberal use of reporters' first names, and charming light banter.

Hillary Clinton's Senate career was changed forever by the events of September 11, 2001, including how she has been perceived and how she has been covered by the Old Media, nationally and, especially, in New York.

Like Bush, Clinton can invoke the Al Qaeda attacks on the World Trade Center towers and the Pentagon to stir emotion and put a protective coating over whatever other points she wants to make. 9/11 has elevated the importance of her platform as a senator from New York. This raised stage allows her to demonstrate competence, doggedness, bipartisanship, and political skill on the most serious and high-profile matters of terrorism and homeland security. At a time of war, those are important qualities for any politician, but particularly for a woman with no personal military record.

The before-and-after is stark. The pre-attack newspapers on New York's newsstands the morning of September 11 had a rather commonplace range of stories about Hillary Clinton's first year in the Senate. *Newsday* featured a fund-raising appeal from Rick Lazio, trying to retire his 2000 Senate campaign debt by invoking the "latest round of Clinton scandals." The *Daily News* wrote about a whistle-blower's attempt to expose a "herbal supplement kingpin" who had paid Hillary Clinton's brother Hugh Rodham $200,000 to help get a pardon from President Clinton for "a 1983 mail fraud conviction he received for selling a product that he falsely claimed cured baldness."

The *New York Post* printed a couple of gossipy items about her appearing with Paul McCartney and about her $8 million book advance for *Living History* (more, the *Post* said, than what Elizabeth Taylor got for her memoirs).

After the airplanes struck the World Trade Center, the press coverage of Clinton changed almost instantly. As with President Bush, her role and consequence were reborn. The *New Republic* noted that one of the most important after-effects was on Clinton's relationship with the *New York Post,* whose conservative owner Rupert Murdoch she heavily courted. "How the *Post* and Clinton found ideological middle ground is no mystery: the politics of 9/11. . . . *Post* editorial page [editor] Bob McManus said, 'She began to exhibit some leadership qualities that we didn't see that were there.' " The tabloid sensibilities of New York City's media overall were reined in by the attacks, and Clinton benefited widely. The *Post,* in particular, still wrote its share of negative news stories and editorials about her. But there was an unmistakable change in its posture.

Along with her seat on the Senate Armed Services Committee; her frequent trips to military facilities in New York and overseas; her actions on behalf of veterans; and a series of hawkish votes, Clinton's 9/11 credentials positioned her in a comfort zone on national security with members of the Gang of 500, families of the victims, defense and foreign policy officials, and segments of the general public in New York. And also, her advisers hope, with voters around the country.

· · ·

As HILLARY CLINTON prepared for her Senate reelection campaign, there was no more vivid example of the new toughness injected into her operation than the encounter with writer Ed Klein. Earlier, her team had brooded and fussed over what to do about the likes of Gail Sheehy and Jerry Oppenheimer. The Klein book, by contrast, demonstrated how she had learned to dispatch the Freak Show with clinical efficiency, surpassing what was done in the past. The handling of this episode from June 2005 showed how prepared she has become for the inevitable assaults should she run for president.

In *The Truth About Hillary: What She Knew, When She Knew It, and How Far She'll Go to Become President*, Klein made the usual charges, assertions, and suggestions about Senator Clinton, including theories on her sexuality, marriage, habits, and temperament. It was heavily hyped by its publisher and flagrantly fanned by Drudge. And Klein brought some journalistic credibility to the fight, having worked at the *New York Times Magazine* and *Newsweek*.

Portions of the right-wing Freak Show maintained the fervent hope that Klein's credentials and his assurance of careful research would insulate the book from what they expected to be a pugnacious Clinton response.

John LeBoutillier, a former Republican congressman from New York, was a friend of Klein and had communicated with him regularly during his research and reporting process. On the eve of the book's release, LeBoutillier wrote on the conservative website NewsMax.com:

> It is safe to say that none of the dozens of biographies of Hillary Clinton have ever been as well-researched as this one. Nor have any of them been written by a professional journalist with such impeccable credentials. Team Clinton undoubtedly plans a fierce counter-attack on Klein as soon as the book is published—that is always their MO—but with this author they are going to have a tough time. . . . this particular book serves an invaluable purpose: cutting through the mainstream media's pro-Hillary propaganda and giving readers a look at the lying, manipulating, dishonest—and extremely dysfunctional—former first lady, who has been on an inexorable march to the Oval Office for over thirty years.

Hillary Clinton's team prepared industriously for the release of Klein's book. They worked their sources to discover what juicy bits would be included. They browbeat television bookers to discourage them from inviting Klein on their shows. (At one point, Klein complained to blogger John Hawkins on RightWingNews.com, "Because of my book . . . Hillary and her war machine have called every major television network in the United States and suggested to them that if they have Ed Klein on to discuss his book, they can forget about Hillary being a guest on their network.")

Clinton's advisers researched the flaws in Klein's past texts. They put together talking points and lined up appropriately reliable surrogates. As with the Sheehy book, they resolved to respond only to select portions of the book, those they considered particularly innocuous or particularly outrageous. Somewhere Dan Bartlett was smiling—or, at least, proffering professional respect.

The author's most titillating assertion (something to do with Mrs. Clinton being a latent lesbian, or wanting to be, or some such thing) was heaven-sent as far as her advisers were concerned. Except on the far end of the Freak Show, the charge was seen as old, extreme, and overly personal. Like Sheehy before him, Klein made some factual errors regarding Clinton lore and basic historical information, which her aides used to help neutralize his arguments.

The book sold reasonably well at first, but the reviews were brutal and it largely was ignored or denounced, even by the Right. The *New York Post* called it a "hatchet-job." Fox News's Bill O'Reilly declined to interview his "colleague" Klein on his show, saying, "It is not that the book is defamatory. It is simply negative . . . that's not hard to do. Writing a book or article that slams somebody is simple. Just line up the person's enemies and let fly. They do that stuff to me all the time and to every other successful person in the media or politics. . . . If you want to read Ed Klein's book, fine with me. . . . But understand what you are reading. Don't think there's anything fair or objective about it."

Klein's work seemed to offend even the sensibilities of Dick Morris. Echoing the sentiments of a surprisingly large number of conservative voices from newspaper columns, the Internet, talk radio, and cable television, Morris condemned the book in his column in *The Hill*: "I am no defender of Hillary Rodham Clinton's, to put it mildly. But the recent charges in Ed Klein's book to the effect that she is a closet homosexual or that Bill raped her and that this act triggered Chelsea's conception are as crazy as the list that was circulating around of the 20 or so people the Clintons allegedly had killed. These accusations do not belong in our public dialogue."

• • •

HILLARY CLINTON'S TRANSFORMED standing in the world meant that many of her customary critics were doing something totally antithetical to Freak Show norms: evaluating the veracity and appropriateness of an attack on a prime target, and denouncing a strike fired from their own side if it crossed a line of rectitude.

But that was not the only reason that some Freak Show performers distanced themselves from Klein. Morris, again emblematic of the way in which many conservatives reacted, said that the book's charges "hit below the belt and tend to discredit the more serious and sober concerns so many of us have about the danger she would present in high office." In other words, *Don't screw up our chance to destroy this woman when the time comes!*

Morris was on to something. Clinton's team had learned that certain attacks are almost welcome, because of the understanding and application of this Trade Secret: *You can use an attack meant to weaken you as an opportunity for a counterattack that will make you stronger.*

When Clinton's team anticipates a challenge from a critic, it assumes that the attacker inevitably will make a mistake that can be exploited. Then, when the accuser has been forced to lose control of his or her public image, there are benefits to reap. (Bush's team has followed this same strategy.)

First, the Old Media begins to see the critic as some combination of goofy and extreme, and everything the person does, says, or writes is viewed skeptically. Rove's operation, for instance, used derisive humor, scornful Internet videos, and tirelessly repetitive talking points to turn liberal icons such as MoveOn.org, Al Gore, and Howard Dean into wild, left-wing caricatures. True, not everyone in the Old Media was swayed, but the opinions of many Old Media–ites could be colored this way.

Hillary Clinton's operation has used similar techniques in both Senate campaigns. Her team labeled Rudy Giuliani as "angry" during the 2000 race. (Republicans have made use of the same prejudicial word to define such adversaries as Gore and Dean, not to mention Clinton herself.) When the Clinton camp twisted Rick Lazio into a "Newt Gingrich clone," a "hypocrite," and a "menacing" Republican, they succeeded in defining him for much of the media and the electorate.

Clinton's advisers do not win every Old Media news cycle, but they are adept at getting the press to cast a number of daily developments as just the latest manifestations of their opponents' clownishness and extremism.

A second benefit of counterattack: The activists on the same political side as the disfigured accuser are demoralized and defanged. Ed Klein's overreaching gave anti–Hillary Clinton reporting a bad name, just as CBS News's bogus piece on Bush's draft record served to put that topic off-limits. Pros on both sides who understand the game (such as Morris) realize that the capacity to criticize, on any topic, is undermined after such a well-publicized misfire.

Third, traits that have been attached to old enemies can be affixed to any new aggressors that come your way. *Rick Lazio is angry, just like Rudy Giuliani. These angry attacks won't fool the people of New York.*

Finally, demoralizing the other team and polluting your accusers are great ways to rev up your own base. Every new embarrassing error exposed or outlandish statement uttered just makes your base more committed. Each additional Old Media reinforcement of a foe's negative image gets the base jazzed up, because sophisticated supporters rightly see such coverage as a victory.

• • •

AROUND A DOZEN Republicans seriously contemplated challenging Hillary Clinton in the 2006 election. None was close to what would be considered a first-tier candidate; none was a statewide officeholder or a United States representative; and none was a brainy, self-funding multimillionaire willing to spend copiously to defeat her. In fact, all the potential nominees found raising money to be more difficult than they expected.

And any candidate who displayed the slightest bit of political or media traction found themselves the victim of some combination of leaked opposition research and intensive battering-by-press-release from the New York state Democratic Party. This reflected tactics being used by Clinton's political advisers. The strategy requires relentless focus and constant application.

First, aggressively define potential opponents from the start, so the public's initial impressions of them are negative, reducing their chances of building up voter support. Then use the party committee apparatus as the main agent in the public effort to solidify the negative impressions, thus insulating the campaign and candidate from any countercharges that they are engaged in sharp-elbowed schemes.

In a Rove-like fashion, Clinton's advisers have made sure that the Democratic Party does things the way they want them done. Even as Democrats continued to dominate party registration in New York and win their share of statewide elections, the state party remained relatively disorganized from the time of Hillary Clinton's election until she geared up for 2006. In 2003, in part to watch over the senator's interests, one of her political consulting firms became paid advisers to the New York Democratic Party, a position from which they could better protect her. This included the assurance that press statements about potential opponents were researched and written smartly, and distributed quickly and efficiently.

Throughout Clinton's reelection campaign, her team has used these opponent-defining Trade Secrets with unabashed repetition. The most

brazen ploy involves giving a piece of opposition research to an amenable reporter (such as Fred Dicker of the *New York Post*), with a pledge from the
journalist not to reveal the information's source.

The reporter writes an article, getting big play because it is an exclusive.
Such stories typically quote two people, a spokesperson for the sandbagged
victim (usually defensive and wobbly on the facts) and someone speaking on
Clinton's behalf (combining a feigned lack of interest, delicate screw tighten-
ing, and humorous quips).

The initial item leads to television and radio news pickup of the story.
Then the next day's papers have follow-up pieces, with off-balance quotes
from Clinton's opponent attempting to offer an explanation of the unexplain-
able, riddled with holes, flaws, understatements, and overstatements.

Sometimes, the reporter who received the original tip will be given an additional nugget of opposition research for the second-day story. (This detail
might have been withheld from the first article either by the campaign or the
reporter, as a way to heighten the buzz or control the story.) Such a maneuver may ratchet up the controversy another notch.

To keep the saga going and shape the tone, some friendly entity (usually
the state Democratic Party) then will put out a news release, reciting the
unanswered questions, contradictions, and blooper-reel replies from the rival
campaign. And if more information surfaces or the candidate under siege
continues to bobble, the Democrats will spend the next news cycle breath-
lessly speculating that the victim's campaign is in disarray and contouring the
facts of the controversy to illustrate whatever negative traits the Clinton campaign is trying to burn into the voters' minds at that moment.

• • •

To BE SURE, there have been controversies during Clinton's Senate years besides the Klein book, including the federal criminal trial of one of her aides
related to a fund-raiser he organized for her in 2000 (he was acquitted); her
2006 Martin Luther King Jr. Day remark that the House "has been run like a
plantation"; her several acrimonious verbal clashes with Republicans; and
fallout from the actions and relationships of her two brothers and, of course,
her husband.

But one of her husband's relationships has substantially improved her
image. President George H. W. Bush's public chumminess with Bill Clinton
has compelled many Republican activists and fund-raisers to complain that
such amity is serving to rehabilitate Hillary Clinton. In truth, a review of
Clinton's Senate career to date suggests that, if there is blame to assign,

Newt Gingrich, Tom DeLay, Sam Brownback, Bill Frist, and many others deserve their share as well, as they have enjoyed plenty of public acts of goodwill directly with the senator herself.

Hillary Clinton is now a respected United States senator. Even the opposition treats her seriously, although she will always be a target. But she has reached the same level of resistance to Freak Show attacks as President Bush. There is no clearer indication of the distance she has traveled.

44! (Assets)

★ ★ ★ ★ ★

FOR THOSE READERS who think she cannot win, get over your delusion.

If Hillary Clinton chooses to run for president in 2008, she can win. That is not the same as saying she *will* win, or even that she is *favored* to win. But if she decides to run, she will be a formidable candidate, with significant advantages over every other plausible Democratic candidate, and over every plausible Republican candidate, with the exception of Arizona senator John McCain.

The simplest way to understand this is to ask yourself if you believe it is feasible that she *could* win the electoral votes of all the states taken by John Kerry in 2004, and then add either Florida or Ohio. Of course she could.

Unlike Kerry, she would not be running against an incumbent in 2008. Whatever has occurred in the war in Iraq and the war on terrorism, and whomever the parties nominate, the chances are good that the Republicans will not have the same dominance on national security in 2008 that they had in 2004. There are no other broad historical, demographic, or issue developments that would make the terrain more favorable to the Republicans than during the last election.

If anything, there are factors (such as eight straight years of Republican control of the White House) that likely would benefit whomever the Democrats nominate. And no probable Republican nominee, with the exception of Senator McCain, has the experience and skills to be considered at this stage a favorite, let alone a prohibitive favorite, to beat Clinton, if the Democrats choose her to represent them.

Part of the denial of some on the right who insist she cannot win is based on the fact that they live in a bubble of interlocking conservative communities in which *everyone* hates Hillary Clinton. This gives them the impression that the woman could not wangle a single vote outside of the Bluest precincts of left-wing America. In their mental scenario, they are matching Clinton up against *herself*, rather than against an actual Republican opponent. This is the same mistake that Democrats made in 2003 and 2004, when they imagined that George W. Bush was too unpopular and fallible to win reelection.

Part of the argument that Clinton cannot win is based on public opinion polls indicating that many Americans would never vote for her for president under any circumstances whatsoever. No first-time presidential contender ever has entered a race for the White House with literally tens of millions of Americans ideologically and emotionally opposed to that candidacy. Her supporters say this is because the Freak Show has kept most of the country from knowing the real Hillary Clinton. Those who cannot stand her say Americans know the real Hillary Clinton all too well.

Starting off with such a committed opposition would make Clinton's challenge trickier. But the difficulty of winning should not obscure the fundamental truth, stated again for emphasis: Hillary Clinton *can* be elected in 2008. If she chooses to run, the real question will be, *what will determine if she wins?*

Every candidate has a balance sheet that defines his or her chances, the pros on one side, the cons on the other. For most candidates, even ones who are relatively well-known national figures, or who have run for the office before, both sides of the ledger are filled with question marks. *How will they handle pressure? Do they know enough people who will help them? How many skeletons remain in the closet? Can they deliver a truly inspiring stump speech? Will they work hard enough? Do they know the way to win?*

Hillary Clinton has her own balance sheet, but it is different from everyone else's. Her ledger has the typical items but also some unique elements. These factors relate to her chances to be nominated by the Democrats, as well as win a general election.

Assets (with Caveats)

1. Fund-raising

The most obvious and dramatic advantage Hillary Clinton would have as a presidential candidate is her ability to bring in money. There is no doubt that she could raise the funds required for 2008, and do so with an ease matched by only one other nonincumbent candidate in modern American political history—President Bush. And *how* she could raise her stash would be almost as important as *how much* she could raise.

In the typical presidential campaign, candidate and spouse scheduling, travel, staff meetings, media strategy, and spending decisions must be geared toward the imperative of fund-raising. Candidates burn an enormous amount of time asking people to help raise money for them and even calling donors personally to request individual contributions. Clinton would be free from the trauma of this relentless struggle. Having strenuously built up her contacts with rich people over the years, Hillary Clinton could delegate most fund-raising chores to her experienced staff and surrogates.

Like Bush before her, if Hillary Clinton runs for president, she can rely on several built-in fund-raising networks, including from within her wealthy mega-state base (Bush had Texas; she would have New York), but also from the other states that contribute a disproportionate share of campaign money (such as California, Illinois, Massachusetts). She herself could host gatherings that would raise in excess of, say, a quarter of a million dollars, but other events could be anchored by Bill Clinton or one of her many prominent supporters, which would attract donors in droves. Also like Bush, she has collected chits across the country from politicians for whom she has raised money in the past. These officials also would be enlisted to help secure funds. She has a valuable roster of past donors who have given to her various causes and campaign committees, and would have access, of course, to all of Bill Clinton's premium lists and contacts, too. Hillary Clinton received contributions to her 2006 Senate campaign from over 250,000 individuals, representing all fifty states and the District of Columbia.

In addition, Senator Clinton would be able to use any residual funds in her 2006 account after her Senate reelection was over. But the leftover money would not be as precious as the lists she would have compiled in raising it.

Cash not only pays the bills, but is the chief measurement that the Gang of 500 uses to determine which candidates are viable. Hard dollar figures affect who gets the most favorable press coverage, which enables a candidate to raise even more money. (Conversely, stories about weak or disappointing fund-raising keep checkbooks firmly shut. No one likes to waste their money on a loser.) And money is a factor from the very start of the so-called Invisible Primary.

This is the period that begins the day after a presidential election and ends with the Iowa caucuses of the next election, during which the potential candidates of both parties jockey for position among an ever-widening circle of opinion leaders. Everyone eventually weighs in: the Gang of 500, the party interest group activists, the major fund-raisers, the press corps, the political junkies, and, these days, the Internet bloggers. With Iowa, the Invisible Primary gives way to the actual voting season.

Historically, almost every candidate who has won a party's Invisible Primary has also won its nomination. The most important category in the Invisible Primary is fund-raising, and doing well in many of the other important categories derives from fund-raising strength. If Clinton runs, she would almost certainly win her party's Invisible Primary. Her money would get her better press coverage, more endorsements, the best staff, and a heightened sense of electability.

Clinton's fund-raising advantage would be even more pronounced than in past seasons because of an expected change in 2008. Many analysts expect campaigns to disregard all spending limits by refusing federal money in the nomination fights, and possibly in the general election, too. Most candidates, including Clinton if she runs, likely would choose this option. Thus she could be sitting pretty with multi-millions pouring in and no regulation on how much she could raise or how to spend it. In contrast, less fortunate hopefuls would face big decisions and a lot of work.

If Hillary Clinton runs for president in 2008, it would not be *all* about the money. But money would give her a titanic advantage.

Caveats: none at all—as long as her campaign avoids taking any illegal contributions that cause her embarrassment, and as long as the Right cannot effectively link the reports of her swollen coffers to her old image of extreme ambition and greed.

2. CONVENTIONAL POLITICAL ADVANTAGES

Pretend for a moment that Hillary Clinton is not *Hillary Clinton.*

Wipe away her White House years, her husband's iconic identity, and every wisp of Clinton Fatigue.

Imagine instead a senator from New York who dominated the field for her party's nomination in every national public opinion survey taken in the years leading up to the election; who had a strong record as a legislator; an authoritative command of policy issues across the board; unparalleled ties to her party's interest groups, activists, and elected officials; the ability to call on many of the party's leading strategists, in addition to national and key state operatives; vast media experience; the capacity to make news and get on network television without effort; a household name to capture the imagination; and unquestioned star power.

As noted, the biggest two challenges for most first-time presidential candidates are getting known and raising money. Clinton would start the race with both fund-raising strength and full control of the fame game. A typical presidential candidate after campaigning for months can still sit unmolested at the Applebee's in Concourse C at Chicago's O'Hare International Airport. If she runs for president, Hillary Clinton will generate a frisson of excitement every time she walks into a room or strides through a terminal (as she does now, but more so). The potential of the historic first of a woman president would add yet another level of magnetism to her mien.

In 1998, Bush was leading in national polls for his party's nomination, but stayed at home to focus on his gubernatorial reelection, while other potential candidates were frantically traveling to Iowa, New Hampshire, and other key states; signing up advisers with presidential campaign experience; and cultivating interest group and elite national support. Since being elected senator, Hillary Clinton, likewise, has done some national travel but remained mostly focused on her reelection bid.

Clinton's self-made résumé and life experience would allow her to enter the race on her own schedule. She would have no difficulty attracting first-rate policy staffers, Iowa field operatives, or advance men and women. She would never show up at an event in New Hampshire to find just a dozen people milling about, with only a casual curiosity in hearing her speak. She would have no shortage of volunteers.

She would receive many interest group endorsements, from labor, civil rights, and social service constituencies allied with the Democratic Party. She could leverage these endorsements and her own celebrity to build excitement and win more endorsements.

Although the crush of the worldwide media attention would tax her staff no matter how many press aides were hired, Clinton's capacity to appear on television whenever opportune would give her an advantage over her rivals. During the nomination fight or in a general election, network bookers always would seek her reaction to the latest developments in the campaign, around the country, and around the world. Other candidates would be frustrated by, and envious of (though surely not surprised by), the attention she would receive.

Despite what would be a vast retinue of aides, a massive security detail, and the ambience of senatorial First Ladydom, Clinton and her advisers would replicate the "listening tour" sensibility of her first campaign. Clinton knows that part of the way to win involves convincing voters, particularly in the states with early nominating contests, that someone is committed to appealing to them directly. She knows she will have to shake hands for hours on end, eat local specialties (Philly cheesesteaks, hold the Swiss; deep-fried candy bars; foot-long corndogs), attend state fairs, remember names, pose for photos, and seem positively delighted to receive her umpteenth high school sweatshirt and hand-knitted scarf. She knows how to appear magisterial (necessary to be seen as presidential material) rather than regal (a turnoff).

Caveats: The infrastructure of the extended Democratic Party family, including the labor movement, interest groups, and state parties, is weaker than it has been in the past or compared with its Republican equivalent. Every time a fund-raiser or operative who worked for Bill Clinton defected to another candidate, Hillary Clinton would get some bad press. Additionally, having served only one full term (plus change) calls for finesse when it comes to credentials.

3. The Only Woman in the Race

Besides Clinton, there are no other likely 2008 Democrat or Republican presidential candidates who are women (Secretary of State Condoleezza Rice's sporadic, ambiguous statements aside). In any field with just one female candidate, the sole woman almost always has an advantage, assuming she passes a threshold credibility test. In such cases, the woman is able to stand out in debates, in advertising, and on the ballot as the only choice for voters searching for something different. The topic of a historic Hillary Clinton candidacy will dominate the dialogue.

Simply put, at this moment there are only a few women in the United States who are positioned to be realistic candidates for president. Clinton would be the first woman ever to be the front-runner for a major party nomination. She would represent for many older people perhaps their single opportunity to see a woman elected president. Groups such as the White House Project and EMILY's List, the most formidable fund-raising force in Democratic politics, would almost certainly put their muscle behind Clinton. Gaining even a few more percentage points of the women's vote, or increasing turnout with the promise of making history, could secure the White House.

Caveat: Interest groups itching to see a woman elected president might feel that Clinton falls short of their ideal because of her controversial past.

There is no way to know if the United States is prepared to elect any woman as president, particularly at a time of national security crisis.

4. The Best Political Strategist in the Democratic Party
(and Plenty of Other Good Ones, Too)

Bill Clinton has made it clear through his public and private comments that he will do whatever he can to assist his wife's political career. And unlike Al Gore (who often refused to listen) and John Kerry (who listened but could not execute), you can bet that Hillary Clinton would hear her husband loud and clear and put his advice to use.

In addition to the nucleus of skilled advisers from her Senate campaigns, notably pollster Mark Penn and media strategist Mandy Grunwald, Hillary Clinton would have her pick of many of the most experienced national strategists throughout the party, plenty of whom worked on Bill Clinton's presidential campaigns.

Caveats: Bill Clinton might be a consummate strategist, but he would not be involved in the granular detail of day-to-day and long-range planning as Karl Rove was in Bush's presidential campaigns. He also has been said to be too psychologically close to the situation to consistently give his wife's campaigns the same crisp political advice he dispenses to others. And while Hillary Clinton's inner circle is reasonably disciplined and stable, and has not fallen prey to the teeming rivalries of Bill Clinton's campaigns and administration, obvious tensions remain. Strategist Harold Ickes, for instance, possesses fund-raising and political contacts vital to a presidential effort, but clashed with the Clintons during their White House years. Some believe Hillary Clinton's team is too insular and reluctant to tell her hard truths, and too competitive as well. The alpha dogs all straining to pull Clinton's sled inevitably will bark, growl, and snap as they jostle for primacy.

5. The Trade Secrets of Bill Clinton,
George W. Bush, and Karl Rove

For six years, Hillary Clinton has been able to cherry-pick from the Trade Secrets of the Clinton years and the Bush years, selecting what works and what does not. She has put these lessons impressively into practice to shore up her own political position and achieve her own political goals. Indeed, she has excelled at some of the most important Trade Secrets in this book.

Hillary Clinton's operation reflects the Republicans' Trade Secrets in the way it deals with its political opponents and the Old Media. Senator Clinton might not advance the delegitimization of the press as aggressively as Karl Rove, but she understands how to benefit from the Old Media's diminished status.

She has made herself an expert on the strengths and weaknesses of the two major political parties, much in the manner of the two most recent presidents.

She knows that showing interest in serious policies generates sophisticated and solid political support. Her decades-long participation in her party's Conversation will provide access to the best ideas should she become a candidate.

Senator Clinton also is a loyal friend to her natural allies, which is smart substantively and politically. In the months leading up to her 2006 reelection campaign, she headed up an effort to develop a fresh agenda for the centrist Democratic Leadership Council, and has worked with the Center for American Progress, an activist think tank run by her husband's former chief of staff John Podesta.

Politically, she understands the importance of putting people first. Her operation emphasizes "relationships over transactions." Clinton herself reaches out to the key state and local politicians (when they experience legislative victory or defeat, win elections, battle illness, or have grandchildren). She also has analyzed the gap between her party and the Republicans in areas of technical competence and toughness.

Caveats: Understanding a Trade Secret does not mean one actually can benefit from it, or execute it efficiently. And without her own Karl Rove eternally planning, plotting, maneuvering, and laying the groundwork for a presidential run, she has not been able to establish the full systems and staffing that buttress the Bush-Rove Trade Secrets.

6. A Freak Show Veteran

Hillary Clinton and her chief political adviser/husband are the Democratic Party's foremost experts/guinea pigs on how the Republican machine separates Democratic candidates from their public images. The Clintons draw on their own experiences, of course, but they also are well versed in the narratives Republicans crafted for other Democrats of recent decades. Every Democratic president or nominee of their adult lifetimes lost control of his public image for at least a time. Carter was reduced to a weakling. Dukakis was portrayed by George H. W. Bush, employing the advice of strategist Lee Atwater, as weak, weird, and possibly unstable. Gore was stiff and a petty liar,

Kerry an insufferable phony. Bill Clinton, too, lost control of his public image, but of all these Democrats he was the only one who managed to reclaim it.

Clinton gave behind-the-scenes advice to the past two Democratic candidates about how to deal with attacks but by Election Day, they had failed to deploy his Trade Secrets and save themselves. If Hillary Clinton runs for president in 2008, she could lose for a lot of reasons, but she will do her darnedest to avoid image troubles, working hard to follow her husband's advice, and the example set by Bush and Rove.

Bill Clinton believes that what separates winners from losers in competitive activities, such as sports and elections, is psychological. Who can handle pressure and avoid being overwhelmed by attacks?

Voters have proven to be less interested in the specifics of allegations about a candidate's past (short of egregious criminal acts) than they are about how a potential president handles adversity. They can forgive previous mistakes and foolishness, but not present deception or weakness. A candidate must respond briskly to charges, rebut them aggressively, and then promptly turn the dialogue back to the policy issues in the race. Bill Clinton says that candidates "have to get to a point where they don't allow the other people to define them as either people or political leaders, or their worth as human beings or their worth in this particular campaign.

"Our people have got to be more psychologically prepared for it and there has to be more distance between them and these withering attacks. They have to be able to know that this is sort of a part of the landscape, and that the voters are looking as much to see how they will react to it as to hear the substance of what" the charges are.

Bill Clinton believes that any Democrat is going to take hits to his or her reputation. "If you're a Democrat you can never give up, you can't let this stuff lie, and then you've got to keep giving the election back to the public. You have to keep redefining what the election's about. They try to define the election one way, then you have to win the definition battle. Then you can fill in the specifics."

Candidates can "not be paralyzed by personal attacks. You just have to know that they're coming in different ways and you just can't let yourself be defined by them.

"Only a small percentage of what [voters are] looking for in the campaign is whether any of this stuff is true because all of them have had problems in their life. What they're really looking for is to see, how is this person going to react to it?"

And even if the charges are "absolute lies," Clinton continued, if "you've never been attacked personally before, you wind up thinking everybody's heard them and everybody believes them and pretty soon it gets in your head that that's the person you are. And then you're disabled from the fight.

"The person out here looking from the point of view of his or her life thinks, 'I'm out here carrying stones all day, barely paying my bills, and I have three kids at home.' What they really want to see is, is this person tough enough and strong enough to lead me, is he going to lead me, is he going to be on my side? And if he is on my side, can he fight for me?"

Republican National Chairman Ken Mehlman has followed Hillary Clinton's growth and he does not underestimate her. "If you think about who are the kinds of people that are good. . . . They're people that know what they want to do and develop a proactive plan to do it, and they're people that are good at pivoting. We know she's good at pivoting. Is she going to be good? Absolutely. She's going to be looking tactically and technically unbelievably competent."

Mehlman claims that Hillary Clinton's record as a liberal would be enough to derail her campaign, but he says he is worried that some on the right will "probably also bring up, unfortunately, stuff about Whitewater and all that. And why is that unfortunate? . . . It's not relevant to people's lives."

Mehlman believes that "One of the mistakes the '92 [Bush] campaign made was by obsessing over bimbo eruptions, they lost credibility to take on Clinton on the real stuff and that's a danger."

Finally, Mehlman says that the Clintons are unique in their ability to thrive even when they do not have control of their public images. "What the Clintons do better than anybody else is judo," he says. "They essentially pivot off of circumstances that are either beyond their control or bad circumstances they've made to benefit themselves."

Caveats: Martial arts aside, Hillary Clinton, for all her edification as the spouse of a presidential candidate, first lady, a Senate candidate, and a senator, has never dealt with the Freak Show as a presidential candidate. On the national stage, when the curtain goes up, the orchestra begins to play, and the actors start to sing, anything can happen.

• • •

THOSE ARE SUBSTANTIAL assets. But Hillary Clinton would bring substantial liabilities to a presidential race as well.

44? (Liabilities)

LIABILITIES

I. THE FREAK SHOW STILL HATES HER,
AND NOW SOME OF THE LEFT DOES, TOO

Should Hillary Clinton choose to run for president, she automatically would make history as the first serious woman presidential candidate. She also might make history as the first candidate to be a primary target of both the right-wing and the left-wing portions of the Freak Show.

The Right's antipathy toward her has been well documented. But the dedicated activist forces she would need to counteract those of the Right have not been marshaled. In many left-wing precincts of the online crankosphere, she is at best a disappointment, at worst an ideological traitor. Many consider her too accommodating toward President Bush's agenda, and decry her vote authorizing the Iraq war; some disparage her for appearing too calculating; others fear she is unelectable. In fact, she faces the perilous possibility that the Left might turn on her during the nomination period or even in the general election. The ire of the left-wing portion of the Freak Show might not do serious damage in the nomination season, but should she face a strong Republican, such as Senator McCain, in the general election, such defections could be lethal.

With some luck and skill, the accommodationist charge is unlikely to be a problem by the 2008 presidential election. Clinton evinces as much anti-Bush scorn as any potential Democratic presidential candidate. Her votes authorizing the Iraq war and approving its funding are at least partially balanced by her standing as one of the party's most effective critics of Bush's overall foreign policy record. She has solid support from many groups in the liberal wing of her party, including women, nonwhites, union members, health and welfare advocates, and lesbians and gays. And, in any case, the views of the Left might not be determinative; the modern Democratic Party has nominated relatively centrist candidates every four years in the modern era.

It is the second allegation—too calculating—on which Clinton has made the least progress in controlling her public image. As an elected official, Hillary Clinton began her career with a notable presumption-by-marital-association that she would shift her positions to suit her short-term political needs. In the Freak Show, politicians face two special challenges regarding their views. First, electronic data retrieval and cutting-and-pasting tools mean that no past position is ever forgotten and is always subject to distorted recall. Second, opponents across the polarized divide (and sometimes alleged allies) will seize on any apparent shift and attach to it high moral outrage.

On balance, Hillary Clinton's record does not demonstrate any more flip-flopping than your average politician. She has always favored the death penalty; abortion rights tempered by consideration for those who differ with her and an articulated resolve to reduce the number of abortions performed in America; strong U.S.-Israel ties with a search for a solution acceptable to the Palestinian people; free market remedies to many health care and social service problems; education reform that challenges (somewhat) the education establishment; an honored place for faith in public life; and a strong role for the American military. Although Clinton has been fairly consistent on all these often difficult issues, she nonetheless has given off an impression of vacillation.

On a few issues, Clinton has given her opponents more to work with. Even so, her squishiness in support of free trade and her sponsorship of a bill to ban flag burning are not greater signs of political opportunism than, say, fiscal conservative and straight-shooting George W. Bush's support for the largest entitlement expansion in a generation and multibillion-dollar agriculture and transportation laws. Or consider Bush's decision to sign a campaign finance bill he had deemed unconstitutional while a presidential candidate. And if you think that Bush is not the standard to use for consistency, pick virtually anyone in elective office and the result of the comparison will be the same.

If Hillary Clinton is not the biggest flip-flopper in the tank, her image as too flexible for her own good is a real problem, and one that will receive constant scrutiny. She has not been able to put this notion to rest, and it could present a genuine predicament in a presidential campaign.

The final reservation Democrats raise about Clinton—that someone with her baggage cannot possibly be elected—is, in the end, a question about her relationship with the Freak Show. Overall, as shown, she has made much progress in disarming her enemies, deciphering the Old and New Media, and practicing the Trade Secrets of Karl Rove and Bill Clinton.

Still, in 2008, conservatives can be expected to launch an aggressive effort at defining Clinton's public image, with or without the assistance of Rove.

The Republican National Committee, which Rove currently oversees, tracks Clinton's every word and is not shy about putting out well-researched press releases casting her as *arrogant* ("The Hillary money machine rolls over everything—and everyone"), *power-hungry* ("Clinton exploits Katrina tragedy for cold hard cash"), *corrupt* ("Clinton delivers the partisan attacks her big donors pay for"), *harsh* ("Clinton Assaults Bush to Win Left-Wing '08 Primary Votes"), *hypocritical* ("With her eye on the presidency, Clinton's interest in New York wanes"), and *liberal* ("Left is left"). And that's all from just a single RNC press release of September 13, 2005.

The RNC has plenty of files and video left over from the 1990s and has carefully accumulated every new thing Clinton says and does. With adversaries in the left wing of the Freak Show as well, Clinton would have a struggle to keep control of her public image.

2. The Past

Hillary Clinton would not be immune from the Trade Secret that affects all presidential candidates, every four years, no matter what they have done in their lives before or how much scrutiny they have gotten.

Even more than in Clinton's Senate race, if she becomes an official presidential candidate, the media and her opponents will scrutinize the greatest hits of past Hillary Clinton controversies, plus some additional all-new bonus tracks from her Senate career.

How *did* she make those enormous cattle futures profits? How *did* those long-missing billing records turn up in the White House? What role *did* she play in those infamous end-of-presidency pardons? What *really* happened with her staff and the indicted (and acquitted) fund-raising aide from her first campaign? What *exactly* is up with her marriage? And: *pretty much everything about her brothers.*

It is not clear which of these old scandals will still have life years later, or what other imbroglios will surface. Whatever the case, brace yourself for renewed television booker interest in Susan McDougal, Gennifer Flowers, and Paula Jones. And Dick Morris would probably have to sleep on a cot at the Fox News Channel studios to fulfill the demands on his time.

3. WEAK CANDIDATE SKILLS

The gap between Hillary Clinton's intellectual understanding of the way to win and her underwhelming performance skills suggest why the conservative columnist George Will would have trouble hitting a professionally pitched fastball. Will has written best-selling books about baseball for many years, but no one has drafted him to play in the major leagues. Senator Clinton is no Natural.

She simply does not possess the same candidate skills as Presidents Bill Clinton and George W. Bush. She cannot give as good a speech, or as convincingly evince a sense of optimism. Like her husband and unlike Bush, she often agonizes over decisions in a way that is not practical in the heat of a presidential campaign. She insists on consultation when action is the right course.

In addition, she sometimes violates the Trade Secret shared by 42 and 43 and does her own rhetorical dirty work (accusing Republicans of running Congress like a "plantation") rather than staying above the fray and leaving the task to others.

Although Clinton is an experienced television performer, public speaking could be her biggest obstacle. Hillary Clinton is not the sort of candidate who puts an audience to sleep; she is far too charismatic, famous, and fetching. But she does not exactly invite listeners to hang on her every word or follow her every thought. Her cadence, moreover, remains flat and twangy. When a candidate gives a speech, the big lines should make people want to cheer and applaud, not make them feel obligated to do so.

4. THE CLINTON BRAND

Just as George W. Bush faced a challenge in remodeling the family name brand in 2000, so would Hillary Clinton need to finesse the Clinton trademark. She and her strategists would have to determine the value of the Clinton Brand within the party and among general election voters. Some of the brand's upside would be determined by the status of the Bush presidency, just as the younger Bush benefited in some quarters because of the comparison to the status of the Clinton Brand in 2000. But she would have to address the downside of the family brand (as Bush did, too) and the possibility of Clinton Fatigue still lingering within portions of the electorate.

Bush was able to overcome the concerns about "restoration" of the family regime when he ran in 2000. Hillary Clinton would have advantages over Bush, particularly given fond memories of the strong economy during the Clinton years.

On the other hand, through message discipline, George W. Bush conveyed the distinct impression that his father (and his father's most prominent advisers) would play no substantive role in his administration. Hardly any voters, whatever they think of Bill Clinton, would believe he would have no influence in a Hillary Clinton White House. As a senator, Hillary Clinton has rarely attended substantive or even political events with her husband. Partly this has been a function of their schedules, which often have them in different cities and, given his globe-trotting ways, different countries. But the couple clearly sees the benefits of her flying solo. The two most obvious: She is able to establish her own independent identity and she minimizes the prospect of taking on his negative baggage. How much his public role would increase in a presidential campaign is an open question, and a thorny one at that.

Then there is the unmentionable question, which actually is mentioned, albeit privately at dinner tables and uneasily in offices, more often than virtually any other topic relating to Hillary Clinton's 2008 plans. Will Bill Clinton's complicated private life, which has shadowed his entire political career, once again go public in the midst of her presidential campaign? It is difficult to understate the amount of speculation that goes on at high levels of the Democratic Party about the possibility of Clinton's continued romantic involvement with other women. Leading Democrats who otherwise would strongly support Hillary Clinton if she ran for president express grave concern that nominating her would be like staking the party's future on a top-flight race car that contains a ticking time bomb.

Former Clinton cabinet officials furtively bring up this topic themselves with journalists. So do senior political advisers to Hillary Clinton, major donors, top operatives, and rank-and-file party members. Often they cite the latest tabloid stories and photographs suggesting possible ex-presidential mischief-making—a striking example of the casual and everyday way that Freak Show platforms now shape elite attitudes.

No one outside a small circle knows for sure the reality of Clinton's personal relationships. And no one knows for sure the political impact of a credible allegation. Perhaps voters would shrug off such a story line as familiar and irrelevant. Or perhaps the public would express weary disgust, leaving Hillary Clinton as the last and final victim of Bill Clinton's indiscretion.

At one point in 2005, the rumors and speculation in Democratic circles became so intense that former party chairman Terry McAuliffe, a close friend of both Clintons, took it upon himself to travel to their Chappaqua, New York, home to ask Bill Clinton about the matter directly, according to several Democrats who said McAuliffe recounted the conversation to them. The former president assured McAuliffe that there was nothing to the rumors, although Clinton had been known to make such promises in the past. Meanwhile, others in the party believe Clinton has at last learned from his errors, and would bring only support and good behavior to a Hillary Clinton presidential campaign.

5. It's All About Her, Until There Is an Agenda

Perhaps Hillary Clinton's greatest weakness as a presidential candidate is the lack of a clear rationale and message. Such a rationale is essential to winning, but Clinton does not seem to have formulated one, let alone conveyed one to the public. The ultimate question of what a Hillary Clinton campaign and administration would be *about* is unanswered.

Of course, very few of the other possible candidates in either party have developed platforms of their own, but their short-term need is not as profound. Until and unless Clinton comes up with some policies and ideas to give the press and public something on which to focus, the void will be filled by a laserlike concentration on her as a person.

Clinton's listening tour in 2000 worked so well because it took the spotlight off her character and personal motives and onto her evolving substantive professional vision.

When Bill Clinton saved his candidacy in 1992, and when George W. Bush shaped his campaign in 1999 and 2000, they succeeded because they got the media and the voters to concentrate on their agenda, rather than on their personal lives or family ties.

Rest assured, the Old Media would want to cover any Hillary Clinton campaign as "Redemption Tour II," with questions focused on the past and the personal. Clinton's challenge would be to make a race about things bigger than herself, about the future not the past, and about serious subjects that absorb voters and bore the Freak Show.

And quite a challenge it is. In July 2005, Gregg Birnbaum, the political editor of the *New York Post,* reflected the prevailing zeitgeist by starting a website (JustHillary.com) exclusively devoted to the political aspirations of Hillary Clinton. The site's tag line: "It's all about her."

Dealing with that sensibility will not be easy. And even when Clinton comes up with a rationale, the press and her enemies still will be inclined to focus on just one thing: *her.*

6. Bush Politics or Clinton Politics?

Hillary Clinton would face a critical choice in choosing between Clinton Politics and Bush Politics as the way to win in 2008. Her husband's experience and Bush's adoption of Clintonian centrist appeal on some issues in 2000 suggest that the proper path is an emphasis on Clinton Politics. But the Republican victories in 2002 and 2004 indicate that Bush Politics may dominate.

As she ponders the correct balance between Clinton Politics and Bush Politics, Hillary Clinton must confront several realities. Given the numerous centrist positions she has taken during her time in public life, she will never unify the activist wing of her party the way George W. Bush did in 1999 and 2000, making Bush Politics look like a dicey proposition.

Hillary Clinton's once-burned-twice-shy experience with the failed health care reform plan in 1993 instilled in her an incremental approach to achieving major policy goals that is antithetical to Bush Politics. She generally has refused entreaties from liberal interest groups and the netroots to take the lead in championing causes dear to them, such as directing the opposition to President Bush's Supreme Court nominees, calling for American troops to be brought home from Iraq, and highlighting certain social issues. So Clinton Politics seems like the solution.

But wait: With few exceptions, she has not designated herself a "different kind of Democrat," even rhetorically. And unlike the two former Southern governors who have demonstrated the way to win the presidency in the current polarized era, Clinton would run as a legislator. Despite her work with Republicans on some issues, her Senate record is distinctly partisan and liberal-leaning, according to nonpartisan groups that analyze congressional voting patterns. She has positioned herself to the left of her husband's governing record on some issues, most notably on free trade.

The few times she has staked out more centrist positions, such as her call in January 2005 for more tolerance for contrary views on the "tragedy" of abortion, she has drawn fire from both the Left and the Right. In fact, one of

Clinton's disadvantages as a presidential candidate attempting to practice Clinton Politics is that she would be practically incapable of a Sister Souljah moment.

Neither the Right nor the Left would accept that she actually believed whatever criticism she was making of her party, and, therefore, they loudly would presume that her motives were strictly craven and political. Despite her great progress, Clinton's failure to regain full control over this aspect of her public image would weaken her chances to win and make it more difficult to practice Clinton Politics.

Perhaps Clinton's Senate reelection campaign agenda and her work with the Democratic Leadership Council will define the dimensions of a presidential campaign based on Clinton Politics. But like every actor in the Freak Show, Hillary Clinton cannot avoid the powerful incentives that draw those seeking power and influence toward the extreme rhetoric of Bush Politics.

· · ·

BILL AND HILLARY Clinton's anger at how they lost control of their public image in the 1990s remains just inches beneath the surface for both of them. Her determination and proven ability to avoid a repeat of this experience is what pegs her as arguably the most important politician in America besides President Bush. Every political move Hillary Clinton has made for the past six years reflects lessons she learned the hard way in the nine years before. Every important question about her political fate between now and 2008, and beyond, hinges in great measure on whether she can adapt these lessons to what would be new and more challenging circumstances.

SECTION X

CONCLUSION

CLINTON POLITICS VERSUS BUSH POLITICS

★ ★ ★ ★ ★

ONE OF THE STATUS MARKERS in any White House is presidential travel. Even the most senior aides crave the glamour of traversing the country and the world on Air Force One. All staffers prize the opportunities for casual and extended encounters with the president—much more common on the road than in the regimented formality of the West Wing.

Karl Rove, however, never showed much interest in claiming a seat on Air Force One. Secure in his relationship with Bush, hardly lacking for private time in the Oval Office, Rove concluded early on in his White House tenure that it was not efficient to venture too far from home and headquarters. Exceptions arose when an outing involved a major policy event or a visit to a place with particular political relevance. Thus, during Bush's first year in office, Rove happened to accompany the president on a trip to Florida, a state that naturally was an obsession of the White House political team after the 2000 election.

The date was September 11, 2001. That evening, after a day of horrific news, chilling images, and near-constant transit, Rove returned with the president to Washington, and, later, recalled the stark scene that greeted them: "We were in Marine One, the helicopter, coming out of Andrews [Air Force Base]. And we came up over the Maryland hills, and you could see the trail of smoke from—flow in from west to east, coming out of the Pentagon. And [the president] was sitting in the left-hand seat. And I'll never forget it. He said very quietly, 'Take a look. You're looking at the face of war in the 21st century.' "

This has been a book about techniques, what the best political strategists do to achieve success. But such techniques are significant only at the margins of history. Rove's meticulous wall calendars and compulsive PowerPoint presentations were worthless on 9/11. The day was a violent break in the continuities of American life, and an abrupt turn in Bush's presidency.

Where might Bush and Rove have traveled without that turn? In the summer of 2001 the Bush presidency was steadily losing momentum. The economy was in the doldrums. Budget surpluses, an accomplishment of the Clinton years, were turning to deficits. Bush's approval ratings were sagging. In the wake of the Florida recount, questions of legitimacy lingered. 9/11 changed all that.

On September 10, the Bush presidency principally was a domestic administration. From September 11 onward, national security was nearly all-consuming. In this new context, Rove, whose background almost entirely involved domestic matters, would no longer be a principal policymaker on the most consequential governmental decisions. In other ways, though, Rove's transition to the age of anxiety launched by the terrorist attacks was surprisingly smooth.

What we call Bush Politics—a political strategy based on expanding executive power, drawing sharp ideological divides between the parties, defying rather than compromising with adversaries, marginalizing the Old Media, and exploiting the New Media—was already well in place during the first months of Bush's term. But a decade after the demise of the Cold War, the reemergence of national security as the supreme issue in presidential politics infused Bush and Bush Politics with new energy and plausibility. Rove skillfully took advantage of both the Al Qaeda threat and the conflict in Iraq. Those two battles made possible Bush's successes on behalf of Republicans in 2002 and on behalf of himself in 2004.

Now the question is whether the Iraq war has made his subsequent failures inevitable. In the spring of 2006, nearly two-thirds of the country believed the war, the central project of Bush's administration, was a mistake. Bush's job approval rating had plunged to around 30 percent, one of the lowest levels recorded for any modern president. Of those who disapproved of his performance, nearly half identified Iraq as a reason.

Bush professes indifference to poll numbers, and expects to be judged, and vindicated, by history. Even if Bush is wrong and history's judgments are severe, the implications for Karl Rove's legacy are ambiguous. The problems in Iraq chiefly reflect defects of military strategy and policy planning, not political strategy. Yet Rove was instrumental in shaping how the war was presented and promoted to the American public: the extravagant claims about what the intelligence reported about weapons of mass destruction, the tendency to trample skeptics and stigmatize second-guessers. The most important political adviser to a wartime president cannot avoid culpability if that war leads to a broken presidency. In the long run, the victories that have been the focus of this book might be seen as mere asterisks when set against Bush's greater failures.

In the short run, including the two years leading up to the 2008 election, Rove still looms much larger than an asterisk. Candidates and their strategists must consider the ways in which the 2000, 2002, and 2004 victories transformed national politics, and weigh them against how the Rove style of politics contributed to Bush's eventual difficulties. The list of those travails has grown: the collapse of Social Security reform and the second-term "ownership society" agenda; the inept performance of the government during the immediate aftermath of Hurricane Katrina; and the swelling disaffection of conservatives about Bush's leadership and his apparent willingness to forsake limited-government ideals.

Did Bush's problems begin when he abandoned the Trade Secrets described in these pages? Or are his stumbles the logical consequence of a political strategy that produced short-term victories at unsustainable costs? Maybe the questions themselves are irrelevant in the face of a more powerful dynamic. Bush was popular when he was perceived as winning at war, and unpopular when he was perceived as losing. By this light, war trumps everything.

At least some things, however, have been left untouched by war. Many of the dynamics that defined American politics before 2001 persist today. Despite Bush's promise to be a "uniter not a divider" and to "change the tone," the nation's capital and wider political culture have become more acrid and contentious than ever. The changes have been almost all for the worse. The Freak Show, which reached maturity during the Clinton years, has roared on in the Bush years, impervious to war and the widespread expectation after 9/11 that the lethal threat of terror would restore sobriety and civility to politics. Looking back at the generation of Bush and Clinton presidencies, what is most striking is that the incentives embedded in the media and political cultures for personal attack, unyielding partisanship, and prurient indulgence have proven so durable.

When he was inaugurated as the forty-first president in January 1989, just as the seeds of the Freak Show were taking root, George H. W. Bush lamented how in America there "has grown a certain divisiveness. We have seen the hard looks and heard the statements in which not each other's ideas are challenged, but each other's motives. And our great parties have too often been far apart and untrusting of each other." He intended to begin "the era of the outstretched hand." Instead, Washington's fists stayed clenched—and swinging.

When he was elected as the forty-second president in November 1992, Bill Clinton rhapsodized on his dream "to bring our people together as never before." He was still dreaming four years later at his second inaugural. Noting that a Democratic president had been returned to power along with a Republican Congress, Clinton commented that the American people surely "did not do this to advance the politics of petty bickering and extreme partisanship they plainly deplore." Citing biblical verse, he pledged to be a "repairer of the breach," and chided his opposition, "Nothing big ever came from being small." As testament to his breakdown at breach repairing, Clinton's presidential library includes an alcove devoted to his impeachment, "The Fight for Power," in which he excoriates his partisan opponents for engaging in the "politics of personal destruction" that "fueled the media's hunger for constant scandal, real or imagined."

Then, in 2001, George W. Bush began his presidency with a commitment to break the cycle of polarization. "A civil society demands from each of us good will and respect, fair dealing and forgiveness," he intoned at his first inauguration.

Were all three presidents simply being disingenuous with these vows? If not, why did all of them fail so extravagantly in their professed ambitions?

· · ·

THOSE QUESTIONS FRAME the 2008 election. And the answers define how presidential candidates will choose to run.

As we have shown, some of the Trade Secrets in this book can work for liberals and conservatives alike. The Bushes and the Clintons won their elections in part because they were happy to borrow from each other. Most important, George W. Bush and Rove were impressed by Bill Clinton's ability to recognize and compensate for the political weaknesses of the Democrats, and used that paradigm as they tried to compensate for some of the Republican weaknesses in the 2000 campaign. Extending the pattern, Hillary Clinton and her strategists are intrigued by Rove's application of technology as a tool to motivate partisans, and she is determined that Democrats follow his example and compete on more equal terms in 2008.

In the end, however, these two dynasties come to the arena with fundamentally different assumptions about how to confront the reality of polarization and Freak Show politics. Why is the electorate divided? And what can national leaders do about it? Bill Clinton and George W. Bush have different answers, and in this sense their most crucial Trade Secrets are not interchangeable.

Clinton saw the job of the president as being a national synthesizer. He aimed to select the best ideas from all parts of the ideological spectrum and reassemble them in ways that met the practical needs of an electorate interested in results instead of ideology. He embraced some traditionally conservative goals, such as balanced budgets and the elimination of a 1930s-era welfare system, but tried to preserve liberal principles in the implementation. He took some traditionally liberal goals, such as expanding access to higher education, but pursued them through conservative means, such as tax credits. He was convinced that many of the disputes of the modern political arena were artificial, deliberately manufactured, or at least exaggerated, by candidates, operatives, and interest groups inclined to exploit conflict, not facilitate consensus.

Clinton's challenge, as he perceived it, was to soar above these conflicts and unify the country. He fumbled partly because of his personal lapses but also because conservative Republicans did not want unity. They were implacably opposed to his leadership and had powerful incentives to foster his failure. But the Arkansan's objective itself, building a durable centrist majority largely by transcending ideology and splitting the difference when possible, remains the essence of Clinton Politics.

George W. Bush saw himself as a national clarifier. In the main, he and Rove believed the disputes that animate American politics are deep and genuine. While preaching the virtues of civility, Bush was willing to split the country over what he considered to be basic points: Are taxes too high or too low? What is the proper balance of force versus persuasion in America's relations with the world? Are liberal interests disproportionately influential as measured against the views of the majority?

Bush and his team felt Clinton had squandered his time in office through inconstancy and the pursuit of high popularity for frivolous ends. "For eight years the Clinton-Gore administration has coasted through prosperity," Bush said at his 2000 nomination acceptance speech. "The path of least resistance is always downhill." For Bush, dividing the electorate was an acceptable avenue to a consequential presidency, one that would make the country's policies and institutions more conservative than they had been for generations.

Bush's problems in the second term mostly have arisen because the public has turned "sour" on the Iraq war, as Rove put it in the spring of 2006. Even as the cause in Iraq has grown unpopular, Bush has persevered in his foreign policies with no less ardor. Bush's second-term troubles also include the erosion of conservative support, something that was never supposed to happen in Karl Rove's political shop. Bush and Rove always wanted to do more than just win elections for themselves. They aspired to a transforming realignment of American politics, in which the Republican Party would dominate both Washington and the country. By their own standards they have stumbled, and there is little prospect of improving this record in the next two years.

Despite these declines, the bigger focus of building a durable conservative majority by embracing ideology and highlighting clear differences between the parties continues as the essence of Bush Politics and the animating force of the Bush presidency.

. . .

THERE WERE TIMES when Bush made accommodations to political reality by following the logic of Clinton Politics, just as there were times when Clinton executed a strategy that looked more like Bush Politics. Ultimately, however, a leader's core values shine through in his or her political strategy. Clinton and Bush bequeathed two distinct political models that will outlive their presidencies. The 2008 candidates will be confronted with their own choice: Do they believe in Bush Politics or Clinton Politics? At the most practical level, which model is more effective?

When we began this book, shortly after the 2004 election, the advantages of Bush Politics seemed particularly evident. Bush had indeed divided the country, but on terms favorable to him and his values. He had spent much of his first term signing laws and executive orders that moved the country in a more conservative direction, routinely backed by the fervent support of a bare majority of Congress, rather than by overwhelming public enthusiasm.

Measured as a percentage, Bush had beaten John Kerry by a modest margin, but he also had won more total votes than any president in history. Unlike Clinton, whose support among the most committed Democrats often was tepid and ambivalent, Bush enjoyed fanatical devotion from his core followers. Many of them seemed to regard him less as a politician than as a visionary and deliverer who was serving as God's own instrument in leading America.

Now, in the days before the 2006 election, the defects of Bush Politics are acutely evident. Bush Politics works only when it is harnessed to clear policy successes. Bush's impassioned base gave him 51 percent of the country in 2004, but the campaign strategy of confrontation guaranteed that a hefty chunk of the losing 49 percent was equally impassioned in their scorn. This exposed Bush and Rove to constant risk that the percentages would reverse themselves, which occurred, and then some, in the second term. By 2005, Bush's base sensed his weakness. No longer certain he shared their conservative commitment, no longer fearful of his power, Republicans turned on Bush in ways that would have been unthinkable a few months earlier. The backlash was evident on right-wing blogs, on talk radio, and on Capitol Hill. Liberals watched with glee.

Bush's political strategy left him little room for error. His governing strategy produced many mistakes. This may have been more than coincidental. Many of the White House's setbacks seemed to flow from an attempt to apply Bush Politics within the executive branch. Analysts at the intelligence agencies cautioned that the data about Iraq's suspected weapons of mass destruction was wobbly and ambiguous. Army generals warned that the invasion force was not large enough to secure the peace for reconstruction. Bush, Cheney, and Secretary of Defense Donald Rumsfeld, distrustful of the bureaucracy and disdainful of excessive caution, discounted such arguments. The same dynamic played out in domestic decisions. A financial expert at the Department of Health and Human Services counseled that the cost of expanding the Medicare program for seniors to include a new drug benefit would be vastly higher than public estimates. Confident that the program promised to be a political boon, the White House dismissed this information, too, later to discover that they had misgauged the eventual public and congressional reaction to the cost and efficacy of the new plan.

Perhaps by some historical measure Bush will be seen as a success, and his great wager in Iraq, despite tactical missteps, applauded as visionary. But for now, the evidence has mounted that Bush Politics, while it can be a brutally effective strategy for winning elections, entails risks for the long haul. Clinton Politics, with its emphasis on high approval ratings and its constant shifting and improvisation, may be less emotionally satisfying for partisan loyalists and less conducive to producing major ideological change, but it is a reliable means of maintaining a politically resilient presidency.

There is another manner in which Bush Politics, while offering a way to win elections in these times, was a failure. It was incompatible with Bush's professed desire to change the tone in Washington. This is one area where

Bush, generally loath to concede defeat, has acknowledged that he has fallen short of his goals. He and his aides ascribe the blame to the Democrats, asserting that the president fought to change the name-calling, payback-driven culture of Washington, but the Democrats kept playing by their old rules. Bush and Rove fingered Democratic leaders such as Representative Richard Gephardt of Missouri and Senator Tom Daschle of South Dakota, whom they considered shameless partisans who coupled liberal stances with disingenuous devices and constant posturing.

Even if this explanation is sincere, it is not serious. A president committed to making national politics more civil must expect to occasionally pay a price. He would have to take a hit from the opposition, even if he thought it was unfair. He would have to refrain from delivering a blow, even if a good opportunity appeared. Bush rarely was disposed to turn the other cheek, and Rove often indulged in the kind of tactics and rhetoric that spurred Washington's cycle of escalation in the first place.

Where does this checkered record leave Rove? He remains one of the most important political strategists of his generation. But his own misjudgments and misfortunes have ensured that his White House years are not only an example of the way to win but a cautionary tale of how to fail.

· · ·

STILL, THE ARGUMENT is far from over. Even as Bush's support faltered in 2005 and 2006, Bush Politics remains an attractive political strategy for many people, Democrats as well as Republicans. Impatient with the cautious, defensive-minded maneuvering that they correctly associate with Clinton Politics, many left-wing partisans are eager for their own side to embrace the confrontational, unapologetic brand of politics associated with Bush and Karl Rove. What some want is a liberal version of Bush Politics.

Let's finally get tough and do to them what they did to us, many Democrats bellow. The incentives and imperatives of the Freak Show draw some liberals to a strategy that emulates Bush and Rove, with many persuaded that fulfilling a liberal agenda, including ending the war in Iraq, paying for universal health care coverage, and raising taxes on the wealthy and corporate interests, requires such a posture.

Liberals may well get a presidential nominee in 2008 who practices Bush Politics. Al Gore, who repeatedly has said he is not running for president but often acts like he is, at one time was known for his muted centrism. Now he regularly indulges in the kind of caustic and ideologically charged rhetoric,

such as calling Bush's White House "a renegade band of right-wing extremists," for which like-minded partisans thirst.

Gore once commented that if he ever ran for president again he would
reject the artifice and anxious calculation, traits identified with Clinton Politics, that marked his joyless, rigid 2000 campaign. "One of the things I have
learned," he told Charlie Rose in November 2002, shortly before he announced his decision not to challenge Bush in 2004, "is that it's always a mistake to hold back in any way." If there were to be a next time, he promised,
he would "just let it rip and let the chips fall where they may."

Bill Clinton would never make such a statement. And if he did, he would
not mean it. Clinton knows, and Gore, too, in his more self-aware moments,
that it is hard to win the White House just by speaking one's mind and free-
ing one's soul.

Even Clinton's achievements, however, do not impress many of the
Democrats who have been radicalized by the Bush years. In 2008 the yearn-
ing for impassioned oratory and ideological purity will be felt as strongly by
the Left as by the Right. These passions are complicating life for many
Democrats contemplating 2008, but above all for Hillary Clinton, the politician most logically associated with Clinton Politics. She faces criticism from
opposite directions. There is widespread opinion that she is not the politician
her husband is. Among the Democratic Party's agitated netroots, liberal bloggers fear that she is, in fact, too much like her husband: another triangulat-
ing Clinton more concerned with advancing herself than advancing a cause.

The irony is that there is barely a blogger in America who could match
Hillary Clinton in contempt for the Bush administration. While Bill Clinton
was a natural accommodator, Hillary Clinton's instincts are more confrontational and less compromising. Rarely does she give voice to those instincts in
an unfiltered way. One instance when she did let loose was in June 2005, at
a fund-raiser in New York City. "There has never been an administration, I
don't believe in our history, more intent upon consolidating and abusing
power to further their own agenda," she thundered. "I know it's frustrating for
many of you, it's frustrating for me. Why can't the Democrats do more to stop
them? I can tell you this: It's very hard to stop people who have no shame
about what they're doing. It is very hard to tell people that they are making
decisions that will undermine our checks and balances and constitutional
system of government who don't care. It is very hard to stop people who have
never been acquainted with the truth."

Some Democrats wish Hillary Clinton made such proclamations more often. If she were a less disciplined politician, she might do so. In any case, the New York comments caused a stir inside her own camp, where some of her advisers cringed at rhetoric they worried was too strident. Still, those who expect a politician named Clinton not to practice Clinton Politics probably are asking too much.

This leaves room for a Democrat in 2008 to run for the nomination practicing a liberal version of Bush Politics. Perhaps this will in fact be Gore. A number of political journalists and hobbyists would relish the prospect of a Hillary Clinton–Al Gore showdown. In all likelihood, should she run, the drama of Clinton having to defend her left flank and liberal bona fides would come with less historical and personal baggage, from a less conspicuous figure such as Wisconsin senator Russ Feingold. But someone almost inevitably would fill the role.

Indeed, it seems possible that both parties in 2008 will have nomination contests in which Bush Politics faces off against Clinton Politics. These groupings will not determine every tactical move. All politicians will have moments when it suits their purpose to strike a conciliatory pose, and moments when they choose to storm the barricades. In broad terms, though, every 2008 candidate will make a fundamental choice: Do they wish to base their candidacy on unifying themes and crossover appeal between the parties? Or do they wish to accept the divisions in the electorate as essentially unbridgeable and strive to win an ideological and partisan argument?

By coincidence, two potential presidential candidates from the state of Virginia help illuminate the distinction between Bush Politics and Clinton Politics. Democrat Mark Warner, a Virginian by way of Connecticut who made a fortune in the cell phone business and went on to a successful term as governor, is maneuvering to become the chief alternative to Hillary Clinton, buoyed by carpers who think Clinton is unelectable. Republican George Allen, a Virginian by way of California who served a term as governor before being elected to the U.S. Senate, is venturing to become the chief alternative to John McCain, urged on by grumblers who think McCain is insufficiently conservative and a slavish practitioner of Clinton Politics.

In many of his early speeches, Warner has struck themes that reflect the heart of Clinton Politics. At a May 2006 commencement address at Wake Forest University, he denounced the media's tendency to be consumed by conflict and preached a message of unity: "Turn on the TV. Listen to the radio. Click on almost any blog. And you'll see what I'm talking about: personal and partisan attacks, complex issues reduced to easy-to-digest sound bites, and way too much cross-fire and not nearly enough cross talk."

Warner counseled the graduates: "Reject the cynicism and shallow posturing that dominate our media. Tune out the shouting and background noise that masquerade as meaningful commentary. Instead, wrestle—wrestle— with those complex issues, be respectful of those with whom you disagree and always remember that despite all our differences there is that common bond that draws us together and binds us together as Americans."

These words could easily have been articulated by Bill Clinton. George Allen, by contrast, has in twenty years in politics, from his days as a young, bolo-tie-wearing state legislator from Charlottesville, uttered precious few sentiments that sound like Clinton Politics. The son of the legendary Washington Redskins football coach, Allen is a man of genuinely and instinctually conservative leanings. He is positioning himself in 2008 as the purist Republican in the field, and he has been critical of Bush from the right on numerous occasions. Allen was practicing the elements of Bush Politics long before George W. Bush entered the national scene. When he ran for governor in 1993, Allen urged his home-state Republicans at a party convention to beat Democrats by "knocking their soft teeth down their whiny throats."

• • •

AFTER HILLARY CLINTON, there is no potential 2008 candidate whose choice between Clinton Politics and Bush Politics is more interesting than John McCain's. But he is the one presidential contender who, by virtue of his own past and his outsized reputation, may not have to choose. He so far is running simultaneously on both Clinton Politics and Bush Politics, or perhaps a blend of the two, flavored with his own maverick style.

McCain is nationally famous, popular with members of both parties and with independents, and capable of raising enormous funds. He also is an experienced candidate with an accomplished staff, including strategist John Weaver, who once worked with Karl Rove and who comprehends as well as anyone the tactical Trade Secrets that have contributed to the Bush-Rove campaign success.

But McCain also is, at this writing, the strongest candidate in the field because he himself understands many of the broader Trade Secrets that Bill Clinton and George W. Bush employed so adroitly. McCain appreciates the importance of knowing the substance of his agenda; of projecting optimism;

of defining public policy decisions in terms of values unique to his political philosophy; and, finally, of grasping the strengths and weaknesses of both the opposition party and his own.

McCain's current platform is distinctive for three reasons. First, his understanding of those strengths and weaknesses puts him head and shoulders above all other plausible candidates except Hillary Clinton. Second, his program derives, as did Bill Clinton's and George W. Bush's, from his personal life experience and long-standing principles. Third, his platform is fairly specific.

A McCain presidential campaign would focus on campaign finance and lobbying reform; limiting corporate welfare; deficit reduction; and modulated environmental policies—all representative of Clinton Politics. But McCain also is hawkish on the Iraq war and foreign policy generally, the very foundation of present Bush Politics.

The Arizona senator has another big advantage. McCain's willingness to shatter conventions and to speak with candor (or, as some critics would quibble, the appearance of candor) have resulted in lavishly favorable treatment from the Old Media.

There rarely has been a presidential candidate in the Freak Show era who has received such fawning press coverage as McCain enjoyed during the 2000 race and beyond. He is fond of joking that his "base" is composed of members of the media. Such wry humor was backed up by reams of news clips and yards of video. This is an exceptional feat for a Republican.

The senator's recipe for success is to follow a model of openness, quite different from what George W. Bush and Hillary Clinton have adopted. McCain loves going on television, loves talking to reporters, and loves taking questions from all comers. He is a great performer from the point of view of the press: witty, accessible, compelling, dramatic, and candid. These same traits also have made him a darling in some quarters of the New Media, where he has prominent allies such as Don Imus, Jay Leno, and Jon Stewart.

McCain as a presidential candidate and potential president is a beguiling figure for another reason. Because of his ability to speak to conservatives, centrists, and even some liberals, and because of the unique power of his personal biography as a military hero, he would seem to have more potential than any of the other 2008 contenders to transcend the Freak Show, to break its cycle of political attack and retribution. But one should not underestimate his vulnerability to the Freak Show. If he runs, it is virtually assured that

McCain's opponents will try to wrest control of his public image by painting him as hypocritical, angry, and mentally unbalanced. He has been called these names before, and the consequences were as unattractive as they were effective.

Part of the lore of the 2000 campaign is how Bush's allies were able to eliminate McCain from nomination contention even after the Arizona's senator's 19-percentage-point victory over Bush in the New Hampshire primary. What is well remembered is that McCain endured a series of attacks from the Right, with wild accusations ranging from the personal (McCain had fathered a child with a prostitute; McCain's wife was addicted to drugs) to the political (the longtime Vietnam-era prisoner of war was insufficiently concerned about the well-being of America's veterans). In the popular retelling, McCain lost a series of primaries, starting in South Carolina, because conservative voters believed these allegations and rallied around Bush.

It is true that such charges were leveled, and they doubtless had an impact on McCain's fortunes. The Right had an incentive to take McCain out, in part to help Bush, but also because it detested McCain's support for campaign finance law changes it decided were abridgments of the First Amendment and would hurt the Republican Party, and because it was wary of his support among liberal elites, such as the press.

What is less well remembered is the period before this rancorous onslaught. In advance of McCain's Granite State conquest, with encouragement from a frustrated Bush campaign, the Arizonan's record in the Senate was subjected to some Old Media scrutiny. A flurry of stories began in the early winter of 1999, detailing a portrait of McCain at odds with the public image he had crafted. None of the pieces accused McCain of breaking the law, but they illustrated a Beltway-business-as-usual coziness with lobbyists and corporate interests.

As chairman of the Commerce Committee, McCain had exercised influence on behalf of companies that had supplied him with political contributions and let him use their corporate jets for campaign travel. McCain denied any quid pro quos, but acknowledged he was "tainted" by the system, and canceled at least one fund-raiser for appearance's sake.

The stories did not seem to damage McCain before his New Hampshire primary triumph but they kept up afterward, and the Bush campaign used the theme to chip away at the maverick's reputation for straight talk. Bush began to refer to his rival as "Chairman McCain," who he said was trying to "get away with this Washington doubletalk." "He has been in Washington long enough," Bush added, "to earn a very important committee chairmanship. He has used that position skillfully to forward his campaign."

McCain's advisers, more than a few of whom were themselves professional lobbyists, reached out to their colleagues for more financial support in the wake of his New Hampshire win, touting the prospect that McCain could end up being the Republican nominee. The Bush campaign continued to flog the issue of McCain's alleged hypocrisy and abuse of his power, as well as his high percentage of contributions from lobbyists. Demonstrating he was wise to Freak Show politics, Bush admitted that he "got defined" in New Hampshire, but declared he was now "going to take it" to McCain. "On the one hand he preaches campaign finance reform. On the other hand he passes the plate," Bush sneered. Behind the scenes, Bush allies, including those on Capitol Hill, accelerated a campaign they had begun in the late fall of 1999, whispering that McCain was mentally unstable and had a volcanic temper, even by the standards of elected officials.

The stories kept coming, and were then joined by the accusation that McCain's record on veterans and defense matters was not consistent with his strong national security image. After first stating that he was "not going to get mad about it" or "lose my temper," McCain boiled over, putting an advertisement on television labeling Bush "untrustworthy" and someone who "twists the truth like Clinton."

One of Bush's South Carolina strategists, Tucker Eskew, well versed in the Freak Show game of candidate definition, said at the time that McCain's camp was "squawking because we hit them where they hurt. . . . McCain and the media created a myth . . . and we exploded that. We challenged him on his greatest point of pride, and they stomped their feet, pointed fingers, and whined."

If the Old Media's favorite politician can suffer such a severe challenge to his public image, there are two lessons. First, it can happen again to McCain if he runs in 2008. And, second, it can happen to anybody.

• • •

WE SET OUT asking how American politics became a Freak Show. Some may have been troubled that our answers were presented with a certain detachment. The politicians who exemplified the way to lose—whose message and reputation were hijacked—perhaps deserve more explicit sympathy. The people who did the hijacking—those in politics and media who practice and profit from Freak Show tactics—perhaps deserve more explicit condemnation. It may seem at times we celebrated the latter for knowing the way to win, with little regard for *how* they won and to what ends they wielded their power. By professional habit, we analyze politics as it is, not as it ought to be.

But the logical next question must be addressed: How can American politics *stop* being a Freak Show? The Freak Show in one sense is a vivid if sometimes vulgar expression of democracy. It emerged as both the political process and the media became less controlled by elites and more accessible to diverse competing voices. The old Establishment consensus, stretching across party lines and including think tanks, interest groups, and news organizations, has been demolished. The result has been unruly, but there is no going back to the way things were. That would not be a good thing even if it were possible.

But nor is the current condition a good thing. The anger and negativity of the Freak Show have supplanted the genuine and productive arguments that should be at the center of national politics. Debate requires at least a modicum of agreed-upon facts. It requires also a willingness to engage with the views of the opposition, if only to demonstrate why they are in error. While the Freak Show creates the impression of nonstop discussion, the reality is that it is producing very few authentic conversations in which those on either side speak and listen in a spirit of frankness and good faith. The result is a form of corruption, as malignant as a politician accepting an illicit suitcase of cash. If one side can dismiss the other as not simply wrong but irredeemably flawed and unworthy, then a politician has little to fear from public criticism except when it comes from his or her own party. The rest can be ignored as the usual ranting and background noise. This is why the Freak Show has made politics less accountable, and why the Freak Show is not an expression of democracy but its enemy. It is urgent that someone or something break the cycle. Three presidents promising civility did not do it. Terrorist attacks did not do it. Hillary Clinton and even John McCain are unlikely to do it. Who then?

Since the Freak Show exists in politics and the media as the response to incentives, it can be eradicated in only two ways. Those who profit from the status quo could choose to reject the current incentives in sacrifice for the greater good. Or news consumers and voters could cause the Freak Show's incentives to evaporate by refusing to respond to or reward prevailing standards.

In our ideal world, the first scenario might be plausible. In the real world, it is scarcely worth discussing. Politicians and their advisers who live amid the depressing, withering conditions of the Freak Show, from interest groups, to fund-raisers, to campaign strategists, and even to presidential candidates, recognize the corrosive effect it has on them, and on the country. If a truce somehow could be called, many would sign on. Instead, new fronts open up nearly every day in the nation's political wars, driven by polarization, which discourages concession or compromise. If some political players tried to abandon the Freak Show fight, motivated by disgust, principle, or a desire to make America better, they most likely would be scorned by their base and squashed by their opponents. People in politics want to win elections, and the accumulated evidence over more than fifteen years suggests that the donors, volunteers, activists, and above all, voters necessary for victory in 2008 respond favorably to the dark incentives of the current system. Unilateral disarmament in the Freak Show is tantamount to political suicide.

Similarly, people in the New Media have no motive to spurn the Freak Show. From Fox News commentators to Matt Drudge to the *Daily Kos,* the current system has showered them with money, celebrity, and clout.

People in the Old Media, on the other hand, are eager to end the Freak Show. Most journalists would prefer to work in a profession in which Matt Drudge had less influence and Jim Lehrer had more. From the outside, it might appear that Old Media leaders have all the power necessary to restructure the landscape, to make choices that reflect their ostensible standards rather than mirror Freak Show doctrine. From the inside, it is clear that the Old Media is afflicted with a pervasive sense of fading power and diminishing options. Matt Drudge thrives because he is an entrepreneur who brilliantly has exploited the opportunities of a free market. Lehrer's *NewsHour* survives because he is insulated from the free market through a combination of private donations and government subsidies. That model works for public broadcasting, but not for the rest of the Old Media. Journalism is a public trust, or should be, but it is not a charity. News is expensive to produce and can be sustained only as it responds to the demands of its restless, jaded, rapidly dispersing audience. Serious, substantive work is still being done, but more commonly in a climate of falling circulation and ratings, strained budgets, and anxious executives.

The power to improve journalism remains above all with the audience, just as the power to improve politics remains with voters. A generation ago, it was editors and producers who were the filter enforcing standards of seriousness, relevancy, and fairness in public debate. Now, individuals must serve as their own filters, and set their own standards. Nearly everyone agrees in principle that journalism and politics need to improve. That will never happen in practice until people decide to turn away from attack and distraction— even when one's own side is the beneficiary. The Freak Show will fade away when its audience does.

Someday, an enlightened public will punish the politics of cynicism and destruction and reward the politics of creativity and civil dialogue. That truly will be the way to win.

AUTHORS' NOTE AND ACKNOWLEDGMENTS

★ ★ ★ ★ ★

THIS BOOK WAS WRITTEN over several months of intense work in 2005 and 2006. But the ideas and observations on which it was based were developed over many years. Mark Halperin was present at Bill Clinton's arrival on the presidential stage, and at times was the only journalist traveling with him during the fall and winter of 1991 as he began his campaign for the White House. John Harris came along a bit later, covering the Clinton presidency for the *Washington Post* from January 1995 to its conclusion in January 2001, then staying with the subject for another several years to write a history of the administration. Together, we felt we knew the Clinton story well, and also perceived the ways in which the ample Clinton mythology did not always match reality as we had witnessed it.

We felt the same about Karl Rove, a political strategist Halperin first met in 1998, just as George W. Bush emerged as a likely contender for the presidency. Harris covered the 2000 and 2004 elections, and from 2005 onward has supervised the *Post*'s coverage of national campaigns and the Bush presidency. Cumulatively, this experience left us eager to tackle the question that seemed to be on the minds of people of all partisan stripes following the president's 2004 reelection: How did Bush and Rove do it?

In the days after the election, Jonathan Karp, then of Random House, proposed that we address this precise subject. We were intrigued but proposed a wider lens, to explain the transformation—historic and sometimes disturbing—in the technology, values, and standards that animate campaigns and the media coverage of politics. We also thought that there was much to be learned from a comparison of the Clinton experience and the Bush experience, and the political lessons suggested by both.

The story, however, was a moving target. A triumphant figure when we began the book, Rove was a beleaguered one for much of the time we were writing it. Our aim was to reflect news as it unfolded without being unduly buffeted by the headlines, and to remember the purpose of the book. With both Clinton and Rove, the primary assignment was identical: to explain why they excelled at winning elections, especially those lessons that are relevant to 2008. The secondary assignment was to reveal how campaigns have implications for governance. The particular ways Clinton and Rove won elections are connected to the successes and failures of the administrations that followed.

The exercise of developing, writing, and sharpening the arguments in this book was a concentrated version of discussions the two of us have had over the past decade—a near-constant conversation about all aspects of politics that was at the center of our friendship. We gossip, joke, and very often brood about the topic, and the ways modern campaigns fall short of the ideal—all the while critiquing our own coverage and that of friends and competitors. Although we generally share similar views on these topics, we engaged in a dialectic of sorts. Harris lives in Washington, Halperin in New York—a physical distance that at times has stimulated a useful difference in perspectives. We sent our drafts back and forth, one person writing and the other editing, and then vice versa. The collaboration produced something that neither one of us could have done individually.

One person, above all others, contributed to this book well beyond what any two authors could ask for. Karen Avrich devoted countless hours to making sure that what was written was as good as we could make it. Karen understands American politics, history, good writing, human nature, deadlines, hard work, and how one procrastinating author can reinforce the bad habits of another. Whatever a reader thinks of *The Way to Win*, we can assure you it is significantly better than it would have been without Karen's brilliant, generous, constant, and vital participation in its writing.

Many people granted on-the-record, background, and off-the-record interviews for the book. Thanks to all of them, including those who asked that they not be named here. All our sources had little to gain except a chance to contribute to an accurate historical record of our era, which we hope we have produced. We wish to express our gratitude especially to former president Bill Clinton, Vice President Dick Cheney, and Karl Rove for sharing their thoughts with us.

Among those who gave us substantial time and assistance were Dan Bartlett, Jay Carson, Matthew Dowd, Mark McKinnon, Ken Mehlman, Steve Schmidt, Stuart Stevens, and Nicolle Wallace.

Others who provided key cooperation included Congressman Joe Barton, David Bates, Becky Beach, Paul Begala, James Carville, Jim Dyke, Mindy Tucker Fletcher, Joe Gaylord, Karen Hicks, Taylor Hughes, Chris Lehane, Mary Matalin, Lea Anne McBride, Mark Mellman, Karen Modlin, Terry Nelson, Jack Oliver, Jonathan Prince, Daron Shaw, Tracey Schmitt, Karen Skelton, Heath Thompson, Margaret Tutwiler, Lorraine Voles, and the staff of the George H. W. Bush Library.

We also are indebted to several readers who helped us markedly improve the final version of our text from early drafts.

Ann O'Hanlon, who is experienced in politics and journalism, brought her grounding in both to a reading of the book. The fact that she was skeptical about some parts of our argument made her all the more helpful as an editor. It also made her praise for the final product that much more gratifying.

Dan Balz of the *Washington Post* has known and covered Bill and Hillary Clinton, George W. Bush, and Karl Rove for years, and we have benefited greatly from his nuanced understanding of their strengths and weaknesses. Dan read a version of the book at a critical time and offered wise, good-natured suggestions.

Bill Nichols of *USA Today* also read the manuscript and gave us excellent advice on how to sharpen and clarify our ideas about the workings of the modern media.

Steven E. Schier of Carleton College is a brilliant political scientist who has written extensively on the Clinton and Bush presidencies. We appreciate his comments. Richard Ward is a highly skilled Washington lawyer who in another life might be a journalist or political operative—he would be superb as either one. He gave us impassioned and valuable comments on an early draft.

Thanks to Lisa Chase, who offered a keen eye on the text and suggested how to tighten both the length and the logic.

Two previous books about Karl Rove were helpful: *Boy Genius: Karl Rove, the Architect of George W. Bush's Remarkable Political Triumphs* by Carl M. Cannon, Lou Dubose, and Jan Reid, and *Bush's Brain: How Karl Rove Made George W. Bush Presidential* by James Moore and Wayne Slater.

Anyone interested in Rove's career would do well to look at the supporting material and interviews that were compiled for the 2005 PBS *Frontline* documentary *The Architect.*

We benefited from the wisdom of many colleagues through both conversations and their writings about Bill Clinton and Karl Rove, especially Rick Berke, Ronald Brownstein, Ron Fournier, John Harwood, Gwen Ifill, Nick Lemann, and Adam Nagourney.

Also giving us insight into Karl Rove were the works of several other reporters who know him well, including Fred Barnes, Robert Novak, and Howard Fineman.

Jonathan Martin of *The Hotline,* who helped us with research, is an enthusiastic and shrewd student of politics. He has a bright future in journalism. So does the *Washington Post*'s Zachary A. Goldfarb, who lent a hand on research. Olwen Price rapidly transcribed major important interviews.

Random House is the ideal publisher for this book because it is filled with smart and creative people who really enjoy and understand politics. Editors Will Murphy and Jonathan Jao were in the trenches with us every step of the way (*usually* with us, and even when they were against us it was for good reason). The sage Gina Centrello and Daniel Menaker always dispensed their wisdom at exactly the right moment. Barbara Fillon is enthusiastic and effective; there is no better combination for a publicist. Steve Messina knew the last-minute production challenges of working with John Harris from a previous book, but took us on anyway, only to discover that the second book was twice as hard.

Andrew Wylie, our agent, showed his typical confidence, creativity, and ingenuity throughout the process.

MARK HALPERIN

JOHN F. HARRIS

July 27, 2006

FROM MARK HALPERIN:

ABC News has been my only professional home, and I have always valued its commitment to serious news and its familial atmosphere. ABC has given me the opportunity to spend a year following presidential hopeful Bill Clinton as he campaigned across the country; to cover the White House; to report internationally; to learn about the business and craft of broadcast journalism; and to concentrate on the world of American politics.

David Westin, Paul Mason, Amy Entelis, Kerry Smith, and Robin Sproul of ABC News management offered me unqualified encouragement during the writing process, as they have throughout my career.

I am grateful to the terrific and terrifically talented David Chalian and Teddy Davis, and past members of the ABC News political unit, for their professional and personal support. My eighteen years of conversations with George Stephanopoulos have given me the equivalent of an advanced degree in political science, and I thank him for the free education. I also have had the honor of working with and learning from such journalistic legends as Sam Donaldson, Charles Gibson, Cokie Roberts, Diane Sawyer, and Jim Wooten, who have taught and inspired me.

Two other people from ABC News warrant special mention. I have covered every election during my career with Nancy Gabriner and Peter Jennings. No one in American political journalism ever has had two better colleagues. Nancy and Peter gave me the chance to learn to be a political reporter, the capacity to understand the country through the prism of campaigns, and the companionship to make the job fun. Peter Jennings was a splendid journalist and a great friend, and he was a paradigm in the news business of perseverance, integrity, grace, vigor, and decency. His memory and legacy continue at ABC News, and will not fade.

Also, thanks to Gil Fuchsberg, Deborah Needleman, and Eileen Prince for their good spirit, good humor, and good advice.

Thanks to my family, including Laura and Peter Hartmann for critiquing the cover, and Hannah and Madelyn Halperin for more esoteric assistance.

Karen Avrich's professional contributions are detailed above. As for the personal:

She made certain that I never lost focus, confidence, or an understanding of what it takes to write half a book. Throughout this grueling process, she remained what she was before, and what she is today: my best friend, the funniest, most wonderful, and most interesting person I know, and the joy and love of my life.

FROM JOHN HARRIS:

As an editor, I'm a bit further removed from the front lines of politics than I was in the previous twenty years as a reporter. Much of what I learn these days is second-hand. But they are excellent hands: my *Washington Post* colleagues who cover the White House and national politics. They are the best team in the business. Special thanks to Mike Abramowitz, Peter Baker, and Mike Fletcher at the White House, and to Dan Balz, David S. Broder, Chris Cillizza, and Jim VandeHei on politics. Others who have other editors but are surrogate members of my team are Chuck Babington, Jeffrey H. Birnbaum, Dana Milbank, Shailagh Murray, and Jonathan Weisman. Every day this group shows how to cover politics seriously and still have fun.

I am in particular debt to my fellow editors on the national desk at the *Post,* starting with National Editor Liz Spayd, a boss, friend, and mentor. The editors with whom I work most closely on politics and government coverage are my friends Eric Pianin and Maralee Schwartz, but editing at the *Post* tends to be a collaborative affair and I work side by side with skilled collaborators: Lenny Bernstein, Scott Butterworth, Nils Bruzelius, Pat Gaston, Steve Holmes, Dan LeDuc, and Scott Vance.

This book returns often to the subject of media failures. It is not simply job protection that prompts me to point out what an admirable exception the *Post* is to these trends. For the twenty-one years I have been in the newsroom, and for a lot longer before that, the *Post* has been living by its ideals of fair-minded, aggressive, and serious journalism, paying little mind to controversy or cost. The credit goes to the people who lead the place, so let's give them credit: Don Graham and Bo Jones, the two publishers during my time at the *Post,* and Ben Bradlee and Len Downie, the two executive editors. Phil Bennett is the latest in a succession of splendid managing editors, and he presses everyone who works at the *Post* to be thinking of ways to demonstrate the vitality and relevance of old values in a chaotic new age. These people have made the *Post* a great newspaper and a great place to work.

Finally, thanks to my family. I wrote this book mostly on the night shift or the early morning shift, or on weekends—arguably not the ideal way to do it with three young children, who so far are more interested in the way to win at soccer than presidential campaigns. My wife, Ann O'Hanlon, is my friend and partner for everything that matters. We love each other in part because we love so many other things together. She did far more than her share to hold down the fort over the past year. And my children—Liza, Griffin, and Nikki—ensured that our household continued to be the most fun fort of all.

NOTES

★ ★ ★ ★ ★

There are many references in this chapter to news accounts. Where the source and day are obvious in the body of the work, there is no note below.

Section I • The Freak Show

THE WAY TO LOSE

6 With a well-timed placement: Interview with RNC sources.

6 "**Exclusive**" promised the *Drudge Report: Drudge Report,* December 3, 2002 (all direct quotes from the *Drudge Report* come from www.drudge reportarchives.com).

10 "He looks French": Adam Nagourney and Richard Stevenson, "Bush's Aides Plan Late Sprint in '04," *New York Times,* April 22, 2003.

11 *You know it's true:* According to people present for the exchange.

12 This essentially took place: Blaine Harden, "A Seething Dole Intensifies Attack; Candidate Lobs FBI Files Accusations," *Washington Post,* October 26, 1996.

12 Polier later traced the story: Alexandra Polier, "The Education of Alexandra Polier," *New York,* June 7, 2004.

12 Drudge was still hovering: *Drudge Report,* March 17, 2004.

13 While the *New York Times* put: David M. Halbfinger, "Amid Natural Splendor in Idaho, a Weary Kerry Gets Away from It All," *New York Times,* March 19, 2004.

13 Drudge trumpeted it: *Drudge Report,* March 19, 2004.

13 The *Boston Globe* picked up the baton: Patrick Healy, "Kerry Seeks Balance, Bush Readies Barrage," *Boston Globe,* March 21, 2004.

13 Republican officeholders fanned the flames: Congressional Record, July 12, 2004.

13 The line Drudge picked up: Michael Manville, "French Going Wild for Senator Kerry in Election Fever," *New York Sun,* March 15, 2004.

13 A few days later, an Associated Press story: "Kerry's Relatives in France Say Dem Candidate Is 'All-American,'" Associated Press, March 30, 2004.

15 A few days later in the *New York Times:* Adam Nagourney and Richard Stevenson, "Bush's Campaign to Intensify, with Emphasis on His Record," *New York Times,* February 1, 2004.

17 CNN's Candy Crowley: *NewsNight,* CNN, April 26, 2004.

17 But the *Washington Post:* Howard Kurtz and Dan Balz, "Leaks About Foes Seen as Routine in Campaigns," *Washington Post,* April 29, 2004.

17 In the fourth paragraph: Jim Rutenberg and Jodi Wilgoren, "1971 Tape Adds to Debate Over Kerry's Medal Protest," *New York Times,* April 26, 2004.

18 "It is interesting that John Kerry": Kurtz and Balz, "Leaks About Foes Seen as Routine in Campaigns."

20 Initially, coverage was limited: Jim VandeHei and Mary Fitzgerald, "McCain Criticizes Ad Attacking Kerry on Vietnam War Record," *Washington Post,* August 6, 2004.

20 A week later: Paula Zahn special, CNN, August 30, 2004.

22 As Kerry's pollster Mark Mellman: Interview with Mark Mellman.

The Profile Primary

26 The setting was Kerry's Georgetown home: Mark Leibovich, "The Heart of Politics; One Woman, Two Senators and Presidential Ambitions: The Washington Tale of John Kerry and Teresa Heinz," *Washington Post,* June 2, 2002.

26 In January of 2004: Mark Miller, "'I Refuse to Be Categorized,'" *Newsweek,* January 17, 2004.

Freak Show Politics

31 "Well, he is sort of a phony, isn't he?": Michael Kranish, "With Antiwar Role, High Visibility," *Boston Globe,* June 17, 2003.

31 "He was in Vietnam": Ibid.

31 Years later: Richard Nixon, *RN: The Memoirs of Richard Nixon,* New York: Simon & Schuster, 1990, pp. 763–64.

31 In a less reflective mood: Charles Colson, *Born Again,* Old Tappan, NJ: Chosen Books, 1976, p. 45.

32 "Nixon understood before": Interview with Ken Mehlman.

32 Nixon himself studied the draft: William Safire, *Before the Fall: An Inside View of the Pre-Watergate White House,* Garden City: Doubleday, 1975, p. 352.

32 On November 13, 1969, Agnew flew: Spiro Agnew, speech to the Midwestern

Republican regional conference, Des Moines, Iowa, November 13, 1969 (Agnew's speech is easily accessible online; full text and audio can be found at www.americanrhetoric.com/speeches/spiroagnew.htm).

33   Frank Stanton, the president of CBS: Paul L. Montgomery, "3 Networks Reply to Agnew Attack," *New York Times,* November 14, 1969.

33   Senator Edward M. Kennedy: "Kennedy Criticizes Speech as Divisive," United Press International, November 14, 1969.

33   A few weeks earlier: Spiro Agnew, speech to Pennsylvania Republican fundraiser, Harrisburg, Pennsylvania, October 30, 1969.

34   One day during those years: David Broder, *Behind the Front Page: A Candid Look at How the News Is Made,* New York: Simon & Schuster, 1987, p. 140.

34   During Bill Clinton's first presidential campaign: Donald Baer, Matthew Cooper, David Gergen, "Bill Clinton's Hidden Life," *U.S. News & World Report,* July 20, 1992.

36   Republican congressman Dick Armey: Kenneth Cooper, "Crime Bill Blocked in House, Health Vote Put Off; Gun Control Opponents Prevail in Stinging Defeat for Clinton," *Washington Post,* August 12, 1994.

36   Describing such treatment: Interview with Bill Clinton.

37   "transformational figure": Dan Balz, "The Whip Who Would Be Speaker; Gingrich Sees Role as 'Transformational,'" *Washington Post,* October 20, 1994.

37   "renew American civilization": David E. Rosenbaum, "Republicans Offer Voters a Deal for Takeover of House," *New York Times,* September 28, 1994.

37   Al Gore, as environmental evangelist: Al Gore, *Earth in the Balance: Ecology and the Human Spirit,* New York: Plume, 1992, p. 269.

37   The third trend: Carl Cannon, "State of Our Disunion," *National Journal,* January 21, 2006.

38   At every turn: Interview with Ken Mehlman.

41   So Rush Limbaugh gets a seat: *Tim Russert,* CNBC, November 21, 1998.

41   Or *Good Morning America* covers: *Good Morning America,* ABC News, June 24, 2003.

45   Kerry often used: Patrick Healy, "Kerry Emphasis Shifts from War Cry to Policy," *Boston Globe,* March 29, 2004.

45   When introducing Edwards to his flock: Edward E. Plowman, "Pulpit Politics," *World,* November 6, 2004.

How Matt Drudge Rules Our World

53   Members of the Gang of 500: David Grann, "Inside Dope; Mark Halperin and the Transformation of the Washington Establishment," *New Yorker,* October 25, 2004.

54   They dined at the Forge: Interview with RNC sources.

55   Ken Mehlman, the RNC chairman: Interview with Mehlman.

57   Not long after the election: Eleanor Clift et al. "The Inside Story," *Newsweek*, November 15, 2004.

58   The *Miami Herald* quoted him: Richard Pachter, "Linking News Sites, Matt Drudge Creates Internet Success," *Miami Herald*, September 1, 2003.

59   "All three stories": Howard Kurtz, "Out There: It's 10 Past Monica, America. Do You Know Where Matt Drudge Is?," *Washington Post*, March 28, 1999.

59   "This is just the first flare": Gabriel Snyder, "Is Matt Drudge Too Far Ahead of *The Times*?," *New York Observer*, September 25, 2000.

60   Responsible *Times*men were not amused: Ibid.

60   A total of perhaps twenty minutes elapsed: *Drudge Report*, May 30, 2005.

62   When his 1984 graduating class: Kurtz, "Out There."

62   So he would "walk by ABC News": Matt Drudge, speech to the National Press Club, June 2, 1998.

62   During one visit, Bob Drudge: Charles Winecoff, "Tattle Tales: In her Dish-y New Book, Jeannette Walls Traces the Rise and Rise of Gossipmongering in America," *Entertainment Weekly*, March 10, 2000.

63   In contrast to the taut, exclamation-spiked style: *Drudge Report*, July 10, 1995.

63   Even then, updates on the legal and personal travails: *Drudge Report*, March 4, 1996.

64   Thanks to his delving inside news organizations: Matt Drudge, speech to the National Press Club, June 2, 1998.

Section II • Bill Clinton's Trade Secrets (and Al Gore's)

1992

69   His tutor was his longtime aide: David Maraniss, *First in His Class*, New York: Simon & Schuster, 1995, p. 441.

70   After a couple more days: Ibid., p. 443.

73   One day in 1992: Thomas M. DeFrank et al., *Quest for the Presidency 1992*, College Station: Texas A&M University Press, 1994, p. 267.

75   "Democratic Senator John Kerry": Mickey Kaus, "Kerry Withdrawal Contest," *Slate*, December 5, 2003.

75   When Clinton's staff: Interview with 1992 Clinton campaign official who participated in the conversation.

78   New York's George Pataki: Adam Nagourney, "Pataki Has an Audition on the National Stage," *New York Times*, February 24, 1998.

CHANGING THE CONVENTIONAL WISDOM ABOUT BILL AND HILLARY CLINTON

82 As Margaret Carlson wrote in *Time:* Margaret Carlson, "Bill's Big Bash; In a Rare Show of Unity and Hollywood Razzmatazz, the Democrats Pull Off the Perfect G.O.P. Convention," *Time,* July 27, 1992.

WEAK AND WRONG

86 "He wants to help": Ruth Marcus, "Clinton, Hill Leaders Hail New Teamwork; President-Elect Calls First Meeting a Step Toward 'Shared Responsibility,'" *Washington Post,* November 17, 1992.

86 Clinton's articulated analysis: Ruth Marcus, "Clinton Hosts Meeting with Top Hill Democrats," *Washington Post,* November 16, 1992.

86 He heralded a "new ethic": Ruth Marcus, "Clinton, Hill Leaders Hail New Teamwork," *Washington Post,* November 17, 1992.

92 When on one of those jogs: White House pool report, March 9, 1993.

92 In the middle of an interview: Jann S. Wenner and William Greider, "The *Rolling Stone* Interview with President Bill Clinton," *Rolling Stone,* December 9, 1993.

92 Some of his advisers realized: Ann Devroy, "Clinton Foes Voice Their Hostility, Loud and Clear; On Talk Shows and in Angry Mail, 'Visceral Reaction' to President Seems Unusually Intense," *Washington Post,* May 22, 1994.

93 Clinton witnessed a stark illustration: Interview with Bill Clinton.

93 Clinton never used the word "Bush": William J. Clinton, speech to the Democratic Leadership Council, New York University, New York City, December 3, 2002.

BUBBA DOES IMUS (AND VICE VERSA)

95 "All the media types": Paul D. Colford, "Hopefuls Warm Up to Shock Talkers," *Newsday,* April 2, 1992.

96 As Imus later admitted: Marci McDonald, "Campaign Carnival," *Maclean's,* April 13, 1992.

96 "Butter Butt": Don Kowet, "N.Y. Media Dent Teflon Candidate Bill Clinton," *Washington Times,* April 6, 1992.

97 "Let's not all pretend": Shauna Snow, "Morning Report," *Los Angeles Times,* March 26, 1996.

STRONG AND RIGHT

98 Bill Clinton, says a political adviser: Dick Morris, *Behind the Oval Office: Getting Reelected Against All Odds,* Los Angeles: Renaissance, 1999, p. xiv (This paperback edition of Morris's book includes memos and other primary documents from the Clinton presidency).

98 His wife, this adviser believes: Ibid. p. 10.

98 One adviser who worked just as closely: Dick Morris, *Rewriting History,* New York: HarperCollins, 2004, p. 42.

99 Distraught after the 1994 election: John F. Harris, *The Survivor: Bill Clinton in the White House,* New York: Random House, 2005, p. 154.

100 Morris advised him: Morris, *Behind the Oval Office,* p. 38.

100 An October 1995 memo: Ibid., p. 483.

101 Morris's numbers: John F. Harris, "Policy and Politics by the Numbers," *Washington Post,* December 31, 2000.

102 "Do not fight," Morris urged: Morris, *Behind the Oval Office,* p. 353.

103 As Morris defined it for Clinton: Ibid., p. 80.

103 Years later, Morris released copies: Ibid., p. 419.

103 Morris himself observed: Ibid., p. 11.

104 In an interview, Clinton cited: Interview with Bill Clinton.

107 "the enemy of normal Americans": Ann Devroy and Charles R. Babcock, "Gingrich Foresees Corruption Probe by a GOP House; Party Could Wield Subpoenas Against 'Enemy' Administration," *Washington Post,* October 14, 1994.

107 "I think most of us learned": Ann Devroy and Eric Pianin, "Clinton Offers Balanced Budget Plan; Preserving Education, Controlling Medicare Are Priorities in 10-Year Program," *Washington Post,* June 14, 1995.

107 "The number one fact": Ron Hayes, "Newt-Wit a Hot Commodity," *Palm Beach Post,* January 22, 1995.

107 His own political action committee: Charles Roos, "If You Think Dems Stink, Take a Whiff of the GOP," *Rocky Mountain News,* November 4, 1994.

107 Over time, however, he concluded: Dick Morris, *The New Prince: Machiavelli Updated for the Twenty-first Century,* Los Angeles: Renaissance, 1999, p. 37.

107 The Clinton style of negative campaigning: William J. Clinton, speech at Georgetown University, Washington, D.C., July 7, 1995.

107 "I want to begin by saying": William J. Clinton, speech at Hartford, Connecticut, October 6, 1996.

108 "I can't believe any thinking American": Thomas Hardy, "Dole Keeps Hammering on Ethics; California Gets Extra Attention in Campaign's Last Days," *Chicago Tribune,* October 28, 1996.

Clinton Versus Drudge

110 An ambivalent source, Willey: Michael Isikoff, *Uncovering Clinton: A Reporter's Story,* New York: Crown, 1999, p. 115.

111 Among the first people: Ibid., p. 149.

111 "What's this all about?": Ibid.

111 The very same Independence Day: "The Findings of Independent Counsel Kenneth W. Starr on President Clinton and the Lewinsky Affair" ("The Starr Report"), Narrative, Section VIII: June–October 1997: Continuing Meetings and Calls, Subsection C: July 4 Meeting.

111 Ten days later: Isikoff, *Uncovering Clinton,* p. 150; "The Starr Report," Narrative, Section VIII: June–October 1997: Continuing Meetings and Calls, Subsection D: July 14–15 Discussions of Linda Tripp.

112 Drudge delighted in the distress: Howard Kurtz, "A Reporter's Net Loss; Details of *Newsweek* Story Appear Prematurely on the Web," *Washington Post,* August 11, 1997.

112 When Isikoff was quoted: Howard Kurtz, "Cyber-Libel and the Web Gossip-Monger; Matt Drudge's Internet Rumors Spark Suit by White House Aide," *Washington Post,* August 15, 1997.

112 "It's a freak show": Edward Helmore, "Keep Up with the Story on the *Drudge Report.* They Do at the White House," *Observer* (UK), August 10, 1997.

112 Within days of his Kathleen Willey triumph: *Drudge Report,* August 10, 1997.

112 Drudge's response to the resulting furor: Howard Kurtz, "Blumenthals Get Apology, Plan Lawsuit; Web Site Retracts Story on Clinton Aide," *Washington Post,* August 12, 1997.

113 "I have no editor": Matt Bai, "Whispers on the Web," *Newsweek,* August 18, 1997.

113 "You don't get a license to report": Matt Drudge, *Talkback Live,* CNN, January 29, 1998.

113 "We have a great tradition": Matt Drudge, speech to the National Press Club, June 2, 1998.

114 What the Kennedy assassination: Michael Kinsley, "In Defense of Matt Drudge," *Time,* February 2, 1998.

114 Drudge's sketchy scoop: *This Week,* ABC News, January 18, 1998.

115 Conservative commentator George Will: *This Week,* ABC News, January 25, 1998.

115 Shortly after the story broke: There are several books that chronicle the links between Drudge, conservative activists (such as Coulter and Brock), and the Starr prosecutorial team. In addition to Isikoff's *Uncovering Clinton,* see Sidney

Blumenthal's *The Clinton Wars,* New York: Farrar, Straus and Giroux, 2003, and Jeffrey Toobin's *A Vast Conspiracy,* New York: Random House, 2000.

116 *New York Times* columnist: Frank Rich, "Journal: The Strange Legacy of Matt Drudge," *New York Times,* December 4, 1999.

How the Freak Show Killed Al Gore

125 a *Washington Post* story dubbed him: Bob Woodward, "Gore Was 'Solicitor-in-Chief' in '96 Reelection Campaign; Some Found Vice President's Directness Inappropriate," *Washington Post,* March 2, 1997.

128 One of Gore's communications directors: Eric Boehlert, "The Press vs. Al Gore: How Lazy Reporting, Pack Journalism and GOP Spin Cost Him the Election," *Rolling Stone,* December 6–13, 2001.

129 As *Rolling Stone* pointed out: Ibid.

132 Speaking to several hundred: Frank Bruni, "Bush Ridicules Gore's Proposals for Tax Cuts," *New York Times,* October 25, 2000.

132 But Bush continued to taunt Clinton: *Nightline,* ABC News, October 24, 2000.

132 Clinton was old enough to remember: Interview with Bill Clinton.

Section III • "Evil Genius"

Who Is Karl Rove?

137 Rove was treated: Sidney Blumenthal, "Counterinaugural at the Clinton Library," *Salon,* November 25, 2004.

138 "Hey, you did a marvelous job": Interview with Bill Clinton; interview with Karl Rove, 2005.

139 The national College Republicans sent him to Illinois: *Frontline, Karl Rove—The Architect,* PBS, April 12, 2005.

141 Typical of the standards used: Joshua Green, "Karl Rove in a Corner," *Atlantic Monthly,* November 2004.

142 Early in 2005, *Time* magazine: James Carville, "Karl Rove: A Brilliant (Ouch!) Political Strategist," *Time,* April 18, 2005.

143 Rove was once asked: Interview with Rove, 1999.

144 "GOP Probes Official": *Frontline, Karl Rove—The Architect,* April 12, 2005.

146 His wife, Darby Rove: Melinda Henneberger, "Driving W.," *New York Times Magazine,* May 14, 2000.

147 "a very unique": Dan Balz, "Team Bush: The Governor's 'Iron Triangle' Points the Way to Washington," *Washington Post,* July 23, 1999.

147 "When Mr. Rove talks about": Frank Bruni, "Behind Bush Juggernaut, an Aide's Labor of Loyalty," *New York Times,* July 11, 2000.

147 Rove once put it: Ibid.

148 During an unusually prickly interview: Elisabeth Bumiller, "A First Lady Fiercely Loyal and Quietly Effective," *New York Times,* February 7, 2004.

149 In 1999, Rove was asked: Interview with Rove, 1999.

149 Six years later: Interview with Rove, 2005.

150 "If he worked for a candidate": Interview with Stuart Stevens.

151 Just a month before: Richard L. Berke and Frank Bruni, "Crew of Listing Bush Ship Draws Republican Scowls," *New York Times,* July 2, 2001.

152 That led Associated Press reporter: Darlene Superville, "Karl Rove's Garage Proves to Be Typical," Associated Press, October 17, 2005.

152 Typical was a 2005 *Boston Globe* editorial: "Rove's Role," *Boston Globe,* August 28, 2005.

Section IV • Serious Rewards

IDEAS MATTER

159 "I am the leading expert": Interview with Rove, 2005.

160 A *New York Times* story: Elisabeth Bumiller, "A Democratic Rallying Cry: Vote Bush Out of Rove's Office," *New York Times,* January 19, 2004.

160 "It is because of the ideas we hold": Karl Rove, speech to the Conservative Political Action Conference, Washington, D.C., February 17, 2005.

161 "It's the performance in office": Karl Rove, interview with Paul Stekler, *Last Man Standing: Myth vs. Reality in Texas Politics,* PBS, July 20, 2004

161 One of the best articles: Sidney Blumenthal, "The Anointed: Bill Clinton, Nominee-elect," *New Republic,* February 3, 1992.

163 One of Rove's: Stuart Stevens, *The Big Enchilada,* New York: The Free Press, 2001, p. 94.

165 Bush himself said the book: George W. Bush, quoted on the cover of Myron Magnet, *The Dream and the Nightmare: The Sixties' Legacy to the Underclass,* New York: Encounter Books, 2000.

166 After being exposed: Interview with Mark McKinnon.

PLAY TO YOUR STRENGTHS (AND AWAY FROM YOUR WEAKNESSES)

177 As Broder later recalled: *Frontline, Karl Rove—the Architect,* April 12, 2005.

178 Rove was galled: Interview with Rove, 2005.

Section V • Putting People First

Know a Lot of People

190 Thirty years later: Interview with Rove, 2005.

191 David Bates, who was a school friend: Interview with David Bates.

194 Beach's memories of Rove: Interview with Becky Beach.

196 Matalin said he focused so intently: Interview with Mary Matalin.

196 Rove told the governor: Interview with Rove, 1999.

196 Says Mary Matalin: Interview with Mary Matalin.

Relationships, Not Transactions

198 After the two '78 races: Interview with Rove, 2005.

198 The questions in Texas: Ibid.

199 As Rove understood: Ibid.

200 "Churches, like any large voluntary organization": Malcolm Gladwell, "The Cellular Church: How Rick Warren's Congregation Grew," *New Yorker*, September 12, 2005.

Karl Rove in Your Mailbox

204 In those days, Gaylord recalled: Interview with Joe Gaylord.

206 "They were both very fiduciary": Interview with Joe Barton (this chapter relies heavily on our interview with Barton).

210 In a 1985 interview: "Karl Rove: Direct Mail Consultant," *Austin Business Journal*, September 2, 1985.

211 "Direct mail caused me to think": Interview with Rove, 2005.

Comity Is Pretty

214 "No," he answered: Interview with Rove, 1999.

214 "Karl is the kind of guy": Interview with Stuart Stevens.

215 As Bush strategist Mark McKinnon recalled: Interview with Mark McKinnon.

215 During the 2000 campaign: George W. Bush, *A Charge to Keep*, New York: William Morrow, 1999, p. 100.

Section VI • The Effective Executive

RENAISSANCE, MAN

219 So there you have it: Interview with Mark McKinnon.

221 As Ken Mehlman has said: David Postman, "State Bush Campaign Betting on Grass Roots," *Seattle Times,* May 23, 2004.

223 Stuart Stevens observed: Interview with Stuart Stevens.

224 Pressed then: Interview with Rove, 1999.

MACHINE POLITICS

229 In 1999, Rove reflected: Interview with Rove, 1999.

232 The hard-to-please Democratic team: James Carville and Paul Begala, *Take It Back: Our Party, Our Country, Our Future,* New York: Simon & Schuster, 2006, p. 27.

MAKE YOURSELF THE CENTER OF THE INFORMATION UNIVERSE

235 One of the few articles written: Thomas B. Edsall and Dana Milbank, "White House's Roving Eye for Politics; President's Most Powerful Adviser May Also Be the Most Connected," *Washington Post,* March 10, 2003.

236 "He was the Ohio College Republican": Interview with Rove, 2005.

Section VII • Leave Nothing to Chance

DAILY PLANNER

244 Asked once what Bush would say: Interview with Rove, 1999.

248 As Bush political operative: Interview with Terry Nelson.

252 "What it generated": Ibid.

252 Rove handled the logistics: Ibid.

253 The *New York Times* the next day ran: Richard L. Berke, "Bush Tests Presidential Run with a Flourish," *New York Times,* March 8, 1999.

253 Rove did a huge: Interview with Rove, 1999.

253 Rove remembered: Ibid.

CONTROL FREAK

268 Nelson, like Rove: Interview with Terry Nelson.

268 Starting in the fall of 2003: Interview with Heath Thompson.

269 Right-wing interest groups: Center for Reclaiming America for Christ, "Florida Parental Notification Measure on November Ballot," May 7, 2004.

269 Thompson said: Interview with Heath Thompson.

Metrics

275 As Mehlman said: Maura Reynolds and Doyle McManus, "GOP Focus Is Already Fixed on Endgame," *Los Angeles Times,* February 1, 2004.

275 Mehlman was not interested in reaching: Interview with Ken Mehlman.

276 "The old model": Ibid.

277 Mehlman believed that so-called earned media: Ibid.

278 That did not happen in 2004: Ibid.

Section VIII • Mastering the Freak Show

Introduction

283 Cheney said this new arena: Interview with Dick Cheney.

Understand and Control the Old Media

286 By November of 1999: Karl Rove, remarks at "Political Discourse" panel at the Penn National Commission on Society, Culture and Community, University of Pennsylvania, November 8, 1999.

287 "These are indeed": Karl Rove, speech to the American Society of Newspaper Editors, April 11, 2003.

288 In March of 2005, with Bush safely reelected: Karl Rove, speech for Washington College's Harwood Lecture series, Washington College, Chestertown, Maryland, April 18, 2005.

289 Bush's political team was certain: Ken Auletta, "Fortress Bush: How the White House Keeps the Press Under Control," *New Yorker,* January 20, 2004.

289 To the Bush administration: David Shaw, "Media Matters: Is Bush Really Implementing a Full-Court Press on Media?" *Los Angeles Times,* March 12, 2005.

289 Dick Cheney, too, has weighed in: Interview with Dick Cheney.

292 As Cheney chuckled wryly: Ibid.

Rally the Base

296 As Rove once said of his boss: Interview with Rove, 1999.

296 As Rove's longtime friend: *Frontline, The Jesus Factor,* PBS, April 29, 2004.

296 "I'd send him an e-mail": Todd S. Purdum and David D. Kirkpatrick, "Cam-

paign Strategist Is in Position to Consolidate Republican Majority," *New York Times,* November 5, 2004.

296 Reagan generally is considered: Interview with Dick Cheney.

297 "Personally, I tend to doubt": Nicholas Lemann, "The Speech: Reagan's Break from the Past," *Washington Post,* February 22, 1981.

301 The *New York Times*'s Rick Berke: Richard L. Berke, "Bush Adviser Suggests War as Campaign Theme," *New York Times,* January 19, 2002.

301 The never understated McAuliffe: Ibid.

302 When Rove was asked: *The Charlie Rose Show,* PBS, March 11, 2002.

302 Years later, he said: Interview with Rove, 2005.

303 So on that night: Karl Rove, speech to the New York Conservative Party, June 22, 2005.

305 As the conservative writer: Rich Lowry, "Bush's Well-Mapped Road to Victory," *National Review,* November 29, 2004.

306 "I liked Dean": Faye Fiore, "Many New Hampshire Voters Still Comparison Shopping; With Hours Before the Polls Open for the Nation's First Primary, Democrats Look at the Candidates Up Close and Focus on Beating Bush," *Los Angeles Times,* January 26, 2004.

TRANSCENDENCY, TRANSPARENCY, AND DESTRUCTION

312 Bartlett claimed nothing: Interview with Dan Bartlett.

313 The uproar that greeted: Interview with Rove, 2005.

314 In 2006, Bartlett acknowledged: Interview with Dan Bartlett.

315 "I've told the American people": *Today,* NBC, August 20, 1999.

316 The book's allegations: Howard Kurtz, "Bush Accuser Is Said to Be Ex-Convict; Publisher Halts Release of Biography of GOP Candidate," *Washington Post,* October 22, 1999.

318 After the publication of the Associated Press account: Interview with Howard Wolfson.

320 According to the *New York Observer:* Robert Sam Anson, "Kerry-Loathing Swift Boaters Sinking Facts," *New York Observer,* August 30, 2004.

320 At his Wisconsin press conference: George W. Bush, press conference, Milwaukee, Wisconsin, November 2, 2000.

321 The Democrats, meanwhile: Dan Balz, "Bush Acknowledges 1976 DUI Arrest," *Washington Post,* November 3, 2000.

321 Bush himself asked: Ibid.

321 She tossed around: John Podhoretz, "D-Dubya-I: The Fallout Truth and the Fog of Political War," *New York Post,* November 4, 2000.

Section IX • Hillary Clinton, the Freak Show, and the Presidency

INTRODUCTION

336   Hillary Clinton closely watched: Interview with Hillary Clinton.

337   Rove attributed this change: Interview with Rove, 2005.

LOSING TO THE FREAK SHOW

341   A quote Hillary Clinton uttered: Gwen Ifill, "Hillary Clinton Defends Her Conduct in Law Firm," *New York Times,* March 17, 1992.

342   "We're all that way": Interview with Bill Clinton.

343   As Bill Clinton famously teased: William J. Clinton, speech at the Radio and Television Correspondents' Association Dinner, March 18, 1993.

344   Richard Nixon told *Time* magazine: Michael Kramer, "The Political Interest: It's Not Going to Be Pretty; A High-Minded Debate of the Issues? No Way. The Roughing Up of Bill Clinton Has Just Begun," *Time,* April 20, 1992.

346   But throughout her remaining days: Interview with Ken Mehlman.

346   As Bill Clinton said: Interview with Bill Clinton.

347   That February day, in the Map Room: Hillary Rodham Clinton, White House transcript, February 11, 1998.

349   For years afterward: *Drudge Report,* February 12, 1998.

CHALLENGING THE FREAK SHOW

354   Yet the money raised: Clifford J. Levy, "Clinton Rivals Raise Little Besides Rage," *New York Times,* October 27, 2000.

354   "Wherever Hillary goes": Jane Gross, "Undecided: The Soft Money Issue," *New York Times,* October 27, 2000.

355   Sheehy had trekked from Little Rock: Gail Sheehy, "Hillary's Choice: Inside the Clinton Marriage," *Vanity Fair,* February 1999.

355   That same week Carl Bernstein: Letta Taylor and Paul D. Colford, "Flash!," *Newsday,* January 6, 1999.

356   the context of Al Haig's memorable: Lloyd Grove, "The Reliable Source," *Washington Post,* December 10, 1999.

356   "Sheehy once made": Lloyd Grove, "The Reliable Source," *Washington Post,* December 9, 1999.

356   "It is worth noting": Lloyd Grove, "The Reliable Source," *Washington Post,* December 8, 1999.

357   "There's a piece of the book": *Larry King Live,* CNN, November 30, 1999.

357   "I feel mousetrapped": George Rush and Joanna Molloy, "Babs and Bill a Real Head-Scratcher," *New York Daily News,* December 3, 1999.

357 "The White House spin": "Spin 'N' Bear It for Hillary Scribe," *New York Post,* December 15, 1999.

357 "Unfortunately for Sheehy": Thomas M. DeFrank, "Hil Chooses to Cite Book Goofs," *New York Daily News,* December 12, 1999.

357 "My book will survive": "Spin 'N' Bear It for Hillary Scribe," *New York Post,* December 15, 1999.

359 "New Yorkers will be subjected": Robert Hardt Jr., " 'Jew' Slur Charge Has Hill in Denial," *New York Post,* July 15, 2000.

359 "It's unfortunate that people": Gregg Birnbaum, "Hill: Believe Me, I Never Uttered Vile Jewish Slur," *New York Post,* July 17, 2000.

360 "It is clearly designed": Edward Lewine, "Ex-Aide Confirms Hil Slur," *New York Daily News,* July 16, 2000.

360 Senator Schumer was heartfelt: Marc Humbert, "Mrs. Clinton Ends Slur Charge Talk," Associated Press, July 19, 2000.

360 Rudy Giuliani gave a press conference: Michael Blood, "Rudy Backs First Lady in Slur Flap," *New York Daily News,* July 19, 2000.

360 Presidential candidate George W. Bush: *Larry King Live,* CNN, July 20, 2000.

360 "This is sort of a": *Crossfire,* CNN, July 19, 2000.

361 During a debate: Gregg Birnbaum, "Hill and Rick Go from Nice to Nasty: Praise 'N' Barbs in Final Debate," *New York Post,* October 28, 2000.

362 "I think we send": Gregg Birnbaum and Maggie Haberman, "Rick Rips Bill for Castro Greeting," *New York Post,* September 9, 2000.

362 "It wasn't a kiss": Stephanie Saul and Herbert Lowe, "No Apology over Arafat Handshake/Lazio Assails White House over Photo," *Newsday,* September 11, 2000.

362 Wolfson mused: Gregg Birnbaum and Robert Hardt Jr., "Rick Labeled a 'Hypocrite' over Arafat Handshake," *New York Post,* September 10, 2000.

362 "You'll have to ask": Adam Nagourney, "White House Enters Senate Race with Release of Photo of Lazio and Arafat," *New York Times,* September 11, 2000.

362 The following evening: Noreen O'Donnell, "Clinton Campaigns for First Lady, Scolds Entertainment Industry," *Journal News* (Westchester County, New York), September 12, 2000.

362 Giuliani told reporters: Elisabeth Bumiller, "Giuliani Criticizes Lazio over Arafat Handshake," *New York Times,* September 12, 2000.

363 The Clinton campaign: Adam Nagourney, "Lofty Talk Discarded, Senate Race Ends in Brawl over Narrow Turf," *New York Times,* November 5, 2000.

363 And, finally, a Gotham City–style Trade Secret: Adam Nagourney, "White House Enters Senate Race with Release of Photo of Lazio and Arafat," *New York Times,* September 11, 2000.

Mastering the Senate, and the Freak Show

364 At her freshman orientation: Joel Siegel, "She's Set to Join the Club; 1st Lady Ready for Low-Key Role as Frosh Senator on Capitol Hill," *New York Daily News*, December 7, 2000.

365 At once representative: Al Kamen, "In the Loop," *Washington Post*, March 20, 2006.

367 "I would have guessed": Thomas Ferraro, "Senator Clinton Works with Husband's Ex-Foes," Reuters, April 10, 2003.

367 Representative Thomas M. Reynolds: Phil Fairbanks, "First Lady Goes on Erie Radio, but This One's in Pennsylvania," *Buffalo News*, July 27, 2000.

367 "I like Senator Clinton": Raymond Hernandez, "As Clinton Wins G.O.P. Friends, Her Challengers' Task Toughens," *New York Times*, March 6, 2005.

367 Clinton even co-authored: Hillary Rodham Clinton and Tom DeLay, "Easing Foster Care's Pain Unites Disparate Politicians," *USA Today*, February 26, 2003.

368 In May 2005: "Hillary Clinton Looks Like a Winner," *New York Observer*, May 2, 2005.

370 *Newsday* featured a fund-raising appeal: Elaine S. Povich, "Payback Time for Lazio; He Bashes Clintons," *Newsday*, September 11, 2001.

370 The *Daily News* wrote: Kenneth R. Bazinet, "Pardon Made Him Do It; Whistleblower Testifies vs. Herbal Supplement Kingpin," *New York Daily News*, September 11, 2001.

370 The *New York Post* printed: Allyson Lieberman, "Liz Inks a Deal to Dish on Gems and Men Behind Them," *New York Post*, September 11, 2001.

370 The *New Republic* noted: Ben Smith, "Post Election," *New Republic*, January 16, 2006.

371 On the eve of the book's release: John LeBoutillier, "Hillary's Denials About Book Won't Work," NewsMax.com, June 7, 2005 (www.newsmax.com/archives/articles/2005/6/7/123857.shtml).

371 "Because of my book": Rachel Deahl, "Did 'The Truth' Hit the Buzzsaw?," *Herald News* (Passaic County, New Jersey), July 17, 2005.

372 The *New York Post* called it: "Hillary Basher Is Error Prone," *New York Post*, June 10, 2005.

372 Fox News's Bill O'Reilly declined: *O'Reilly Factor*, Fox News Channel, June 20, 2005.

372 Echoing the sentiments: Dick Morris, "Personal Attacks on Hillary Will Only Embolden Her," *The Hill*, June 15, 2005.

44! (ASSETS)

384   Every Democratic president or nominee: Interview with Bill Clinton.

385   Bill Clinton believes: Ibid.

386   Republican National Chairman Ken Mehlman has watched: Interview with Ken Mehlman.

386   Finally, Mehlman says that the Clintons: Ibid.

INDEX

★ ★ ★ ★ ★

About the Authors

MARK HALPERIN is the political director of ABC News and the creator of "The Note," a daily online publication on ABCNews .com, described by the *New Yorker* as the most influential tip sheet in Washington. He has covered five presidential elections.

JOHN F. HARRIS is the national political editor of the *Washington Post.* He is the author of the *New York Times* best-selling biography of Bill Clinton *The Survivor.*

About the Type

This book was set in Fairfield, the first typeface from the hand of the distinguished American artist and engraver Rudolph Ruzicka (1883–1978). In its structure Fairfield displays the sober and sane qualities of the master craftsman whose talent has long been dedicated to clarity. It is this trait that accounts for the trim grace and vigor, the spirited design and sensitive balance, of this original typeface.

Rudolph Ruzicka was born in Bohemia and came to America in 1894. He set up his own shop, devoted to wood engraving and printing, in New York in 1913 after a varied career working as a wood engraver, in photoengraving and banknote printing plants, and as an art director and freelance artist. He designed and illustrated many books, and was the creator of a considerable list of individual prints—wood engravings, line engravings on copper, and aquatints.